THE REAL COLD WAR

featuring

"JACK IN JOE'S LAND"

by

CHRIS B. TYE

First published in 1995 by

CHRIS B. TYE
5 Begonia Avenue
Gillingham
Kent ME8 6YD

ISBN 0 9524692

Cover Picture:
'Ice on Gun Barrels of HMS King George V'

Cover:
by Peter Gunthorpe

Typeset and Produced by:
Delco Creative Services Ltd, Strood, Rochester, Kent.
Tel: 01634 297444

S. BATEMAN
70 NICKLEBY HOUSE
ALL SAINTS ROAD
PORTSMOUTH
PO1 4EL
TEL. 0705 817775

THE AUTHOR

THE AUTHOR joined the RNVR at Chatham in September 1939. For over 3 years he served in various shore bases in the UK before being drafted to the staff of the Senior British Naval Officer, North Russia at the Naval Base at Polyarnoe, Kola Inlet where he was promoted to Leading Writer.

In this book he has brought together the individuals who took part, the men who were there, the eye witnesses, both ashore and afloat. In 1984 he was the founder member and secretary of the North Russia Club. Initially with 35 members, it has now enlisted over 1800 members including many from overseas. He is now President of the Club. From these members, valuable research material and over 65 personal accounts have helped to make this book possible.

List Of Photographs

THE REAL COLD WAR

by

Chris B. Tye

This book is dedicated as a tribute to the men who served on or around the Russian Convoys, whether afloat, ashore or in the air - to those who did not return and those who survived

"THE REAL COLD WAR"

Dear Reader,

Now the story can be told by the men themselves - the men who defied bombs, torpedoes and the cruellest seas in the world to deliver vital war supplies, tanks, lorries, engines, ammunition, stores and aviation fuel to Russia in the most inhospitable theatre of war, where the worst enemy was the weather.

The gallant Merchantmen and Escort crews showed true courage on what became known as the "Hell Run".

Where they suffered, the lost band of officers and ratings ashore in Russia at Polyarnoe and Murmansk (Naval Party 100 - of which I was one) and at Archangel (Naval Party 200) only endured.

Read on, witness their experiences and hope, as we who survived do, that it will never be repeated.

Sincerely

Chris B. Tye

Chris B. Tye

Foreword

(By W.B.C. Evans, Captain (S) RN Ret'd.)

On 21st August, 1941 the first convoy of seven ships sailed for North Russia. In the following four years there were a further 40 convoys outward and 35 homeward. The last convoy sailed for home on 23rd May, 1945. During this period 98 vessels were lost by enemy action.

These figures give the bare bones of the story. In this book Chris Tye has brought together the experiences of individuals who took part, the men who were there, the eye witnesses. It is none too soon; time is passing and the veterans are fast fading away.

The operational control of these convoys in Russian waters was the responsibility of the Senior British Naval Officer North Russia at Polyarnoe. Admiral Sir Douglas Fisher held this command for nine months in 1942/43 and Admiral Archer for the remainder of the time. The Admiral also had the task of co-operating with the Russian Naval Commander in Chief - Admiral Golovco - in regard to the reception and protection of the convoys, which was not an easy matter. On the whole, the Russian naval authorities were inclined to be helpful.

The Author served in the Admiral's Office at Polyarnoe and was well placed to observe all that was going on. He was thus well qualified to write this book, which has been a labour of love. The story is set against the background of terrible weather and Arctic ice. It is an epic of courage and endurance. It deserves wide attention.

W.B.C. Evans

"He that outlives this day and comes safe home will stand a tip-toe when this day is named"

Preface

Much has been said about Russian convoys and their gallant escort crews and merchantmen. Their suffering, courage and losses. Little, if any, of the lost band of Officers and Naval ratings of Naval Party 100 based ashore at Polyarnoe and Murmansk and Naval Party 200 at Archangel, under the command of the Senior British Naval Officer, North Russia.

They endured the atrocious weather, lack of fresh food and mail, the continuous darkness for over 100 days. The problems with, and lack of cooperation from, the Russians with their mistrust, suspicion, secrecy and censorship.

Many of these men, as communication ratings, served aboard Russian destroyers and icebreakers because of the Russians inability to understand the international morse code.

This story is not so much about the characters but their individual experiences, both afloat and ashore.

We did not suffer, only endured, as each man became a "Jack in Joe's Land".

INTRODUCTION

THE ARCTIC CAMPAIGN

The convoys which took war material to the USSR via the Northern Trade Route during the Second World War have a special place in the history of the war at sea because of the unequalled hardships they faced. After being assembled in the grim harbour of Hvalfjord in Iceland or a remote Scottish loch the convoys would sail through the Norwegian and Barents Seas to the Russian port of Murmansk in the Kola Inlet or Archangel on the White Sea. The route the convoys had to follow is notorious for bad weather and conditions which border the limits of human endurance. In winter the northern latitudes produce conditions of continuous darkness while from May to August there is perpetual daylight. The fierce storms which frequently battered the convoys caused ice to build up on ships' superstructures and deck fittings, and this had to be chipped away to prevent the vessels from becoming top-heavy. This was treacherous work, and a man's chances of survival should he fall overboard into the icy waters were very slim.

As if the appalling climate were not enough, the convoys also faced continual attack since they were always within range of German airfields in Norway. The Norwegian fjords also sheltered U-boats and capital ships like Tirpitz, which meant that considerable British and American forces were needed to cover the convoys when they could have been deployed in other theatres.

Under these conditions the men of the Royal and United States Navies, together with their colleagues in the Merchant Marine, laboured to bring material to Russia.

In all 21 Allied warships were sunk and naval casualties amounted to 1,944. Merchant Navy losses were 98 ships and 829 men.

ACKNOWLEDGEMENTS

The author acknowledges with grateful thanks the contributors who served in the ships, ashore in North Russia and others associated with events mentioned in this book and with special gratitude to:

Naval historian Frank Pearce for permission to use excerpts from his books:

"The Ship that Torpedoed Herself"

"Running the Gauntlet"

"Last Call for HMS 'Edinburgh"

"Sea War"

Admiral Brian Schofield "The Russian Convoys" (Batsford 1964).

Captain W.B.C. Evans RN (Ret'd.), the Foreword.

Ronald Wren, Secretary Arctic Campaign Memorial Trust for Introduction.

Dick Squires MBE, Editor "Northern Light", the official publication of the North Russia Club, for permission to use excerpts, analyses and convoy data, etc.

Chris Darge, my young "Minder" who has been my sounding board, patient researcher of ideas and photography throughout the writing of this book, constantly around to kick me when needed.

Peter Gunthorpe, naval historian.

David Meaton, schoolteacher as literary adviser.

F. Roy Chappell of Tasmania, author.

Alfred Lewis for editing and proof reading.

Jackie Williamson for valuable assistance with compilation and editing.

Wendy Roberts for the arduous task of manuscript typing.

The Imperial War Museum for use of photographs.

The Public Record Office for use of documents ADM116/4972, ADM1/3272 and FO447 53 HN01273.

The Author acknowledges with grateful thanks the CONTRIBUTORS without whose reports, stories and eye witness accounts the book would not have been possible. * Denotes since "Crossed The Bar".

ASHTON	Dick	Signalman	ONSLOW
BAKER	Ben	Telegraphist	NAVAL PARTY 100
BALAAM	Ted	Leading Signalman	SHROPSHIRE
BARTLE	Arthur	Leading Seaman	HONEYSUCKLE
BATES	Bill	Telegraphist	GOODALL
BEARDMORE	John	Lieutenant RNVR	POPPY
BEDBROOK	Denys	Ldg. Telegraphist	NAVAL PARTY 100
BIRKETT	Maurice	Able Seaman	CASSANDRA
BRAGG*	D.L.	Ordnce Artificer	OBEDIENT
BROOKE	Denis	Sub-Lieut. RNVR	POPPY
BULL	Ken	Ldg. Sick Berth Att.	NAVAL PARTY 100/200
BUTLER	Jim	Telegraphist	NAVAL PARTY 100
CHALLANDS	Jack	Coder	LORD AUSTIN
CONLEY	Sid	Master-At-Arms	NAIRANA
COOLEY	Ronald	Telegraphist	ESCAPADE
CRAIG	David	Radio Officer	DOVER HILL
CREEDY	Archie	Telegraphist	NAVAL PARTY 100
CREWE	Freddie	Sergeant Pilot	151 WING RAF
CROSS	Maurice	Signalman	SEAGULL
DEVAL	Charles	Leading Seaman	LONDON
DOWNING	Alex	Ldg. Telegraphist	NAVAL PARTY 100
DYSON	George		
EDWARDS *	Jim		LARK
ELDRED	John	Ord. Seaman	HARRIER
FIRTH	Alan	Aero Engine Fitter	151 WING RAF
FORBES	Jim	Ldg. Supply Assistant	SCYLLA
FRENCH	Joe	Writer	NAVAL PARTY 200
GOLDSMITH	Arthur	Leading Signalman	BELFAST
HOLMES	Edward		
HORTON	John	Radio Operator	MATCHLESS
HOUGH	Les	Ordnce Artificer	SNOWFLAKE
INGLE	Harry	Leading Signalman	EDINBURGH
JEWETT	Fred		
JOHNSTON	Bill	Coder	NAVAL PARTY 100
KIRBY	Stan	Asdic	ASPHODEL
LAWRENCE*	Les	Telegraphist	WESTCOTT
LAY	Sid	Stoker PO	CASSANDRA
LOADES*	Bill	Leading Signalman	NAVAL PARTY 100
LOWE	Jack	Petty Officer CR1	KENT
LOWE	John	Signalman	NAVAL PARTY 100
LUCK	George	Petty Officer St.	SUBMARINE P.614
MADDERN	John	Leading Signalman	GOSSAMER
MATTHEWS	Ralph		
McALLISTER*	Tony	Petty Officer	SAVAGE
McHUGH	Jimmy	Able Seaman	ACHATES
NEALE	Henry	Flight Sgt.	151 WING RAF
NELSON	Oliver	Ldg. Telegraphist	WHITEHALL
PARRY	Eric	Leading Seaman	SCORPION
PLATT	Arthur	Ldg. Aircraftman	151 WING RAF
RATHBONE*	Eric	Signalman	NAVAL PARTY 100
RICKETTS	Gerry	Signalman	PUNJABI
ROBSON	Edward	Leading Signalman	NAVAL PARTY 200
ROBINSON*	George	Signalman	EMPIRE TIDE
RISLEY	Bob	Signalman	NAVAL PARTY 200
SHAW	Eric	Lieut-Commander	RCN NENE
SKELTON*	Ernie	Leading Signalman	NAVAL PARTY 100
SPITTLE*	H.S.	Lieut-Commander RN	SECRETARY TO SBNO
SQUIRES MBE	Dick	Petty Officer LTO	MATCHLESS
TANNER	Les	Able Seaman	SAVAGE
THAKE	Ron	Leading Seaman	APOLLO
UPTON	Tom	Signalman	ONSLOW
WHITEHOUSE*	Dennis	Ldg. Telegraphist	NAVAL PARTY 100
WHYTE	Eric	Signalman	KING GEORGE V

Additional photographs kindly supplied and donated by:-
BAKER, Henry; CREWE, Freddie; DOWNING, Alex; FRENCH, Joseph; FLOYD, Charles; ROBSON, Edward.

Yesterday's Memory

Cast back the hands of time to other days,
Neath sullen ice cold skies, over Arctic waterways,
Where wartime convoys Russian bound, their perils fought,
And victory if won was dearly bought.

Then men and ships were hammered by the foe,
Relentlessly from air, U-boats below,
And nature with her frozen hell, gave help,
In adding to the misery they dealt.

To those ashore midst Russia's winter snow,
When daylight scarcely came and then a murky glow,
Or in the summer when each day was full of light,
No darkness fell to shield the convoy's plight.

And we on Kola Inlet's shores endured in turn,
When all around, midst bombs the buildings burned,
Yet helped survivors with what succour we could spare,
Little enough, but it was gladly shared.

Ah yes, Ah yes, those distant days long gone,
Yet down the years the memories live on,
The friendships made, back in those valiant times,
And sealed, through common bonds, in Arctic climes.

Bill Johnston

1941

- *Eden's trip to Moscow via Kent*
- *A dummy run called "Dervish"*
- *Bearing gifts to Uncle Joe*
- *Hurricanes in the Arctic*
- *Setting up shop in the wasteland*

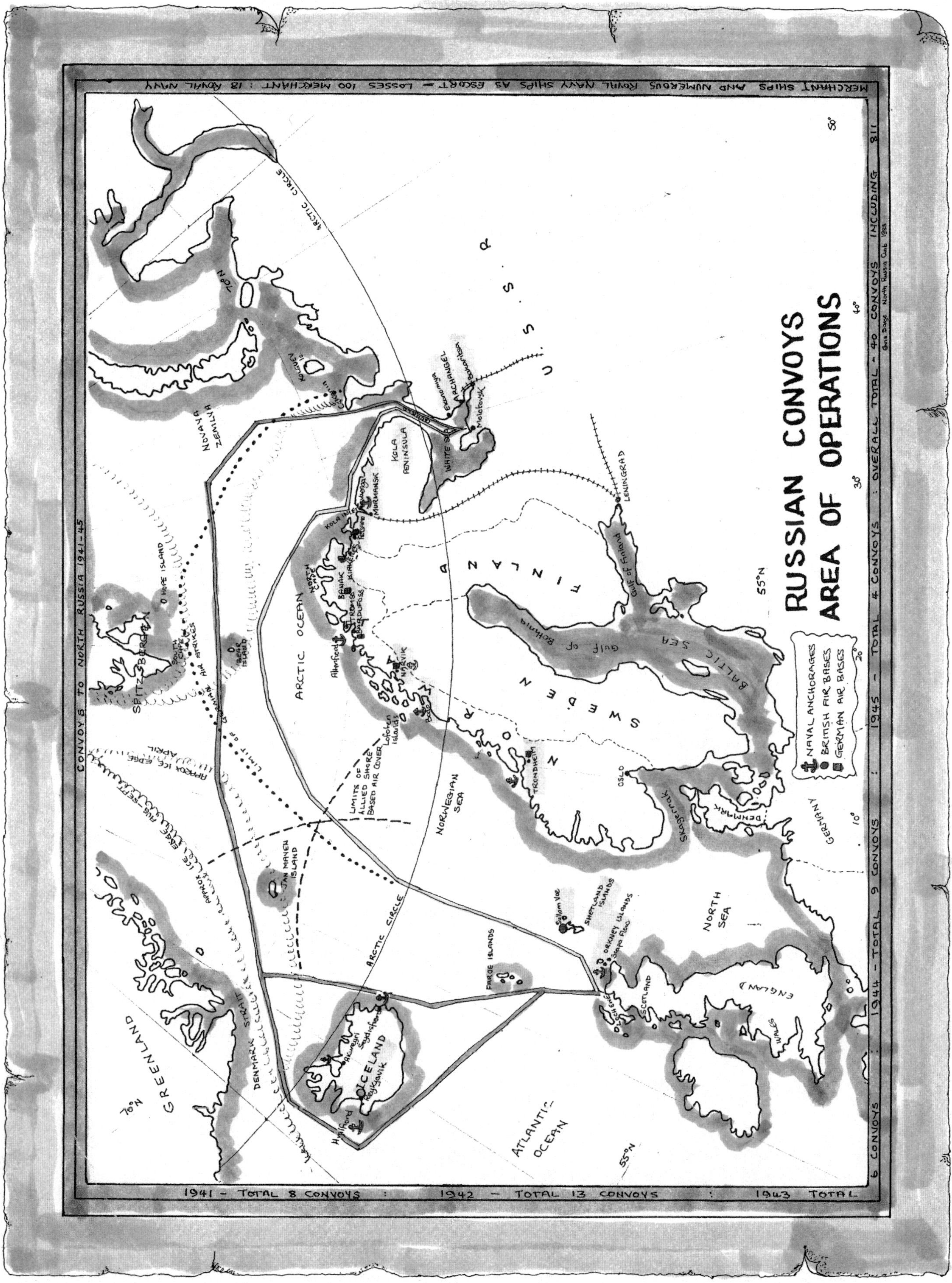
RUSSIAN CONVOYS
AREA OF OPERATIONS
CONVOYS TO NORTH RUSSIA 1941-45
1941 - TOTAL 8 CONVOYS : 1942 - TOTAL 13 CONVOYS : 1943 TOTAL 6 CONVOYS : 1944 - TOTAL 9 CONVOYS : 1945 - TOTAL 4 CONVOYS : OVERALL TOTAL - 40 CONVOYS INCLUDING 811 MERCHANT SHIPS AND NUMEROUS ROYAL NAVY SHIPS AS ESCORT - LOSSES 100 MERCHANT : 18 ROYAL NAVY
NAVAL ANCHORAGES
BRITISH AIR BASES
GERMAN AIR BASES
ARCTIC OCEAN
NORWEGIAN SEA
ATLANTIC OCEAN
NORTH SEA
ARCTIC CIRCLE
GREENLAND
ICELAND
SPITZBERGEN
NOVAYA ZEMLYA
KOLA PENINSULA
WHITE SEA
ARCHANGEL
MURMANSK
LENINGRAD
U. S. S. R
FINLAND
SWEDEN
NORWAY
DENMARK
GERMANY
ENGLAND
SCOTLAND
WALES
BALTIC SEA
Gulf of Bothnia
Gulf of Finland
JAN MAYEN ISLAND
BEAR ISLAND
HOPE ISLAND
FAROE ISLANDS
SHETLAND ISLANDS
ORKNEY ISLANDS
LIMITS OF ALLIED SHORE BASED AIR COVER
DENMARK STRAIT
Skagerrak
OSLO
TRONDHEIM
NARVIK
NORTH CAPE
Lofoten Islands

During winter the Arctic ice barrier moves so far as to leave a navigable stretch of water barely 200 miles between it and North Cape. Convoys were sailing past the Germans doorstep, while at the same time struggling to overcome navigational hazards. Freezing spray from the huge waves formed layers of ice on ships' decks so thick that smaller vessels were in danger of capsizing. Red-eyed lookouts peered through sleet-laden darkness fearing they might crash into the ship ahead or the ship at rear collide with their stern.

As the convoys moved slowly on their voyage each ship would be fighting against the storms ploughing through great seas, climbing foaming crests, sliding into troughs with 35° on the roll indicators. In temperatures as low as 40° below freezing where crews dare not place a hand on bare metal for fear of leaving skin behind. Eyelashes froze together, nostril hairs became little needles, a touch on the nose would bring streaming blood.

The Arctic climate cultivated fear of what would happen if ships were torpedoed and had to take to the rafts, even worse how quickly death would come if it meant trying to swim for it.

In the harsh desolate waste of the sea framed by the ice masses, the pitiless cold, the savagery of the sea, the loneliness and presence of an enemy would undermine the will to survive. Such were the conditions facing and endured by these merchantmen and escorts on the Road to Hell of Russian Convoys.

It is difficult for anyone who has never experienced the intense cold of the Polar regions to comprehend fully what superhuman endurance was called for from the ships' companies of warship and merchantmen so engaged. The escort vessels patrolling ceaselessly round the convoys shook and shivered as they climbed to the crest of each foaming, mountainous wave, hesitated, then plunged to wallow for a moment in the trough. The process being repeated with exhausting monotony.

Guns, ammunition, torpedoes and depth charges became coated with ice and frozen spray so it was one long struggle to keep them free of ice and ready for use in an all too likely emergency. To touch bare metal without a glove was to invite painful ice burns.

The weight of clothing one had to wear, in what was generally an unsuccessful attempt to keep out the cold became a burden almost too heavy to bear as the long hours of the watch dragged on. The faces of officers and lookouts peering over the edges of exposed bridges were whipped by driving snow and sleet until icicles formed on eyebrows, noses and beards.

In 1941, before the convoys commenced, **HMS KENT** sailed from Scapa Flow - on board was Anthony Eden and M. Maisky, the Soviet Ambassador, bound for Murmansk from where they were to fly to Moscow for important meetings at the British Mission.

HMS KENT, unescorted, made a fast passage at 32 knots steaming to the extreme north until she reached the ice packs as far away from Norway as possible, meeting on the way the atrocious weather of the Arctic in continuous darkness and the heavy seas around Bear Island.

Anthony Eden not being a very good sailor was violently sea sick, spent considerable time in the Sick Bay and the rest of the time in his cabin.

In June 1941 Philip Vian, an outstandingly brilliant Naval Officer was promoted to Rear Admiral. Late one evening in July he received a telephone call with the message to pack what was necessary for a week's travel and report immediately to Sir Dudley Pound, the First Sea Lord, in London. Arriving early next morning he was introduced to General Golikov, Vice Chief of the Russian General Staff, Captain 1st Grade M. Vorontsov, a Russian Colonel and an Interpreter who had been sent to seek British assistance with an invitation from Kuznetsov, the Soviet Commisar for the Russian Navy, to send a force to the White Sea or Murmansk.

The First Sea Lord told Admiral Vian that General Golikov, and his associates, were returning to Russia the next day and he was to accompany them to discuss with Kuznetsov what their part of the proposed operations would be and to examine the bases proposed for our naval force. Leaving the same day for Greenock, he was joined there by Group Captain Pearce who was to study the air defence side of the project. A twin-engined Catalina of the R.A.F. awaited them to take the party to Archangel, a flight of 22 hours. On arrival they were met by Rear Admiral Geoffrey Miles, who had recently been appointed for naval liaison duties in Moscow.

Next morning the party of VIP's flew a further 800 miles to Moscow and on arrival were driven to the British Embassy for lunch with the Ambassador, Sir Stafford Cripps, who immediately warned Admiral Vian that he would not find Kuznetsov, a young politician, easy and who would resent any view different from his own. This soon became apparent but, nevertheless, politely said that he was very glad to meet the Commander of the British Force who was to cooperate with the Russian Navy in the far north against the Germans.

On 22nd June, 1941, Hitler invaded Russia having intimated earlier he would overrun them in six weeks. Churchill and Roosevelt having promised aid to the Russians, the Lease-Lend Bill being founded, now had the task of fulfilling that promise.

Following talks between Stalin and Churchill regarding supplies, what then was to be the best route? The Pacific from USA to Vladivostok then by rail across Siberia, the Mediterranean to the Persian Gulf, Port Hormuz, Basra then overland, or Britain via Iceland and North Cape to Murmansk and Archangel. It was agreed and decided the latter as being the shortest route, a distance of 2000 miles, could be covered by the naval escorts. Nevertheless there were immediate problems at Murmansk as the port seemed inadequate and left much to be desired as no cranes were available to lift more than ten tons, so one of the first ships sent had to be a Crane ship to lift the heavy equipment. - The sailing of the convoys to Russia were soon to begin. . . .

Churchill having given a warning to be prepared for heavy sacrifices in the munitions field had to meet the needs of Russia. Lord Beaverbrook, Minister of Supply, having already visited the United States, was the man to lead the "Mission to Moscow" which sailed in the Cruiser **HMS LONDON**.

With Lord Beaverbrook was Captain H H Balfour, Parliamentary Under Secretary, Major General Sir Ismay Hastings, Senior Staff Officer, Ministry of Defence, Major General Macready, Asst. Chief Imperial General Staff. General F N Mason Macfarlane, Rear Admiral G A Brett and Admiral W H Stanley. On his departure Lord Beaverbrook told factory workers going flat out with increasing production: "I am taking with me to Moscow your pledge and promise to the soldiers and workers of Russia".

It will be noted that from this entourage of high ranking officials there were only two sailors - both Admirals, one English, one American - who had any "Sea time", so this caused problems on outward and return voyages. To the officers and crew of **HMS LONDON** the Minister of Supply became known as the "Beaver".

Leading Seaman Charles Deval who was detailed to look after them recalls an amusing incident.

On entering the notorious Barents Sea conditions were bad and extremely cold and the "Beaver" having been allocated to the Commander's cabin found it was not warm enough for him. He had some kind of electric heater which he was trying to connect to the ships power system. This was discovered by one of the LTO's (Leading Torpedo

Operator) who realised that any tampering with the electrics aboard would have a dangerous effect on degaussing equipment, this making the ship susceptible to magnetic mines suspected to be adjacent to our track on entering the White Sea. This was reported to the bridge through the usual channels. Accordingly Deval was instructed by the Captain to escort Lord Beaverbrook to the bridge who then chastised the noble Lord in no uncertain manner. "I have over a thousand first class men in my ship's company and I will not tolerate stupidity which puts them at risk unnecessarily. We have quite enough on our hands fighting the enemy without having to play nursemaid to His Majesty's Ministers". Great glee spread among the lower deck on hearing the buzz that the pompous bleeder aft had been put in the rattle!

Their Mission to Moscow completed during which no time was wasted. Great Britain and United States having agreed to give aid and to the transportation of materials to Russia, also help with the delivery. The Russians having stated their needs, were told what would be supplied and soon the convoys would be on their way with the materials promised. The entourage of Ministers and Officers were ready to return to the UK in the Cruiser **HMS LONDON** which could not get into Archangel having too much draft to cross the bar at Dvina. So they embarked in **HMS HARRIER** one of the small Fleet Sweepers based in Russia which had the task of transhipping his Lordship and entourage including baggage to get them aboard **LONDON**. It was a hell of a night, terrific seas running **LONDON** was reasonably steady whereas **HARRIER** was tossing about like a toy boat with the Russian Chief of Naval Staff on board and, after several attempts to get alongside, he indicated it was not possible and should abandon the attempt. This of course was sufficient to stiffen the national pride of the gallant Skipper who indicated that nothing was beyond the prowess of the finest seamen in the world. Whilst it might be impossible for others, the Royal Navy could and would do the job.

There were about 40 members of the entourage British, American, Russian Navy, Army and Air Force Chiefs, Civvies, Servants and Secretaries with enough gold carat to tie up the **HARRIER**. Six attempts were made to get the Mission and their baggage aboard with dozens of tin cases 3ft x 2ft weighing 50lbs, meaning each case was sent across separately on a line and the passengers had to wait until the brow of **LONDON** was a reasonable distance from the top of the potato locker then jump for it. In getting them aboard, **HARRIER** had smashed the port whaler, parted four wires, lost four manillas, all heaving lines and stove in several plates on the seamen's mess deck.

As the Cruiser **LONDON** sailed back to the UK and the entourage of the "Mission to Moscow" returned to their offices near the Port after which she was named, the Convoys to Russia becoming known as the "Hell Run" were soon to begin.

Leading Signalman Ted Balaam like hundreds of others, remembers the freezing cold - especially on the bridge of **HMS SHROPSHIRE**.

On one occasion early in 1941 Sir Stafford Cripps and Sir Winston Churchill were aboard, making a high speed passage, for security reasons, for them to discuss convoy proposals with the Russian authorities, including Joe Stalin.

On other convoys, QP15 in particular, in a big storm with eight-foot waves and blizzards all signalmen were warned not to touch a thing on the bridge without sheepskin gloves otherwise it would burn the skin off their hands. The spray when it hit the compass platform was sharp needles of ice as temperatures of -60°F froze you to the bone giving you only two minutes to live if sunk or washed overboard.

We had no warm clothing except overcoats, so many put on extra underclothes and socks only to find a layer of ice between when going off watch. Worse was as the ice thawed out it became increasingly painful.

Three lookouts on the Bridge Wings died standing upright; so in the future part of my duty was to walk around to make sure they were awake. We also experienced the additional need to look out for icebergs the further North they steamed towards the Ice Barrier along with the officer of the watch. A constant reminder of the Titanic, at night they were easier to detect as the air became even colder if that were possible when already -50/60°. When you see the massive lump you must miss you know that 7/8 of the berg is below water and spread out in all directions.

Steaming still northward crashing through the ice **HMS SHROPSHIRE** sustained many dents to her half an inch plating on the ship side making the passage more harrowing.

Following the visit of Admiral Vian to Russia and the Beaverbrook Mission to Moscow, Naval Party 100 was formed on 25th July 1941, just four weeks after Russia entered the war. The original party consisted of the strange combination of one Admiral, one Royal Navy Commander, one Chief Petty Officer Telegraphist and eight Telegraphists. The intention was to set up a radio station to communicate with the submarines **TIGRIS** and **TRIDENT** who were to patrol off the Petsamo coast, showing the Russians our methods of sinking enemy shipping. The Russians had fine large submarines but no idea how to use them. Their patrols started after breakfast then home for tea. The RN submarine patrols had a duration of approximately thirty days. The Naval Party 100 stay at the submarine base at Polyarnoe was intended to last not longer than 3 months.

Telegraphist Archie Creedy was one of the 8 telegraphists sent out to commission the base. The draft from Chatham had an air of secrecy and mystery right from the start.

We were called to the Drafting Office late one evening, issued a revolver, twelve rounds of ammunition and complete kit of Arctic clothing and rushed to the Admiralty in London. An Admiral gave us a lecture saying it would be a great adventure for us and would see many strange things, yet gave no indication as to our destination. We were sent to the Strand for photographs to be taken for passports, much to the annoyance of the photographer who objected to having to open his studio so late at night. We then took the night train to Glasgow.

Prior to departure from Euston Station we met a Lieutenant RNVR who was joining the party. He whispered to me that he was not a sailor, which seemed rather strange for a Naval Officer and I assumed he suffered from sea-sickness. It transpired he was a civilian Russian interpreter and was only given the uniform that afternoon.

Eventually arriving at Dunoon we were taken aboard the Submarine Depot Ship **TITANIA**, issued with two submarine sweaters, filled in a next-of-kin form and within twenty minutes were at sea heading North in the Submarine **TIGRIS**. Until recently the **TIGRIS** had been landing and picking up agents from the coast of France and the crew gave us the impression that this was to be our destination. At first we were most unpopular with the crew of the **TIGRIS**. They resented having 7 extra hands aboard, complete with kit bag, hammock and Arctic gear on an already cramped boat. Even the Davis escape hatch was full of spuds. There was no place to sleep and we were only able to bunk down on bags of stores in the forward torpedo compartment.

The trip took 9 days and it was not until four days out we were informed we were going to Russia. Being unprepared for life in a submarine we were faced with many difficulties. Using the "heads" was most complicated. When dived we had to first ask the Officer of the Watch for permission to "Blow the Heads". Before permission was granted he had "Up Periscope" to see if any surface bubbles could be seen by the enemy. All waste is blown out by compressed air but to the inexperienced it had the habit of coming back at you.

On one occasion whilst on the surface to charge the batteries we were spotted by a German aircraft. We crash dived and within twenty minutes were informed by radio that we had been spotted. The Admiralty had decoded the enemy report, recoded it, and transmitted to us. This shows how efficient the Navy can be.

As we neared the Russian coast and Polyarnoe we were met by a Russian destroyer. The **TIGRIS** signalman was having difficulty in reading messages in broken English from the Russian Aldis lamp. It transpired later that the "Russian signalman" was a telegraphist who had been detached from our party at the Admiralty in London and had been flown out to Russia with the Admiral, Commander and CPO Telegraphist by Catalina aircraft.

As we entered Polyarnoe we changed into our Arctic "long johns" but to our surprise there was no snow to be seen, they were in fact having a "mini heatwave" and the roads were a sea of mud.

Setting up a radio station from scratch in any foreign country would create problems but in Russia the task was enormous. We had only a small portable transmitter and the CPO Tel worked day and night endeavouring to communicate with the Admiralty. He was the finest operator I had met during my time in the service, although bad tempered primarily through having such inexperienced operators, he taught us the ropes which were invaluable later. He hated Russia and never left the building once during his 18 month stay. He was able, somehow, to fiddle a constant flow of vodka and rum.

It was decided that for us to work efficiently it was essential to seek help from the Russians to obtain the use of a more powerful transmitter. The Admiral was a quiet English gentleman, but perhaps too much so to deal with the tough Communist attitude of the Russian Naval Authorities. They treated us with constant distrust so it was many months before the correct equipment was available from the UK.

As the winter days grew shorter bringing the constant darkness, radio communication became even more difficult. This was primarily the effect of the "Aurora Borealis"; we would go days without obtaining contact with UK through interference. It was decided to send a "Geological Boffin" from the UK to take earth and rock samples to try to eliminate the interference. On arrival he requested the use of a horse and drosky to go into the hills with a portable battery radio to test reception. I had great difficulty in obtaining the hire of the sledge but promised to return the horse each day. We set off with a large bundle of hay for the horse; we fed him the entire bale only to find when we returned in the evening this was supposed to have been a week's ration. It must have been the horse's happiest day! The Boffin never did eliminate the interference but had great fun having an earth plate placed in the harbour on his advice.

It was not through lack of trying very hard but we had little success in forming a friendship with the Russians as it seemed to be a form of fear that stopped them from fraternising. However we did make friends with the Russian matelots during trips on the Russian destroyers when they acted as local escort to the convoys, most of them felt rather sorry for us feeling we should have a Revolution to be as happy as they were, little did they know!

A very strange thing was the behaviour of the many wild dogs of Polyarnoe. There were dozens of them which were badly treated by the Russians.

However, as soon as a British sailor set foot ashore he was immediately followed by the dogs as they seemed to sense the kindness of the British but would run away from the Russians.

As the convoys became more frequent it was essential to enlarge the jetty, most of the work being done by prisoners and the poor individuals, mostly Mongolian who seemed to have little value for life. Many deaths were caused unnecessarily by logs falling from cranes lifting them from the barges. On one occasion they hooked the crane to a barge and went off for a meal returning to find the tide had gone down pulling the crane into the barge. The antics of trying to lift the crane back to the jetty would have made a wonderful comedy film.

One of my saddest memories of North Russia was the funeral of an RAF Hurricane pilot who was shot whilst on patrol but managed to fly the plane back to the aerodrome at Vaenga. He was buried in a little Russian cemetery high in the hills behind the town. The makeshift wooden coffin was carried by a sledge. His colleagues fired a volley over his grave. I will always remember the echo of those shots over the hills that seemed to go on for minutes. There were no crosses to be seen in the cemetery but each grave had a large red star.

The first convoy to Russia sailed in early August 1941 as a "dummy run" plotting the best course of navigation not to be too close to the German air bases in Norway, or the ice barriers which would extend closer in the winter months ahead, thus establishing a summer route and a winter route. Code named "Dervish" it preceded the following PQ and JW outward bound and QP and RA return convoys.

Western military aid was urgently required by Russia having been overwhelmingly attacked by German military forces. This made Stalin press Churchill for a second front to divert the strain on his forces. Churchill was not ready to assist with a second front but agreed to help with RAF fighters, as British fighter aircraft were considered the most imperative to start with.

At short notice an RAF Wing was designed during late July and early August 1941. Similarly the means of getting the aircraft to Russia and the purpose for it. This obviously had to be a seaborne operation.

The RAF Wing number 151 comprising two Squadrons 81 and 134, totalling some 500 personnel, was assembled at an RAF station in Yorkshire. A number of 12-gun Hurricane aircraft were prepared for transport with other stores and equipment made ready for their final destination, an airfield near Murmansk Vaenga.

The purpose of 151 Wing was to serve a short period of operational flying, to demonstrate the Hurricane as a fighter aircraft, teach and train Russian pilots how to fly and operate them and to train the Russian technicians how to assemble, maintain and service the aircraft before being handed over to the Soviet Airforce.

What then was the best method of transport to release the first Hurricane fighters to the Soviets, with efficiency and obvious secrecy?

With the close cooperation between Royal Navy and Royal Air Force it was decided that **HMS ARGUS** the aircraft carrier would be ideal. Originally built as a liner for an Italian shipping line the Admiralty converted it into the first aircraft carrier with full length flight deck and a lift to take aircraft down to the hangar. Being squat and box-like without masts or obvious funnels it became known in the Fleet as "The Ditty Box"!

In 1941 **ARGUS** had made several trips to the Mediterranean flying off Hurricanes for the relief of Malta; and on another occasion to Takoradi for the relief of the Eighth Army, so was the obvious choice for Russia.

Leading Aircraftsman Arthur Platt of B Flight 134 Squadron of RAF Wing 151 was more than aware at all times what was happening on this epic voyage to Russia.

24 crated Hurricane aircraft were put aboard **ARGUS** with a team of technicians who were to unpack and assemble them during the voyage, with obvious difficulties in the heavy seas in spite of being August, an unusual experience for the RAF chaps. Pilots were aboard to fly them off at a predetermined time and point off Murmansk to the airfield at Vaenga.

Another 24 Hurricane aircraft in crates were put aboard the Dutch merchant ship ALCHIBA for assembly at a Russian airfield Keg Ostrov, air tested and flown by their pilots to Vaenga there being a refuelling station en route.

Arthur was with the main body of 151 Wing personnel aboard the passenger liner LLANSTEPHAN CASTLE sailing from Liverpool to join the other ships at Iceland assembling for departure in the first convoy "Dervish" to Russia. A staff had to be at Vaenga to receive aircraft as they flew in and to assure the Wing was fully operational.

Alan Firth as an Aero engine fitter remembers when overseas units were created in the RAF by selecting from various units airmen by trade and rank only, so it was left to the unit to select who was "on the boat". As a result anyone who was a troublemaker and always on "jankers", or an unknown factor, was invariably the one to be chosen rather than a valued member of the squadron.

For this reason 151 Wing was an assembly of "characters". A pal was chosen to go overseas but as he was married I, foolishly, volunteered to go in his place. No innoculations, I was convinced I was bound for Canada. I took my dancing shoes and a Corporal PT Instructor took his golf clubs.

We formed at RAF Leconfield near Hull and sailed from Liverpool on the LLANSTEPHAN CASTLE. Three weeks later we arrived at Archangel. During the voyage we were asked which fitters were used to Merlin engines which riggers on airframes. 20 assorted tradesmen formed a party at Archangel to unpack the crates unloaded, and assemble the Hurricanes. This was at an airfield on an island in the harbour "Keg Ostrov". We were billeted in a Russian ferry boat. The beds were alive with lice and we went down with stomach trouble from the sour bread and strange food. Our task was to assemble the aircraft by affixing main planes, stern frame, rudder, propeller, prime engine and air test prior to flying to Vaenga. Meanwhile our stores were landed and these and our men went by train from Archangel to Murmansk, not without problems. The rear party were then flown from Archangel to Vaenga at low level in a twin engined Russian transport aircraft.

The airfield was a large sandy plateau surrounded by birch trees, the sand was soft. It snowed in September but did not freeze hard until October. When the snow was still soft we had problems. When Jerry attacked the airfield and the Hurricanes had to scramble the pilots had difficulties in taxiing. The pilots would give a burst of throttle which usually did the trick, if not and the wheels still stuck, the aircraft tail came up and broke the propeller.

The C.O. then gave orders that the ground crew, fitter and rigger, were to sit on the tail of the aircraft whilst it taxied to take off. Unfortunately, and sadly, one pilot forgot about his human ballast and took off. The two aircrew were killed.

The two Squadrons were operational for several weeks shooting down 15 aircraft and five probables for the loss of one aircraft. We were then taken off operations and became instructional. Canada then began to send aircraft to Russia. We taught the pilots and their technicians the armament, engine, airframe, wireless etc.

DIRECTIVE TO THE COMMANDING OFFICER OF FORCE "BENEDICT"

APPOINTMENT

YOU ARE APPOINTED FORCE COMMANDER OF THE R.A.F. IN NORTH RUSSIA (NO. 151 WING).

COMMAND

YOU WILL EXERCISE FULL OPERATIONAL CONTROL OF YOUR FORCE, BUT YOU WILL BE UNDER THE GENERAL COMMAND OF THE COMMANDER OF THE ARMY AIR FORCE OF THE NORTHERN FRONT. (MAJOR-GENERAL FOR AIR KOUZNETZOV).

ROLE

THE PRIMARY ROLE ASSIGNED TO YOUR FORCE IS THE DEFENCE OF THE NAVAL BASE AT MURMANSK AND CO-OPERATION WITH THE SOVIET FORCES IN THE MURMANSK AREA. SUBJECT TO THE REQUIREMENTS OF THIS PRIMARY ROLE, YOU MAY, AT YOUR DISCRETION, GIVE SUCH OTHER ASSISTANCE TO THE SOVIET AUTHORITIES AS THEY MAY ASK FOR.

Sergeant Pilot Freddie Crewe RAF sailed to Russia with other personnel aboard SS LLANSTEPHAN CASTLE to rejoin 81 Squadron at Vaenga - There had been many rumours regarding the destination of the Wing; tropical or somewhere cold? The issue of clothing covered both. However, one bright spark discovered that the only common foreign language among the interpreters was Russian - so Russia it had to be. On board the ship were nineteen crated Hurricanes.

On board the aircraft carrier **HMS ARGUS**, were 24 pilots of 81 and 134 Squadrons whose task was to fly the aircraft direct to Vaenga when some 180 miles from the Kola Inlet. To have launched closer to the coast, would have compromised the security of the operation.

After the crated aircraft had been assembled and test flown at Keg-Ostrov (Archangel) they were ferried to Vaenga via Kandalaksha to join their **ARGUS** launched colleagues. Ground crews and stores arrived mainly by train, some by destroyer, Russian "Dakotas" and Catalina.

On 12th September 151 Wing became operational. After a couple of sorties, it went into action defending the base from reconnaissance and attacking German aircraft. The Luftwaffe obviously now knew that the RAF was in residence.

Freddie Crewe relates his flying experience in Russia.

"My first sortie was reconnaissance, followed by the escorting of Russian bombers to Finland to bomb Petsamo and again to attack the German air base. Altogether six sorties were flown which included scrambling to intercept JU88's which were attacking Vaenga and Polyarnoe.

"When the snow came, we had to be careful when coming into land [there being little with which to judge height]. We used the technique of "feeling" the aircraft down on the main wheels, rather than executing a three point landing."

There were now some forty Hurricanes at Vaenga and, in addition to normal operations, the Russian pilots had to be trained.

My question to Freddie Crewe: "How do you train pilots to fly a single-seated aircraft when you cannot co-pilot the student?"

"You teach them the cockpit checks for each phase of the flight, what speeds to use for landing and taking off, what speeds to use for lowering flaps and undercarriage, what characteristics the aircraft displays in various flight regimes, brief them to avoid tight turns when in the landing configuration etc., specifically pointing out any hazards which can be avoided by good pilotage."

The first solos were made satisfactorily, albeit often in pretty bad weather. Several circuits and landings being made to gain experience in handling the machine. It did not take them long to become operational and take on the defence of Vaenga and the escort of their bombers. Throughout their stay in Russia 151 Wing received the fullest cooperation and unstinted help from the Russians. Whatever was needed, they received; food was plentiful and accommodation good. At Vaenga the Russian Commander, Major General Kouenetzof was concerned that the semi-underground hangars at dispersals, were too small to house the Hurricanes. He stated they must be enlarged immediately, and the task would be completed by noon *tomorrow*. The next morning, as the pilots and ground crew were arriving to set up dawn readiness, they passed a large contingent of approximately ten thousand Mongolian characters. Each was equipped with a pick or shovel. They opened up the semi-underground hangars, enlarged them from twenty-six feet wide to forty-five feet wide. By lunchtime each roof had been replaced, earth and turf put back on top thus providing an ideal camouflage.

Missions continued and by the time the Wing had finished operations, it had accounted for fifteen enemy aircraft destroyed (fourteen to 81 Squadron and one to 134 Squadron) against the loss of one 81 Squadron Hurricane and pilot. Four members of the Wing were awarded the Order of Lenin, the Commander, the two Squadron Commanders and Flt.Sgt. "Wag" Hawe. The whole operation was unique and enlightening. 151 Wing returned to the UK aboard **HMS KENYA** and other destroyers arriving at Rosyth on 7th December.

Regretfully, this early cooperation became spasmodic on future occasions with the materials supplied, as the continuance will divulge, describe and outline.

This first consignment of materials to Russia for their assistance being "gift" aircraft must have been very exciting for the Russians, especially the pilots.

A few of us had the need to travel by train throughout Russia, others journeys, but none to compare with the earlier journey of Flight Sgt Henry Neale and Flight Sgt Frank Loxley of the RAF. Having dealt with the consignment of aircraft and stores at Archangel they had to get to Murmansk to rejoin 151 wing established at Vaenga.

Our journey started from a station just outside Bakaritza aboard a cattle truck. It was night time and there was a lot of noise and activity. By the time we found our train some of our kit had been stolen. We built shelves out of frozen planks of wood to stow our rations, trying to make ourselves as comfortable as possible not knowing the length or time of the journey ahead. We were innocent enough to think the truck was for us when in piled about 20 other people, they were male and female troops bound for the Finnish front. The truck became quite full although the Russians did give us the biggest part.

We pushed off into the night, a long line of trucks. Every time the train stopped it was buffer to buffer everyone being thrown off their feet. The train "chugged" on day after day, night after night, sometimes fast, sometimes slow, through endless forests. Sometimes it stopped for a whole day, to allow the line to be repaired which had been subject to bombing.

At times when the train stopped it was necessary to relieve ourselves so had to take a chance. It was an unwritten law that males jumped out one side and females the other. Then, without warning, there would be a couple of sharp toots on the engine whistle and the train started to move on, so you had to move with it. This proved extremely difficult as there was deep snow at the side of the track and running with your trousers down below the knees in freezing weather made going to the trackside toilet a nerve-racking experience.

Occasionally a station would appear out of the forest so there was a mad rush for hot water and wood for the stove which was in the middle of each cattle truck. This had to be kept going for most of the way for warmth as well as cooking food.

The journey took three weeks before eventually arriving very cold, hungry, dirty, tired and exhausted, at Murmansk, for the last of the journey down river to the airfield at - Vaenga.

Telegraphist Jim Butler was one of the first to join Naval Party 100 with other communication ratings to set up the Signal Station ashore at the Naval Base at Polyarnoe. It was to play such an important part for the control of convoys by keeping in contact with Admiralty in London. The preparation for his sojourn in Russia was also shrouded in mystery and secrecy.

Later in October 1941 I was in the Naval Barracks at Chatham waiting the completion of the refit of **HMS SHARPSHOOTER**. The Tannoy sounded off with the customary preamble "Do you hear there" and went on to announce "The following ratings are to report to Drafting Master-at-Arms in the Drill Shed at the double".

Safe in the knowledge that being **SHARPSHOOTER's** crew this could not possibly apply to me, barely listened to the list of ratings being intoned by that metallic and inhuman voice until, almost after the event, realised that my name had been announced. After giving the repeated announcement full attention the awful truth was confirmed not only by name but by official number.

With dismay I hastened to the Drill Shed to rectify the obvious mistake. But to no avail as I was brusquely informed that there had been no mistake and I had been taken off the **SHARPSHOOTER's** crew and that the draft chit stood. "Get fell in with the rest", I was ordered.

We were then told that we constituted Naval Party 100; no other information was available, we were to pack our kit and report back that same evening. Despite the lower deck grape vine, which usually could be depended on to have a buzz on anything ranging from the conduct of the war and the movements resulting therefrom - to the personal peccadilloes of the Commodore and the barracks in general, our enquiries drew a complete blank. No one knew anything about Naval Party 100, not even the "barrack stanchions". Such tight security was perhaps some comfort to us; if no one knew about the party in Chatham Depot it was feasible that the enemy too was oblivious to Naval Party 100, its formation and its purpose.

That evening we were transported complete with kit bag, hammock and baggage to the dockyard where a steam train with drawn blinds in each coach awaited our boarding. We were each issued with a bag meal and were told not to raise the blinds in our compartments under the pain of dire punishment should we disobey. We boarded the train and shortly afterwards began to move accompanied by the shrill sounds of whistles and the hoarse shouts of unseen dockyard workers. The journey seemed interminable and after wild conjecture about our destination, surreptitious peeps through the blinded windows, we gradually lapsed into sullen silence and resigned fate, fully preoccupied with our own private thoughts of home and loved ones. After many stops and starts we eventually arrived at Thurso, at the extreme NE tip of Scotland. The Party then embarked on **HMS ASHANTI**, a Tribal class destroyer, and were transported to that hell among the Orkney Islands, Scapa Flow. The party was then halved, one group was detailed to take passage in **HMS KENYA** the cruiser and the other in a submarine. I drew the former and considered myself fortunate but fate decided otherwise. We were still oblivious to our ultimate destination.

On sailing, the **KENYA**'s captain announced that we were ordered to Iceland where we were to join up with a convoy bound for North Russia. We then very quickly appreciated what our ultimate destination was to be but could not foresee the purpose which seemingly, at the time, was known by few outside the minds of the Lords Commissioners of the Admiralty. However, we soon had other things to think about when the impersonal voice of the Captain again sounded throughout the ship to inform the crew and those taking passage that, one or more of the enemy's heavy ships had sailed from their Norwegian anchorages and that we had been ordered to patrol the Denmark Straits in the hope of making an interception. After days of fruitless search, we were notified that the alarm was false and that the ship was about to proceed in accordance with its previous orders for which we were duly grateful.

On joining the convoy bound for North Russia we took up station in its centre while the destroyers and other small ships formed a screen to protect the convoy from 'U' boats. As we progressed slowly towards the east the weather gradually worsened until a full gale was blowing. Conditions in the ship became very uncomfortable but compared to what the small escorts had to put up with we were undoubtedly having a fairly comfortable voyage. Nevertheless, a Royal Marine was washed overboard and not seen again, his kit being auctioned before we arrived at our destination. During the voyage the members of Naval Party 100 were employed as additional lookouts, the cold being so severe that the exposure to it for more than an hour in a static position was humanly unbearable. Throughout the daylight hours I stood or rather sat my watch - on the starboard wing of the bridge armed only with powerful binoculars. I was ordered to carry out a sweep on a specific arc on the starboard side and to report immediately should I see anything suspicious. On taking over my initial watch I was struck by the apparent comical situation of five or six faceless ratings sitting in a row cocooned by massive balls of clothing and tinged white with frost, their eyes glued to binoculars trained on their respective arcs of search on the ship's beam. They were so stiffened by the very low temperature that when relieved from their interminable vigil raised themselves from their seats like brittle old men fearful that something might snap. Before my relief was to arrive all thoughts of amusement had vanished from my mind and I was to dread the onset of each watch long before the shores of North Russia loomed up on the horizon. Notwithstanding the inhospitable spectre of the Kola Inlet I must confess that I was pleased to see it - how naive I was at the tender age of 20 years.

After anchoring in the Kola Inlet which led to Murmansk, Naval Party 100 was piped to muster with baggage on the quarterdeck. After a short wait we boarded a small boat which transported the pathetic and shivering party of despondent sailors to the icy shores of Polyarnoe. We were then led to what can only be described, when compared to the surrounding buildings, as a sumptuous block of flats, which was later commonly known among the British sailors as "Navy House"; being greeted by the other members of the party who had sailed in a submarine directly to North Russia and had arrived some days earlier. We were conducted to our accommodation and allocated flats, 3 or 4 to a room. The building was generously heated, the windows were double and sealed, the single beds were quite luxurious, there was adequate wardrobe space for our gear, also bathrooms although the bath water was invariably brown. All in all we found ourselves very comfortably situated. We were introduced to some young Russian girls who were allocated by the Russian authorities to look after our creature comforts - there were some exceptions of course not knowing precisely what these were at the time. Notwithstanding the bleak view from the window our spirits rose and we began to think we might after all be on to a good thing.

Our equanimity was to some extent shattered by the emergence of an elderly and burly Chief Petty Officer Telegraphist - at that time anyone over 30 was elderly - who ordered us in stentorian tones to muster in what later became the wireless office. He brusquely informed us of the reason for our existence in North Russia and that there was work to be done without further delay if the station was to become operative. Despite his forbidding appearance and gruff manner he had a heart of gold and had the best interests of the staff always in mind. He was a hard taskmaster, merciless with 'skates' and malingerers, generous with praise for the conscientious workers, but always scrupulously fair. We grew to admire him and to seek his advice.

Setting up the Signal Station meant working on the aerials on the roof of the building in the intense cold which made the task more difficult. We were warned not to remove our gloves for fear of frostbite and other dire consequences, and not to touch the metal with bare hands otherwise it would stick to our fingers and the skin would be torn off in any attempt to free them. This I did not venture to learn by experience.

We were allocated to watches and I was given the plum job of working the direct line to the Admiralty. This line was usually the busiest and demanded a good speed at both receiving and transmitting morse. When a "Y" station was set up, a few miles from Polyarnoe in the direction of the front line which was then somewhere in the region of Petsamo, the task of transmitting to the Admiralty the intercepted German radio traffic became especially onerous. In due course a relay was fitted which enabled this traffic to be cleared quite readily by automatic high speed morse - it was incredible to be able to clear a signal of, say, 300 groups in a few seconds. There were, of course, occasions in that latitude when owing to the Aurora Borealis radio communication was completely blacked out and sometimes lasted for hours or even days. It was uncanny to sit on watch with earphones glued to ones head with not a peep of morse to be heard. On one occasion, when there was a panic on about the likely interception of a Russian bound convoy by enemy units, we were experiencing a radio black out and, of all times, the Admiral ordered a very high priority signal to be cleared to the Admiralty. I tried all means to obtain an acknowledgement to my transmission to no avail; my lack of success was not received with any enthusiasm and the Chief became frantic. "Keep trying" he moaned. I continued to call any British Naval Station when to my surprise on listening out heard very faint but quite clear cheeps of morse from a naval call sign quite unknown on the frequency I was working. "Chief, Chief, I've got someone", I cried. After frantic scrabbling for the relevant publication listing Naval Call Signs the unknown was identified as a shore station in South Africa. I was ordered to transmit the signal to that station giving instructions that it was to be retransmitted to the Admiralty, which was duly carried out. Great relief was experienced tinged with innate suspicion that we may have been duped by an enemy station. Subsequent events were to confirm that the South African station was genuine and that the signal was in fact received by the Admiralty. Avid discussion ensued among colleagues about this peculiar phenomenon in a vain attempt to rationalise it. They threw in all the ionised layers in the earth's atmosphere not named or identified, the frequency used, but our limited knowledge at our tender ages could produce no satisfactory theory and we put it down to a freak wireless transmission. Perhaps on reflection it was divine intervention.

The Russian girls who looked after us in the way of preparing our meals and cleaning the flat had by now become quite friendly and were beginning to pick up smatterings of the English language. I became fairly close to one young girl called Tanya, who in turn called me Jimisky. We told each other about our upbringing, education, holidays and way of life. I had a photograph album with me at the time and recalled how amazed she was seeing a photograph taken whilst on holiday. "Did I have permission to travel? Why was I released from work? Why did I still live with my parents?" she asked. Explaining that in the United Kingdom citizens were free to do what they wished, she was stunned. She told me she had been taken from her parents at the age of 14 years and allocated to work in North Russia, and had not seen them since. Other confidences were exchanged from time to time and she became quite envious of life in the United Kingdom. Although our friendship blossomed it was definitely platonic and there was absolutely no physical contact whatsoever. Any attempt at familiarity was instantly rebuffed despite the favourable conditions, we usually sat on my bed chatting, looking at magazines or whatever. My mess mates confirmed that the same situation applied to them and we were soon to learn that the girls dare not form any such liaison with foreigners and that prostitution in North Russia was punishable by death. In the event the opportunity of testing this edict did not arise.

The Russian authorities soon became aware of the relationships, albeit innocent, being developed and of the truth about the Western World becoming known to these young girls. Their action was swift and incisive. Almost overnight the girls were removed and we were told that henceforth we had to fend for ourselves. The chore of keeping the flats clean presented no problem since we were used to performing these functions at sea, but the absence of a trained cook did cause some inconvenience. It was not long before a naval cook appeared on the scene to fill the breach but there was no doubt that we missed the girls and their companionship. The Chief Telegraphist then broke the dismal news that the Russian Navy would henceforth augment the escorts of convoys proceeding to and from the United Kingdom by their most up-to-date destroyers and that a Telegraphist and a Signalman from Naval Party 100 would be allocated to each destroyer for convoy escort communication purposes. All too soon my turn came and, in company with a Signalman Ginger, we were told to report to the Russian destroyer **SOCRASHATINI**. Suitably attired in appropriate clothing and armed with a sack of tinned food - the Russian sailors' food was inedible - we made our way unhappily to the jetty. We were received quite hospitably by the Russian junior ranks and shown to our accommodation right forward in the bows of the ship. Access to the compartment was by means of a square scuttle through which we virtually had to crawl; when sailing the scuttle was secured by means of a bolted hatch. Viewing our only means of escape from the compartment with some misgivings we were comforted by the thought that if the ship were to sink, we still had exactly the same chance of surviving. In those Northern waters none at all. After a few days at sea the Russian skipper asked the signalman to seek permission from the senior officer of the escort for the **SOCRASHATINI** to return to the comparative safety of the Kola Inlet. As no reply had been received within an hour the skipper, prompted most vociferously by the ship's commissar, who hated being at sea, asked the signalman to urge the senior officer to reply. His reply explained that the signal had been received by the senior officer and when considered appropriate to release **SOCRASHATINI** would doubtless do so. The Russian captain and the commissar became increasingly frantic when no signal ensued and further pressed the signalman in very unseamanlike language to hasten a reply. Ginger, stung by the obvious slight to the senior officer of the escort, lost all control and castigated the Russian captain, the commissar and all in sight which led to him being removed from the bridge by the British naval liaison officer. Shortly afterwards permission was given for the **SOCRASHATINI** to return to harbour and departing at best speed all seemed well and the incident perhaps forgotten. However it was not to be. On return to Polyarnoe representations were made by the Russian authorities at the highest level and it emerged that nothing less than the shooting of Ginger would be likely to satisfy them. The Admiral was in a dilemma. He had to please the Russians but, of course, had no power to execute Ginger for such a minor offence. Insubordination in the Royal Navy could quite adequately be dealt with by less primitive measures. The Admiral's decision was soon made known - or at least that part of it which we were required to play. One morning those not on watch were ordered to dress in number 3 blue uniforms; issued with khaki belt, garters and 303 rifles and ordered to fall in outside the building. Ginger was then suitably placed in the middle of our ranks and the escort, with rifles at the slope, marched him to the jetty where a British destroyer was waiting alongside to transport him back to the United Kingdom. We were led to believe that dire punishment awaited him on his return to the RN Barracks, Chatham. It was an awesome show and the Russians were certainly given the impression that their honour had been vindicated. I later learnt on return to the United Kingdom, that no further action had in fact been taken against Ginger. He had been given a fright but that was all. There was no doubt in my mind that the Admiral had displayed the wisdom of King Solomon.

On another occasion of sailing in the Russian ship when the cold was even more severe than usual, we found on returning to our anchorage in the Kola Inlet that the sea was rapidly freezing. Requests for a boat to take us back to Navy House were made in vain; it could not penetrate the icy barrier and we were marooned aboard until the weather relented or until an ice-breaker could be sent to free the boat's passage. Since the latter required the cooperation of the Russian authorities the position was fairly hopeless.

We had run out of our tinned food and were thus dependent on the Russians for sustenance. The Russian sailors were very sympathetic and when the midday meal was served we started off with a small raw fish, something like a sprat, which they considered to be a rare delicacy. They eyed us with pleasant anticipation, waiting to see grateful appreciation for their obvious generosity, but were appalled because there was no way that we could digest uncooked fish, which appeared most revolting, endeavouring to explain in our totally inadequate grasp of the Russian language. They were puzzled and a pregnant pause ensued until one young Russian sailor who had a smattering of English suddenly beamed upon us and indicated that we should await his return. An embarrassing silence reigned in the meantime. He returned, with a wide grin, brandishing a bottle of vodka. Nethertheless, a few tots of this fiery liquid not only numbed the senses, but sharpened the appetite and it was not long before I found myself consuming the fish with some gusto, although feeling nauseated at the thought of it.

Fortunately we were soon rescued from our plight and transported back to the comfort of the block of flats. Once in my room I threw off my clothing, which had been worn without change for about ten days, and sank gratefully into a bath filled to the brim with piping hot, rusty-brown water and dreamed of the delights of the table which, I anticipated, were soon to follow. Alas the chef plied us with the same old monotonous food, corned beef hash and rice, which we had been forced to consume interminably as any supplies of food sent by sea from the UK always seemed to be stored in a ship which inevitably was sunk on the way up. The chef did his best and our diet was to a limited extent augmented by what the Russians could spare. They supplied yak meat which needed to be chewed until one's jaws ached and still without any impression on it. They supplied what they called butter - which defied description - and tins of thick condensed milk, but we soon learned to drink tea the Russian way: out of a glass and without milk.

Having settled back into the watchkeeping routine and being between convoys things were generally quiet. I decided in my youthful ignorance and naivety, to pay a call on the **SOCRASHTINI** moored alongside the jetty, to thank them for their hospitality on my last trip, and to provide them with some magazines, which were now surplus to our requirements. Picture Post was one, others that had been sent from Canada. The Admiral having connections in Canada asked for comforts to be sent to us. I was received most hospitably and the magazines were taken with obvious relish. I returned feeling quite pleased with myself, having done a kindly deed.

The repercussions were catastrophic! Shortly after the visit to the **SOCRASHTINI** I was imperiously summoned to report immediately to the Admiral's office. I could not imagine what I had done to deserve such a command. At that age I could be relied on to fall foul of King's Regulations and Admiralty Instructions without even trying and had from time to time incurred the wrath of the Chief and on the odd occasion even the Flag Lieutenant. But to be summoned to the Admiral's office was outside my field of comprehension. It has to be understood that the Admiral was so remote from us as to be almost the Almighty himself; Admirals do not deign to speak to Telegraphists. Filled with foreboding I hastened to the Admiral's office and reported my presence to the Admiral's Secretary. After a brief wait I was told to enter the holy of holies. The Admiral rose from his desk, greeted me kindly and bade me sit down in a chair opposite his desk. He addressed me by christian name and went out of his way to put me at ease. My spirits rose, as I was clearly not to be admonished, perhaps even a recommend for an award. The King, Buckingham Palace, my awestruck family, drinks in the local, all flashed before my eyes. Then the Admiral cleared his throat and began. "The reason I have sent for you is because the Russians have made very strong protests about the insidious propaganda being transmitted to the crew of one of their destroyers by a member of the British naval party". Investigations had revealed that I was the culprit, and while the Admiral appreciated that my motives were perfectly innocent this sort of thing could not be tolerated in Russia. I was not to take any books, magazines or other Western literature to the Russian ships. The Admiral gently explained some of the differences between Western democracies and totalitarian states, which of course at my tender age was most difficult to comprehend. The interview made a lasting impression upon me and armed me against left-wing extremism to this day. Although I was to serve under some outstanding Admirals during my career in the Royal Navy never again was I to meet one quite like that Admiral. Reflecting on the awards given at that time for service in North Russia, the Admiral was made a CBE, the Chief Petty Officer Telegraphist was Mentioned in Despatches and a DSM was awarded to one of my colleagues. It was rumoured at the time that one DSM was allocated by the Admiralty to the junior ranks who manned the Russian destroyers and that it was decided to give it to the youngest member among us. Whether there was any substance in this, I must have only just missed it.

The sinking of one of our cruisers in February 1942, brings me back to the conduct of the war which at this particular time was not proceeding in our favour. The Russian front in these latitudes ran from Petsamo roughly down the line of the Finnish-Russian border, which was not much more than 50 miles from the base. Fluctuations in this line occurred from time to time and on one occasion when there was a possibility of the base being overrun a destroyer was ordered to stand by to evacuate us. Fortunately, such an event did not transpire. Worse was to come, however, as one of the most humiliating experiences of the war was soon to occur. During that summer a convoy (PQ17) sailed for Russia and was ordered by the Admiralty to scatter. We in Russia had become used to the Russian ingratitude of our efforts to supply them but could always hold our heads up high because we knew that our seamen, both merchant and navy, were being called on to make sacrifices beyond the call of duty. There seemed no way, however, that the action taken by the Admiralty in this instance could be justified and although every effort was made by the Royal Navy in North Russia to retrieve the situation as best it could our morale was at its lowest. I would liked to have been anywhere but North Russia at that particular time.

After serving in North Russia for just over a year the adverse climate and the inadequate food began to take its toll. On leaving the United Kingdom and being somewhat overweight for my height I could do with some slimming down. North Russia solved that problem by reducing my 13 stones to about 11 stones. In the 13th month at Polyarnoe, however, my stomach reacted to the monotonous diet and developed diarrhoea. The doctor diagnosed something more worrying - gastroenteritis. He warned the naval authorities that no one should serve in North Russia under the existing conditions for more than twelve months and prognosticated that if it were allowed to happen there would be dire consequences, such as loss of hair and teeth and so on. I was then approaching my 14th month of service in that inhospitable country and became somewhat apprehensive and depressive. It was apparent that my decline had been noted by those responsible for the movement of personnel and I was informed that I would be sent home with the next convoy to the UK. In pursuit of this I was required to have my photograph taken by the Russian authorities for the purpose of an exit visa and was duly escorted by a Russian Naval officer, who was assumed to be an interpreter attached to the base. On the way to the photographer he asked how I felt about going home and I rashly replied that I would be glad to leave this Godforsaken country. Although it was nothing but a puerile expression on my part it had a tremendous impact upon his 'Russian' mind and for the remainder of his escort duties he maintained a sullen silence. In retrospect I now felt that my ungracious reply was much nearer the truth than I had realised. In any event no repercussions ensued and shortly afterwards my 'exit' was approved by the Russian authorities. I was ordered to pack my kit and embark on **HMS FURY** for transport to the Royal Naval Barracks at Chatham.

I was extremely glad to see the shores of the United Kingdom. Although having returned safely from the sub-zero temperatures of the Arctic and my sojourn in Russia I could not keep warm during my leave and spent considerable time huddled over a coal fire, probably due to the damp cold and inadequate winter clothing. But I was soon to become overheated as on return from leave found myself, after a few weeks, in the Red Sea.

1942

- *The ship that torpedoed herself*
- *A Tribal Chieftain dies in the Arctic*
- *The agonies of the "Induna" survivors*
- *Crude surgery in a freezing hospital*
- *Four days in an open boat*
- *"Edinburgh's" gold*
- *A disasterous ramming by KGV*
- *Hospitals from the Dark Ages*
- *A fatal signal to "Scatter"*
- *Marooned on an Arctic island*
- *PQ17 through a Nazi periscope*
- *A four day fight with the Luftwaffe in the midnight sun*
- *Hitler's ships repulsed in the Barent's Sea*
- *A scrambling net to safety*

Apart from damage caused by the storms the first seven convoys managed to reach Murmansk without loss. This success was due to almost continuous Arctic darkness as enemy aircraft could not locate targets. Regrettably this good fortune was short lived.

On the 10th January 1942 PQ8 sailed from Iceland to Murmansk. Eight ships loaded with tanks and guns protected by two destroyers, two minesweepers and the new 8000 tonne cruiser **HMS TRINIDAD**.

On January 17th the convoy was nearing the Kola Inlet, the dangerous waters where U Boats gathered. Suddenly there was a violent explosion which lit up the night sky, the convoy's leading ship had been torpedoed. The torpedoes aimed at **TRINIDAD** missed the cruiser by only a few feet and sped on to hit a merchant ship.

Three hours later a U Boat fired two torpedoes. These found their target in the magazines of **MATABELE** sending a sheet of flame 700ft high into the night sky - the destroyer had disintegrated hurling her crew into the icy seas. Several of the destroyer's already primed depth charges set to explode at various depths blew up beneath those who had not been killed. A minesweeper moved in to pick up survivors only to find the sea covered with a thick layer of fuel oil, and through a mass of debris found men in life jackets floating upright but dead. The sea was littered with men in this shocking and gruesome state.

In the space of 3 hours the first merchant ship and Royal Naval destroyer on the convoys had been sunk with four survivors.

On 24th January **HMS TRINIDAD** arrived in the Kola Inlet after normal turn round period escorted one back and on 21st March 1942 called again to escort PQ13 to Murmansk with different circumstances from previous voyage. On the morning of 28th a German shadow plane spotted the cruiser and convoy - reporting position to headquarters, 2 hours later the convoy was attacked by dive bombers hurtling down through the low cloud to release their bombs. **TRINIDAD** escaped, thanks to a barrage of anti aircraft fire by the gun crews. At midnight the same day the cruiser received a report that 3 enemy destroyers were heading towards the convoy.

Suddenly ahead at only one and a half miles were three German Narvik class destroyers each carrying guns equal to the fire power of the British cruiser and much larger than British destroyers and a top speed of 38 knots. Captain of **TRINIDAD** gave the order to open fire with main guns, anti aircraft, pom poms and even machine guns sending a curtain of fire crashing into the leading destroyer immediately setting it on fire. Shells could be seen exploding amidships with flame and smoke. The German ship began to return fire and two shells smashed into **TRINIDAD**'s port side aft. The German destroyer then broke off the engagement and headed north-west into a snow cloud. Captain of **TRINIDAD** then set about attacking the other two destroyers with continued risk of danger of torpedo attack by these modern destroyers. As the cruiser turned to starboard two torpedo tracks were clearly seen passing harmlessly by the port side.

Decreasing visibility caused the second and third ships to lose contact with their damaged leader. **TRINIDAD** decided to chase the first attacker to finish her off as she was only 2 miles away. She soon overhauled the lone destroyer: zig zagging to escape further damage, the enemy was seen emitting clouds of smoke. Many German sailors were seen supported by life jackets; many already dead, they had either been blown overboard or had jumped to avoid being blown up and died in the ice cold water.

To finish her **TRINIDAD** fired 3 torpedoes, two of these were frozen solid in mountings and failed to leave the tubes, but the third travelled on its way towards the enemy until completing a half circle it began to head back towards **TRINIDAD**. The gyro mechanism controlling the rudder had jammed from the effects of the ice cold water. It had the whole Arctic Ocean in which to run wild yet it had swung round and headed straight back for the cruiser.

Officers and look-outs stood helpless as their own lethal missile with 750lbs of high explosive raced towards them. Watching in horror as it neared, knowing it could explode in one of the four magazines and they would be blown up in one mighty flash. Seconds later the torpedo plunged into the port side and exploded leaving a gaping hole sixty feet by twenty. Ironically **TRINIDAD** was the ship that torpedoed herself. The damage caused many casualties, seventeen of the twenty-one men in the oil tanks area drowned in fuel oil. In other parts of the ship the explosion killed another fifteen. It left the cruiser critically damaged, virtually helpless wallowing in the rising sea.

Down below damage control parties were fighting to bring the fire under control and the small arms magazine had been flooded to avoid it blowing up from the heat generated. By now the cruiser was decreasing her list, quite helpless and a perfect target as with only one boiler operative her speed was only 4 knots. Then the engines stopped as salt water had found its way into pure water needed to feed the boilers, which had to be shut down to prevent more damage, so the cruiser drifted to a standstill. The engine room staff alive to the danger of the situation worked hard to solve the problem. The weather changed, the wind dropped, the clouds dispersed, out came the moon which lit up the ocean even better than the sun the previous day. Apprehension among the crew rose knowing that **TRINIDAD**'s black silhouette against the silver sea would be framed in periscopes of waiting submarines. At first only one sound, the lapping of the water against the hull, then the clang of hammering would create fears of discovery as every U Boat would hear the noise. **TRINIDAD**'s luck held, as a sitting duck they were spared the destruction that seemed certain. At last, repairs completed, she was on her way again, the ship alive and full of hope. Came the dawn and Kola Inlet. Only five miles away when finally with great thankfulness she arrived to anchor opposite a dry dock at Rosta.

After some entirely unnecessary negotiations the Russians finally gave permission for the damaged cruiser to enter the dry dock. They were most unhelpful only allowing use of the dock if their crew did the docking themselves. Incessant bombing had put the electric power out of action so the ship had to be pulled into dock manually by the weary and exhausted crew, following their recent harrowing experience after being nearly sunk by one of their own torpedoes.

Once in the dock massive tree trunks had to be cut to size to shore the ship in place. As the water pumped out the full extent of the damage could be seen, a gaping hole, three decks laid bare and many bulkheads completely disintegrated. Steel plates were needed to repair the ruptured hull, but requests to the Russians for these plates were in vain. There were plates somewhere in the dockyard, but were buried under tons of snow so impossible to find. An urgent signal was sent to Admiralty for suitable plates to be sent in the next convoy - not due to arrive until mid April. The crew remaining although safe, were stranded in Russia at Rosta with nothing around them except snow and ice with constant gaze at their ship in which so many lives had been lost through previous action by the enemy and the malfunction of their own torpedo.

On Wednesday 9th April 1942 PQ14 of twenty-three merchant ships and eight anti-submarine trawlers and minesweepers sailed from Iceland for Murmansk with intention to rendezvous with a strong destroyer and corvette escort and the 10,000 ton cruiser **HMS EDINBURGH** carrying a deck cargo of steel plates for the damaged **TRINIDAD**.

On Saturday 19th April **EDINBURGH** accompanied by two destroyers entered Kola Inlet. Immediately barges came alongside to unload the huge steel plates and take them up river to the stricken **TRINIDAD**; these were soon put to good use. Russian women welders were employed to fasten them into position and build supports out of massive timbers as the Russians had no steel girders to spare, so it was only a patch up job. The best that could be done, but would they stand the strain put upon them in the Arctic storms to be faced on the return voyage?

By 12th May **TRINIDAD** was ready to sail as could be. She took aboard sixty **EDINBURGH** survivors and equal number of merchant navy survivors. Leaving on the 13th, with the intention of reaching Philadelphia USA for permanent repairs and refit, was thought a bad omen by the men, with fears that the voyage might end in tragedy.

In March **TRINIDAD** and other ships had been hidden from dive bombers by snow, fog and mist whereas this time there was to be twenty-four hours of daylight. Very soon the radar screen was full with formations of aircraft approaching from all directions followed by the alarm bells hailing the call, 'Action Stations, prepare to repel enemy aircraft'. Then out of the sky came the hum like a swarm of angry bees as formations of Junker 88's came screaming down at vertical angles to low altitude to release their bombs, followed by the deafening barrage of anti aircraft guns from the cruiser.

For two hours the attacks continued, **TRINIDAD** shuddering under impact of so many, fortunately, misses as the ship swung to port and starboard to avoid once again being ripped apart. If not, how long would the welded plates and the ruptured torpedo hole take the battering from near misses.

As if two hours of dive bombing were not enough, with the gunners fighting off planes overhead, coming in low over the horizon were Heinkel 115's and 111's each carrying two torpedoes. Skimming just above the sea in they came releasing torpedoes at surface level. Fortunately the tracks could be clearly seen and **TRINIDAD** was able to swing clear of the trails and see the deadly tin fish go speeding by on either side.

Again the Heinkels circled and came in for another torpedo attack. At the same time a Junker appeared overhead roaring down releasing four bombs at only 400 feet.

As cruisers cannot be made to turn and dodge about, as little ships, in the middle of a turn to port to avoid three torpedoes heading straight for her, **TRINIDAD** was immediately in line of the falling bombs. The 500-pound bombs were on target falling straight on the bridge superstructure through the Admiral's Sea Cabin. Fleet Air Arm Office, canteen and exploding in the stoker and Petty Officers' mess deck. The blast went upwards hurling bridge personnel into the sides of the bridge, blowing away the port side of B gun deck and making a huge crater in the fo'c'sle deck. Within minutes the crater was ablaze with fire spreading rapidly to other mess decks. Another bomb skimmed along the side of the ship exploding just under the water line tearing off the temporary plates and allowing tons of water in, creating a list to starboard. The other two bombs grazed down the port side fracturing the forward compartments causing flooding. The damage to the ship was disastrous. The Junker that caused the damage was blasted by a stream of pom pom shells as it tried to escape and plunged into the sea.

The crater was now a cauldron of fire creeping towards the water mains necessary for fire fighting and uncomfortably close to the forward magazine containing cordite and shells. **TRINIDAD**'s Captain now had to make an agonising decision: should he stop the ship to prevent wind fanning the flames becoming an easy target for the enemy, or keep going to dodge the torpedoes when the fire might become out of control. Already more torpedo bombers were forming for attack. He decided to keep going. The recreation spaces filled with returning passenger survivors were only a few feet from where one of the bombs exploded. Few, if any, of the men in these sections survived.

Rescue parties found a scene of utter destruction. The huge crater in the deck, the massive gun turret pushed up at a crazy angle, part of the ship's side had gone, within the crater sounds of cries for help as ropes were hurriedly lowered.

The whole situation was tragic and disastrous. By now the flames had reached the repair work carried out at Vaenga the timber shores and oil fuel leakages were igniting.

At midnight the sun still above the horizon, the fires raged out of control. Below, those still alive, dazed and wounded, were groping their way past flames and through choking smoke to safety. Compartments with men in them were sealed off by the flames, the bridge was becoming a chimney for the fire below and flames were up the bridge companionways and ladder openings.

The state of the ship was so grave and with further attacks expected Captain of **HMS TRINIDAD** decided to abandon ship. The engines were stopped and the crew ordered to muster on the quarter deck. The destroyer **MATCHLESS** was alerted to come alongside, nosed in carefully with regard for the exploding ammunition and the flames roaring round the ship. Stretcher cases were first loaded on to her decks followed by the many wounded who were able to get aboard with assistance. On the bridge the Captain turned to his officers and signalmen. It was time to get out before being burnt alive.

Frank Pearce, friend and fellow author, was among the many who were thankful to clamber down the escape ladder. Three other destroyers circled around to provide a screen to keep the U Boats away from any further attack.

The four destroyers stood off to watch the last moments of the gallant cruiser **TRINIDAD**. To hasten her end the Admiral now aboard **SOMALI** gave the order to **MATCHLESS** to sink **TRINIDAD** with torpedoes. The crew and survivors watched the two steel torpedoes streak through the water to their ship. A breathless hush came over everyone as, in the seconds that followed they entered the side under the bridge, a third torpedo almost cut **TRINIDAD** in two who then slowly moved forward and down.

On the decks of the destroyers the survivors watched in silence with the knowledge that a great number of their shipmates were being committed to the deep as **TRINIDAD** sank in a huge cloud of smoke and steam.

Both **EDINBURGH** and **TRINIDAD** had experienced the same fate within 2 weeks of each other.

John Eldred, Ordinary Seaman, aboard **HMS HARRIER** in the first month of the worst year of losses, witnessed the sinking of the first naval ship to be lost on the convoys, **HMS MATABELE** a Tribal Class destroyer.

On the afternoon of 16th January 1942, all was well with Convoy PQ9, some bad weather and the occasional 'Ping'. We were not far from the Kola Inlet and safety. It was my first voyage to North Russia. With only two Tribal Class destroyers and two fleet sweepers we were not much protection for the convoy.

My oppo pointed to a strange cloud formation, "Looks like a destroyer" he said, "that means one of them will cop it". We all immediately dismissed this as "Rubbish". In the evening a merchant ship was damaged by a torpedo and **MATABELE** was soon there to ascertain the damage. She signalled "Should be able to make harbour".

In the early hours of the 17th my warm cocoon of a hammock was shattered by a large explosion, together with the ship's alarm bells sounding "Action Stations". When I reached the upper deck **MATABELE** was broken in two and the bows and stern were pointing skywards. A few desperate cries were heard as we stopped to lower our whaler and scrambling nets.

The first man the whaler approached called out in a calm parade voice, "Don't stop for me - some of my men are in real trouble over there, pick me up on your way back". This was a brave act of self-sacrifice, we all knew you lasted only a couple of minutes in that sea. This unknown hero was never to be seen again, and we managed to pick up only three from the sea. The rest would have gone straight down with the ship.

The men that we saved were smothered in oil fuel and although it was terrible to have it in your lungs, no doubt it gave them a precious few moments to survive the savage cold.

It was said afterwards that **MATABELE** had towed the merchant ship for a while, and then kept a close eye on her and so, when expecting further trouble, switched on her searchlight to investigate, making a perfect target for the U-boat.

Telegraphist Ron Cooley has sad memories of his 21st birthday on January 3rd 1942.

The destroyer **ESCAPADE**, my ship, was tied up alongside the **EDINBURGH** in Murmansk.

I was a 'Sparker' and kept the First Watch the night of the 3rd, my 21st birthday. At that time the Bos'n was a three badge A.B. and a terrific seaman. Built like a bull with a round rosy face, a wonderful character.

It had been a rough trip weatherwise, high winds and heavy seas, which had meant lots of work for him. As a result he had promised himself a big 'piss-up' once he got alongside. To fulfil this promise to himself he had saved his daily tot - illegally, of course.

So, it was to be on the evening of 3rd January. And to savour it in his preferred company, he had invited aboard two of his old cronies from **EDINBURGH**. Of course, the 'bubbly' soon began to get low, and to top it up they had somehow obtained some methylated spirits from the **EDINBURGH**.

This, they boiled up on the galley stove to make a rather fierce concoction. This was later added to by adding wood alcohol, drained from the cruiser's Walrus aircraft. I came off watch at midnight, and the mess deck reverberated with the thumping of metal pots and raucous songs which went on well into the early morning. I had sippers of the stuff they were drinking, and almost lost the back of my skull.

About three in the morning I woke to a horrible moaning sound. Of course, the moans came from the Bos'n whose hammock was always slung below mine. I looked down at him and a mountain of froth, which went up and down with each breath, covered his mouth. Though his eyes were open, he obviously was unable to see, indicated by some choice description of me because I wouldn't switch on the lights which were fully illuminating the scene already.

I was very concerned and turned out the Sick Bay Tiffy. He in turn went aboard **EDINBURGH** for a doctor who came and immediately ordered we get him on to the cruiser. Imagine the struggle we had to get this 15-stone man up the restricted ladders and hatches and into the cruiser's sick bay. They immediately administered oxygen, but he died and was buried ashore the same day.

Bill Short, Engineer Officer, was aboard SS INDUNA when sunk by torpedo of **U140** on 29th March 1942, 170 miles from Murmansk.

He was preparing to go on watch when the torpedo hit. He immediately went to his boat station. The lifeboat he should have been in had already been launched as the weather was so bad. The lifeboat had been cut adrift, so he ran round to the other lifeboat to discover it also had been launched and had a full complement. He then realised that if he was to get off that ship, he would have to jump into the sea. Eventually he was picked up by an overloaded lifeboat designed to take 25 persons but found there were already 34 aboard. The lifeboat had been damaged when it was launched, because of the heavy weather. It was leaking badly and survivors were actually sitting in a waterlogged lifeboat; and with so many in it they were packed like sardines in a tin. There was no room for any movement whatsoever, but there was every hope of being picked up knowing that an SOS had been sent and perhaps a naval ship would be sent out to search for them. Hope for the first day was high, but as night fell they realised that it was going to be a bitterly cold night, sleet, snow and 40ft. waves were experienced in that lifeboat.

Little did Bill Short realise at that moment the most awful experience that was to follow, one of courage and endurance as he relates:-

There has always been the impression that if you had a tot of rum or something, it kept the cold out. There was whisky aboard the lifeboat and some indulged and drank too much, and now it is known that whisky does not help to withstand the cold, what happened proved it. Those who overindulged went to sleep and no matter how much they were shaken they did not stir, as by now they had hypothermia - they went to sleep and never woke up. Sadly that night six people died, and all we could do was reverently put the dead over the side. They were given a sea burial, their grave being the Barents Sea. This went on for four days and eventually more dropped off to sleep never to awaken. A donkeyman who had been badly burned in the engine room after a flash over, was lying in the bottom of the lifeboat and there was nothing we could do for his wounds; he eventually died and was actually frozen to the bottom of the lifeboat. We could not move him. The water keg was frozen stiff, so we were licking ice. Water had got into the wireless transmitter so we could not send an SOS. All the rations that would sustain us were frozen so could not be used, so all we could do was break ice and lick it.

At the end of 4 days out of 34 there were 17 left, more dead than alive. One man went mad - the sea spray was freezing on the gunwale and he started to lick. His tongue became swollen and he became deranged and eventually died of suffocation by his own tongue. At the end of four days, more dead than alive, we had given up hope of rescue, and from time to time we sighted land but it seemed so far away. When the INDUNA was torpedoed we were 175 miles from Murmansk. When we were picked up we were told we were 25 miles from Murmansk, so in 4 days the lifeboat had drifted 150 miles.

The first sighting of our lifeboat was by a Hurricane - one given by Britain to Russia. Sadly the Russians were so incompetent at navigating that they never went out of sight of land so they could see their way home. We were eventually picked up by a Russian minesweeper.

By now being so weak we were hauled aboard by a rope round our waists. I actually tried to walk to keep circulation going in my legs but it was impossible. My legs were swollen and they would not support me. We eventually landed at Murmansk and vaguely remember it was the most bumpy ride I have ever known in any vehicle. Murmansk had been heavily bombed and there were craters everywhere. I was eventually taken to this makeshift hospital. All the hospitals had been bombed. All that was left standing were schools which were commandeered as military hospitals. I was covered with goose grease and bandaged from head to foot to try to warm me up. They put a tube down my throat to my stomach and poured tepid water down to clear the ice that had formed there. They managed to get that cleared up and then when they took the bandages off they realised that gangrene had set off in both my legs. There were screens all round me and no one was allowed to come near. I was eventually taken down to a makeshift theatre, a school classroom where there were six operations going on at one time. Put on an ordinary table, a white sheet was put up in front of me and someone in broken English said to me: "We are going to cut your legs off!" I was given no general anaesthetic; no preparation; medical supplies were non-existent. All I can remember after that was an excrutiating pain in my legs before I passed out. When I came too I was told I had been delirious for 3 days. After some time I was eventually given a blood transfusion. It was rather comical - in that hospital the conditions were unbelievable. The school had huge windows, and the German bombers came across from Petsamo every hour, on the hour. They had blown all the windows in, these had been boarded up - no ventilation getting in, the stench was awful. The school room was jammed with beds, all with wounded, their wounds spewing out gangrene - the smell was unbelievable!! When taken from the operating theatre and more aware of my surroundings I discovered that both my legs had been taken off, one below and one above the knee and there were great incisions to the stumps in order to drain the gangrene away which just flowed onto the bed. No-one was allowed near me for risk of infection. My legs had been literally chopped off, just like chopping a piece of meat and the bones were sticking out, the nerves exposed - so when anyone came near the nerve ends reacted. It seemed very crude. I would not be here today if they had not cut the diseased parts away thus saving my life. The dressings which came once a week were just pure hell. To take the dressing off was like taking paper off raw meat literally coming off raw flesh. Then they sprayed hydrogen peroxide on the raw flesh - the idea being to try to heal the wounds because in the climate of Murmansk wounds take a long time to heal.

The conditions were just unbelievable. If frostbite affected fingers or toes - they let them go black then snipped them off. Food was not nourishing - for 5 months we had rice - fried, stewed, boiled, every conceivable way. Sometimes just what was supposed to be YAK - we joked there must have been more amputations that day, the only way we could keep each others spirits up - crude humour but it seemed to work.

By now my weight was 6 stone (normally 12 stone) - I was like someone from Belsen, bones sticking out all over - close cropped hair!!

Toilet facilities were non existent - with no legs my bowels etc. were evacuated direct on to the bed.

It was always a long time before I was cleaned up, very few nurses - too many patients - very upsetting situation, but we were all so weak we could not do otherwise - bowel control being non existent through weakness.

When they took me to the theatre for a blood transfusion I was so emaciated that 5 attempts in each arm to find a vein proved fruitless. A senior doctor finally just stuck a needle in me and I got a transfusion, the transfusion being 4 months after the operation.

The Russian answer to frostbite was amputation. British doctors thought otherwise but sadly they were not allowed to assist/operate ashore by the Russians. Maybe part of my legs could have been saved. (It was sometime later that R.N. medical personnel were allowed ashore to set up a hospital).

Five months passed, my wounds were never stitched, the bones were sticking out, Naval ships were having a job getting through. We were taken by ambulance to **HMS LEDA** for sending home. I went to Polyarnoe, on to **LEDA** and thence to Archangel. Whilst there we had better food. At Archangel there was a massive air raid - the nurses were panic stricken - we were reassuring them - not them - us!! We were then put on board the **USS TUSCALOOSA** - it was pure heaven to be on board in the American sickbay. We had ice cream, fruit - pure luxury.

We had a destroyer escort for the homeward trip. We came under attack by German ships - a German destroyer was sunk and a survivor was brought on board into **TUSCALOOSA**'s sick bay with us. Guards were posted - we weren't sure whether they were to protect us from him, or him from us!

We eventually came back to the Clyde and disembarked at Greenock where I was taken to Haremarsh Hospital in Glasgow for two further operations by Canadian surgeons who made my stumps suitable for wearing artificial limbs. Eventually I went elsewhere to be taught how to use artificial legs, leaving hospital in June 1943.

Austin Byrne, Naval Gunner, joined SS INDUNA at Greenock. A rusty old ship full of cargo petrol in drums - a floating bomb. If that lot were to be hit by the enemy there would be little chance of survival for anyone aboard - a chance any ship in any convoy was to take en route to Russia. It was his first voyage to sea.

Down to the cabin, what a shock! I did not want a lot but this was spartan. I went aft onto the poop deck and through a trapdoor of sorts down into a dark hole with two wash basins and toilets; into the cabin a room 15ft. square for 12 people. When in your bunk you could reach the table. Luckily it was not full so you could keep kit bags on the spare bunks. In the centre was a stove to keep warm, for coal you went down to the stokehole and carried it up. Barracks were bad enough but this was not any better - well it was a ship. The deck had a thin coat of red flooring but it had not been put down right so when it got wet later it was like walking on three-quarters of an inch of mud.

In the cabin were nine people, six army gunners for the bofors gun which was aft, also aft was a 4" gun, on each side of the bridge were gun pits with a hotchkiss in each pit. These were relics from 1914-18 and fired .303 rounds of ammo, also the para and wire device to fire at planes. The machine-guns had a range of 400 yards so were told to fire at 600 yards to hit any planes. After unpacking and settled in, the gunlayer said: "Get all the sleep you can as it will be watch and watch. Four hours on, four off. Washing, eating and other things done in your off watch which cuts it down a bit".

The second day was cleaning guns. The bunks aboard were just wood, no springs. Just like a shelf with a board so you did not fall off. The mattresses, for want of a better word, were bad so were dropped over the side. We slept on our hammock mattress. SS INDUNA sailed in Convoy PQ13 with other ships from the Clyde. During the voyage, the gunners were on watch 2 hours on, 2 hours off; daylight hours in the gun pits, on the bridge. It was cold up there, sleep when possible was not often in the cabin but in the gunlayer cabin below the bridge, on the deck, so as not to take sea boots off. Sleeping with all gear on, duffle, gloves, hat, but this was to be a godsend very soon. At first light on 29th March, 1942 INDUNA was attacked by a U Boat, one single torpedo was all it needed to set the cargo of petrol ablaze and very soon she was sinking fast. She was hit in number 5 hold starboard side and settling by the stern. I was on the bridge at the time. The Captain and First Mate realised how serious the fire was so with the ship sinking more rapidly by the stern ordered "abandon ship, get to lifeboat stations".

The stern was now well ablaze where she had been hit. The explosion had blown the cargo on to the top of the deck cargo, that is barbed wire on to the top of blazing petrol. Those who were aft were in a bad way. Some were on fire, and jumped over the side, others tried to run through the flames. With the problem of not being able to see where they were putting their feet in the flames, scrambling over a pile of burning barbed wire.

Many jumped over the side. About 4 or 6 got through the flames, one dropped at the side of the lifeboat and did not move again. The lifeboat was now ready to launch, everyone getting wild and excited, the mate picked up an iron bar 4 foot long and just said "Don't move" - no-one did.

Orders were then given to "Lower the boat to deck level". Everyone hurriedly clambered aboard. The last one, an American, very badly burnt wearing just a shirt and pants, no shoes. At last the lifeboat was lowered down to the water.

By now the ship had settled. The water aft was still alight with the petrol. Some of those in the water were still screaming.

The sea now started to smash the boat out from the side of the ship, and hurl it back again. The mate looked down, shouting orders for them to row round the stern to take the others off, to avoid the boat being broken up on the side of the ship.

Casting off was very frightening. The two gunners were trying to hold the boat off the ships side, so it did not break up, but all it did was smash the oars. The hook on the falls are sharp and the blocks very big, so these were removed with difficulty with the lifeboat bobbing about like a cork.

At last we cast off, to move her round to the stern of the sinking ship. We took an oar each and the others who did not want to do anything, just got into the bottom of the boat. We set off, two rowing, one steering and the rest moaning. The need to get clear of the flames, and the stern pulling against the sea was slow. At last, some way from the ship, all we could do was pull, pull and hope. After what seemed an age, the boat cleared the ship to go round the stern. The sea seemed to carry us clear. At last nearer to the ship, a rope ladder was put over the side to get into the lifeboat when it got there. There was another huge explosion and she went. We thought she got hit again, but it was the boilers. We were not far away when she went. As she slid down we kept rowing. Then the bits started falling out of the sky, some very big ones, if any of those had gone in the lifeboat we too would have gone. Then the sea was calm and huge bubbles came up very near us, what bubbles and what a glug as they burst.

That was all, no ship, no men, we were in the calm and we saw no one come up. The sea took over and all that was left was wood and petrol drums, pushed away with the remaining oars. Then we were alone in the lifeboat. Looking round at the desolation we saw the U-Boat with three men in the tower with one machine-gun. It cruised around, so we got down into the bottom of the boat. After a short while they took the machine gun off its mounting as the U-Boat disappeared below the surface. Now we were completely alone, 3 Americans, a Belgian, a cabin boy, 2 firemen, a bofors gunner, Robby by name, and myself. Our first thoughts were to get near to the other boat for help and instructions on what we should do, but the seas were so high they were only seen once, and waved like mad standing on the seats. We were now completely alone, already exhausted with attempts to save our shipmates, sad, hungry and frightened yet still to face the Arctic weather in an open damaged lifeboat. The sea was getting worse all the time with snow and sleet in the wind.

The Belgium, Third Mate survivor Robby put out a sea anchor, to keep us straight to sea to avoid turning over. After a short while the water in the boat began to rise, so we had to commence the task of bailing with one keeping hold of the tiller. The rest were in the bottom of the boat, except one American who was badly burnt. He was on a seat and ice was forming on him, so after a short while he could hardly move. A coat was put around him, the side of the boat was cold and wet like all of us. Worried and frightened he was told to get down into the boat. The cabin boy was scared, the poor lad was only 16 years old. I told him to pray for help. He said he did not know how, or that he was that frightened he had forgotten how. He was told to talk to God in his mind, just any way and God would hear him. At this another survivor, a fireman, said that there would be no praying as he was an atheist. We were all praying as we needed help. So the boy carried on. He was not well clad for the weather, in fact only the two gunners were well clothed.

At this stage the Belgian found a bottle of brandy which was opened and passed round for warmth. When INDUNA was hit no one had had any breakfast so we were hungry. After a drink all round the bottle was passed back but regretfully the cork was not put on and the rest was spilt into the bottom of the boat.

After this a bottle of rum was found and passed around, but soon we were cold again, and with the boat rolling everyone felt sick and it all came up. It was just as warming when it came up as when it went down.

By now it was a few hours since the sinking so we were getting our minds clear, but it did not seem as if help was coming for quite a while so we were all feeling cold and miserable. The Belgian had got out of the wind, and as the boat filled up again, turns would be taken to bail, but the rest did not want to know, as the cold had begun to get to them.

The Americans in the lifeboat were all now saying they did not think the big bonus they were getting for going there was worth it, and were shocked at naval pay. But money is not worth a lot in a boat; in fact the cabin boy dropped two pound notes and a ten shilling note in the bottom of the boat, if just floated about. He was told to put it back in his pocket but there was no interest. By now it was afternoon and all had got down out of the wind, it was decided that as the rest were not going to do much, we put a piece of wood over the side and watched it drift.

It was thought that you can drift at one mile an hour and would be in the end of the Gulf Stream. The sea anchor was taken in and kept the stern to the waves to go the way we wanted. It was agreed to steer south-east because not being too sure where we were, we did not want to hit land occupied by the Germans. It should take about six days to do the trip to land. Being the only two interested we took turns to steer and bail and were now very hungry, so we looked to see what there was to eat. Something called penpigan was made by Bovril. The water barrel was frozen solid so had some Horlicks tablets instead.

Then it was night. We put the anchor out, bailed the boat and got down out of the wind and weather, but not for long. The water came up again so we did not sleep but kept warm together - the first day had gone. The sea was cruel, and there were many bad moments when the sea was high and rough. Without the sea anchor the lifeboat would have gone over. The salt out of the wind dried on the lips and also the part of faces uncovered. When the waves hit the side of the boat it froze before it hit the occupants. If when bailing or sat high up, and a wave hit the boat it would go on our backs and freeze so with movement it broke the ice on the back. Bailing had to be constant, one filled the bucket in the bottom of the boat and passed it to the other to put over the side. On day two with a little more to eat and after a while I needed to open my bowels. What a problem. Did not fancy sitting with my arse over the side so I dropped my pants and got Robby to hold the tail of my coat and about an hour later did the same for him.

That was day two, so we cut the second knotch in the gunwale of the boat to mark time and settled down to talk, pray, steer, and bail. Not a lot happened, except that we just talked about home. It was cold and rough and the wind blew but still moved nicely through the water. We sat with hope in our hearts, getting colder and colder and more uncomfortable as each hour passed. The Yanks were suffering now, also the fireman of INDUNA They could not move much. The cabin boy was down in the dumps but encouraged to keep going. Those at first who thought thet could miss their share of the work and save themselves, were disappointed. The most cheerful chap was the badly burnt one. Several had wet themselves to keep warm, what a price to pay. Later they discovered they had scabs all down their thighs, and were bad with the cold, the poor souls were now suffering. So ended day two, just cold, wet and rough. Day three started just the same as the others. Now it seemed a long time since the ship had sunk. Legs and thighs ached with the constant roll of the boat, and we were very tired and to keep moving was a must, looking at the others knew they must. So now it was day three, another cut to mark the days, and much the same, bail and pray and steer. The Yanks said that they would not go to sea again, but should be expected to, as there was a war, and the navy would expect me to. At this time they got to think we were their only hope. To keep the spirits up they all said we could have half of their pay off, if we got to land. As day three wore on we were eating some tablets and sucking some ice, I broke two teeth on the ice and biscuits, but by now was really thirsty and wanted to urinate so I put some bits of ice in a cup and piddled into it to melt the ice, then drank it. At least it was wet, looked like whisky, but did not taste too good. About mid afternoon, whilst bending up from bailing, a ship was seen not too far away on the port side. Everyone waved like mad and shouted. At last we were safe, were our thoughts, but no it did not see us. It just turned and went out of sight. The bottom fell out of our world.

We tried to get the sail up, but could not lift the mast. The others were no good at all. Then we put an oar up with a bit of bunting on top, a bit late, all that hope and a let down, what an awful day.

Day four, all the time we had wind, snow, sleet, rain, ice and cold. As time passed, we ached even more. We took in the sea anchor with difficulties, talked about just anything but always thought we would get through all this and just prayed and prayed over and over again. Then the fireman, who had said he was an atheist, suddenly and bravely said: "I think we should pray, as only God can save us now". My quick reply was: "I have four days start on you". There was nothing different on day four and of what was thought a six-day trip. The weather was good in the late afternoon when Robby thought he could see land. He was right, it was land a long way off, but land, which land. Thoughts were was it, is it German land?, and of a long train ride on wooden seats with a guard and a corner seat all the way down Norway.

Everyone felt better at the sight of land, but now found the boat did not move so well as it was lower in the water. We scraped the ice off the gunwales and the air tanks and then when looking over the side, and on the ropes that run round the boat to handle her on deck, we found ice had formed on all of them. Movement through the water, and now it was slowing it down so we decided it must be removed. With Robby, sitting on my legs, I hung outboard chopping away with an axe tied to my wrist. Whilst doing this not knowing where it came from, a brown duck appeared in the water. It could not fly as its wings were wet. Feeling really hungry, I grabbed at the duck, but missed, the intention being to chop off the head, and drink its warm blood. All I could say was "ducky, ducky come to me", but no duck came my way.

Then Robby shouted: "I can see a ship", then "two" then "three". Hanging over the side nothing could be seen. If he were to stand up I would be in the water. Back in the boat we wondered, are we all mad, and seeing things. Alas we had not gone mad and were saved. But by who? We stood on the seats and waved and waved hugging each other. What were the ships, Russian or German? One said to shout comrade, others said all shout in English. If we shouted comrade and they were Germans they might shoot thinking we were Russians. If they were Russians they might think we were Germans shouting Kamerad. At least we were still thinking straight. The fireman said he would shout comrade, but was told in no uncertain words that as we were stood on the seat and he was in the bottom of the boat he would have the back of his head kicked in. We have not come so far to die, so it was decided everyone shout in English. Very soon the boats came alongside from three points. Little patrol boats all with guns manned and aimed at the now very weak survivors, still not certain they were being saved. One boat came alongside, the other two circled round; the man on the small bridge pointed to come aboard. Putting my arms on to the rail to pull myself up I found with my clothes on, and sheepskin at the bottom wet, and with no sleep for 4 days and 3 nights, there was no pull left. So two Russians grabbed me, pulled and held tight. The man in some language said something like "Ingleas?" and gesticulating with arms "bombed?", replied "No, torpedoed". "How long ago?" "Four days". When we were pulled on board noticed the red flag at the stern. What a relief and a wonderful sight.

We wondered what we would have done if they had been Germans. Soon all were lifted on board. The Russians who lifted the others aboard also got the lifeboat rations. They soon had the chocolate and such on board. The rest were soon down below, the boat in tow and the three ships under way. I was kept on deck. The Russians wanted to see some identification but all that was now available was an identity disc. I was allowed to go below finding warmth at last. Off came my gloves and coat. The cabin boy was on a bunk groaning and delirious. The captain came down with a bottle of vodka and a mug, pouring everyone a drink and said to drink quick - Russian style. He said something in Russian, shook hands and went back on deck. Soon each had another large tot: on a very empty stomach vodka Russian style was good. The Russian was having trouble with the cabin boy getting his clothes off. Offers of help were refused. He was blue with cold all his legs and back and thighs were black with big scabs, and so bad were his clothes which had to be left on. The American who was burnt still had his coat frozen to his body and was also in a bad state. The Russian seemed to be satisfied, the boat was going fast, we were at last warm, and went and got something to eat. It was a piece of raw fat about 9 inches square. Our first meal for over 4 days, welcome but not very appetising. More vodka straight down, soon everyone was happy, singing with sheer relief and the vodka. Soon the boat slowed and the engine stopped, they had arrived somewhere. We were told to put coats on, and helped onto deck, so weak and tired with a Russian at each side. As we came on deck we saw the flag on the stern, stopped, made the Russians stand back and saluted their flag in proper RN style, in appreciation of their rescue and saving our lives. Shouts, all stopped, the Captain and all the crew came and hugged us. We then went down the gangway saluting the other ship that was to take us to Murmansk. On arrival we went into a mess hall to find with great joy and excitement a reunion with the survivors from the other boat. They had both been picked up about the same time having been sighted by aircraft. We were safe.

The rescue ship arrived at Murmansk at first light and so to hospital. The American and the Cabin Boy died the next day.

Early in April 1942, the crew of the Flower Class Corvette **HMS SNOWFLAKE** were relaxing after another Atlantic convoy and were dreaming of a short leave or at least the comforts of Londonderry. Their dreams were quickly shattered when a signal from Admiralty ordered them to proceed with all speed to Reykjavik in Iceland. The weather was terrible and with a full gale blowing, their Captain pushed on bravely through mountainous seas to arrive at their rendezvous ahead of time.

Les Hough, Senior Ordnance Artificer aboard **SNOWFLAKE** and whilst ashore in Reykjavik had heard about a ship on a previous Russian convoy whose guns had frozen solid in the terrible Arctic conditions and were completely out of action. He went ashore and obtained some special non-freezing grease. This was fed into all the gun mountings and working parts. As each watch came on duty the guns were constantly trained and elevated, keeping them free and ready for action at all times.

As the convoy was mustering and **SNOWFLAKE** was repairing storm damage, they received great encouragement from a surprise visit from the Rear Admiral aboard **HMS EDINBURGH** who was duly piped aboard **SNOWFLAKE** and with the crew mustered on the quarter-deck, he sprang a few rungs up the bridge-ladder, turned about and said: "Take a good look at me lads - you don't see a bloody Admiral every day of the week". This went down great with the crew and he continued: "And don't think that because I'm in a bloody great cruiser that I don't think of you chaps tossing about in the small ships". He went on to tell them of the dangers that lay ahead and the importance of their convoy. His visit was a real tonic to all and helped to allay the anxieties that everyone felt before embarking on this hazardous journey.

As the convoy was nearing Bear Island, **SNOWFLAKE** was attacked by four German HE111's but due to the alertness and accuracy of the 2lb pom-pom and only 2 Lewis gun crews, the attack was beaten off without damage or casualties; sufficient enough to put them off, ineffectively letting torpedoes go at long range.

Such inefficiency and lack of experience was just a lick and promise to what was to come later with more massive, fatal and successful convoy attacks and the crew were rightly proud of this early abortive attack and more than relieved to hear all guns firing without jamming or stoppages. He remembers his old pal John Burlinson the yeoman, jumping on to the Lewis guns and blasting away at the enemy. The guns got so hot that his hands were burned by the flying empty cartridge cases. But far better this than having frozen guns, which could have made **SNOWFLAKE** easily one of the earliest casualties of the convoy.

And so the little corvette pressed on unharmed, and after hair-raising experiences in the Arctic ice barrier and seeing the convoy attacked again and again by a relentless enemy they finally made it to Murmansk. The sight of the cruiser **TRINIDAD** in dry dock with a huge torpedo hole in her side did not lift their spirits and a trip ashore only emphasised the terrible hardships that the Russians and our own base staff were having to endure in the frightful conditions.

On the return journey the sight of Reykjavik was more than welcome, and although **SNOWFLAKE** lived on to take part in the final battle of the Atlantic, there was not a man aboard who would forget that 'suicide' run to North Russia.

Stan Kirby, known as the "Ping Bos'n" aboard **HMS ASPHODEL** one of the many Flower Class corvettes describes life aboard one of the small ships escorting the convoys and recalls the loss of the **BLUEBELL** with all hands save one.

Can you imagine building a house with a hundred-foot-long garden, and then putting the kitchen at the end of the garden? This is how the Flower Class corvettes were built.

The living quarters for the crew at one end of the ship and the 'galley' at the other end.

The Admiralty must have recruited their naval architects from Wormwood Scrubs!

The original design incorporated a short fo'c'sle with a 'well deck' forward of the bridge. When we encountered bad weather, these corvettes had a horrible habit of rising on the crest of the wave, sliding down the other side, and then digging her nose completely under the next one. This filled the well deck with tons of water which then rolled forward into the fo'c'sle messdeck. With only one access door it was, necessarily, more open than shut. As a result the messdeck was permanently filled with eighteen inches of sea water.

As the ship pitched and rolled so the water would rush from one side to the other, bearing all before it!

Articles of kit, cap boxes, ditty boxes, kit bags, hammocks, mess traps, knives, forks, spoons, sea boots and spew! This went on night and day through the interminable weeks of convoy duty, in the ever atrocious weather.

A complete absence of any normal comforts - not even a hot meal. At least, until some bright spark developed the practice of rolling the pusser's cocoa issue (six inch squares of solid cocoa, one inch thick, and as hard as a bullet) in a cloth and bashing it on the iron deck with a hammer, together with the hard tack (ship's biscuit) the same as Lord Nelson's men had, chucking it all in a mess fanny, taking it down the boiler room and putting it under a steam drain valve, like our 'Espresso' machine.

This was then suspended from the deck head and one dipped a mug into it before it got cold. Once it cooled off it went solid.

With no refrigerator, once the tinned grub had gone, that was the only nourishment we had.

The only consolation was that it was the same for the enemy. A U-Boat on the surface would be thrown about as badly as we were.

The ship's cook did his best with a coal-fired galley range. Even if a meal was successfully cooked, the journey along the deck and back again was so hazardous that one often had to jettison the grub to save being washed overboard.

This then was the daily grind for all on board, permanently wet, hungry and cold. How we managed to stay cheerful under such conditions (and we did) has constantly amazed me! We drew strength from each other, and never doubted that we would win in the end.

"SHEPHERDS OF THE FLEET"

There was Primrose and Petunia,
And Rose and Tulip too,
Verbena and Azalea,
Good ships through and through.
Shepherds of the Fleet, they were
To all we owe a debt,
Each one a gallant fighting ship,
A 'Flower Class' Corvette!

They hastened not, but rested not,
And saw their duty done
From the icy Russian Convoys
To a blistering tropic sun.

Crewed by men of iron will,
Who neither flinched nor fled
When duty called to give their all,
And the sea consumed their dead!

Such pretty names these small ships had,
Each one belied their name,
For where else can you find a flower
In a fighting 'Hall Of Fame!'

There was Orchid, Honeysuckle,
Dianthus, Hollyhock,
And the only time they paused for breath
Was 'repair time' in a dock!

Built to withstand a raging storm,
And still fight tooth and claw,
They proved their worth to a still free world
As countless millions saw.

There was Snowdrop and Snapdragon,
Carnation and Dahlia too,
Geranuim and Gardenia,
Good ships through and through.
Shepherds of the Fleet, they were
To all we owe a debt,
Each one a gallant fighting ship,
A 'Flower Class' Corvette!

Denis J. Woods

With **HMS TRINIDAD** in Dry Dock at Rosta after attack by German destroyers - causing damage worsened by that of her own torpedo that accidentally went amuck - she needed new plates in the shortest possible time.

On Wednesday 9th April 1942 PQ14 sailed from Reykjavik for Murmansk to rendezvous with the 10,000 ton cruiser **HMS EDINBURGH**, who was carrying a deck cargo of large steel plates for **TRINIDAD**, arriving at Kola Inlet on the 19th. Immediately barges were alongside to unload the large steel plates and take them up river to the stricken **TRINIDAD**

In the days **EDINBURGH** was in the Kola Inlet she took aboard badly injured merchant seamen, survivors from bombed or torpedoed ships, many mutilated seamen who had miraculously survived awful conditions in open boats. Many, with limbs amputated under the primitive conditions in the Russian hospitals because of frostbite, turned gangrenous. Most survivors were happy and relieved at going home. Those with drastic amputations had little will to live knowing that if they reached Britain there would be little satisfaction in life, their bodies needing attention for the rest of it.

Two days before **EDINBURGH** was due to sail she took aboard a seemingly strange cargo. One of the crew who had been asleep for an hour was awakened by the sound of the bugle calling for both watches of the duty hands to fall in. Looking at his watch he thought: "What the hell's going on, it's quarter to bloody midnight?" Arriving on deck he could not believe what he saw, it was like something from a film.

Tied up to the side of the ship were two barges, all around Russian soldiers armed with guns held at the ready. Also on the flight-deck and ladders of **EDINBURGH** their own marines were on guard. A tarpaulin covering the barge cargo, when drawn back revealed ammunition boxes. Why all this security at nearly midnight for a routine job? Very soon the truth became evident. The boxes did not contain ammunition, but over 5 tons of gold bullion to be stored in the cruiser and shipped to the UK. Each rope-handled box needed two men to lift, carry up to flight deck then lower to a room three decks below.

At the time of unloading the gold, there seemed present an aura of evil, a very uncomfortable feeling amongst the crew - superstition being a strong characteristic of sailors. Sleet started to fall and the heavy red printing on the boxes ran freely to make a trail of scarlet on the snow-covered decks, making the crew think even more of the trip ahead seemingly carrying Russian gold dripping with blood. The value of the bullion was thought to be £5 million, and was a down payment from the Russians to the United States Treasury for thousands of tons of war materials delivered to equip the Red Army.

On the morning of 28th April with the gold stored below **HMS EDINBURGH** left to escort QP11 back to England, steaming patiently behind the 6 knot convoy, its crew aware of the responsibility to protect the convoy and the importance of safe delivery of the vast fortune of shining gold.

By 29th April convoy had been sighted by German "shad" reconnaissance plane and reported to Norway. All knew attack would be inevitable by German destroyers which would be **EDINBURGH**'s function, whereas the frequent sighting of U-Boats kept the escorts alert, instead of trailing convoy at only 6 knots. **EDINBURGH** was ordered to move twenty miles to north-west and zigzag to avoid U-boat attacks. The crew somewhat mystified by no destroyer escort had to obey orders.

At the end of the 20-mile patrol - disaster! Submerged across her path lay **U456**, not believing the cruiser was alone without escort. Firing her last two torpedoes, the first hit **EDINBURGH** amidships in the forward boiler room killing everyone in the explosion area and flooding mess decks with oil and water. The second crashed into the stern smashing the rudder and two of four propellers. By now with tons of sea water filling the ship **EDINBURGH** slowed to a stop listing to starboard. Hand the U-boat one more torpedo **EDINBURGH** would have surely sunk altogether. From the bridge the officers gazed in disbelief at the damage, **EDINBURGH** had been ripped open, some sixty feet of the stern a tangled mess of wreckage, but she was still afloat.

The convoy moving westward had been sighted by submarines, but with knowledge of the cruiser's plight two destroyers were sent to assist. It was decided to attempt to tow her back to Kola Inlet some 250 miles away with the help of its one working propeller. A difficult task with the knowledge of U-boats around. Would she make it?

By now the ship was almost uncontrollable, yawing about, going round in circles and leaving a tell-tale trail of oil astern. Reports were then received that enemy submarines were in its path to Kola Inlet, and, even more serious from Admiralty Intelligence, enemy destroyers had left Kirkenes to intercept the convoy, **EDINBURGH** or both. The good news, however, a Russian tug and four minesweepers were on their way to help.

Could the crew, this wounded ship and the vast amount of gold, be saved? As if not in enough trouble a further signal advised the pocket battleship **ADMIRAL SCHEER** (sister ship of **GRAF SPEE**) had sailed from Trondheim.

Still with another 200 miles to go, speed now only 2 knots, it would be four days and nights to reach shelter. **EDINBURGH** with most of her guns out of action would be a sitting target.

On the morning of 1st May the three German destroyers set a course towards the convoy and the crippled cruiser knowing it could be attacked and destroyed at any time as it was barely moving. Nine hours later the convoy was attacked, **EDINBURGH** being made aware, was ready.

Later at 1800 with two thirds of their ammunition used in the convoy attack and being beaten off, the Germans abandoned the fight and broke off the engagement. They headed south-east to find the crippled **EDINBURGH** which had made little progress. The crew hungry, cold and exhausted were much in need of sleep.

By now the four minesweepers had arrived at the scene joining the two destroyers, screening the ship from further U-boat attack.

To the north the three German destroyers raced through the night at 35 knots towards **EDINBURGH**. They knew following withdrawal from convoy attack this one should succeed.

At 0600 on 2nd May the German force came upon the long oil slick, the rest was easy.

The enemy's guns found range, the two British destroyers raced in with all 4-inch guns firing against the enemy's twelve 5.9-inch guns giving them superiority in fire power. Our destroyers turned together and fired a spread of torpedoes. Each time the German destroyers crossed the line of fire. **EDINBURGH** although nearly stopped, her remaining guns flashed out. The German plan for a concentrated spread of torpedoes was confused by the attack strategy of our own destroyers.

EDINBURGH's gunfire smashed into one of the German destroyers; both engine rooms were destroyed and it drifted to a stop. A bitter battle followed, now two against two, one of our destroyers was hit by five enemy shells, killing many of the crew after two direct hits. The other racing in to defend her partner received two direct hits, killing many of her crew. At this moment the crew above decks watched in horror as two torpedoes were seen coming towards them. Frozen into inaction, waiting for the explosion that might send them into eternity. But in that moment of horror and despair the torpedoes passed under the ship and sped onward to the circling, crippled cruiser, striking **EDINBURGH** dead centre for the third time in three days. It was the death blow as she lifted and shook from the impact, but still her guns kept firing, her shells falling around the German ships. Also, one of the now crippled British destroyers, still firing, scored a direct hit on the enemy. With one sinking and another damaged, one was scuttled by depth charges, the other loaded with survivors, gave up the fight, and disappeared into the mist.

All the problems and attempts to tow, trying to make headway on remaining operative engines, unable to steer correctly, the final torpedo striking the cruiser had almost cut the ship in two. It had ripped out the centre and killed many more below decks. The situation had become hopeless and thinking she might fall apart at any time the Admiral gave the order to "abandon ship".

Two minesweepers secured alongside to take off the wounded and survivors, a difficult task with the ship listing and decks at different heights. Some fell off stretchers crashing to the deck, others, naked, fell over the side to become entangled in safety nets, nearly freezing to death in the bitter Arctic winds.

Salvage of the mass of gold bullion aboard was out of the question.

Finally, the Admiral and Captain left the cruiser for the last time, the two minesweepers pulled away from **EDINBURGH** and other escorts stood off to watch her go down, this she seemed reluctant to do. One of the destroyers was ordered to fire her one remaining torpedo. Slowly the cruiser **EDINBURGH** rolled over on to her side. As the bows rose high the stern disappeared below the surface with the bodies of those killed aboard. Only the stench of fuel oil drifting over the freezing water remained. Not far away the German destroyer settled on the ocean bed with her dead. For both there had been neither victory nor defeat.

The Captain of **HMS EDINBURGH** sums up the dramatic situation in his report to Admiralty.

HMS EDINBURGH
BFPO Ships

FAIR COPY OF THE REPORT ON THE LOSS OF HMS EDINBURGH ON SATURDAY 2 MAY 1942 BY CAPTAIN H FAULKNER ROYAL NAVY.

Sir,

1. I have the honour to submit the following report on the loss of **HMS EDINBURGH** under my command on Saturday 2 May 1942.

2. On receiving the first damage by two torpedoes at 1613B on 30 April 1942, I was proceeding in accordance with your verbal instructions in position 73° 08'N 33°E ahead of convoy QP11 on a Mean course of 205 at a speed of 19 knots and carrying out zigzag No 34. The convoy was steering 295 and **EDINBURGH** had previously been steering 315 to keep clear of submarines which D/F bearings indicated might be in the convoy's line of advance. At 1606B course was altered to 205 to cross the convoy's track, before turning to remake contact on the course of 115.

3. At 1607 course was altered 20 degrees to starboard to carry out the first leg of the zigzag. The ship had steadied on the new course when she was struck by one torpedo between Station No 70 and 87. Within two seconds a second torpedo struck her between stations 248 and 260.

4. The ship continued to steam circling to starboard to 020 and I tried to establish communication with the Lower Steering position, or Damage Control Headquarters, but could get no reply. No communication could be obtained with either the After Damage Control Party in "Y" Cabin Flat or the Engine Room and the ship took on a list of about 7 degrees. I had all damage control parties piped to close up and ordered the torpedoes on the starboard side to be fired to reduce the list.

5. Communication was soon established by telephone to the Type 279 RDF Office, CCO and Engine Room and a report was received stating that steam pressure was maintained and that all four shafts were rotating. Shortly afterwards I received a report that the stern abaft "Y" turret was demolished except for some wreckage, it broke off finally two hours later at about 1830 from abaft the armoured bulkhead No 238 carrying with it the port inner "A" bracket and propeller.

6. I realised that the rudder had gone and that the port inner shaft could not be expected to remain serviceable for long.

7. I then tried to bring the ship to an Easterly course by varying the revolutions on the remaining two shafts; this was found to be impractical, and as it was possible that further attack could be expected and since no escort was available I continued steaming in a North North Easterly course at about 10 knots, which was the highest speed obtainable without risk of further damage.

8. A full report of the damage contained and the action taken is contained in Enclosure 1.

9. Immediately the ship had been struck, CS18 ordered a signal to be made to **BULLDOG** and at 1730B **FORESTER** arrived to screen me, followed by **FORESIGHT** at 1800B and the two Russian destroyers at 1832B. **FORESTER** proceeded to investigate a S/M sighted to the North Eastward returning at 1920B.

10. Preparations were made for a destroyer to tow ahead to assist in steering the ship and at 1950B **EDINBURGH** was taken in tow by **FORESTER**. Unfortunately, the ship, which was now 7ft down by the bow and had no stern and probably two damaged shafts hanging well below her bottom, came rapidly up into the wind immediately she gathered headway.

11. After parting the tow, the attempt to tow from forward was abandoned and preparations were made to take a destroyer on aft.

12. Before this could be done, however, **FORESTER** sighted a submarine on the surface about 4 miles distant and made off to attack.

13. In the meantime a report of the damage had been received, flooding boundaries established, and the list had been taken off the ship; the Engineer Officer informed me that 120 revolutions per minute on the two outer shafts could be maintained without risk of further damage. This report was confirmed by the Executive Officer, and Shipwright Officer.

14. When the **FORESTER** returned, **FORESIGHT** was taken in tow aft and an attempt was made to maintain a course towards Kola Inlet, using the towed ship to control the steering.

15. This method proved reasonably efficient and a speed of advance of about 3 knots was attained between 2330B/30 and 0600B/1.

16. The ship was then estimated to be 240 miles from Kola Inlet and, as a report had been received from SBNO North Russia that a tug and further escort of minesweepers were being sent out, there appeared every hope that the ship might be brought back to harbour, though it was realised that, as this would take four days, I would have to be prepared for increasing attack from submarines, aircraft and light forces.

17. At 1600 Russian destroyers, who had been making signals about their fuel shortage for some hours, reported that they must now return to harbour owing to shortage of fuel and as it was considered essential that at least two destroyers should be used for screening the ship, the tow was cast off and an attempt was made to steer the ship by use of main engines only.

18. The wind being from NNW it was found that she could only be pointed to her course by gathering slight sternway. When her head was pointing about 110 degrees, and swinging to Starboard, headway was gathered and the swing maintained as far as possible by control of the engines. After passing through 140 degrees the swing was stopped at about 200 degrees and the ship swung rapidly back to 110 degrees. In spite of every effort to reduce this swing to port it could not be done without gathering slight sternway. After letting her head pass through 110 sternway was again gathered and the process repeated.

19. By tacking in this manner a speed of advance of about 2 knots was obtained inspite of having to gather sternway about every 5 to 10 minutes. This tortuous track could be seen winding astern, indicated by the oil, and occasionally the ship got completely out of control and swept round in a complete circle. The engine room register shows that in one watch 64 orders were executed on one shaft alone.

20. This progress was maintained for about 23 hours and although it was a considerable strain on all concerned, the ship did advance in the right direction.

21. Submarines were continually in the vicinity as homing signals were received, and there was no doubt that **EDINBURGH**'s movements were being reported.

22. Attempts were made by **FORESIGHT** and **FORESTER** to drive off submarines and their efficient screening and general alertness during this trying time undoubtedly saved **EDINBURGH** from further attack, as the ship was an almost stationary t arget.

23. Reports received from SBNO of D/F fixes indicated that many submarines were taking up their positions between **EDINBURGH** and Kola Inlet, and reports from **BULLDOG** indicated that enemy destroyers were at sea and might reach us any time after midnight.

24. The hands were kept at Action Stations, but the extreme cold (17°F) and lack of electrical heating, made the duties of all men in exposed positions extremely arduous, especially as the destruction of the mess-decks forward had deprived a number of them of warm clothing.

25. Before the Russian destroyers left me I took the opportunity of mustering a representative proportion of the ship's company on the flight deck and informing them of the situation.

26. I told them that I had high hopes of getting the ship back to harbour, and the way they responded to these remarks convinced me that my hopes were shared by them all, that morale was high and that there was no indication of our danger in the behaviour, conversation or other actions of any officer or man with whom I came in contact.

27. In fact we soon began to re-establish communications, restore amenities, such as cooking facilities and SRE gear, which made life seem almost normal.

28. At 1800/1 a vessel was sighted bearing approximately 210 and at first this was thought to be a German destroyer. The armament was trained onto the target, but at the same time the vessel made an identification signal and gave her name as the Russian gunboat **RUBIN.**

29. **HUSSAR**, in company with a tug, joined at 2345/1 followed by **HARRIER, GOSSAMER** and **NIGER**. The tug was taken on ahead but was not sufficiently powerful to keep the ship from coming into the wind. A further attempt was made towing the tug astern, but this was again found to be impracticable.

30. The possibility of towing or steaming the ships stern first was again considered but the Warrant Shipwright informed me that the movement of the after bulkhead every time the ship had gained any sternway indicated that such action would be attended with grave risk and could not be entertained.

31. At 0530 the tug was again taken on ahead and **GOSSAMER** astern to act as a drogue. The ship was hauled round till her head was pointing in the desired direction and then went slowly ahead on both engines.

32. She was proceeding on a course of 150 with a speed of about 3 knots with the tug fine on the Starboard bow and **GOSSAMER** broad on the Port Quarter. There seemed every hope that by this means the desired course could be made good, but the arrival of the German destroyers made it necessary to slip the tow before sufficient advance had been made to prove this conclusively. Although I very much doubt if a speed of more than 3 knots could have been obtained which would have meant a further 3 or 4 days at sea with attendant difficulties of fuel requirements of tug and escort.

33. At 0600 gunfire from **HARRIER** on the Starboard quarter indicated the arrival of enemy vessels which proved to be three German destroyers. The tows were slipped and **EDINBURGH** proceeded at her maximum speed of about eight knots. As from previous experience it was realised that it was hopeless to try to steer the ship except by gathering sternway, no attempt was made to steer by main engines. The ship circled round to Port sometimes rapidly and sometimes on a wider curve.

34. By this time **FORESTER** and **FORESIGHT** had moved out to engage the enemy destroyers and **EDINBURGH** concentrated all her efforts on assisting them as much as she could.

35. The visibility was very bad and only one enemy destroyer was visible at any one time. The remainder being hidden by smoke or snow flurries, and it was always difficult to distinguish our own from enemy vessels.

36. As the ship was continually altering course and all turrets were in local control, it was only with great difficulty that the armament could be kept on the target and, in addition, to safeguard **FORESIGHT** and **FORESTER**, it was essential to withhold fire until the target could be clearly identified.

37. The Gunnery Officer was in control of "X" Turret, and the foremost group controlled by a Lieutenant in "B" Turret was conned onto the target by the bridge and by this means did some very effective firing at the destroyers which attempted to close **EDINBURGH**. On three occasions determined attempts were driven off before torpedoes were fired but on the fourth occasion the enemy was in sight for such a brief period that torpedoes must have been fired as soon as the ship was sighted.

38. "A" Turret could not pick up the target and did not open fire. Nearly all salvoes from "B" Turret seemed to fall in line and on two occasions hits were reported.

39. At 0652 torpedoes were seen breaking surface about 5000 yards on the Starboard beam and it seemed certain that they would pass well astern.

40. The ship's head, however, was swinging very slowly to Port and the tracks were lost sight of. The ship started to swing rapidly to Port and the tracks were again sighted on the Port side and it was thought that they would pass astern, which, in fact, two of them did. However, one torpedo, running deep, was seen close to the ship and it was realised that no action could be taken to avoid it. Another track was seen to pass close ahead.

41. One torpedo struck the ship between frames numbers 87 and 108 and she listed rapidly to Port to an angle of 12 degrees and continued slowly to increase the list. The Engineer Officer reported that steam was failing.

42. I received a report, whose origin I have not been able to trace, that "A" Boiler Room was flooding and I ordered the Engineer Officer to stop Main Engines and to get the Engine Room and Boiler Room personnel on deck.

43. "B" Turret was still engaging the enemy when in accordance with your orders **GOSSAMER** came alongside Starboard side and **HARRIER** Port side.

44. The list had by this time increased to 17 degrees and orders were passed to transfer all sick and wounded to minesweepers and men not required to man the armament to embark.

45. At this time **FORESIGHT** was seen to have been hit and stopped although still in action with the enemy. **FORESTER** was not in sight. **HUSSAR** laid a smoke screen to cover **EDINBURGH**.

46. The list prevented **EDINBURGH** making use of her armament at close quarters on the engaged side. I ordered "A" and "B" Turrets' crews to leave their turrets and the ship to be completely abandoned, in accordance with your verbal orders.

47. When I had been informed by the Master-At-Arms and Executive Officer that all men were up from below, that all upper deck hatches that could be reached had been opened, I then left the ship myself and boarded **HARRIER**. In accordance with your orders, **HARRIER** lay off to wait for the ship to sink.

48. The wind having gone down and there being no sea, the list only increased very slowly and as the action with the destroyers was still in progress, attempts were made to hasten the end by firing a few 4-inch shells from **HARRIER** and dropping depth charges close alongside. This proved unsuccessful and **FORESIGHT** who had one torpedo remaining and was now again under way was ordered to sink her.

49. On being hit by **FORESIGHT**'s torpedo the ship immediately started to turn over and within 3 minutes was completely submerged.

50. I have no doubt from seeing the effect of the final torpedo, that the ship had previously been in a very bad state; had another torpedo hit her before the ship's company was taken off, only a very small proportion would have been saved; the temperature of the water being so low that no men could have lived if not picked up within a few minutes, and even those who could have been saved would probably have been maimed by frostbite as they would not have been given proper attention in the limited space available in the minesweepers.

51. **HARRIER** and **GOSSAMER** then proceeded to Murmansk at their best available speed and during our time onboard we were shown every consideration and given every comfort available. All officers turned out of their cabins to provide accommodation and the captains' cabins were given over to the sick and wounded.

52. On arrival at Polyarnoe all men were mustered by the open list on the jetty and the total number of casualties established. After I had addressed them they were split up into groups as required by local accommodation. One third of them remained at Polyarnoe and the rest re-embarked in **GOSSAMER** for transport to Vaenga, the sick and wounded being sent to Murmansk.

53. The ship's log and ledger were saved. Confidential Books and Charge Documents, which were in a locked stowage were not transferred to **HARRIER** as it was considered better for security reasons that they should be sunk with the ship. **HARRIER** herself was in the presence of the enemy, was most unlikely to have a suitable stowage onboard and, above all, the time and the risk of transfer could not be accepted.

54. The only other stores saved were two pairs of binoculars from the Captain's sights which were removed by the bridge personnel before they left the ship, have been transferred to **HARRIER** who has taken them on voluntary charge.

55. The ship's company's behaviour during these three trying days left nothing to be desired and although they had to work continually in severe cold with makeshift meals and almost continually at Action Stations when not repairing damage or handling tows, all orders

were carried out cheerfully and enthusiastically. All emergencies were met with such confidence and calmness that they ceased to be emergencies.

56. The work of the Damage Control Parties under Commander Jefferis, Sub Lieutenant (E) Cox and Mr Dudding calls for special commendation, the careful planning of the damage control organisation with the many weeks of training proved its worth on this occasion as never before. In fact both hits had actually been exercised before and although the damage visualised was almost correct in the case of the forward torpedo, the complete collapse of the stern had not been foreseen. In the drawing up of the DC organisation and planning the training I was fortunate in having Construction Commander Skinner onboard whose help and advice proved invaluable.

57. Throughout the whole three days, the work of all men below decks and in particular the Engine Room Department was beyond praise and their behaviour and bearing were in the highest traditions of the Service. At no time was there any panic or selfish thought. Every man worked for the good of his messmates and the ship. Commander (E) Dathon was always intent on keeping the ship steaming and the great work of the engine room department was largely due to his leadership and determination. Total casualties were 2 officers and 58 ratings killed, one officer and 24 ratings wounded.

58. Surgeon Commander Lacelles and his staff who had been working almost unceasingly in attending to the many sick and wounded which we carried continued to the end calmly and methodically doing everything that was necessary for the casualties and the efficient evacuation of the disabled reflects the greatest credit on him.

59. An efficient well trained ships company have been saved for further service. I think that we have all been hardened by our experience. It is our one desire that we may be kept together to man another ship as soon as possible and see another convoy through.

60. The way the ship stood up to her punishment has restored the confidence of all officers and men in our ships.

I have the honour to be,

Sir,

Your obedient Servant,

H FAULKNER
Captain Royal Navy
Commanding Officer.

On our arrival ashore from the escorts, deep in the heart of the Arctic Tundra, the survivors were formed up for a muster and for the first time they realised who had been lost in the final action. Then the long march began, none of them knew where they were going. They were hungry and cold, and dressed in awful clothes, some wearing trousers, some in singlets, others wrapped in woollen blankets.

Finally they arrived at the camp set up for the survivors and were of course, looking forward to a substantial meal. What they actually got on arrival was a piece of black bread each, followed by a breaker of pine needle tea, made by bruising and boiling pine needles and tasting just as you would imagine, dish water being used for washing up plates aft er a meal of mutton.

Some of the survivors were to remain in Russia for months sharing the incredible hardships of the Russian people, and many were to lose their lives as ships taking them back to the UK were sank. Some stayed at Vaenga, a long coastal community. Others at Polyarnoe. The wounded were sent to a Russian hospital in Murmansk. The conditions at Vaenga were so sub-human, with food so short, the civilian population had barely enough to live on. Conditions at Polyarnoe were a little less harsh, but by any standards life in both places was primitive, although the survivors agreed they were no worse for the Russian people themselves.

Leading Signalman Harry Ingle a survivor from **HMS EDINBURGH** has vivid memories of the sinking of his ship and the equally enduring yet safe time ashore.

In our survivors' camp in Northern Siberia we were put with hundreds of other survivors of naval and merchant ships brought ashore in all stages of health and disarray. Everything was primitive, but the best the Russians could provide under the circumstances of wartime was in regard to our most basic daily need. To our dismay, and that of even our most hardened matelots, the Russians had dug a big 20 foot pit on the top of a hill at one end of our camp with a very long board about a foot from each side - we climbed up there, turned round in two rows loosened our clothes and gingerly lowered our backsides on to the board, first providing ourselves with a handful of snow in lieu of paper. As there was about 20 foot of snow all round it was regularly covered over all day. At the end of May came the dawning of the Siberian Spring and on the 1st of June we awoke to find all the snow had vanished and melted clean away, although the constant German bombing of the nearby airfield still carried on! But worse was the odour from the hill-top which the Russian soldiers were busy covering with soil, as fast as they could, our primitive Winter toilet.

This was May, snow and ice were still everywhere. September was to come before the last of the survivors left after sharing the hardships. **HMS EDINBURGH** lay at the bottom of the Arctic waters more than 200 miles from Murmansk after being crippled by three German torpedoes and finally sunk by the torpedo of one of our own destroyers.

The school that housed the survivors was bombed the day after they left to return to the U.K. Was this a coincidence, was this a mistake of one day, as no other buildings were bombed? The bodies of the Russians were blown out of the building in a mangled mess. A woman went to one of the bodies, picked up what was left by the hair, looked at the face, didn't recognise anyone, so dropped it and walked away.

EDINBURGH'S GOLD

That gold was in safe keeping
t the bottom of the sea;
It was no trouble to leave it there
Why couldn't they let it be?
Is this world a better place
Now they have taken it from the dead.
Who had guarded it with watchful eye
Upon that ocean bed?
God ordained that it should lie
Within that cruiser's womb
And who are we that's mortal
To vandalise this tomb?
It was watched over by heroes
Friends of you and me
In that cruiser "Edinburgh"
In that cold North Arctic Sea.
Their bones have long been bleached
By the seas these many years
And when that gold was taken away
Many folks shed tears,
Wives, mothers, friends of loved ones
That trod that cruiser's deck,
To them it was a war grave
To gold seekers just a wreck
But judgement day will surely come
And debts be fully paid
They'll find it better to have left
That gold where it was laid.

Ralph Matthews

THIS GREED FOR GOLD

Haven't they had their fill
These vultures of the deep,
Wandals of this war grave
Where valiant sailors sleep?
Must this greed for gold go on
For avaricious personal gain,
Have they no thought at all
For those who suffered pain,
The heart of losing loved ones
In the Barents Sea up there
On board the cruiser "Edinburgh"
This pain they had to bear;
No gold for them to replace this loss
On a day so long ago
Those widows, orphans, mothers
Of men that history know,
No gold for them to replace a son
A father, husband, friend
Who gave their lives on that ship
This cargo the defend.

These greedy vandals knew not
The toil, the struggle, the strife
They knew not these gallant men
Who sadly gave their life,
In Britain's fight in icy seas
With nare a cross to show
On this sea where they fell
And now are sleeping there below.
Must these human vultures once again
Disturb their sea bleached bones,
For this awful greed for gold
That no-one really owns,
I believe it belongs to those
In that cruiser's womb
They have guarded it and they own it
Cradles in that iron tomb
So let us in this country now
Rise up and take a stand
This gold must remain and stay there
Away from this thieving piratical band.

Ralph Matthews

Captain E. Fox MN was at the age of 30 Third Officer to the M.V. HOPEMOUNT a tanker of 4529 tons, which left North Shields on 24th April 1942, for a voyage to Murmansk. Yet another ship to find itself marooned, with a full load of fuel and deisel oil.

Loading completed, we sailed with a small convoy to Hvalfjord, to await other ships. With all ships and escorts assembled we set sail for Murmansk - so we thought!

From the start we encountered poor visibility and then ice, with these adverse conditions it was not long before some of the ships were missing from the convoy, and it was presumed that they had returned to Iceland. Worse was to come, proceeding at a slow speed we reached a point to the north of North Cape, when we suffered a combined attack by aircraft and U-boats. The first casualty was the Commodore's ship, the S.S. EMPIRE HOWARD, sustaining two torpedo hits and sinking in a matter of seconds. Losing the Commodore was a double blow, but then a miracle happened. The fog came down in a thick blanket and visibility was reduced to just a few yards. I recall the fog lasting until just before arriving off the Inlet. The HOPEMOUNT was the only tanker to get through, in company with six other vessels.

At Murmansk we had a busy time, oiling ships and constantly changing our anchorage because of the two or three daily visits from German aircraft from the captured port of Petsamo. We worked in Murmansk from arriving until the end of July, by which time we had completely discharged all of our precious cargo. Our spirits were lifted, with the thoughts of once again returning to U.K. and home. However, those joyful thoughts promptly had the damper put on them, with orders to proceed to Archangel to await further instructions. At Archangel we were promptly despatched to another White Sea port. It consisted of a wooden jetty where we loaded Russian oil, and were then instructed to join a convoy of Russian vessels for another destination - Vladivostok, north about!

Having been at Murmansk for nearly five months, and as the ship only set off with stores for a six-month period, our big problem now was food. We were right out of stores and we knew that several food ships had not got through to Murmansk. However, the Russian authorities did their best and gave us crates containing thousands of bottles of beans, and sacks of Russian flour which, no matter what way it was baked, was always sad and saggy. Little did we know that before our Arctic voyage was finished we would treasure this. Also provided were about twenty yak carcasses of varying sizes. Unfortunately, our fridge was the old ammonia type and as this ammonia was not available the fridge was useless for keeping meat fresh. We were told not to worry as we would soon be in the icefield and the freezing conditions would keep the meat frozen. One good thing that the Russians gave us was special clothing for the extreme cold we were to encounter.

So, with three Russian ice pilots aboard, (one for each bridge watch) we proceeded out of the White Sea, turning east along the northern coastal lane of Yugorski Sha, at the entrance to the Kara Sea. In the Yugorski Strait we did some re-fuelling of vessels and were joined by two ice-breakers. With these, and about twelve other Russian vessels we left the straits and proceeded up the Kara Sea, and clearing this sea, we proceeded further eastward to Dickson Harbour 73°30" N 80°45" E. Then on anchoring at Dickson Harbour fresh orders were received from Moscow. These were interpreted by the ice pilots, then up anchors and so once more we headed north until we reached Cape Cheliuskin 77°40" N 104°15" E. Here we had a setback, as the breakers reported the icefield to be too thick, so we back-tracked to a little island called Neilosenn Island, where we anchored until conditions improved. The three pilots were captains who had vast experience of the severe conditions that we were encountering. Our stay here was short, as information was received that a German light cruiser was dogging our steps. Thick ice or no, we set off for Cape Cheliuskin and into the ice field.

We followed the ice breakers, only a few yards behind them, and what an experience. Pushing through the ice was like grating a piece of iron along a brick wall, and this continued, day and night, until we managed to find a lane through. I could not see us getting through the dense ice that we had encountered. We steamed eastwards and eventually got Tiksi, which is something like 73° N 141° E. We remained here alone, as the Russian vessels and the breakers departed without us. Several days later the breakers returned, in company with three Russian Navy destroyers. We joined the destroyers for the long haul back to Kola Inlet, refuelling them on the way. We arrived back there during the middle of December and sailed for home on New Year's Eve.

The first thing we did was to have a good meal, for after four months with beans for breakfast, beans and flapjack for lunch, beans for tea and coffee with only brown sugar and tea with milk only, but not the both! However, the various Unions took this up with shipowners, who grudgingly awarded each member of the crew with the princely sum of five pounds - for the food they had not had!

Needless to say, the ship was a wreck after the voyage, two well bent propeller shafts with twisted blades which reduced the ship's maximum speed to eight knots, and a ship's bottom that looked more like a switchback railway. In the whole of the war this was definitely the worst voyage I experienced.

On 1st May 1942 outward bound convoy PQ15 sailing to North Russian ports was shrouded in heavy mist and fog. Although the sea was calm, danger was always there from enemy surface raiders such as the giant German battleship **TIRPITZ**, likely to appear on the horizon at any time, from beneath the waves, U-boats with their deadly torpedoes at the ready, or should the fog clear for any length of time from the German bomber and torpedo bombers from the air.

Escorts were a group of destroyers covering force aft being the battleship **KING GEORGE V**. aircraft carrier **VICTORIOUS**, **USS WASHINGTON**, **USS WICHITA** and **USS TUSCALOOSA.**

But death came suddenly to the men on the Tribal Class destroyer, **HMS PUNJABI**. By accident, with one of the larger ships of the covering force, whilst manoeuvring in the fog she was sliced in half by the battleship **KING GEORGE V**. - the silence being shattered by an explosion sending a shock wave through the ships in the area.

A signal had been sent to **PUNJABI** to watch out for a floating mine and to avoid this she had turned to starboard, and cut across the bows of **KING GEORGE V**. unable to avoid the collision. As the two sections began to sink and with the crew jumping into the water there were more explosions as the primed depth charges rolled off the stern into the water amongst the crew. A great personal tragedy amongst officers and men of the ships concerned, particularly the **PUNJABI**. The two sections fast sinking were surrounded with blood, oil debris and bodies of the crew in the wash of the grey silhouette disappearing into the fog. Although realising something awful had happened yet unaware of the reason or result, it was assumed to be a torpedo or mine.

Signalman Eric Whyte was in the communications mess waiting to go on watch on the flagdeck of the **KING GEORGE V**.

Suddenly I felt the ship make a violent turn and seemed to heave out of the water. Soon after a loud explosion could be heard along with ship's side. Hands to mine stations was piped. My station was amidships near the catapult, visibility was poor. Although there was plenty of activity on the signal deck we seemed to be proceeding as normal. A destroyer on port screen signalled intention to haul out of position to aid the now known crippled destroyer **PUNJABI** astern of us. We then learned our bows had cut her in half and as a result of the collision her primed depth charges had rolled off the stern and exploded near us and in the area of the doomed **PUNJABI.**

I was given to understand this tragic accident happened because the destroyer was out of position at the end of a manoeuvre and perhaps did not carry out the correct procedure. The sad fact remains that loss of life had been suffered and one of our own destroyers had been sunk and we felt for those lost and the thoughts of the Captain of this tragic accident.

Seaman Gerry Ricketts aboard **PUNJABI** luckily survived the tragic sinking of his ship. He relates:

The sea was calm with frequent snow showers and dense fog patches, so the opening and closing of distance between the big ships and escorts was frequent and often frightening. As the fog closed in the escorts with fog buoys streamed formed port and starboard screens.

PUNJABI was second in the starboard column following the leader. As she turned towards the big ships to close the distance the fog buoy of the leader was lost. Within minutes **PUNJABI** now blind crossed the line of advance of the 35,000 tonne flagship **KING GEORGE V**. who struck our port side aft of the engine room slicing through us like a knife through butter. The tremendous crash was heard, all power and lighting failed as the ship lurched violently to starboard with everything crashing around us. As the ship was slowly returning only temporarily to even keel we scrambled to the ladder and on to the upper deck when it was obvious that half had disappeared. We stood on deck the angle getting steeper every minute.

On the part side our stern could be seen vertical, some yards away and appeared to rise up out of the water as the depth charges exploded throwing up water and wreckage.

Looking aft the battleship **USS WASHINGTON** loomed out of the fog and altered course to starboard. Looking forward the huge hulk of the carrier **VICTORIOUS** swept across our bows. It became very obvious this was the time to leave so went over to the starboard side. The ship's whaler was some distance and the water was rising fast up to my knees. Steadying myself on the boat davits I stood on the top guard rail when within seconds the water rose suddenly floating me off and away. I joined a messmate and shared his wooden staging where we could. I saw **HMS MARTIN** and **HMS MARNE** coming towards us to pick us up as thankful survivors. Whilst in the water, oil, wreckage and other less fortunate bodies of our shipmates. **WICHITA** and **TUSCALOOSA** passed close by before we were rescued by **HMS MARTIN**.

For many of my shipmates the cold and oil fuel was too much and fifty-two of the crew of **PUNJABI** died that day.

Stoker 1st class George Stacey was aboard **MARNE**, one of the rescue ships taking aboard survivors. He was on duty in the boiler room when engine room rang for more steam.

We thought contact had been made with a U-boat. Then the buzz went round the ship, that one of the escorts had been sunk. We raced to the scene of disaster, then bridge rang down to stop engines. I came off watch and was standing on the upper deck. I have never seen such fog. Everything was deadly still, quiet and eerie.

As we drifted along silently, the sea became calm, all round was thick, black, oil fuel and trying to swim for their lives were the poor devils from the **PUNJABI**. Others that were past swimming just floated by looking terrible, just black oil covering their lifeless bodies amongst the wreckage.

Again the silence was broken by further explosions from the depth charges rolling off the sinking stern of the doomed ship causing further havoc, injuries and death to the crew, before finally disappearing below the surface.

A dreadful tragedy not by enemy action, but accident between two of our own ships.

Although hundreds of allied merchant sailors and naval personnel lost their lives in getting supplies to Russia from 1941 to the end of the war in Europe, Russia has maintained an official silence on the value of this assistance in defeating Nazi Germany.

The Commander-in-Chief of the Soviet Northern Fleet, despite limited forces at his disposal "supported the allied effort to the best of his ability", but when hundreds of injured allied seamen were being treated in primitive medical conditions in Russia, it is difficult to forgive the grudging eventual permission to land the medical unit brought out by **TUSCALOOSA** only after the intervention of Churchill/Stalin level.

These seamen had taken part in a heroic struggle not only against a determined enemy, but the other enemy of gales, fog, snow and cold of such intensity that death was swift when thrown into the icy waters.

Considering naval personnel sent to Russia to administer the arrival of merchant ships and escorts in and out of Kola Inlet and diversion to Archangel, unload, refuel, turn round and return to UK, all part of the assistance to Russia with supplies of war material, it was, nevertheless, more than surprising and beyond all comprehension that the Russians made it a necessity for us to have a visa to enter their country to assist them.

This became paramount when reports from medical offices ashore in Russia outlined to Admiralty the awful conditions prevailing in the Russian hospitals and the somewhat mediaeval treatment given to survivors. The urgent need for a medical unit with sick berth staff to be sent became obvious if convoys were to be continued, and the number of casualties requiring hospital treatment must be expected to increase beyond present level, as naval personnel risked their lives to bring convoys to Russia. This resulted in due consequences with many difficulties to be overcome, as after all the organisations by Admiralty and medical branch in UK the Russians for reason of suspicion, jealousy and pride refused to allow the unit to land on the ridiculous grounds that the men did not have a visa.

2046B/31st May
SECRET MESSAGE

From S.B.N.O. North Russia

Date: 1.6.42
Recd: 0132

Interdepartmental Cypher (O.T.T.) by W/T

Addressed: Admiralty. Repeated: C. in C. Home Fleet, Admiral Miles, S.B.N.O. Archangel.

110. If convoys to North Russia are to be continued on present scale the number of casualties requiring hospital treatment must be expected to increase well beyond present high level. Although I am satisfied that Russian Authorities give our men equal if not better treatment than their own, their methods are below our standards and I feel that our men are enduring much greater suffering than should be necessary.

A hospital ship equipped to deal with at least 100 cases is an unostentatious necessity, but if this cannot be provided a British or American hospital unit of similar capacity should be sent out at the first opportunity and a hospital established ashore at the convoy terminus.

Supplies of hospital stores are very difficult to obtain in North Russia especially plaster of Paris M and B, Gentian violet and all forms of anesthetic. The unit should therefore be self contained both in personnel and all stores. Admiralty pass to C. in C. Home Fleet.

2046B/31.
Passing action being taken by War Registry

1st Lord		
1st S.L.	N.A.1st S.L.	O.D. (5)
2nd S.L.	Nav. Sec.	D. of P (3)
4th S.L.	D.P.S. (2)	M (4)
V.C.N.S.	D.N.I. (5)	D.T.D. (M)
A.C.N.S. (F)	D.T.D. (4)	D. of S.T. (2)

SECRET

H.M.S. "Ashanti"

23rd July 1942

Medical Services in the KOLA INLET existent on the arrival of Convoy P.Q.16.

Sir,

I have the honour to submit the following report concerning the medical services existent in the Kola Inlet based on personal observations during my stay in Murmansk five weeks ago, when for five days I was acting Base Medical Officer owing to the latter being on sick leave.

2. There are four Russian hospitals in the Inlet which accepted and dealt with surgical cases. Their primary dutico wcrc to act ao baoc hoopitalo for oaoualtioo roooivod from tho front and ao ouoh, therefore, were always overcrowded with serious and invariably septic cases.

POLYARNOE

3. This hospital is situated at the submarine base. There are about 50 beds with facilities for surgery (with limited equipment) and an X-ray plant available.

VAENGA

4. This hospital proved to be nothing more than an improvised sick quarters in the basement and on the ground floor of a block of flats. There were about 40 beds. Conditions were appalling and

require to be seen to be believed. There was no ventilation, constant smoking by the Russians (including the staff), stale spit bowls and urine bottles on the floor. This mingled with the odour of sceptic wounds and suppurating compound fractures in plaster made the foulest atmosphere conceivable. Treatment was lacking and extremely inefficient and generally the standard of medical practice was very low.

5. I beg to give two illustrations of this:

(a) Intravenous anaesthesia had never been seen before and when Pentothal was given by a Surgeon Lieutenant ex **H.M.S. EDINBURGH**, to a case of severe compound fracture with osteomylelitis of the tibia and fibula for re-application of P.O.P. and removal of sequestra the Russian doctors were amazed; so much so that the patient came round almost before the operation had been commenced.

(b) In a 40' x 20' room where all our wounded were warded, 10 in number, excluding a few Russians, the cases were mixed. Thus one found cases of clean burns of hands and face (incidentally being treated with Tannic acid and having severe flexion deformity six weeks afterwards), suppurating compound fractures and clean primarily sutured wounds all mixed together.

6. The beds, as seemed to be the practice in most hospitals, were grouped in twos making double beds, as it were.

7. The food was nauseating, a type of brown gelatinous bread, rice and yak meat served in the most unappetising manner possible. This monotonous daily diet was without variation. In my view the wounded of the western allies should not be sent to this hospital.

GRASNERE

8. This hospital, a further 6-7 miles up the inlet towards Murmansk, was the better of the hospitals in the area with full facilities for major surgery and a modern X-ray plant. It could take about 50 cases. I personally did not visit this hospital although I sent the major wounded cases of **H.M.S. GOSSAMER** there.

MURMANSK

9. This hospital is a converted school and stands on a hill dominating the town - its vast white walls making an obvious landmark. This presumably accounted for the fact that in two days, June 12-13th, the hospital had sticks of bombs within 200 yards on three sides of it. No visible red crosses were shown on its roof. There are about 300 beds. The administrative services and departments are on the ground floor. Russian wards are on the first floor and in what was the school hall on the second floor are housed the wounded PQ and QP convoy survivors. 99% of the window space was boarded up and therefore fresh air was non existent. Incidentally I had great difficulty in persuading the authorities to remove various pictures and busts of noted Bolsheviks and weighing upward of 10 cwt. from the walls. These swayed around in a most alarming manner during the frequent raids and in themselves were capable of proving lethal weapons.

10. No words of mine can describe the deplorable conditions under which the patients were treated. "Bloody awful", in its literal sense, is the nearest I can get. The cots were placed together in twos with an eighteen inch space between each pair. There were no smoking restrictions, not even amongst the staff. If a patient wished to open his bowels at a mealtime then he did so, without screens around his bed. Should epidemic disease occur under these conditions it would be impossible to control it. The 60 patients in this hall were indiscriminately mixed both as regards race, rank and disease: Poles, Americans, Hindus, Portugese and English with diseases as variant as pneumonia, clean compound fractures (at least so on admittance), fractured spines, with incontinence and bedsores, malaria and about 15 cases of gangrenous extremities following frost-bite.

11. As regards the treatment of frost-bite, and especially the surgical treatment following gangrene and sepsis, the Russian doctors seem to lack the very fundamentals of medical and surgical practice. A typical case would be one in which gangrene of the hands or feet seq. frost-bite had been treated by amputation through the line of demarcation and not at the site of election with a consequent sepsis, sloughing and osteomyelitis necessitating repeated re-amputation. Plantar and Palmar infection of the feet and hands followed upon amputation of the digits with monotonous regularity. The Russians seem to favour Lisfrancs operation for gangrene of the toes (an operation leaving a stump, in any case ill

designed for weight-bearing) but this was always followed by a boggy cellulitic foot and an ascending osteomyelitis which in one case caused an amputation through the mid third of the femur.

12. Dressings were usually done on the ground floor out of the wards. Here under conditions vaguely simulating a dungeon, where no screams could be heard, major dressings such as those involving packing the shoulder joint with reapplication of plaster of Paris would be conducted without anaesthesia. Young cabin boys, of whom I saw three aged 14, 16 and 16 respectively with arms and/or legs missing and with unhealed stumps were subjected to this medieval medicine.

13. It was tragic to observe these emaciated patients, with no hope of cure under these conditions, subjected to an average of eight air raid warnings a day and including an average of three severe raids during which the building would literally rock. Naturally they were terror stricken to such an extent that the absence of arms and legs proved no hindrance to their diving under their beds, as a result of which, as often as not they injured and hurt themselves and would have to have their wounds redressed.

14. The operating theatre contained two tables and two benches and here, following the arrival of a convoy, or after an air raid, the wounded were operated upon en masse. I saw, following one blitz, cases of compound fracture of the spine, shrapnel wounds of the abdomen with evisceration and a lacerated wound involving the elbow joint and a compound fracture of the lower end of the humerus, all operated upon at the same time from a communal table of instruments.

15. The case of the elbow injury will linger long in my memory. It was a case of a Russian soldier who was being held down by two orderlies whilst three people probed the joint and manipulated the fracture. Some type of local anaesthetic was injected into the raw surfaces of the wound but no time was given for it to act and anyway it was totally ineffective. I am extremely doubtful if anyone of these three persons treating this case was qualified in medicine.

16. During these operations, as often as not, someone would be smoking in the theatre. Even in seriously shocked cases preliminary resuscitation was reduced to a minimum with the obvious results.

17. Improvisation, and the infrequency with which wounds, requiring repeated dressings, received attention, illustrated only too well the shortage of medical equipment.

18. The Russians would not allow British doctors to assist in the operations on our casualties, but earlier had allowed us to dress our own cases: even this was soon withdrawn. All we could do was to maintain a constant watch to ensure that no obvious surgical blunders were made or the diagnosis of complications missed, to our knowledge.

19. I have already made mention of the hospital food but at Murmansk especially its poorness in quality and the unappetising way in which it was served defy all description. Were it not the illicit traffic of food into the hospital by the friends our casualties whose ships were in harbour, supplemented by intermittent supply from official British sources, the patient's diet would have been a starvation one.

20. An opinion grossly unfavourable to our Russian allies may be construed from this report but I must point out very definitely that their men had exactly the same treatment, the low standards of medical practice being entirely due to the fact that they assess the value of human life at a lower value than we do. I therefore hold the view that if a man (or woman) becomes a casualty he is no longer of use to his country and a minimum of time and expense is wasted upon the patient. If a casualty has an injury of such a nature that it is obvious he will soon become physically fit for battle, then attempts are made to help his recovery; but should the reverse be the case then little is done to obviate his sufferings and at the very best he eventually recovers to remain a permanent cripple. This Russian attitude towards their casualties is unfortunately (but quite naturally) also held towards ours.

21. I made repeated efforts to persuade the authorities to evacuate our casualties to the U.K. in destroyers - in my humble opinion this is the safest method of transport. However the official attitude is that these survivors shall remain in Russia until either:-

(a) they are physically fit - it seems problematical if a man minus arms and/or legs will ever become fit. Nothing short of a miracle will cause a cure under the present lines for the majority of cases there in the Kola Inlet.

(b) the present war ends.

22. On about June 14th after two days of continuous air raids I made a strong recommendation that all our cases be evacuated to the hospitals at Grasnere and Polyarnoe and the non-cot cases to the **EDINBURGH** survivors camp at Vaenga. This was done by the Base Medical Officer who had then returned, I having gone sick with acute gastro enteritis no doubt due to the fact that by that time all the main water and drainage were out of action and rats were everywhere.

23. The non-Russian cot cases from Murmansk were eventually sent by train to Archangel. The following day the Russians, acting on our example, also evacuated the hospital.

24. Such were the medical facilities at Murmansk and the conditions under which our men, already having undergone hell at sea, were subjected to. Of British medical stores, beyond many bandages and a few odd drugs I saw nothing. The base seemed to be dependent, at that time anyway, by being supplied by H.M. Ships, mostly destroyers who came into the Inlet.

25. It is worthy of mention that even before the raids started all water had to be boiled before it could be drunk with safety.

RECOMMENDATIONS

26. A. That an R.N. Hospital or Sick Quarters capable of dealing with major surgical cases, especially orthopaedic cases be established in North Russia. I would suggest that the minimum size be 40 cots. The establishment of our own hospital in my opinion is essential because of the peculiar ideas the Russians have of aseptic technique, the treatment of shock, surgery (especially orthopaedics) and the treatment of burns.

B. An ambulance launch is required, because of the terrible state of the roads.

C. Full stores are required including reserve supplies for ships engaged in North Russian convoy and mine-sweeping duties whose supplies may become exhausted following one action alone would suggest that particular attention be paid to the following items of stores:

(a) hypnotics and anaesthetics.
(b) dressings.
(c) plaster of Paris.
(d) M and B 693.
(e) Anti-Gas Gangrene serum, preferably polyvalent. Cases of this disease are very frequent during the cold months.

I have the honour to be,
Sir,
Your obedient servant,

Commanding Officer,

SECRET

In view of the unsatisfactory hospital conditions reported by S.B.N.O. North Russia, the Naval Staff arranged for a medical unit, consisting of 7 Officers and 36 ratings, to be despatched on the **USS TUSCALOOSA**. On security grounds, owing to the special nature of the operation, the prior authorisation of the Soviet Foreign Office was not obtained and Admiral Miles was asked to make the necessary arrangements for visas only a few days before the medical personnel landed on Russian soil. Two doctors and six ratings were landed at Vaenga and the remainder at Archangel.

2. Admiral Miles, in his 1256/12, reported that Molotov had refused landing permits to the personnel at Archangel and that they are returning in Q.P.14, which sailed yesterday. The signal does not make it clear whether Molotov is aware of the medical personnel having been landed at Vaenga. We had some doubt yesterday whether the Archangel party had in fact been placed on board Q.P.14, as the Russians might not have had time to do this, but H.M. Ambassador's telegram No. 135 has just come in, dated 12th September, in which he says that Admiral Miles is instructing the party to return home. It therefore seems probable that they did, in fact, catch Q.P.14.

3. Molotov's action in denying our wounded and sick Naval and Merchant Seamen personnel in North Russia the services of British medical personnel, is quite unspeakable, but we are also ourselves to blame. We have several times had trouble with the Russians over visas and in January last Molotov said explicitly that the Soviet could "not agree to the practice of sending British Military personnel to U.S.S.R. without entry visas in anticipation of special arrangements being made at the port of landing". H.M. Ambassador thereupon expressed the hope that all Service Departments would be impressed with the absolute necessity for obtaining visas in all cases and warned us that next time the persons concerned would probably be sent back.

4. Admittedly, the Russian delays in granting visas are intolerable and obstruct the administrative arrangements for working the Russian convoys, but in trying to overreach the regulations we were asking for trouble in this instance - and have got it.

5. A further difficulty, of course, is that the Russians probably resent the implied criticism of their own arrangements and would be disposed to make difficulties about receiving British medical personnel in North Russia in any case.

6. On the other hand, we are under a heavy responsibility to our own men to improve their conditions, and the present passage of another P.Q. convoy to North Russia is likely to emphasize this obligation. We must, therefore, it is considered:

a) try to keep the Vaenga party in Russia, if possible, and

b) if, after all, the Archangel party are not on board Q.P.14, we should try, once more, to obtain permission for them to land, making a frank admission that in making operational arrangements the error had been committed of not obtaining diplomatic sanction for the arrival of the British medical personnel.

7. It is to be feared that no further diplomatic representations will make the slightest impression on Molotov, whose heart is completely stony in these matters. Moreover, it is thought that it would be dangerous to leave our men at Vaenga without finding out whether Molotov is aware of their presence there and has acquiesced in their remaining. If he were to find out subsequently, he would be quite capable of locking them all up. It is therefore proposed that H.M. Ambassador should be asked to inform M. Molotov of the Vaenga party, if he is not already aware of them, and to request most urgently that they be permitted to remain.

8. If Molotov refuses to give the Vaenga party landing permits, the only way in which we can overcome the difficulty is for a personal telegram to be sent by the Prime Minister to Stalin. Similarly, it is thought this would be the only way of obtaining the landing permits for the Archangel party, if these have not already sailed in Q.P.14. It is a question, however, whether the Prime Minister would wish to take a matter of this kind up with Stalin at this juncture.

9. There remains the further question whether the requirement for British medical personnel at Archangel is so pressing that, notwithstanding the mishap in this case, we must make a fresh effort to obtain landing permits for a British party. This also affects a recent proposal of V.C.N.S. that a small team of three nurses and one doctor should be flown out by Catalina. Unfortunately, the fact that we have put ourselves in the wrong makes it more difficult to ask the Prime Minister to take the matter up with Stalin. Nevertheless, every convoy is likely to be attended by heavy casualties, and if we are to continue them during the coming months we must give our merchant seamen and naval personnel the best possible chance of decent treatment the other end. Molotov is reported in Moscow telegram No. 135 to have returned a flat negative to all our Ambassador's pleas, even after full apologies had been made. It therefore seems as if the only possible action is at the highest level, if the Board wish further efforts to be made.

10. A signal has been sent to S.B.N.O., North Russia, requesting an immediate report whether the Archangel party was, in fact, put on board Q.P.14. It is proposed:

(a) That the Foreign Secretary should be asked to consider whether in all the circumstances it is possible for the question to be re-opened by the Prime Minister with Stalin. The psychological moment will clearly be at the conclusion of the present convoy, particularly if a reasonable number of ships get through with important supplies. It will be necessary frankly to admit our error, and to emphasise the discomfort caused to our men by language difficulties, and the great assistance to their morale by their being able to discuss their difficulties with doctors and nurses of their own race. V.C.N.S.'s proposal for a special nursing interpreter unit to be flown out in a Catalina might be included in the representations, if so desired.

(b) To call the Foreign Office's attention to the fact that it may be dangerous to leave Molotov in ignorance of the Vaenga party, if he is not already aware of them. They may then decide to send a separate telegram to H.M. Ambassador on this point.

11. D.N.I. has been consulted, and concurs in the above. Submitted through Dof P to consult the F.O. as proposed.

C.H.M. Doland

Military Branch
14th September, 1942.

SECRET

2. This is a most unfortunate occurrence and the Russians are clearly very annoyed, not only because we failed to make timely application for the visas, but because we did not do so until about two days before **TUSCALOOSA** was due to arrive at Archangel. They also, no doubt, resent what appears to be a hidden implication that their own medical arrangements are inadequate. However adequate the Russians may consider their arrangements to be, there could be little doubt that their standard falls far below our own. This is clearly brought out in the report contained in U.C. No. 238 which has been inserted, and from which it will be seen that the existing conditions leave a great deal to be desired. We owe it to the wounded and those who suffer from extreme exposure to insist that adequate provision is made for the comfort and peace of mind of our naval and mercantile personnel.

3. The Foreign Office seem to think there is extremely little hope that normal diplomatic representations will succeed in persuading M. Molotov to agree to our establishing a medical staff in North Russia.

4. I would, therefore, urge that the Prime Minister should be invited to consider taking up this matter with M. Stalin as being the only course which is likely to produce the desired results. As M. Branch observes the arrival of P.Q.18 would seem to present a most favourable opportunity for this to be done.

5. The Foreign Office are already considering taking action on the lines proposed in (b) of paragraph 10 of M. Branch's minute.

Charles Lambe

Director of Plans,
15th September, 1942

Kuibyshev no 1250 is attached, which has arrived rather belatedly. Clearly normal diplomatic channels are hopeless. If Stalingrad should fall, this also may affect the question of whether an approach to Stalin is feasible.

[illegible]
M. Branch
15/9/42

Concur generally with M. Branch
Even though we have admittedly not failed to meet the Russian wishes regarding visas the situation as between allies is becoming intolerable in that the Russian attitude in this & similar matters constantly hampers proper cooperation.
The request should therefore, I suggest, be very firm – with perhaps the suggestion that if this goes on we may have to restrict the facilities given to the Russian mission here.

[illegible] 15/9

THIS DOCUMENT IS THE PROPERTY OF HIS BRITANNIC MAJESTY'S GOVERNMENT

MOST SECRET Copy No. 33

[N 5181/23/38]

Mr. Eden to Sir A. Clark Kerr (Moscow)
(No.311.)

Sir,
Foreign Office, October 5, 1942.

IN the course of our conversation to-day, the Soviet Ambassador said that he brought me the attached replies to two personal messages, one for the Prime Minister and one for myself, from M. Molotov on the question of British medical personnel in Soviet northern ports. When I had read the answer, I said that I was completely puzzled by the Soviet Government's attitude in this matter. Here were our sailors risking their lives to bring these convoys to Russia and, when we wished to send hospital units to help the wounded, the Soviet Government made difficulties. I should have thought that these units would have been warmly welcomed.

2. The Ambassador said that surely I must know that this was not the real difficulty. The difficulty had arisen because these units had been sent without any kind of warning to the Soviet Government. If he might speak off the record, he would like to tell me what he believed to be behind his Government's attitude. They were, unfortunately perhaps, always ready to resent any action which seemed to show that their feelings or their point of view need not be considered. As a result, when we sent troops or detachments or individuals without warning to Russia we inevitably caused offence. It surely should have been possible in this case for warning to be given. The Ambassador added that, in order to avoid

future friction, he asked that the Service Departments and the Ministry of War Transport should be strictly instructed to give notice in advance to the Soviet Government and obtain their consent before despatching special units or individuals. He was quite sure that, if only notice had been given in this instance, none of the difficulty would have arisen. As it was, he much hoped that I would accept the offer which M. Molotov had made. It would, however, no doubt be possible to go into the matter further and increase the facilities if it was still desired a little later on.

3. I said that, while I admitted that proper notice was not given in this case and that this was an error for which we were responsible, I still felt that the Soviet Government should have overlooked this in the greater interests of the crews who were working for Russia. I undertook to examine M. Molotov's reply.

I am, &c.
ANTHONY EDEN.

Enclosure 1.

Personal Message from M. Molotov to Mr. Churchill.

IN my letter to Mr. Eden I asked him to acquaint you, Mr. Prime Minister, with the contents of my reply on the question of the British medical personnel in Archangel and Vaenga (Murmansk). I think that if you glance at the Memorandum of the Soviet Foreign Office of the 27th August and my letter of the 12th September addressed to the British Ambassador, Sir Archibald Clark Kerr, you will have the full information on the matter and will be in a position to draw the necessary conclusions as to the real state of affairs, particularly in regard to certain irregularities in the actions of the respective British naval authorities. I think also that the solution of this question as set out in my message to Mr. Eden corresponds to the wishes you have expressed.

V. MOLOTOV.
Moscow, October 2, 1942.

Personal Message from M. Molotov to Mr. Eden.

THE circumstances and the reasons which prompted the respective Soviet authorities to take a decision on the question of the group of British medical personnel in Archangel were set out in the Memorandum of the Soviet Foreign Office of the 27th August, delivered to the British Embassy in Kuibsyshev, as well as in my personal letter of the 12th September to the British Ambassador, Sir Archibald Clark Kerr, the contents of which are already known to you. A similar decision on the same grounds has been taken with regard to the British medical group at Vaenga (Murmansk). It therefore seems to me that it would be hardly necessary once more to reiterate all the circumstances. I think perhaps I need mention only two fundamental considerations which prompted these decisions: (1) the Soviet medical institutions have all the necessary means and personnel to render hospital treatment to all British seamen who are in need of it in the U.S.S.R., which makes unnecessary the organisation of special English hospitals in Archangel or Vaenga (2) the above-mentioned groups of British medical personnel arrived at Archangel and Vaenga without any previous warning being given to the respective Soviet authorities as to their arrival.

I hope you will agree with my view that before any British Service personnel is sent to the Soviet Union the respective British naval authorities could, at any rate, raise this question with the Foreign Office and the latter surely would raise it with the Soviet Embassy in London. This should be done before any such personnel is sent on board ship to the Soviet Union. The difficulties and complications which unfortunately arose in this case would have been avoided had this been done.

We note your desire that there should be a certain number of British medical men among the Soviet medical personnel to treat the sick and wounded British seamen, who have had in the past and will in the future have the full care and attention of the Soviet hospitals. In view of the wish expressed by the Prime Minister and yourself, this can be carried out in Archangel as well as in Vaenga. The necessary instructions will be given to the Soviet medical authorities and the Soviet medical institutions in Archangel and in Murmansk.

May I request you to acquaint the Prime Minister with the contents of this letter?

V. MOLOTOV.

Moscow, October 2, 1942.

Leading Sick Berth Attendant Ken Bull with his staff sailed in the American Cruiser **TUSCALOOSA** loaded with equipment to set up the Royal Naval Auxiliary Hospital at Vaenga, Kola Inlet, North Russia. The equipment included beds, bedding, medical instruments, lighting, operating theatre equipment. The purpose, to improve the primitive conditions and lack of medical attention for our injured. It was intolerable that British Seamen wounded while carrying supplies to Russia should be exposed unnecessarily to the mediaeval treatment prevailing in the bleak Russian hospitals.

On arrival and subsequent unloading of the medical equipment, absolute shock and disgust faced Ken Bull and his team. Ahead of them the arduous task of making a practically derelict old school into a Naval hospital in the tradition of other Naval hospitals, and civilian, elsewhere. Carried out in the atrocious weather of the Arctic in general, but at this time of year, in particular.

As **Ken Bull** relates:-

There were no facilities to set up a sick bay, let alone a hospital. The building was filthy. No quarters were ready for use, we slept on hammocks, rolled out on the floor, rats running about during the night.

The Russians did not treat frostbite, they amputated there being no other alternative as antibiotics were neither considered or available.

Many an experienced SBA and others, were sickened at the sight of a hospital orderly walking around with amputated limbs carried in a bucket.

Jerry kept coming, dropping bombs, so these patients, victims as survivors, had to be carried down into the cellar. One was just a torso, both arms and legs missing. Their nerves were terrible; with each raid they got worse. Gradually by hard work of the team and assistance of the, as always, Russian women, the building was cleaned, decorated, fumigated, disinfected throughout and eventually made habitable and suitable as a hospital for medical treatment for naval personnel. Logs had to be chopped for heating and it was no surprise to see the women humping the trees before cutting. After a raid on Vaenga airfield it was decided to help Russian casualties. They arrived on lorries - dead, dying, sick and wounded piled on top of each other - a Russian sister guiding us as to where to place or take the casualties, or more or less sorting out who was worthwhile to treat - officers had priority, any small ranking body if badly injured left to die. Another raid hit the village - civilian casualties ignored - we went to help but they were more interested in having a roll call counting the rifles which were stored in the building that had been damaged.

It was decided to hold a party to try and get to know, or at least unfreeze the very tense atmosphere with Russian staff. Plenty of rum and some so-called vodka had been found for us. Magazines and pictures of our wives and families were shown. Not true they said - all propaganda - no buses or trains in London - our clothes specially made to go to Russia in - photos special for propaganda purposes. We really very poor, not like Russian people.

A Russian lad in one of the beds who was dying for the lack of attention and need of oxygen, asked if we could look after him, they said we could do what we liked as he was only small. It was great and rewarding to see the response of the patient. They always tried to put a show on when we went into the Russian hospital ward in order to impress us. No matter how trivial the visit we were made to put a gown and hat on before entering their ward. To my amazement, I was invited to attend and witness two operations in the Russian hospital theatre, noticed some of the theatre staff wearing footwear they had been wearing outside the hospital. The operations were done under local anaesthetics and left much to be desired in the way of sterilisation of a hospital theatre. However by agreeing to attend these operations it was one more way of unfreezing the hostile atmosphere. During later talks on the medical subjects VD was discussed and were assured in no uncertain terms there was no VD in Russia which was later found to be untrue.

There was some concern about the food store being robbed but the liaison officer a Russian by birth, not in the Navy, was reluctant to complain because of what the consequences might be. However it got so bad that it had to be reported. Two days later a Russian Army officer and two privates turned by carrying tins of corned beef. They informed us that they had caught the thieves and for them life was now finished.

It was about this time when one of our destroyers tied up alongside at Vaenga. They had political prisoners working in all their docks. The destroyer's gash was ditched overboard and two prisoners looked around and thought they were unobserved by the blue capped guards and grabbed two floating crusts out of the water, they were seen and marched behind a corrugated iron shed and shot. We had a few beds there to accommodate patients who could not get to RNAH Vaenga. One week later I was called to Polyarnoe to take some diagnostic equipment as an officer was ill. It was a very cold morning with a keen wind blowing and it was very slippery all along the jetty, the ice was like glass. After arriving at the sick bay and helping the MO with his examination of the patient we decided to return to the Sub base. What a stroke of luck, it saved his life. As we were making our way gingerly back to the Sub base along the jetty there was the feeling something or somebody was behind. Turning back this bloody polar bear jumped forward grabbing my coat in its mouth. I slipped on the ice flat out and was dragged towards the drink. The MO grabbed my arm and pulled the other way but at times the bear was dragging both of us. No help was offered by the many Russian sailors looking over the ship's side, in fact they seemed to enjoy watching the chance of an English sailor being ripped to bits. Luckily the bottom of my coat and the button holes started to give and rip off, the bear finished by tearing the coat to shreds. The Russians shot the bear and returned the tattered remains of the coat. There was hell to pay over the incident and during the subsequent enquiry the MO complained about the lack of assistance from the Russian sailors. The Russians at the enquiry said the bear was a recent captured one and had broken away from its bonds on one of their ships. I will never forget that bear retreating and dragging the two of us along the deck.

When the Senior MO returned I was told that all the Naval personnel at Archangel and surrounding anchorages were dependant on the Army sick bay at Archangel and they were not very happy. It was decided that we should have our own staff there. I was detailed to go to try and sort things out; to be followed in a few weeks by the MO.

Two days later I boarded a merchant ship at Murmansk, a coal burner the LLANSTEPHAN CASTLE. When shown my cabin he was told not to leave anything edible on the table and to keep a light on all night because of the rats. Also the use of water was very restricted, allowance of one can a day, near enough a gallon. Moored for the night off Murmansk, sailed for Archangel the next morning. What a dirty bloody ship, it was terrible, I turned in early as nothing else to do, and started to read only to be interrupted with the squeaking of rats. There was a beam running through the cabin and the buggers were following each other line astern - dozens of them. They didn't run they just ambled because they were so fat. Gesticulating as if to throw a book at them they stared and didn't flinch a muscle. Getting off my bunk I went towards them but they didn't move until a yard away. They were without doubt the biggest rats ever seen. We went flat out (6 knots) round to Archangel, no escort, one or two scares from the air, and I was glad to get off that packet. The ship returned to Murmansk four days later, and was hit with a glider bomb which blew the cabin previously used to bits, rats and all.

On arrival at Archangel I was placed in Karl Marx House amongst all the other various members of different branches. No one was allowed to go out until cleared by the Russians. I was escorted there the next day and sat at a large table opposite three Russians, and a portfolio on Ken Bull was produced from a cabinet. One or two questions came from the English-speaking Russian and I was given a pass duly stamped and signed. A visit now to the Army Sick Bay. Staff/Captain MO RAMC Sergeant and a Private. Another Sergeant was stationed at a First Aid Post on the other side of the estuary at Bakeritza. The sick bay was a bit of a shambles and left much to be desired. I was invited by the MO to sit in with him on his morning surgery so I could see the way it went. Army personnel first, but I was disgusted with the so-called treatment given. He was the laziest and most incompetent MO every known or worked with.

Things now were beginning to get a bit heated up on board the various merchant ships, through boredom and frustration and lack of co-operation from the local Russian power groups. In a matter of a few weeks there was a case of murder and three suicides. Regarding the murder case, the accused was under guard at the Army quarters, and he joined in card playing with us some nights. He was confident he would get off. However, after sending him back to Scotland on an RN ship we heard news he had been found guilty and later executed. One suicide situation was one of the privates, he lay on his bunk, put his rifle under his chin and pressed the trigger. The bullet went through his head into the dividing wall and just stopped by half an inch into the Sick Bay.

Another one was an American Lieutenant (MN) who had a go slashing his wrist. He was saved but a couple of weeks afterwards he shot himself in the head. One of our own Navy lads slashed his wrists but he was okay and was sent home at the first chance. The general situation amongst our own lads in NP 200 was getting very tense at times and it took the Senior CPO who was responsible for discipline to keep them in check, especially when they witnessed very cruel treatment being dished out by the Russian Police to their own men and women. It could have been disastrous if they had interfered. Some of the instances which caused so much concern were:-

A young lad (13-14 years) climbing over the army fence was seen by one of the Blue Caps (Russian Police); out came a revolver and they shot him dead. He fell beneath the Union Jack. His body laying on the pavement outside Headquarters was only removed after complaints that it had been there 48 hours. A woman attacked by two Blue Caps on the other side of the road from Headquarters; battered, knocked unconscious and kicked in various areas of the body. They stopped a horse and cart and just slung her on like a sack of potatoes. The local Sculks (Black Market to us) was out of bounds to patients from the Russian Military Hospital. One of them was walking around still in his hospital dressing gown; a Blue Cap shot him in the back in front of all the people.

At least once a month we would witness a show of strength from the local NKVD (the green caps, Political Secret Police) dressed in jackboots and all the regalia like Hitler's Stormtroopers. The population were scared stiff of them. They would surround a wooden dwelling and open up with automatic arms leaving it like the top of a pepper pot.

Every morning down the main street you would see the hundreds of political prisoners being herded down to work in the docks. There would be just one guard at the front of the column and one at the rear. That was all that was needed. They looked half dead, hands behind their backs and head bent looking at the deck. Back they would come in the late evening after the day's work.

Loudspeakers, were hung on all the lamp posts and they would blare out periodically during the day: "Slucyee Tavarish, Slucyee Tavarish". Everything had to halt, trams, carts and pedestrians. The old Blue Caps made sure nobody moved, you had to listen to the propaganda being poured out and only move on when it stopped.

I was approached by one or two of the Russian staff at the Karl Marx House for treatment for various ailments. The old odd job man was in great pain with rheumatism and had a job to move around. He didn't want to lose his job because he was living so well, off our food. He was treated and his body responded extremely well; in a month he was a new man. Tears of gratitude used to stream down his face when he tried to express his thanks. Treating him started a rush and I had to clamp down because they were coming to the sick bay at the Army base, using a back door so they wouldn't be seen. However, although I said no more, one little lad was treated. His mother came to the back door carrying him in her arms. He was 18 months old but so very tiny and obviously dying from malnutrition, his eyes bulging out and lifeless. The mother said that on reaching the age of one, his baby rations of milk and baby food stopped, it was just black bread and soup, and in this case he just couldn't take it. He was on vitamins, scrounged tins of full cream milk, milk powder and anything available to nourish him. After only a week there was a big improvement and some of the army chaps were giving any fresh fruit and eggs etc. that came their way. It was very rewarding to see the great improvement and he was soon actually walking on his own. The mother took a great risk coming. Goodness knows what would have happened if the Russian authorities had caught her. She was most grateful and flung her arms around me and cried when she heard I was leaving.

The amount of VD cases had now really stepped up, nearly all amongst the members of the various merchant navies. One very sad case was a young pantry boy, 17 years of age, he had both syphillis and gonorrhoea of particular severity. Treatment couldn't control the infection or make much impact. He had to be sent to the UK urgently on a destroyer which was one of two making a special fast trip to North Russia and back to UK.

The pressure on the small Sick Bay Unit became severe. And because of all his hard work and awful experiences in dealing with dead, dying, sick and wounded, Ken Bull was offered leave in Moscow for a break. But the following day he was told to get kit packed, not for Moscow but UK as his relief was to arrive next day. A decision had been made, this man had been through enough and needed a rest. He was thanked for his efforts and hard work. Quite a surprise as the MO, a brilliant doctor, was a tough, hard Australian, very strict and when roused a vile temper, even to fellow officers, so this was praise indeed. With joy and relief Ken Bull sailed for Polyarnoe en route escorting a tanker round to the Kola Inlet to join other ships and escorts and proceed to UK. But this was short lived, and his hopes shattered as a signal was sent while at sea reading:-

"You have on board an LSBA Bull taking passage to UK. He is NOT, repeat NOT to proceed to UK. You are to disembark this rating at Vaenga where his services are urgently needed at the RNAH".

He was livid as he could not understand why. Landing, sadly but safely, at Vaenga, **HMS BRITOMART** pulled away to join the homeward bound convoy. On arrival at RNAH the MO apologised for what had happened. On enquiry for the reason, there being plenty of staff at the Hospital including Chief PO's with 10, 12 and 18 years in the service - a bombshell dropped.

There were twelve cases of suspected VD but neither MO or staff had the knowledge or experience to know whether they had the disease or not but knew Ken had studied and gained experience with treatment of the disease.

This experience was welcomed and appreciated in the emergency. Leading Sick Berth Attendant Ken Bull returned to UK long after the period of twelve months recommended for personnel serving in North Russia, advised ironically by the Medical Department at Admiralty.

Leading Signalman John Maddern was aboard **HMS GOSSAMER** of the 6th Minesweeping Flotilla escorting ships of the first official convoy PQ1 in September 1941 to Archangel. Leaving North Dvina River on November 27th 1941 after almost getting frozen in for the winter, and hastening to get away as the ice thickened, they got stuck on a sandbank at the entrance of the river and had difficulty getting off - but just in time. With atrocious weather on return the small convoy QP3 split up. **GOSSAMER** was left in company with a Russian ship, but soon lost touch in the continuous darkness. **GOSSAMER** almost capsized with the u-force of the wind and the sea, acting on lack of stability because of the low state of the fuel tanks. It was the worst weather John had ever experienced.

GOSSAMER was based at Archangel on the first trip, but at Polyarnoe on the second stint at the entrance to Kola Inlet, along with others to carry out patrols to sweep for mines and U-boats and as local escorts for incoming and outward convoys. Prior to her second run to Russia **GOSSAMER** spent time in a dockyard at Tilbury for ice strengthening of the plates and insulation inboard of the ship. Unfortunately ice still formed on the ship's side in the messdecks once back in the Arctic winter.

After leaving Scapa, en route to Iceland, the ship ran into a ferocious gale and had to heave-to for over 24 hours sustaining a lot of damage to deck fittings, to say nothing of chaos on the mess-decks, eventually putting into Hvalfjord, Iceland, for repairs alongside a R.N. depot ship. After missing convoy, She proceeded to Kola independently. A hazardous experience. En route she sighted a straggler from convoy QP8 (a Russian ship) and some hours later picked up a distress call 'being attacked by an armed surface raider'.

Probably a destroyer which had been accompanying the **TIRPITZ** seeking convoy PQ12. **GOSSAMER** then proceeded as far north as possible into the ice, arriving again at Kola for escort, sweeping and anti-sub patrols. She was present and involved in the action in which **EDINBURGH** was sunk, taking off more than 400 crew.

On 24th June 1942 **HMS GOSSAMER** was at anchor in the Kola Inlet north of Mishukov Point. The weather was fine, warm and the sky clear but the water cold. The crew were in jerseys, trousers and shoes in the pleasant weather, so different to the freezing cold of the winter months.

Then came the warning of approaching enemy aircraft by the shore - based AA guns and warning flags from ships in the anchorage. **GOSSAMER**'s guns crews were closed up and the crew waited for the impending attack - but not for long.

As **John Maddern** relates, the first ones on board to see the enemy were the oerlikon gunners at the stern of the ship.

Five aircraft came out of the sun and at least one attacked with bombs. The gunners opened fire but no hits were recorded. 2 bombs hit us, and one near miss, virtually blowing our stern off at the break of the upper deck and quarter deck. The wardroom just disappeared with our Engineer Officer and two Deck Officers and several crew. A great deal of carnage, *but no panic*. Some men below decks managed to get clear, but others were trapped as the ship was sinking fast. 25 of the crew were killed or drowned. One died of wounds ashore.

After the first explosion, I said to the Captain there seemed nothing for me to do on the bridge - could I help below? I had just got to the ladder when a louder explosion threw me across the wheelhouse. This was the bomb that finished her, as she took a heavy list to starboard. On the upper deck - aft - two seamen were supporting an AB - one of the gunners. We lowered our port whaler to get the wounded away. I looked at some of my mates sliding over the port side whilst on the starboard side the guard rail was the only part above water. I saw a messmate sliding on his backside portside until reaching the bilge-keel and jumping into the water. At the height of our survival he, being a mess-deck wag, was heard to say even at a time of crisis - "Those bloody barnacles ripped the arse out of my pants".

Soon there was only a P.O. and myself on that part of deck and he said the order had been given "Abandon ship: every man for himself". Two stokers appeared from the boiler room escape hatch and went over the side. One I never saw again - one survived. So I decided to jump. The whole business of the sinking took only ten minutes or so. Some small Russian boats headed towards us. We hastily climbed aboard, but our ship was now turning over, and the boat was being pushed under by the mast, so we had to abandon that one and board another in the vicinity.

This then was the sad end to yet another gallant ship and crew with one exception. One of the enemy aircraft, still not satisfied, returned to survey the kill-flying low over the scene, machine-gunning the survivors in the water. It has since been related to me that three of the survivors in the confusion were hit by machine-gun bullets and died whilst swimming for their lives. Eventually **HMS HUSSAR** another fleet sweeper picked up survivors and landed them ashore at Polyarnoe.

John recalls his experience ashore at Vaenga and Polyarnoe as a survivor to this most awful place - if only for a rest from sea duties.

My first few days were in a school type of building at Vaenga. I had to walk some distance to a Russian Army barracks for food. A so-called diet - a sort of greasy 'skilly' with cereals floating about and something that looked like meat scrapings from a butcher's shop, plus black bread. The taste, if any, I could not get used to. But it was the same as the Red Army had. After a while I was transferred to Red Naval submarine base at Polyarnoe where there were other survivors, mostly with injuries from exposure and frostbite. Bare rooms, beds, no change of clothing provided, but we luckily found a store with basic items:- shifts, socks, towels, enabling us to get clean. Food was scarce; you could shower once a week in a separate shed a distance away with water supply timed. Very primitive (nevertheless a luxury as we had to bath in a bucket aboard **GOSSAMER**). Our "Heads" (Toilet) was a hole in the floor with foot rests. Some enterprising 'Jack' had scrounged a chair - knocked the seat out - some some rest could be acquired whilst aiming.

Air raids were frequent. Shelter was a stone-built edifice erected against the cliffs. Among the survivors was one from a sunken merchant ship. He had been in a lifeboat for many days. Although sadly some of his companions died, he survived. He had amputations which left him with no arms below the elbows and no legs below the knees, but was surprisingly cheerful - who would have thought it?

We used to call in on the second floor of our building on our dashes to the shelter and pick-a-back him to safety. As this took some time we usually took refuge with him in a sub-basement as by this time bombs would be falling. I often think of this man and wonder if he survived after the war or even got back home. Came the time for the welcome return home as passenger survivor. I was to report to **HMS MARTIN**, which took part in a surface action on the way - with **ONSLAUGHT** and **MARNE**, sinking German minelayer, Sub., and supply ship ULM. There were **GOSSAMER** survivors on all three, and at least one was killed. But what could I wear for the trip? My trousers, jersey and shoes were in a sorry state after the sinking. The problem was solved, somewhere along the line when some Russian uniforms came on the scene. From where, no-one bothered to find out - so a number of us were rigged out in these uniforms with red stars all over them. We were not encouraged to mingle at any stops on the rail journey to London in case we created suspicion. We finally arrived in London at the Union Jack Club where a decent meal had been arranged. The waitresses were very reticent on seeing our uniforms and offered no conversation at all until some cheerful Cockney told them "not to worry, ducks, it's only us red matelots coming home without snow on our boots".

The uniforms disappeared very quickly when we were kitted at Portsmouth. I wanted to hang on to mine as a souvenir - but no such luck!

John Beardmore, Lieut. RNVR, Navigating Officer HMS POPPY, outlines the events of PQ17, the worst convoy disaster of World War 2. Nevertheless, it is largely forgotten that, due mostly to the initiative shown by the smaller escort vessels (corvettes, trawlers and minesweepers skippered by RNR and RNVR officers and crewed by HO ratings), most of whom tacitly ignored the Admiralty's directive to proceed independently to Archangel, headed instead for Matochkin Straits. The remnants of the scattered convoy were eventually gathered together on and off the coast of Novaya Zembla. Over a traumatic period of two weeks, one third of PQ17 were finally shepherded into Archangel intact, together with 1,200 merchant navy survivors from the ships that were lost.

The Admiralty's decision to prematurely scatter the convoy in view of the 'imminent' **TIRPITZ** menace proved, in the end, to be the wrong one. The destroyers under Captain Broome RN withdrew to place themselves between the convoy and a much larger enemy who did not as it turned out, materialise. The smaller escort, corvettes **POPPY**, **LA MALOUINE**, **LOTUS**, and **DIANELLA**, trawlers **LORD AUSTIN**, **LORD MIDDLETON**, **AYRSHIRE** and **NORTHERN GEM**, and minesweepers **HALCYON**, **BRITOMART** and **SALAMANDER**, by then very low on fuel, and two thirteen and a half knot cumbersome 'banana boats', converted to ack-ack ships, **PALOMARES** and **POZARICA**, did the best they could for the surviving ships, under very difficult circumstances.

Within one hour of 'Scatter', the convoy was spread out on a 35-mile front heading in all directions except west. It would have been virtually impossible to reform it again.

The naval crews stranded in the White Sea all that summer, as well as the survivors, suffered unbelievable privations in the land of our brave allies. Those on the naval vessels ended up by having to open the tins of ship's biscuits, lashed in their own lifeboats, to supplement their low rations and later suffered the stigma of 'ratting on the convoy' when many of the survivors were repatriated. The Admiralty remained silent and it was not until twelve years after the war had ended that Admiral Tovey (C-in-C Home Fleet at the time of PQ17) was allowed to publish his own despatches in the 'London Gazette', telling the whole truth and apportioning the blame, where it was due, not on the R.N. afloat, but on the Admiralty in Whitehall. Obviously (and how easy it is to be wise after the event), PQ17 would have stood a better chance had it been allowed to stick together as a convoy, in spite of the threat of the **TIRPITZ**, the 240 air sorties and the two dozen U-boats that we afterwards learned were directed against it.

PQ17 was doomed from the start and became the 'Balaclava' of World War 2.

Signalman George Robinson was aboard the catapult assisted Merchant Ship M.V. EMPIRE TIDE in Convoy PQ17 when, after loading of cargo completed, proceeded to Belfast Lough, where her aircraft, radar and armaments were tested; then on to Iceland where he spent four weeks at anchor. During this period there were visits from various ship's companies including an American Admiral Henry and his Flag Lieutenant Douglas Fairbanks Jnr. It was suggested that a dummy aircraft be made so that it could be fitted to the launching catapault to deceive the enemy. This was done and secured to the fore hatch, but it was smashed and washed overboard later in heavy weather. The various captains were briefed and PQ17 convoy of 34 merchant ships departed from iceland and formed into columns before rounding the northern coast of the island; course was set for Jan Mayen Island and Spitzbergen. Fog came down as we sailed through ice-floes and small bergs. One ship crashed into one of these bergs and was so badly damaged that she asked permission to return to Iceland. Some time later the first enemy aircraft appeared to be joined later by another. On 4th July 1942, EMPIRE TIDE was attacked by large formations of torpedo bombers, coming in from the starboard quarter, their 12-pounder gun scored a direct hit on one plane which burst into flames and dived into the sea. Another plane which was also hit by gunners was finished off by the ship on the port bow. Some ships were lost but the convoy sailed on. His ship had been damaged by low angle cross-fire; rigging, derrick spans and gun telephones had been shot away as well as holes in the hull.

The only casualty was a defensively equipped merchant ship gunner, Mr E Haddell who was seriously wounded in the thigh and as the ship had no doctor on board he was attended to by the Second Officer and the Chief Steward who put seventeen stitches into the wound. Later that evening the convoy was ordered to scatter and George watched in amazement as the Naval escort took off at high speed to take up formation with the main fleet which was sailing to the south-west of the convoy. Some of the merchant ships ran straight into the packs of submarines which were waiting for them but luckily the Captain, sailing north and passing from one bank of fog to the next, managed to escape the submarines, but could still hear the enemy planes overhead. So hoisting the protective balloon perhaps the German airmen, seeing our Hurricane fighter, with propeller revolving, thought it safer to give us a miss.

EMPIRE TIDE sailed north to latitude N77°25' E then east along the ice barrier until the Captain decided to seek an anchorage being Goletz Island. The charts showed a depth of seventeen fathoms of water but running at dead slow ran aground on the rocks. Instead of the crew getting a night's rest, which was the intention, hours were spent pumping out water and fuel tanks to a bare minimum and also running the main engine full astern for hours until the ship slid off the rock. Luckily the fore peak had been filled in with concrete so it did not take in water. It was then decided not to risk finding another anchorage as they had now expended most of the ammunition and being provisioned only for a short voyage were now very short of food and water. It was decided to run south towards the White Sea along the coast of Novaya Zembla. On 7th July they caught up on another ship when she was torpedoed. This was plainly seen, also the three submarines on the surface. Reversing course immediately, they headed north at maximum speed being followed by one of the submarines which eventually gave up the chase, possibly after seeing the 4 gun on the stern. They once again had to find a safe anchorage at all costs, so the ship entered Nayezdnike Roads, behind Karmakulski Island and entered a little bay which was hidden from view from the open sea. A small coaster was anchored in the bay and there were some small huts ashore. So two Russian Officers aboard for transport from Iceland on passage to Archangel went ashore and acted as interpreters. This was a meteorological and trading station and had a short wave wireless station on the hill, so were then able to contact the Soviet authorities to ask for medical help for gunner Haddell whose condition was now serious. Living off sea birds' eggs and water shipped from a smal fresh water lake stored in a steel-hulled lifeboat.

On 11th July a Catalina flying boat arrived and the pilot instructed the Captain to remain in the bay until receipt of further instructions, also that a coaster had been sent to search for other survivors along the coast of Novaya Zembla.

The Germans were still actively hunting for survivors of the convoy and had broadcast that PQ17 had been destroyed, also that EMPIRE TIDE had been sunk, even mentioning the Captain and Air Force officers by name. The Catalina had brought a medical doctor and attendant who examined gunner Haddell and decided that he needed an immediate operation so he was taken from the ship to the aircraft and flown out. Survivors from various ships were now arriving and on 14th July, forty-one officers and men arrived from two American ships. Later the coaster brought a further one hundred and seven survivors from four other sunken ships. She also had six of the lifeboats in tow from these ships and luckily one of the boats contained tins of Spam and bags of beans and flour which helped to supplement their diet of sea birds and eggs. Twenty-seven of these men were taken ashore to the settlement, some of them were badly frost-bitten and required to be flown to Archangel for amputations. There were over one hundred men on board over and above the usual complement, so food rations were again cut down, although the fresh water situation was greatly improved thanks to the steel lifeboat. On 17th July a German aircraft flew over the ship. Some of the survivors wanted to live ashore and two small camps were set up for this purpose.

On 19th July, the Catalina again flew over but did not land, but later on a corvette **LA MALOUINE** entered the bay and gave instructions to prepare to sail. By now there were over two hundred men on board, so all the additional lifeboats were shipped and all survivors allocated to their own ship's lifeboats. The corvette returned with some provisions and a medical officer and on 21st July, in company with five other ships a small convoy was formed and headed for the White Sea. After three days they arrived at Bakaritsa, Archangel.

Due to the heavy losses there were over one thousand survivors there awaiting passage home.

Alongside the jetty, an armed Russian guard was placed at the top and bottom of the gangway and whenever anyone went ashore to check the ship's draft they were followed by a guard with fixed bayonet. They were not allowed to visit any other ships moored alongside and when a naval rating brought a bag of mail to the foot of the gangway the crew were not allowed to bring it aboard. The Captain then ordered that all steam be shut off from the winches, leaving planes, ammunition and all sorts of cargo left dangling in mid-air. The local commissar duly arrived with interpreters and complained, but the Captain stuck to his word and the mail came aboard and cargo unloading recommenced. There was one incident which shook everyone aboard. A lifeboat had been broken into and the incident reported to the authorities. The following morning an armed guard arrived on the quay, six stevedores were stood out and shot dead, no mercy was shown at that time.

Other indignities were suffered by the Captain, which although committed without the knowledge of the authorities made him refuse a Soviet decoration. After discharging the cargo, the outbound cargo was loaded at the White Sea ports of Ekonomya and Molotoysk. Time spent around these ports became very boring although there was some entertainment at the International Club, an Intourist Hotel. The weather in Archangel was very warm but the mosquitoes were numerous and savage. The ordinary people had very little comforts, with black bread and soup their daily ration. Anyone who had had the wisdom to store some chocolate or the like could get a very good rate of exchange. At Ekonomya, EMPIRE TIDE was the only merchant ship along with seven naval ships.

The Captain of EMPIRE TIDE was the first Merchant Navy officer to be awarded the Distinguished Service Cross along with the Chief Officer and the Chief and Second Engineers. Also Distinguished Service Medals were awarded to some of the crew. Sailing for home on 13th September each officer had to double up with a survivor.

This crowded ship, the normal completement doubled by survivors from PQ17, was again subjected to submarine and air attack. Although other ships around them were lost, she arrived safely 13 days later in Scotland.

In the mind of Charles de Val the convoy that stands out clearly against all others is PQ17. **LONDON**, **NORFOLK**, **TUSCALOOSA** and **WICHITA** were the close cover cruiser force during one of those glassy summer periods without even darkness as an aid. We had already weathered some days, wherein we had fought off the worst of the air and submarine attacks, when we heard our Captain address the ship's company on the SRE syst em. He told us that the convoy had been ordered to "scatter" due to a threat from superior surface ships from Norway, which was believed to include **TIRPITZ**, **SCHARNHORST** and **HIPPER**. In consequence of this we had received orders from the Admiralty to withdraw and join the Home Fleet, which was hurrying north from Scapa Flow. When nothing larger than a sparrow could go unobserved and Faithful Freddie, usually a Blohm & Voss 140 seaplane, circled around our convoy just out of reach of even our 8" guns had it been possible to use them against an airborne threat. In those conditions it was often necessary to refuel destroyers and frigates in company whilst still keeping pace with our convoy, later, by which time most of the horrific losses of PQ17 had already occurred. That withdrawal from the convoy made him and many of his shipmates in **LONDON** feel very nearly mutinous. Records show countless instances of the folly of fighting naval engagements from a desk, far removed from the action by ageing warriors whose current experience is second hand at best. He is still convinced that, had we been allowed to fight our way through, the losses would have been smaller. It was fortunate that soon after this the convoys were accompanied by some air support.

"PQ17" THROUGH THE EYES OF A U-BOAT OFFICER

We well and truly cursed the fog, the officers and I, at the continually shifting vision, at the same time swearing. Come what may, we would be tough, wily and patient, like a true fox on the trail - our emblem was a fox's head painted on the conning tower.

At last, fortune relented. After thirty hours of groping through dense fog, we came out of it at last and turning south lay in wait off the Matotschkin Straits. Sure enough there she came rearing her fat funnel right into the fox's jaws . . . . improved position slightly, then a textbook runout. We couldn't miss, but to make sure, we gave her a salvo. Two explosions. She stopped, took on a list. Boats lowered. One more from the stern tube, to finish her off. She split open and sank. From a raft, with our scraps of English, we managed to get her name and tonnage: the American ship ALCOA RANGER, 10,000 tons - some hors d'oeuvre! The boats had red sails. We handed them bread and water and gave them a course for far off Novaya Zembla - they'd have a rough trip before they reached their 'friends'.

Victory mood in us. We signalled headquarters with a suggestion that the ships of the convoy had been told to try to reach Novaya Zembla - we turned out to be right. Our long chase at high speed had brought us to the van of the scattered merchant ships hurrying to reach safety, while their escorts were busy scrapping with other U-boats further north or picking up survivors of ships sunk by the Luftwaffe.

Soon another pair of masts came out of the fog towards us, followed closely by two more. The traffic here was about as thick as that encountered off the American coast earlier in the year - the U-boat paradise all over again, except that this one was rather colder. We had to fire at the first ship at an acute angle because the second was almost on top of us, and we missed. As a result, both got away. But we had no need to chase after them, for at that moment a third conveniently put in an appearance to the northward. This time the torpedo found its mark. Then we got up the ammunition, and the sailors were allowed to amuse themselves gunning her from the surface with the 88 millimetre. They left the good ship OLOPANA a blazing wreck. We were getting our hands in now, and soon after our cannon claimed another victim. The gun's crew were right in their element. Smothered with smoke and steam, another steamer went to the fishes.

By now the area must be getting a bad name, we felt, so we headed southwest to a position on the escape route to the White Sea, where Russian ice breakers had cleared the approaches to Archangel. One morning off the Kola Peninsula we saw a strange sight - two enemy merchant ships with an escort apparently sailing upside down in the clouds, their inverted masts balanced on the tips of the real ones which at that moment were coming over the horizon. We wondered whether our outline was similarly in the sky. Soon, in fact, the Russians did send a rickety byplane after us and we had to cover a good distance underwater before the perpetual daylight would allow us to escape at high speed to the north. Concluding U-boat operations against PQ17, those boats not yet run out of fuel were ordered to comb certain areas of the route over which the convoy had passed so as to pick up any stragglers. We were allocated the northernmost sector, extending to latitude 76°, then south to Bear Island and home via Andfjort and Narvik. We came upon a Dutch ship the PAULUS POTTER, stuck fast in pack ice and abandoned by the crew. She had been torpedoed from the air and her engine room was under water. The crew had obviously left in a hurry - the breakfast was still on the table - and we found a deed box, stove in but the contents intact, that no one had bothered to throw overboard. Among other useful information it contained the new signal book for convoys and a complete list of all ships in the convoy. Thanks to our find the German High Command was able, a few days later, to announce the fate of the famous PQ17 before even the enemy knew it himself.

THE ENSIGN AND THE PLANK

When you've pulled a man from the freezing sea,
All black with ship's oil fuel -
ou've cleaned him off, seen his wounds
And wondered what to do -
You see the whiteness of his ribs,
Where steam has skinned him too -
The guilt you feel when you look at him,
Feeling glad it wasn't you -
And all you have to ease the pain
Is aspirin and "God" -
You fear to look him in the eye,
For the question you know will be there -
The answer you know is certain death,
And there's nothing more you can do -
You light him a fag and give him your tot,
As he looks for the rest of his crew.

When you lay him down on the iron deck
Knowing that's his lot -
Briefly wondering if you did right
By giving him your tot!
For the rest of the watch, with a sailmaker's palm
With needle and the thread -
You sew him in his canvas shroud,
With the rest of last night's dead -
A dummy shell between their feet
Makes certain that they'll sink -
You sit and sew 'till the morning glow
Amid the mess and stink.

By dawn's grey light you carry them aft
To the ensign and the plank -
The hands off watch gather around
All bleary-eyed and dank -
Then the skipper with Bible, says the Sailor's Prayer
'Our Father, which art in Heaven' (we hope you're really there)
One by one, the dead are gone, slid from the greasy plank -
The hands go forward, feeling chilled
Thinking of those that were slain -
With the certain knowledge, in a while we'll do it all again.
Each one, being still alive, gives a silent prayer of thanks,
Wondering, with a cold dark fear,
Will I be next on the plank!

Stan Kirby

PQ17 through the eyes of an English submariner George Luck, perhaps slightly in more comical vain. For those of you who experienced the "pleasures of the Cruises to Russia by courtesy of HM Grey Funnel Line. I appreciate you know all about it so forgive me. To those who didn't, count your blessings".

Early 1942 - I was a young P.O.S.T. on the submarine depot ship **FORTH** in Holy Loch, Dunoon, on the Clyde. Sadly I 'fell foul' of the O.O.W. and, to avoid losing my Rate, the Regulating Coxswain gave me a 'Pier Head Jump' to **H.M.S/m P614**. This was one of four submarines built for Turkey, and with **P615** (later lost with all hands) retained for service with our submarine service. They were ghastly 'boats'.

Within minutes of getting down the boat, our captain took us out, we did a patrol and finished up in Iceland, where a convoy was being assembled. We, **P614**, tied up alongside **POZARICA**, topped up with fuel and water and set forth as escort for what was designated Convoy PQ17.

Our job with **P615** was close escort, in case any major German units emerged. Contrary to most notions we did the whole trip on the surface, except when during the latter part of the voyage, we were so 'iced-up' that we were in danger of not being able to dive, due to the Kingston Valves (Diving vent valves) icing-up. We then for a short while dived to melt the ice, then belted after the convoy and resumed station, making signals to all and sundry to say that we were a jolly little British submarine, and not a horrible German U-boat.

Conditions on a small submarine are, at the best of times, unsocial and not for the squeamish, but **P614**, being built to Turkish specifications, was in a class of its own. Obviously the brainchild of a deranged sanitary engineer. As I recall, we carried 800 gallons of water for everything. (Well, everything was cooking and living). My last wash was aboard **FORTH**, my next was weeks later. Kit was what I stood up in, plus an extra S/m sweater, a pair of overalls and that was it, thanks to my Pier Head Jump.

Because I was excess to complement I kipped down wherever possible, occasionally 'hot-bunking' if someone else was on watch. Being young I suppose we took the situation in our stride. What did concentrate our thoughts was the regular loss of ships and knowing that we could not help. A body in those waters could expect a merciful end in a very few minutes.

Of course, few on board, if any, knew of the drama that was then unfolding, or the awful outcome that was to befall PQ17. **P615** was ordered to patrol to the south, nearer North Cape. Two Russian submarines were also in this area. Further to the west **STURGEON** was patrolling off Northern Norway.

Having taken my watches as lookout I began to accept the lessening number of merchant ships each time I was 'up-top', but as I recall, it got worse as the days went by. I was down below when the 'Scatter' signal was received, so I cannot visualise the scene. Suffice to say that when next I was up on the bridge it was to realise I was on a very small submarine, all alone in a very rough, very large, and awfully cold ocean, and having to accept that 'something' had gone wrong. History shows just how few made their way to Russia. **P614** eventually picked up a convoy of 'empties', and set off for home. Again, more losses.

Because of desperate fuel shortage we were diverted to Scapa Flow instead of going round to the Clyde. We 'borrowed' a cutter from somewhere and in a pea-souper fog I was ordered to set off with as near a gang of pirates as you ever saw to the depot ship; for emergency rations to tide us over. Only to fall foul of the two-ring, wavy navy, O.O.W. He said something about: "How dare you come here in that filthy state? With men, dressed like that!"

I agree that "That" only needed a couple of wooden legs, a black patch or two and a parrot for Long John Silver to have been proud of us. O.K. we were dirty, we did smell, we were not 'pusser', but that's life in the boats! Next question : "What do you want and where have you come from?" Meaning, I suppose, which of His Majesty's are you currently serving on? Foolishly, I forgot the "Sir" and replied: "Food, please, we've just called in on our way from Russia".

Peering at some of the boys, and then down at our cutter tied up at the gangway, the O.O.W. hesitated, and said: "Oh no, not in that". I replied, "Certainly not sir, we were in a little submarine built for Turkey". Result - utter confusion. Eventually, sanity returned, we got our stores and somehow found our way back to **P614** in the fog.

The following day, having refuelled and taken on water, we went round to the Clyde and 'home' to **FORTH**. Exactly half-an-hour after we had tied up, the pipe, "Liberty Boat for **P614**, in 15 minutes". So, wipe the face, hands and wrists, on clean shirt, down to the liberty boat, and away to Liverpool and home.

While in the bath, father decides to burn my singlet and underpants! Well I had not washed or changed for just over six weeks, so I couldn't complain.

"PQ17 ROLL CALL"

Following vessels sunk with loss of lives.

Vessel	Flag	Year	Tonnes	Date	Position	Action	R.I.P.
Chrsitopher Newport	USA	1942	7191	4 Jly	70°N 20°E	Aircraft torpedo	3 dead
Navarino	UK	1937	4841	4 Jly	75°N 25°E	Aircraft torpedo	1 dead
William Hooper	USA	1942	7177	4 Jly	76°N 27°E	Aircraft torpedo	3 dead
Empire Byron	UK	1941	6645	5 Jly	76°N 33°E	U703 torpedo	18 dead
Carlton	USA	1920	5127	5 Jly	76°N 33°E	U88 torpedo	4 dead
Honomu	USA	1919	6877	5 Jly	75°N 37°E	U456 torpedo	19 dead
River Afton (Cmdre)	UK	1937	5423	5 Jly	73°N 43°E	U703 torpedo	23 dead
Daniel Morgan	USA	1942	7177	5 Jly	76°N 33°E	U88 torpedo	3 dead
Fairfield City	USA	1921	5686	5 Jly	75°N 41°E	Aircraft bombs	6 dead
Zaafaran Rescue Ship	UK	1921	1559	5 Jly	75°N 44°E	Aircraft bombs	1 dead
Pan Kraft	USA	1919	5644	5 Jly	77°N 39°E	Aircraft bombs	2 dead
John Witherspoon	USA	1942	7180	6 Jly	71°N 53°E	U255 torpedo	1 dead
Pan Atlantic	USA	1919	5411	6 Jly	74°N 43°E	Aircraft bombs	26 dead
Hartlebury	UK	1937	5082	7 Jly	73°N 52°E	U355 torpedo	37 dead
Olopana	USA	1920	6069	8 Jly	72°N 51°E	U255 torpedo	6 dead

Following vessels sunk without loss of life

Vessel	Flag	Year	Tonnes	Date	Position	Action	R.I.P.
Earlston	UK	1941	7494	5 Jly	74°N 32°E	U334 torpedo	
Paulus Potter	Dutch	1942	7168	5 Jly	77°N 32°E	A/C bomb & U255 guns	13/7
Bolton	UK	1939	5203	5 Jly	77°N 32°E	Aircraft bombs	
Washington	USA	1919	5564	5 Jly	77°N 32°E	Aircraft bombs	
Peter Kerr	USA	1920	6476	5 Jly	74°N 34°E	Aircraft bombs	
Aldersdale (Oiler)	UK	1937	8402	7 Jly	75°N 43°E	U457 torpedo	
Alcoa Ranger	USA	1919	5116	7 Jly	71°N 51°E	U255 torpedo	
Hoosier	USA	1920	5060	10 Jly	70°N 41°E	U376 torpedo	
El Kapitan	Pana.	1917	5255	10 Jly	70°N 40°E	U251 torpedo	

Vessel	Flag	Year	Tonnes	Date	Position
Rathlin Rescue Ship	UK	1936	1600	9th Jly	Arrived Archangel
Donbass	USSR	1931	7925	9th Jly	Arrived Archangel
Bellingham	USA	1920	5345	9th Jly	Arrived Archangel
Zamalek Rescue Ship	UK	1921	1567	11th Jly	Arrived Archangel
Ocean Freedom	UK	1942	7173	11th Jly	Arrived Archangel
Samuel Chase	USA	1942	7191	11th Jly	Arrived Archangel
Empire Tide Cam Ship	UK	1941	6978	24th Jly	Arrived Archangel
Benjamin Harrison	USA	1942	7191	24th Jly	Arrived Archangel
Silver Sword	USA	1919	4937	24th Jly	Arrived Archangel
Troubador	Norw.	1920	5808	24th Jly	Arrived Archangel
Ironclad	USA	1919	5685	24th Jly	Arrived Archangel
Azerbaidjan (Tanker)	USSR	1932	6114	24th Jly	Arrived Archangel
Winston-Salem	USA	1920	6223	28th Jly	Arrived Molotovsk

It was summer in Russia and after the colossal losses in PQ17 following the order to scatter, John Beardmore became marooned and further recalls experiences during his unscheduled stay in the country whose supply ships he had escorted in **HMS POPPY**.

Small wonder that the Russians were bitter - they rightly reminded us that their glorious Red Army was holding the Eastern Front, and were fighting a final battle for Stalingrad, that there was still no sign of a promised Second Front, that they, the Russians were carrying the whole brunt of the war and that we, the allies, should double the flow of supplies on the Arctic route. Instead, the Admiralty postponed all further sailings to Russia during the continuous daylight of the summer months. The British escort vessels now marooned at Archangel were soon moved down river to isolated wooden berths at the wooden village of Ekonomya. At it turned out they were not entirely sorry about this as later that summer there were several fire blitzes on the largely wooden city of Archangel which blazed away like the 1812 Overture.

Somewhere in the wood piles of Ekonomya was a small Naafi type shack (misnamed in Russian 'The Welcome In'). Here our sailors could drink gut-rotting raw vodka and smile at, but not speak, to the waitresses there. They rapidly tired of this and rarely went ashore except to play games on the wooden jetties under the unfriendly eyes of the Russian sentries.

The military guards that had been placed on all ships' gangways were a tiresome lot. They prevented all intercourse with the merchant ships, and the female sentries were particularly zealous in their duties. The gunnery officer (a former music teacher) who had been able to identify the merchant ships of the convoy in the fog banks by the notes of their sirens - "F Sharp, Captain, that's EMPIRE TIDE" - was sent ashore by the commanding officer one day to try to telephone the British Naval Base in Archangel from a hut on the jetty and was confronted by a large woman sentry who shouted to him in Russian. He just smiled and said "Good Afternoon". The next thing he knew there was a bayonet up his backside and he came running back onboard covered in blood and with a very surprised look on his face.

The civilian population, however, were most friendly towards us. Less so towards the officers whom they identified with their own feared green-capped commissars who strutted about arrogantly and were shown great deference. The workers on the river banks invariably waved as we passed and the Russian ships always dipped their flags in salute. One day in Archangel I saw a group of women queuing up, not for bread but for the latest qar poster to be issued, of a Russian mother defending her child from a Nazi bayonet. They were taught to hate the Germans much more than we were.

Although relations with civilians was not encouraged I did manage to meet a young, rather serious schoolteacher named Katrin who spoke some English and seemed anxious to learn more. After a few meetings she brought along her text book of English Literature to show me. It was a potted version of 'Oliver Twist' (Dickens being Russia's most popular English author). It was, therefore, evident that the description of Fagin's kitchen, the slums, the poverty and the crime were pictures of mid-twentieth century London. I explained that this, of course, was not so and that anyway Dickens lived a hundred years previously in Victorian London and was writing about an even earlier period. She was incredulous but believed me. Unfortunately, she went away and told her friends. Sadly I never saw her again but I learned that for her folly in listening to and repeating 'false Western propaganda' she had been sent away - where to I did not discover.

In order to placate the Russians and to be in a better position to obtain food from them, the corvettes undertook certain sea duties. Reluctantly **LOTUS, LA MALOUINE** and **POPPY** were sent out to search for a suspected Japanese raider which had allegedly shelled the lighthouse at Kanin Point in the Kara Sea. Fortunately we did not encounter it but returned with a small supply of cod upon which we had wasted a depth charge when passing through the fishing grounds. So the summer wore on, and we were reduced to even smaller rations. The crews of the naval vessels grew despondent and lost inteest in the many sporting events arranged to occupy them during their spare time. They had long since run out of Tombola tickets, the wardroom's stock of gin was perilously low and rationed. Our daily diet of rice and a little corned beef grew monotonous and, of course, there were no green vegetables, apart from the odd cabbage and a few potatoes stolen at considerable risk from the guarded farm on the Dvina delta. Although some ships had flour there was no yeast, so they could not bake bread. We continued to scrounge from one another and finally opened up the emergency tins of ships biscuits lashed in our lifeboats - we were on 'hard tack'. For the troops however the final blow came when their rum ran out. The Admiralty eventually sailed four of its fastest destroyers to the White Sea. They brought us much needed ammunition, mail, medical supplies and some stores which bolstered up our rations for a while.

The British and American survivors ashore fared even worse. After hospitalisation many had been herded into compounds, issued with shabby institutional clothing in lieu of their own clothes which were taken away from them, and put on Russian rations. Needless to say they (especially the Americans) felt very bitter about their treatment, particularly after all they had endured. We used to visit them and pass on any cigarettes and chocolate that we could spare through the railings. The Dieppe raid occurred in August and the Russian authorities thinking that this was the beginning of the long awaited Second Front showed their delight by delivering to the ships a few bags of cabbages and some scraggy, evil smelling carcasses of yak. The cabbages were welcome but the men refused to touch the yak, as they were convinced that these were the corpses of German soldiers. When a rumour actually went round that an Iron Cross had been found in one - that clinched it. They burnt the carcasses in the ships' furnaces. As soon as it was known that the Dieppe raid had been a failure (just like PQ17, said the Russians) they demanded their yak back. They said it had all been a mistake! Too late!

One must remember that this area of the Arctic was frozen over for much of the year and conditions of living were like something out of Mrs Gaskell's novel, or worse. Russian civilian rations were bare subsistence with one foodless day a week to help the Red Army, though it was suspected that the commissars and officer classes fared much better. When we first arrived earlier in the summer we had noticed old women with long fishing nets who waited for the waste food to be tipped through the shute over the ship's side nearest the jetty. Immediately they fished out the soggy bread remains, dried it in the sun and ate it all. Everyone was deeply shocked and afterwards saved our scraps for these wretched people who were civilians, had no ration cards, were too old or useless to work and contribute to the war effort, and so lived by begging.

There were dozens of young orphans who lived wild on the jetties having lost their parents in air raids. These civilian children were as astute as adults and bartered pocket's full of Red Star badges for cigarettes or chocolate, until these too were in short supply. Many of the ships adopted these 'water babies', the corvette **DIANELLA** adopted a seven year old orphan called Wolfga who they quickly renamed Vodka. The sailors made him a little petty officer's uniform complete with badges, he had his own small hammock and Bosun's pipe, and he ate with the crew. They were very fond of him. When finally, in September we had to sail away, we had to leave behind our small adoptees who watched us go with tears running down their cheeks, their arms clutching presents and woollies for the oncoming winter. There were quite a few tears on the weathered cheeks of the petty officers who had cared for and loved these lost children as they watched them growing smaller on the jetty waving their woollen comforts.

Denis Brooke Sub. Lieut RNVR was safe but marooned after PQ17, and was awaiting escort of the next convoy back. Alongside the timber wharf at Ekonomya near Archangel he remembers how food was getting scarce.

All our efforts through the S.B.N.O. North Russia and the appropriate commissars came to nought and we existed on an interminable diet of corned beef and rice. Only once did the wardroom chef fool us that we'd got something different - he mashed the corned beef with tinned milk into a pale pink paste and froze it in the fridge into a kind of mousse.

Our Number One mounted an expedition to get some potatoes and several officers from the corvettes rowed down stream one night with muffled oars, dark jerseys and gym shoes to a field alongside the river which we had previously reconnoitred. We knew it contained potatoes and was guarded by armed sentries who patrolled the dykes which kept the water out. We chose our time carefully - crawled over the dyke and down in among the potato plants. Keeping flat on our stomachs we wriggled down the rows burrowing in with our hands to get the potatoes without disturbing the plants. We stayed as long as we dared then scurried back to the boat with our spoils in a sack - not a great quantity of vegetables but Queen Elizabeth couldn't have enjoyed Raleigh's potatoes more.

Two events brought us some fresh (yak) meat, flour and green vegetables - the Dieppe landings and Churchill's visit to Stalin in Moscow when he was made aware of our plight.

In the opinion of the Commander-in-Chief Home Fleet:

The order to scatter the convoy had in my opinion been premature; it's results were disastrous. The convoy had covered more than half its route with the loss of only three ships. Now, its ships spread over a wide area, were exposed without defence to the powerful enemy U-boat and air forces. The enemy took prompt advantage of this situation operating both weapons to their full capacity.

Just one of the many situations of the terrible plight of the survivors from the sunken ships of PQ17. These men were in a lifeboat for many days, the fittest amongst them rowing to a hopeful landfall and comparative safety. Eventually landing, tired and hungry on an uninhabited, desolate barren island beach south of Matchokin Strait near Novaya Zembla just visible on the horizon. For protection and reasonable comfort they made a tent from the sails of the lifeboat. Scavenger parties were set up to search for anything burnable to keep a fire going and look for something eatable. A few birds were caught quite easily as they did not seem afraid and a few eggs were found. The birds' feathers came off as a kind of skin, then making a stew by filling a biscuit tin with snow and putting bits of the birds in when it melted.

Whilst away from the camp looking for fuel and food, three men were left by the fire. One was a young seaman with frostbite in both feet, nothing could be done except just comfort him. Whilst he was alone for a short time put his feet in the fire to warm them. Found in this awful state was a terrible sight, his feet looked like two big balloons of raw meat.

Eventually reaching Archangel, after many more days in extreme pain and agony, he had both legs amputated.

The colossal loss of material aboard the many ships lost in PQ17, after the order to scatter because of the threat of attack by the German Battleship **TIRPITZ**, was over 3000 vehicles and 100,000 tons of general cargo including aviation spirit. The scattered ships were attacked by over 200 German aircraft, 138 Junkers 88, 43 Heinkel 111's and 29 Heinkel 115, some being damaged, only 15 were lost.

But still Stalin with Germany entering a second winter of war was urging us to send more supplies, his attitude being, if a convoy was destroyed then send another one and if that were cut to pieces then send another. He did not know the meaning of sacrifice, being interested only in results. What stores, tanks, bombers, ammunition are being sent; how much arrived, and what we did was never enough.

While the Russian Ambassador Maisky said the convoys to Russia are a northern saga of heroism, bravery and endurance, and complained of lost ships being sent, Winston Churchill told the Foreign Secretary Anthony Eden: "I am getting to the end of my tether with these repeated Russian naggings".

In the afternoon of 2nd July 1942 homeward bound convoy QP13 comprising thirty-five merchant ships and an escort of five destroyers, four corvettes, two minesweepers, and two trawlers set sail. 400 officers and ratings, survivors from ships damaged or sunk en route to Murmansk - including thirty-nine from **HMS EDINBURGH** - were distributed according to accommodation availability in the escorts.

The convoy had a quiet passage to Iceland because the enemy were concentrating their attack on PQ17. On 4th July the day PQ17 received the signal to scatter, the result now being known, QP13 had arrived just North East of Iceland. Sixteen of the thirty-five ships were bound for Britain so turned south along the east coast. The other nineteen mainly American headed for Reykjavik on south west coast. That evening the bad weather with poor visibility that had protected them from the enemy became a hazard having only an approximate idea of their position.

At 1900 that evening the Senior Officer of the escort proceeded ahead for a navigational fix. He was aware through prior notification there was a British minefield off the north west corner of Iceland to entrap any German vessel trying to break through the Denmark Straits to the Atlantic, a narrow channel ten miles wide between edge of minefield and coastline. The Senior Officer signalled the convoy commodore to reform convoy into two columns to negotiate this narrow channel.

From soundings, he believed the Iceland north cape had been passed, so he ordered a south west course to sight the coast. Steering through the mist and low cloud he suddenly saw something that seemed like a steep cliff looming up and assumed it must be the north cape after all and realised he had altered course too soon. To rectify this, he immediately signalled to swing the convoy back on a westerly course; in so doing a sudden clearance in the poor visibility showed that what he had assumed to be a cliff face was a massive iceberg. Realising his mistake the Senior Officer was immediately aware they could be in the minefield and hastily signalled the convoy to change course to the south west. But it was too late. Within minutes his ship struck a mine and blew up, her hull torn apart, her back broken and she sank very quickly taking himself, eighty officers and crew including thirty-nine **EDINBURGH** survivors down with her. Moments later a merchant ship hit a mine, cut in two, she disappeared ablaze.

Confusion broke out among the ships following as one vessel after another was shaken by explosions which triggered off other mines in the area creating columns of water looking like shell splashes.

The captains of the merchant ships, unaware of the minefield, immediately assumed they were being shelled by a distant unseen German warship. Within minutes another vessel blew up followed by another leaving the crews struggling in the water; yet another merchantman became a victim, her bows were blown off.

Now it was every ship for itself fighting for survival, in confusion, twisting and turning in a desperate bid to avoid a catastrophe. No further course alterations were given as the vessels yawed around amid the wail of sirens.

Then less than half a mile away another brilliant flash lit up the grey of the Arctic night. A mine had hit the side of a Russian freighter and she immediately listed to starboard. As her rail dipped under, people were slipping and sliding to reach the lifeboats, including women and children.

As the echoes of the freighter explosion faded than yet another vessel astern of her ran on to a mine tearing out the middle of the ship breaking her in two. Then the roar of exploding boilers bringing her to a swift end, spilling out human cargo and thick black oil. The dead and living in the water numbered over four hundred.

The two rescue trawlers were in the middle of all this unaware of the minefield, having assumed that U-boats had intercepted and were firing torpedoes into the group of ships. The remaining freighters were wallowing around as if blinded men on a battlefield. A decision had to be made to protect them. The two trawlers sped into the centre of the area firing depth charges. But in the sea where the ships had foundered were people, terrified, screaming for help, trying to swim through oil fuel. Then came more deafening explosions as the depth charges landed in the sea throwing columns of water into the air with horrifying effect on those in the water who died instantly.

Another ship, assuming the depth charges would deter the submarines, began searching for survivors, still unaware they were moving around in the middle of a minefield. Some had miraculously managed to survive in the cold, oil-strewn water and were helped aboard on the point of collapse. Soon some of the escorts joined the rescue, circled the area of the minefield rescuing 230 people, but 47 of them died later from exposure.

On 19th July 1942 **Leading Telegraphist Denys Bedbrook** and **Telegraphist Ben Bake**r, with other communication ratings, sailed for Russia in **HMS MARNE** to join Naval Party 100. A special fast trip not only to accompany Admiral Douglas Fisher who was to be the next Senior British Officer, North Russia, but to convey the equipment, transmitters, aerials etc. to set up a "Meaconing" station in the hills above Polyarnoe. Billeted temporarily at Navy House, the next few months were spent hauling trees up the hill for construction of huts to store the equipment and others to live in. Each day they waited patiently for the Russian carpenters to arrive to build their quarters. By November, now in heavy snow, the Meaconing station was complete and became known as "M Cottage".

What was the need, aim and purpose of "Meaconing"? To pick up a convoy sighting report, either from the aircraft shadowing the convoy and sending its position back to the German air bases, or the submarines intent on attacking the convoy. Then to re-broadcast it simultaneously to confuse the true bearing by use of the powerful transmitters set up in M Cottage to give a totally different bearing - and it worked - as into 1943 the attacks on the convoys decreased considerably. Denys Bedbrook remembers:

Apart from the occasional disagreement the small party, living as a close knit community got on extremely well and had to be supportive and cooperative with harmony. As it was now winter the extreme cold was felt. As snow and ice covered the hut it became like an igloo. Those not on duty would collect logs and saw them up for the stove. Water originally came from a well which was now frozen as the temperature lowered to 30° below. Then it had to be brought up the hill by sledge again becoming frozen en route so considerably heavier. Food, which was tinned, had to be collected and delivered by the same method.

Christmas came, and by coincidence and extreme joy so did the mail. New Year's Eve saw 1943 in with quite a party at M Cottage, booze had been obtained by some means, devious or otherwise. April was to come but we were still there awaiting relief which eventually arrived after being in isolation for twelve months.

Such was the success of this venture a similar Meaconing station had been set up on the other side of the hill overlooking Vaenga Bay.

In April 1943 **Telegraphist Tom Speirs** with a Petty Officer Telegraphist and five others were seconded to No. 26 Bomber Command R.A.F. at Luton for training in Meaconing as the RAF were using the same system against German aircraft bombing raids on England. Following training this special party sailed for Russia to join Naval Party 100.

At Vaenga. Climbing the hill to the Station they could not believe what they found as Tom Speirs explains:

The Hut was half buried in the ground so it was downhill through the snow to gain entrance, the roof eventually became level with the ground so we could stand on it without climbing. Our rations were brought up the hill by sledge, as was water, in a huge barrel covered with ice. Fresh vegetables and white bread were available only when the convoys were in, so we went by boat around the escorts for potatoes, carrots and anything else available. Normal diet being tinned was supported by a daily dose of tablets. We took turns at cooking on a large grate fired by sawn up logs. Meals were often a disaster with our amateur attempts over an unpredictable stove, but we coped, as we had to, with difficulty. In stark living conditions, we were completely isolated for long periods from any other human contracts. It was bloody cold especially when unable to get the fire going because the wooden block fuel had become waterlogged. The feeling of isolation, was very much felt between arrival of mail from home and being incarcerated inside the Arctic Circle, was always with us.

The phenomenon of the "Aurora Borealis" (Northern Lights) as seen from M Cottage in the hills above Polyarnoe, and from the pen of Denys Bedbrook.

Wondrous ever changing light

Shining brightly through the night

Shedding weird etherical glow

Over mountains white with snow

Red to purple blue to white

Whirling in fantastic flight

In an ever changing flow

Of colours as they come and go

Throughout the icy Arctic night.

As was to be expected the Germans were jubilant at their success against PQ17 but for the allies the consequences of two disastrous voyages PQ17 and QP13 were felt not only in Britain and the United States, but especially Moscow with the news of the loss of 130,000 tons of valuable cargo. 400 tanks, 200 aircraft and 33,000 was received with anger and dismay. America had lost nineteen cargo ships gross gonnage of approximately 115,000 tons.

The Admiralty felt in view of this the convoys must be suspended until the perpetual daylight was over. The Prime Minister did not agree except it could be wise to delay PQ18 for a while. In these circumstances Churchill felt the necessity to inform Stalin of the situation and conditions that brought about the misfortune, his letter read: "We do not think it right to risk our Home Fleet east of Bear Island where it can be brought under the attack of powerful shore based aircraft. If one or two of our powerful battleships were to be lost or damaged while **TIRPITZ**, soon to be joined by **SCHARNHORST**, remained in action the whole command of the Atlantic would be temporarily lost. Besides affecting the food supplies by which we live our war effort would be crippled.

"The great convoys of American troops across the ocean, at present as many as 80,000 in a month, would be prevented and the building up of a strong Second Front in 1943 rendered impossible".

Stalin was not impressed. In his reply he stated his naval experts considered the British justification for cessation of convoys to USSR was unconvincing.

"I never expected the British Government would stop despatch of war materials to us at the very moment when the Soviet Union, in view of the serious situation on the German front, requires these materials more than ever".

Subsequently on 12th August 1942 Churchill flew to Moscow, where frank and constructive talks were held with Premier Stalin. These were much more friendly than Churchill had anticipated and after five days he returned to London with a better understanding of the war material Stalin needed and preparations were made for the sailing of the next convoy.

On 2nd September PQ18 comprising forty merchant ships was heavily escorted and protected by forty-eight warships. Twenty-five destroyers, nine submarines, four corvettes, two tankers, four trawlers, two anti-aircraft ships, three minesweepers, an escort carrier and a cruiser. Approaching Bear Island the notorious danger area and 100 miles north west of it, the convoy was attacked by a pack of U-boats, two merchant ships were sunk. Then followed the most concentrated attack of the war when in mid-afternoon of 12th September when over 90 bombers and torpedo bombers sent 110 torpedoes racing towards the convoy at one time. Eight of the merchant ships were hit.

In two further attacks the bombers failed to score hits due to intense barrage from both escorts and merchant ships and the cruiser's powerful anti-aircraft guns. The Germans lost eight aircraft. On 14th the air battle was resumed when twenty torpedo bombers attacked, the Germans losing another eleven aircraft without a single hit on the convoy. Almost immediately yet another thirty-seven torpedo bombers came over, nine of which were destroyed, but a merchant ship carrying 2000 tons of TNT was hit and blew up giving no chance of survival to fifty of the crew. Within the next twenty-four hours yet again, over seventy aircraft attacked PQ18 without success but losing three more planes.

During the passage of PQ18 in September 1942 **Signalman Joe Robinson** was aboard **HMS SCYLLA** to witness the largest convoy ever sent to Russia get through with vital supplies for our allies. That is the salient fact which emerges from the days of danger which were lived while the convoy forged ahead despite the worst attack by aircraft and U-boats.

The great four-day Arctic convoy battle with Navy and Fleet Air Arm as seen from the bridge of convoy Flagship **HMS SCYLLA**.

The convoy got through, and in getting it through the Navy fought and won the most sustained and heaviest sea-battle of the war.

The Luftwaffe and the U-boats were once again licking their wounds after probably the biggest defeat they had so far received.

It is estimated 40 German torpedo bombers, dive bombers and high level bombers were destroyed. Two U-boats were sent to the bottom and four others seriously damaged.

Some of the German aircraft took part in attacks on successive days and therefore likely air losses amounted to between a third and half of the total planes employed. Our losses were four fighters the pilots of three being saved.

On the return journey the convoy's escort was continuously attacked by U-boats, but no aircraft attempted attack. The gallantry, rugged determination and humour of the British sailor were once again vividly displayed. The Yeoman of Signals on the bridge of **SCYLLA** was a typical sailor. When the first wave of German torpedo bombers was sighted, binoculars to eyes, he counted them aloud: "One, two, three, ten, fifteen, forty-two coming in".

As the planes zoom over the destroyer screen, all hell breaks loose. The guns of the destroyers open up followed by every gun of the convoy ships from the smallest merchant ship to the big stuff of **SCYLLA** - heavy pom-poms, Oerlikons, anti-aircraft guns, machine guns and bren guns. The rattle of shells, bullets, tracers, black, blue, brown and grey smoke bursts. The excitement and fear on the flag deck becomes deafening yet stilled, by the voice of the yeoman who controls everybody in that small space, with a vocabulary of any sergeant major which invariably avoids a possible attack of the jitters.

Then when it is all over the convoy safely in and the escort again in home waters a crisp voice from the bridge loudspeaker: "Those planes above are friendly Hurricanes". Yeoman of Signals: "Cor stone the bleeding crows" all Hurricane's is friendly. Blimey! 'ere comes a good natured, Einkel".

One vivid impression - that of the Padre listening without batting an eyelid to the bridge vocabulary, paying no more attention to the explosion of guns, bombs, shells than he would if the noise had been caused by a Parishioner dropping a hymn book in his church.

A tribute to the reckless gallantry of the Fleet Air Arm fighter pilots was paid by Rear Admiral Burnett commanding the escorts. He added praise by saying: "Don't forget the aircraft carrier. Those lads were magnificent. Never have I seen such courage and daring, magnificent youngsters".

In so doing, he omitted the part he played in the operation; one of the largest and most tricky of its kind.

The amazing small percentage of losses in merchant ships, unlike previous convoy PQ17 is a tribute to his brilliant strategy and direction.

Nearing the end of this awful year of bombing and U-boat attacks on the convoys, yet another ship had a "Misadventure in the Cold" with more tragic loss of life for a different reason and courage and endurance of those who survived the ordeal.

On 31st October 1942 the British CHUMLEIGH (5,445 tons) left Hvalfjord for North Russia, carrying a cargo of government stores. The weather was overcast and heavy snowstorms made it very difficult to fix positions. The Master, Captain D.M. Williams, had made good, though necessarily erratic, progress, when at 2300 on 5th November his ship struck a reef. A snowstorm was raging and visibility was very poor. The CHUMLEIGH, stuck firmly amidships on the reef, with her stern almost out of the water; she was so much down by the bows that the foredeck was almost awash and the Captain was afraid that the swell then running would break her back. A wireless message was sent out, and after an hour and a half the men were ordered to the boats. The Captain remained on board with the Chief Officer and the Second Engineer. The numbing cold so affected the men in the boats that they seemed incapable of action. The Master at length got the engines started, but the ship only settled more down by the head, and finally bogged amidships; the engines were stopped for fear that the ship would break in two. A further wireless message was sent, and by 0400 CHUMLEIGH had been abandoned. The boats seemed to be in a horse shoe-shaped lagoon, with heavy seas running and breakers all around; the boats were kept alongside the ship, as they would otherwise have been crushed on the reef.

At the first sign of daylight they moved off towards an opening in the lagoon; almost at once five German aircraft flew over the ship at masthead height and scored two direct hits with their bombs. A column of black smoke rose high into the air, but the CHUMLEIGH did not catch fire. Captain Williams decided to make for the nearest settlement, which he calculated to be about 150 miles distant. The three boats could not easily keep together, and one of them was soon abandoned after its crew were divided between the others. These then proceeded along the coast, which was generally visible during the few hours of twilight which alone relieved the perpetual night. A gale blew up on the 8th, but on the 9th the two boats turned towards the shore and regained contact with each other. Captain Williams's boat had a serviceable motor and it was agreed that he should go on ahead to the settlement to fetch help. It was very cold and a lot of water was shipped; the wind froze the sails and the clothes of the crew became rigid with frost and ice.

The night of the 9th/10th was so severe that the steward became delirious and died. On the afternoon of 10th November some huts at the entrance to a fjord were sighted, but as they were making towards them the motor froze up and could not be restarted. During the night Captain Williams became delirious and lost conciousness; the Third Officer took command. All the crew were weak and without appetite; there was fortunately still plenty of water, and this was very welcome. The Third Officer decided that any landfall was preferable to further exposure in the boat; he therefore set course on the 11th to the east, and later to the south. The land, when finally located, was so thickly covered with snow that there could be no question of choosing a favourable place; all appeared equally barren. At about 0200, after several hours among the reefs, they were suddenly washed up on the beach, where a heavy sea broke over the party and the Master regained consciousness at the shock. By good fortune they found several wooden huts within twenty yards; two of the crew had died in the boat and another died on the beach, but the survivors managed to reach the huts, although the young boys had to be carried. They at once fell dead asleep. In the morning the twenty-three men who remained from the original ship's company of fifty-eight moved into one of the larger huts. This proved to be quite habitable; it had a small coal stove, and there was enough wood and coal to make a good fire. Although there were no trees in sight there was plenty of driftwood and a great many old boxes. "After we had slept that first night", the Third Officer said "we all felt a little better. We collected what was left of the lifeboat's rations and at once made ourselves hot drinks, coffee and Horlicks, melting the snow for water. This revived us considerably and we became terribly hungry. We also found some tins of corned beef and biscuits in one of the huts, so we managed very well. As long as we had food for tomorrow our morale remained good. Captain Williams encouraged us to take about two hours' exercise each day, but after a time most of us suffered so much from frostbitten feet that it was impossible. Feet and hands became gangrenous and I became very ill".

After a few days on land Captain Williams recovered enough to take charge. Most of the men had swollen hands and feet and could do very little, but the four Army gunners were hardly affected; one man in particular, only four feet and eleven inches in height, was phenomenally tough; the Captain said of the gunners that they "looked after us all, nursing the men who were ill, going out to collect firewood, and generally running things". The Third Officer and a Lance-Sergeant made two attempts during their first few days on land to reach the settlement, but the intervening country was barren and strewn with rocks; deep ravines and great stretches of snow and ice were further hindrance to the explorers, who had to turn back and arrived completely exhausted.

During the first three or four days thirteen more men died from frostbite, gangrene and exposure. "They seemed to give up hope", said Captain Williams, "and then died; but I believed right to the end that we would come through". Expeditions of any kind were never easy; they had only a few hours of twilight in which to work and visibility was often reduced to ten yards. Another sortie, in a north-easterly direction up the fjord, revealed a small hut in which there was a sack of flour and some tins of corned beef and cocoa; this was brought back and the flour, mixed with water and cooked in the form of small cakes, kept the party alive for three or four weeks. There were dozens of boxes of matches in their hut, and with the petrol from the lifeboat's tank they managed to keep two Primus stoves working. They had hot drinks three times a day; and when towards the end the coffee and cocoa ran out they made do with hot water. They also found some tins of whale-blubber preserved in oil; this sustained them for five or six days, and they also drank the boiled oil - "although it was not particularly nice".

A second attempt to reach the settlement was unsuccessful, and towards the end of December the situation was becoming desperate. According to the Master's statement: "By now the Third Officer and an Able Seaman were suffering badly from gangrene, as were several of the others; their feet and hands were discharging and the smell was awful. Another man died on Christmas Eve. I therefore decided to make a final attempt to get help, or die in the effort". When they were half-way to the settlement his two companions broke down and could not go on; so they turned back, and on reaching the hut all three collapsed. On 2nd January one of the gunners went out to collect firewood; almost at once he came rushing back in a state of complete terror. Captain Williams could get nothing out of him, and the nine men who still lived could think only that they were about to be set upon by bears. Happily, it was nothing more fearsome than two hunters who were on a trapping expedition wearing white furs. They took heed of the survivor's plight to the settlement, and a rescue party was sent with sleighs. "We were all in a pretty bad condition", says Captain Williams, "as we had ceased to have the energy to exercise ourselves. Our clothes were soaked with pus from gangreous limbs and gave off a horrible stench". At 2000 on 4th January the survivors reached the settlement, where they stayed until 10th June. After two months in bed they were allowed to get up, and spent most of their time learning to ski. This pastime provides an ironical footnote to the long story of endurance, for Captain Williams adds: "There had been a pair of skis in the hut, and if only we had known how to use them we could probably have got help much sooner".

Even more ironic is the fact that they were within minutes (or yards) of being sighted on the day of the bombing. An excerpt from a letter written by the Commanding Officer of H.M. Submarine **TUNA** explains: ". . . . . I remember the snow cleared about midday and it would have been about then that we might have sighted any survivors . . . . . From notes written at the time it seems that I came on CHUMLEIGH at 0710 in heavy snow and poor visibility . . . . . She seemed to be keel up. I very well remember finding myself in the horseshoe shaped lagoon and gingerly feeling my way out through the only small opening which was clear of breaking water. I was clear by 0800 and it would seem that we might just have stumbled on the boats in the lagoon in this period 0710-0800. I was wholly preoccupied with getting **TUNA** out of the lagoon. I never saw or heard the aircraft which bombed her, though I could not have been far away at the time. By 1100/1200 when the snow storm cleared there was no sign of CHUMLEIGH at all".

As the fateful year 1942 drew to its close there were differences of opinion between Hitler and the Commander in Chief of the Navy Grand Admiral Erich Raeder and between Raeder and the Commander in Chief of the Air Force Reichsmarshall Herman Goering. Raeder had been in opposition to many of Hitler's plans. Although it was realised he was a man of skill and ability Hitler felt the time had come when Raeder would have to go, as attacks on the Russian convoys had not brought the success he had hoped for: its war materials were still reaching Murmansk and Archangel.

By December 1942 Raeder had become impatient at the German fleet's lack of action and repeated his suggestion that a strong surface strike against the convoys in December would be justified by results obtained and with some reluctance Hitler agreed. It was proposed a combined strike be made against the next convoy using the heavy cruiser **HIPPER** and the pocket battleship **LUTZOW** with destroyer escort.

Admiralty made plans to sail a convoy of thirty ships with strong escort, although it was realised such a large convoy could easily be scattered over a wide area. Because of extreme weather conditions making U-boat attacks more vulnerable it was decided that it should sail in two parts.

On 15th December the first section of sixteen ships with a destroyer escort JW51A sailed for Murmansk with close cover of two cruisers and two destroyers and distance cover of two other cruisers. Convoy JW51A arrived in the Kola Inlet on Christmas Eve 24th December after an uneventful voyage. The second part of the convoy JW51B of fourteen ships sailed from Iceland on 22nd December for a Christmas at Sea voyage with an escort of six fleet destroyers commanded by Captain R Sherbrooke senior officer escorts known as Captain S, two corvettes, a minesweeper and two trawlers.

Distant cover was a battleship, cruiser and three destroyers.

When JW51B was mid-way between Jan Mayen Island and Bear Island on 27th December it was hit by an Arctic gale, so severe it became a greater threat than the enemy, separating a column of five ships and delaying the rear cruiser cover. The situation as previously feared had become reality with the sea rising quickly, mountains of water pouring over the ships, the spray sweeping continuously across the decks freezing where it fell. On the bridge binoculars were useless as moisture froze on the lenses making visibility impossible. Below deck water poured down open shafts flooding mess decks, saturating clothing and hammocks. In these terrible conditions it was not surprising that ships became separated from the convoy causing the Captain S, Sherbrooke, much concern as at this time of year the edge of the ice barrier was only 200 miles between the enemy air bases and the convoy was approaching the area where an attack could be made. Even worse the freezing snow and wind made it impossible to keep the guns free from ice.

Captain Sherbrooke ordered the minesweeper **BRAMBLE** to search for and round up the missing ships. By 31st December, New Year's Eve, the sea at last became calm. The day before a German submarine had sighted the convoy, reporting its position to Norway. This gave Admiral Raeder his opportunity to warrant a surface attack and despatched the **HIPPER** and **LUTZOW** with destroyer escort to intercept and destroy the convoy whose position was now known. With two large surface raiders, the pocket battleship **LUTZOW** and heavy cruiser **HIPPER** now at sea, the first of 3 large attacks by sea on the convoys to Russia - the Battle of the Barents Sea - was about to begin.

The comparison of gun power between the German force approaching the convoy and the small British screening force showed an overwhelming superiority in favour of the enemy. Apart from his ship, **ONSLOW**, Captain Sherbrooke had only four escorting destroyers, two corvettes and a trawler armed with World War I 4.7 inch guns, whereas **LUTZOW** and **HIPPER** and the six destroyers had a total fire power of six 11-inch, eight 8-inch, twenty-three 5.9 inch, fifteen 5-inch and twelve 4-inch guns, also 4- to 5-inch armour plating against which the shells of the British destroyers would have little effect.

At this time of year there were only two hours to twilight in the morning giving visibility of between five and ten miles, the rest of the time was darkness, so this was the obvious time for any attack.

HIPPER and **LUTZOW** were ordered to separate to be 70 miles apart. By dawn **HIPPER** to north with six destroyers, **LUTZOW** to the south passing across the stern of convoy twenty miles ahead.

The convoy JW51B was now 200 miles north-west of Kola Inlet. Over 30 miles to the north cruisers **JAMAICA** and **SHEFFIELD**; 15 miles away was the minesweeper **BRAMBLE** looking for missing ships. On the first quarter of the merchant ships was **HIPPER** with **LUTZOW** approaching from starboard, the six German destroyers were in two groups, one shadowing the convoy the other moving eastwards to join **LUTZOW**.

Two destroyers were sighted and reported to **ONSLOW**, indentity being in no doubt as in range of four miles they opened fire and turned away. Sherbrooke had seen the gun flashes and ordered three of his destroyers to join him heading at speed towards rear of convoy leading them to the most advantageous position of defence. The Battle of the Barents Sea had begun.

Meanwhile a British destroyer, **ACHATES**, racing along between **HIPPER** and the convoy, was laying a thick smokescreen to hide the merchant ships. **HIPPER** swung to port to bring her 8-inch guns into range and opened fire with several broadsides, miraculously **ACHATES** escaped damage and continued the smokescreen operation.

Captain Sherbrooke then saw the dark silhouette of a large ship through the twilight haze. He was aware that at least three German destroyers with greater fire power than his were in the vicinity and now the heavy cruiser with her great guns and heavily armoued hull had appeared they could have easily wiped out his group of destroyers then gone on to destroy the merchant fleet and their valuable cargoes. Undaunted by the odds Sherbrooke led around to starboard and closed in on **HIPPER** opening fire at range of five miles. **ONSLOW**'s torpedoes in their tubes were made ready, the only chance of hitting the cruiser would be to fire all at once. As the German cruiser turned to fire her 8-inch guns, he had a broadside view of target. **HIPPER** fired torpedoes assuming a torpedo attack had been made broke off the engagement, racing away laying a curtain of fire from the after turrets on **ONSLOW**, but this was surely not the end. By 1000 another expected attack was launched against the British destroyers, but there was encouraging news that help was on the way as **SHEFFIELD** and **JAMAICA** were racing to join us. Much needed, as **ONSLOW**'s four guns had frozen up, so only six 4.7 inch guns available against the large fire power of the enemy, and where was the **LUTZOW**? Apparently 30 miles away to the south as **HIPPER** made her attack. Again **ONSLOW** turned towards her opening fire with both guns scoring three hits.The cruiser turned away laying a smokescreen, but five minutes later returned to make a fourth attack to bring her 8-inch and 4-inch guns to train on the British destroyers. Four shells landed in quick succession on **ONSLOW**'s causing crippling damage and many casualties; the foredeck a mass of flame and in front of the bridge and destroying the two remaining guns. Sherbrooke received severe wounds and was covered in blood, but in spite of losing one of his eyes, continued to direct operations until relieved on the bridge.

Much to everyone's surprise **HIPPER** did not make a further attack on the other destroyers, but abandoned the action and was seen to turn eastward with no attempt to attack convoy as obviously planned.

In **ONSLOW** the ship's surgeon did what he could for Sherbrooke, by now in his cabin in great pain with his left eye hanging down his cheek, insisting on reports of damage and to issue orders on control of his ship, eventually ordering one officer to take command of the flotilla and another to command **ONSLOW**.

At 1045 **HIPPER** with two escorting destroyers again returned to attack the remaining destroyers who copied the tactics exercised previously with a mock torpedo attack. Meanwhile **ACHATES**, which had been steaming backwards and forwards around the convoy providing a smokescreen, came into view of **HIPPER** who opened fire. **ACHATES** was hit and holed forward reducing her speed. Minutes later more shells struck, one demolished the bridge killing her commanding officer. Another penetrated the hull damaging the boiler rooms. Despite the damage **ACHATES** maintained her smokescreen operation between enemy and convoy, but was sinking fast. **NORTHERN GEM** took off her survivors before she sank. What chance did this defenceless destroyer have against greater odds at close range?

The three remaining destroyers continued to fire their little 4-inch guns at the enemy achieving their object by yet again turning **HIPPER** away. In doing so she ran into the path of the minesweeper **BRAMBLE** who had been previously rounding up the ships of the convoy into some formation. The little ship even smaller and in similar situation to **ACHATES**, defenceless, was blown out of the water by the 8-inch guns of the enemy, and sank very quickly.

The time had come for the expected appearance of the battleship **LUTZOW** as the corvette **RHODODENDRON** reported a heavy ship closing in from the south with escort of three destroyers. Soon the 11-inch shells of **LUTZOW** were straddling the rear of convoy. By now following damage to **ONSLOW** the commanding officer of **OBEDIENT** had taken command of the destroyers, led them round to protect the southern part of the convoy and had a smokescreen between them and the larger enemy. At the same time **HIPPER** and her destroyer escort returned to launch another attack. **OBEDIENT** followed the previous pattern of a mock torpedo attack, again **HIPPER** turned away but in doing so straddled **OBDURATE** causing damage and casualties.

The expected appearance of **LUTZOW** and her intention to wipe out the convoy did not materialise - failing to use her advantage, she just turned away from the smoke and snow clouds. The British force were now depleted with **ONSLOW** useless, **OBEDIENT** and **OBDURATE** badly damaged, **ACHATES** and **BRAMBLE** sunk, only one remained unscathed, **ORWELL**. They had faced a pocket battleship, heavy cruiser and six large destroyers, but help was on its way with the British cruisers **SHEFFIELD** and **JAMAICA** approaching at top speed of 31 knots. **HIPPER** on her last attempt, still fearful of torpedo attack, swinging away to the north ran straight into the gunsights of the oncoming British cruisers. She was hit by four 6-inch shells from **SHEFFIELD** causing considerable damage. One boiler room was flooded and put out of action reducing her speed, shells penetrating the port side started many fires.

Suddenly two enemy destroyers appeared out of the murk. One, the **FRIEDRICH ECKHOLDT**, braodside on, in perfrect position to torpedo the British cruiser. Rear Admiral R.L. Burnett, Commander in Chief, ordered **SHEFFIELD** to steer towards the Germans to avoid a torpedo attack decided to ram the **ECKHOLDT** at the same time at this close range, firing his six guns on the forward turret.

The German destroyer thinking the two ships heading for her were **HIPPER** and **LUTZOW** and caught completely by surprise was soon a blazing wreck. This engagement had allowed **HIPPER** to escape at top speed. Admiral Burnett did not pursue the big ships as he felt his duty was the protection of the merchant ships in case of possible further attack by other enemy ships.

The enemy attack on JW51B had not been as simple as they thought and did not get their own way as Captain Sherbrooke, with his few destroyers, had called their bluff and sent them away. Whilst suffering casualties, he had fought a gallant action against a superior enemy force, saving the convoy from the intended utter destruction.

The Battle of the Barents Sea was over.

Admiral Tovey in **KING GEORGE V** having provided distant cover at rear of convoy summed it all up in his report;

"The conduct of all Officers and Men of the escort and covering forces throughout this successful action against greatly superior forces was in accordance with the traditions of the service. That an enemy force of at least one pocket battleship, one heavy cruiser and six destroyers, with all the advantage of surprise and concentration, should be held off for four hours by five destroyers and driven from the area by two 6-inch gun cruisers, without any loss to the convoy, is most creditable and satisfactory indeed". This message was also displayed on all ships' notice boards on arrival in Kola Inlet.

On 1st January 1943 the badly damaged **ONSLOW** arrived in Murmansk where Captain Sherbrooke badly wounded was transferred to hospital. Whilst there he was told that the King had awarded him the Victoria Cross followed by an announcement in the London Gazette:-

"The King has been graciously pleased to approve the award of the Victoria Cross for valour in the defence of a convoy to Captain Robert St. Vincent Sherbrooke D50 Royal Navy . . . ." The citation continues with the situation now already known.

In response to the overwhelming congratulations from the officers and men of his destroyer flotilla he despatched the following signal:-

"This award is a tribute to the force in general and I hope will be taken by the next of kin of those who lost their lives, as some measure of their country's appreciation".

Able Seaman Jimmy McHugh was abroad **ACHATES**, one of the ships lost in the action when the convoy escort was attacked by **HIPPER**, **LUTZOW** and destroyers remembers.

Unfortunately **ACHATES** became the first target for **HIPPER**, the bridge got a direct hit. Our skipper, Lieutenant Commander A.H.T. Johns R.N., was killed as were a lot of our shipmates whose action stations were on or near the bridge. There was considerable damage to the boiler room and elsewhere. In spite of all this we continued to shield the convoy for another hour and forty minutes. But at 1300 hrs we were compelled to call **NORTHERN GEM** and ask her to stand by, as the ship had turned over on to her port side. We all clambered up on to the side of the ship pulling a lot of our shipmates up with us.

We saw flashes in the distance, a signalman picked up the message - it was **NORTHERN GEM**. Just as she approached the side (which was the bottom of the ship) our bows started to go down.

We all went over into the water and swam to her. Thank God for those scrambling nets and the lads on **NORTHERN GEM**. They ordered us into the engine room area where we got warm and dried out. We had managed to get several of our injured shipmates with us. But there were many uninjured who were not lucky enough to be picked up; there were only 81 survivors. Everyone on **NORTHERN GEM** did all they could for us, they made soup and sandwiches and the skipper ordered an immediate rum issue. We stayed in the engine room area until we heard voices above. **OBEDIENT** was asking where **ACHATES** was. **NORTHERN GEM** informed them that we had been sunk and there were survivors onboard. Our officers' shipmates and myself were issued with clothing and toilet gear. **OBEDIENT** had been damaged during the action and her W/T was out of action. **HIPPER** and the destroyers continued to try to break through to the convoy but were driven back by our destroyers. They eventually withdrew when **SHEFFIELD** and **JAMAICA** arrived to join the escort.

It was established that the German forces had retreated to the north west, but the close escort were unaware of this and we all spent a very anxious night.

Aboard **NORTHERN GEM**, many of the 81 survivors from **ACHATES** were in a bad state. On another destroyer a naval surgeon stood poised on the ice-bound deck awaiting opportunity to get aboard as the ship heaved and plunged in a gale. Slowly the gap between narrowed until as close as they could possibly get and remain in that position for seconds only. The doctor jumped from ship to ship and had he slipped he could not possibly have lived. But he landed safely.

For 30 hours the surgeon operated without a stop on the wounded, many of whom were seriously injured. The operations were carried out on the seamen's mess deck table and continually, throughout those long hours, two ratings supported him as he worked, so that he could keep a steady hand as the ship pitched and rolled. Not one of the patients died.

He was Surgeon Lieutenant Maurice Hood RNVR, who for his courage, endurance, great skill and tireless devotion to duty was awarded the DSC.

Ordnance Artificer D.L. Bragg was aboard **OBEDIENT** in the Battle of The Barents Sea and gives a brief but poignant account of the situation in one of our destroyers.

When the alarm bells rang on the morning of 31st December 1942, I went to my action station just below the bridge on the starboard side. It was still dark; at that time of the year there was little daylight, only twilight. After a while some flashes were seen to starboard, followed by the sound, like that of an express train, and the ocean began exploding all around us. Shortly after we opened fire and then withdrew to put a smoke screen round the convoy.

I was informed that 'A' gun was out of action and on reaching the gun found that a shell had jammed in the breach, which was removed after a struggle. It was found that the chamber of the gun was full of ice. As we were closing with the enemy, later known to be **HIPPER**, I was repeatedly asked how long it would be to put the gun in action. The only way to remove the ice was to scrape with a screw driver and finger nails, the ice burns were something else. Then with the help of the gun crew, the push rods and bazaba brush, the chamber and barrel were cleared off the loose ice. Seconds later we opened fire. The same thing happened to the other three guns in turn oafter a delay in firing.

I saw the port side of **ONSLOW** with flames pouring out of 'B' gun deck. Shortly after that we were peppered with shrapnel, losing our aerials and putting the director partly out of action. Three of the crew were wounded.

Our guns kept firing and I remember the plight of the loaders slipping, sliding and falling on the icy decks, some crying out in sheer frustration.

'Y' gun had no shield and because they were limited from firing due to the safety gear when closing with the enemy, they fired by lanyard. A very dangerous practice, we could see more clearly where they were bearing. It did wonders for the morale of the crew.

> **Signalman Tom Upton** and **Signalman Dick Ashton** were aboard **ONSLOW** on that fateful day 31st December, 1942 when Captain Sherbrooke was injured, lost an eye and was later awarded the VC for his part in the action as Captain. D. Tom Ashton was on the bridge with the Captain and remembers the day he was wounded.
>
> **ONSLOW** had a direct hit on B Gun. A lump of shrapnel from the explosion hit the Captain in the face. Tom thought he was dead when he picked him up. Luckily everyone else on the bridge escaped unhurt.
>
> **ONSLOW** limped into the Kola Inlet and anchored in Vaenga Bay, prior to going up river to Murmansk for repairs. Out of the blue Tom Upton and Dick Ashton were dumped ashore to man a signal station at Vaenga with instructions to maintain communications with ships in the bay and also telephone communication with the base at Polyarnoe. They could see the station to be manned, a small wooden structure; they were dumped on the jetty and away went their ship to Murmansk. Making their way towards the wooden hut with nothing but the clothes they were wearing, and had been since their voyage from England, they found the Russians were billeted there - and what a miserable suspicious lot they were. Tom and Dick relate their plight.

By now we realised that no arrangements had been made for food or anywhere to sleep. The Russians had, with much reluctance, given us a small part of the hospital at Vaenga so when hungry we went there for a hot meal. We were stuck there for three weeks supplementing our daily dinner with what we could scrounge from any of the ships that came in: chocolates, cigarettes etc. There was a cast iron stove in the signal station which was never lit, so we pinched any wood we could find, found a cross-cut saw and used that to cut logs for the fire. The Russians watched with cynical grins but would do nothing to help. We used newspaper to get the wood alight but one of the Russians played hell because they used newspaper to roll their tobacco in.

All the time we were there they never made a friendly or helpful gesture towards us and were armed with rifles and bayonets.

Dick Ashton's words were never forgotten: "These bastards wouldn't piss down your throat if your heart was on fire".

It was extremely cold this day, 40 degrees below zero, there were three air raids and dive bombers hit a British tanker in the Inlet. The Russians were very panicky during raids. By now after two weeks we were extremely fed up and unhappy, no facilities to wash and shave, except at the hospital three miles away, a tramp through heavy snow. By now we were getting to speak and understand a bit of Russian. One does not like us at all and certainly shows it, others were a little more friendly but remained distant.

After 18 days we made a desperate request to be relieved from the station saying: "We are stinking, have been unable to change our underclothes, or have a bath", but had no reply to our request. There were 2 single beds, solid iron with a couple of blankets on them and we had to sleep with our clothes on, having done so all the time there. One morning I was woken by a poking in the ribs of a rifle butt, it was our unfriendly Russian. If ever I felt like hitting a man it was this one but could have ended up in a labour camp like other unfortunate ratings.

Then came the "buzz" that the **ONSLOW** was leaving Murmansk. Thank God for that. The ship was supposed to berth at Vaenga to collect them. First thing that morning we went down to the jetty, it was freezing cold, our ship steamed down the Inlet and carried straight on. We just stood there absolutely flabberghasted, so started screaming and waving like a couple of castaways on an island, - but **ONSLOW** just steamed on.

Dashing back to the station we tried to get on to Polyarnoe which was always an ordeal through the Russian exchange. A vague answer indicated that the ship was berthing at Polyarnoe prior to return to UK, and suggested we went back on board there. But the big question was how? Eventually we arrived there in a small Russian motor boat and rejoined our ship.

Our brief stay "marooned" at Vaenga will live in the memory for ever. To think of the hazards we faced to get the goods to Russia and be treated as if enemies. We came to the mutual conclusion that the convoys were the most futile effort ever thought up in the history of warfare, for what it cost in men, ships and materials was disgusting. The worst part was that the materials that did get there were dumped on the quayside to rot - but maybe we feel reason to be somewhat prejudiced.

As destroyers berthed near **ONSLOW** at Vaenga everyone suffered a repetition of the revulsion they all felt for the place. They were horrified to see - working in sub-zero temperatures - and the continuous Arctic winter darkness old men, young women and children who, without mechanical aids, unloaded the convoy ships. Worst of all were the slave labourers, treated with casual brutality by guards who loosened off their rifles at the slightest provocation. These scenes depressed the British seaman who had grown accustomed to the aggressive unfriendliness and lack of contact with allies for which so much hardship and danger was experienced on the Arctic convoys.

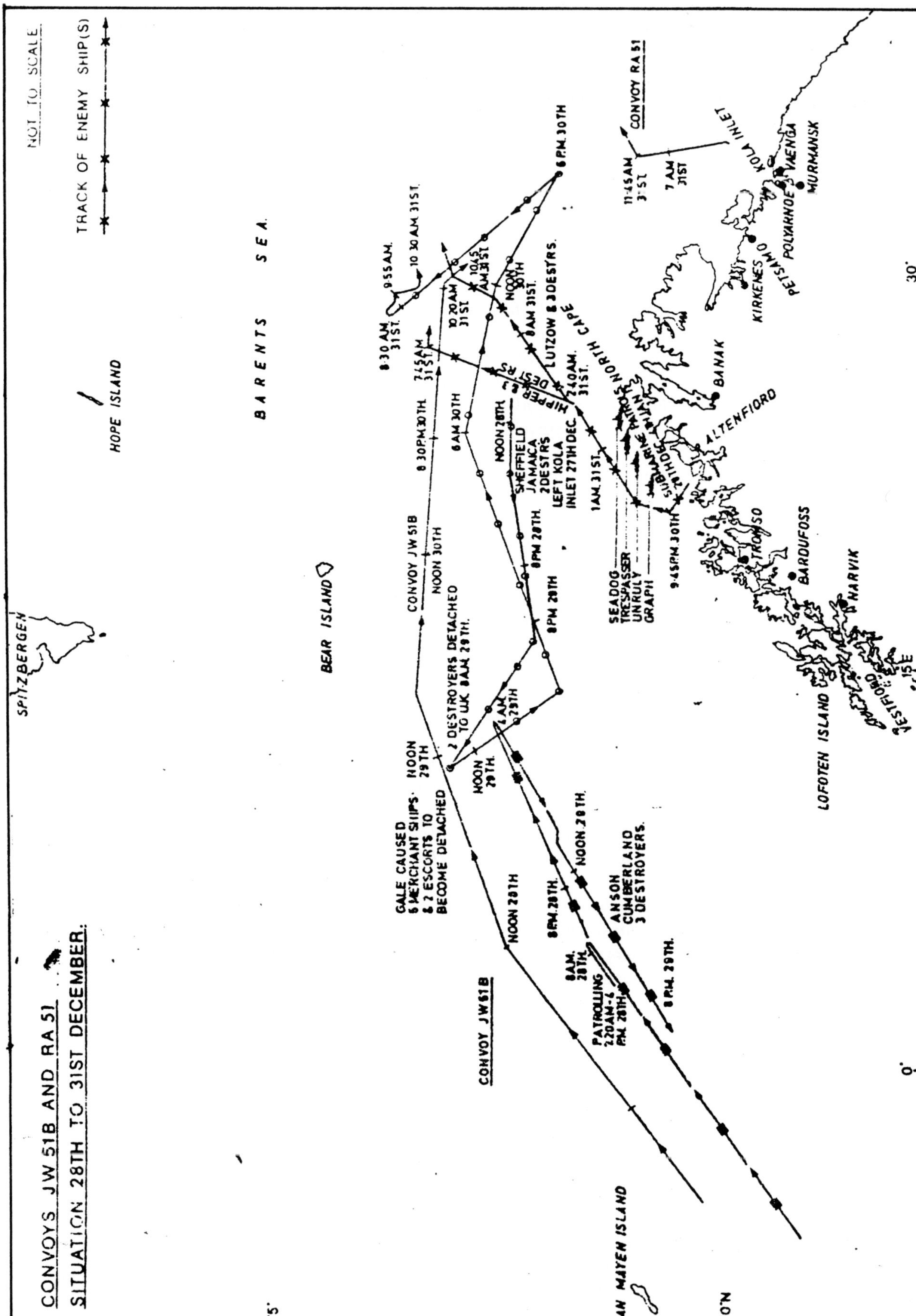

The scenario leading up to the Battle of Barents Sea.

CONVOY P.Q.

I remember the Barents, grey and bare.
Tinged red with the blood of each sailor there.
Escorting destroyers, sleek and proud,
Harrying, their twin four inch guns spoke aloud
Betraying their ally, the silent night
Shattered often, alas, by the doomed plight
Of a Texan, Tartar, or our flotilla.
Or a ship of the sons of the sons of Attila.

Each new dawn broke, we kept vigil upsun
For a Junker, or Heinkel One-One-One,
Or ubiquitous shadowers covering our wake.
To these we were prey if we made a mistake.
But, one Hurricane plane in defiance flew.
Catapulted aloft by a pilot that knew
When his task was complete and he'd smashed an attack.
There was nowhere to land and no way to get back.

Soon the stench of burnt cordite baptized every gun
That killed a few more of the blasted Hun
Whose acoustic torpedoes repeatedly scored,
Ripping open the heart as they suddenly bored
Deep into the hull of another ship -
Thirty odd at the start, few finished the trip.
Their ships of the depths were hammered as well
And sweet was the music that blew them to Hell.

Away on our beam lay the pack-ice reef,
By now, half the convoy had come to grief.
Far ahead lay our target, Archangel port
But we were too busy to give it much thought.
Brilliant firework displays shown at evening time
Supplied by His Majesty's ships of the line.
Intensified, now, concentrated attack
Meant fighting for life with each bullet fired back.

Each hour was a year, each day a decade,
Some seconds eternal as history made
Immortal the dead of each battle-torn ship
That took up the gauntlet and tasted a sip
Of potent war from above and below
By each lethal device employed by the foe.
Now, time has revealed the extent of their toll
And how bitter the fight, by the length of the scroll.

I remember the Barents, grey and bare.
I've forgotten the names of some ships there.
Yet the cold of the night makes me sometimes feel
A 'hard-over' helm meet a shuddering keel.
And ghastly explosions from ghostly ships
With the shriek of men's horror when plunged to the depths.
And as each man fought with the Barents his killer
He cursed all the sons of the sons of Attila.

Fred Jewett

Communications Rating Arthur Goldsmith remembers.

Life aboard the plucky destroyers of World War II was, as those who served on them often relate, a bitter-sweet experience. Conditions were hard, to say the least. The small ships often found themselves pounding for days and nights without respite, through the rough seas and vicious gales of the North Atlantic and, worse still, Arctic seas.

In really severe conditions it was often necessary to rig lifelines around the decks amidships with 'lizards' - shorter lengths of rope with thimbles attached at one end - so that one could move from one end of the ship to the other. Even with the facility, weather conditions occasionally became so serious that crew members were forced to remain at one end until the weather became calmer!

Naturally, during such protracted periods of almost impossible circumstances, tension tended to be high and living conditions became almost intolerable. It was a monumental task to attempt to maintain morale and efficiency and yet the success of these unique vessels was remarkably high.

As can be imagined it took a unique combination of skills and qualities to serve aboard a destroyer. No special privileges were available to a destroyer captain and, as a result, the closeness and fellow feeling with his crew was considerable.

Often spending almost all his time on the bridge and forced to grab what rest and meals he could in an adjoining steel box - generously described as his sea cabin - he was justifiably able to command the respect of his shipmates to a degree rarely experienced on other types of ship.

The result was that these crews fought as tight, efficient units and held a special brand of fraternity with the other destroyer teams alongside whom they sailed.

The island no one will ever forget as the point of possible no return.

BEAR ISLAND

Its just a name, Bear Island, like the Isle of Wight, or a place in America, Coney Island: just a name. But for thousands of others it's a bit more than that. It was like a turning-point, a dividing point in our lives, when we came to know we knew that no name had ever meant so much to us before - that nothing would ever be the same again. Bear Island was the place where boys grew up, just overnight.

It was called the 'Gate'. The Gate to the Barents Sea and the White Sea and those places in Russia where we took those convoys through all the long years of the war. If you passed the Gate and came back again, you were a lucky man: if you did it half-a-dozen times you'd used up all your luck for a lifetime. It was here, in those Arctic waters, that the enemy waited by night and by day and it was here that the enemy struck us down. The fine ships and the fine boys, and the German boys, more of them lie in those waters than anywhere in the world, but the waters run clean now and the blood is washed away. But not in our minds. Years have passed now and we cannot hear the words 'Bear Island' for the blood to run cold.

Motor Launch negotiating ice in Kola Inlet.

Near top Heavy HMS Nigeria.

HMS Sheffield fights her way through heavy seas and Arctic gale.

Hurricane aircraft at Vaenga.

Ice and snow HMS Belfast Forecastle.

Ice and snow HMS Belfast bridge and superstructure

German Battle Cruiser 'Scharnhorst'.

Thawing out anchor chains and winches HMS Scylla.

Escorts assemble off Iceland.

"ARCTIC CAMPAIGN"

JANUARY TO DECEMBER 1942

Jan 2nd	SS WAZARISTAN sunk by U-boat torpedo in position 74°09'N 19°10'E.
Jan 8th	PQ9 sailed from Hvalfiord with 7 merchantmen, arrived at Murmansk on 17th Jan with no losses.
Jan 11th	PQ8 arrived at Murmansk with no losses. (Had sailed from Hvalfiord on New Year's Eve '41).
Jan 12th	PQ7 arrived at Murmansk with 1 loss. (Slow convoy, had sailed from Hvalfiord on Boxing Day '41).
Jan 13th	QP5 sailed from Murmansk with 4 merchantmen. (Arrived at Reykjavik on 24th Jan).
Jan 16th	QP4 arrived at Seydisfjord with no losses. 2 merchantmen returned to Archangel with ice damage. (Had sailed on 20th Dec).
Jan 17th	HMS MATABELE torpedoed and sunk by U454. Two survivors.
Jan 24th	QP6 sailed from Murmansk with 6 merchantmen, arrived at Clyde on 2nd Feb. with no losses.
Feb 1st	PQ10 sailed from Hvalfiord with 10 Merchantmen, arrived at Murmansk on 18th with no losses.
Feb 6th	PQ11 sailed from Loch Ewe with 13 merchantmen, arrived at Murmansk on 23rd with no losses.
Feb 12th	QP7 sailed from Murmansk with 8 merchantmen, arrived at Seydisfjord on 22nd with no losses.
Mar 1st	PQ12 sailed from Reykjavik with 16 merchantmen, arrived at Murmansk on 12th with no losses.
Mar 1st	QP8 sailed from Murmansk with 15 merchantmen, arrived Reykjavik on 11th with 1 loss.
Mar 8th	HM Armed Trawler NOTTS COUNTY sunk off Iceland by mine or torpedo.
Mar 9th	HM Armed Whaler SHERA capsized and sunk in Barents Sea in heavy weather and pack ice.
Mar 9th	Albacore aircraft from HMS VICTORIOUS attacked TIRPITZ at sea.
Mar 19th	HM Armed Trawler STELLA CAPELLA missing with all hands off Iceland.
Mar 20th	PQ13 sailed from Reykjavik with 19 merchantmen, arrived at Murmansk on 31st with 5 losses.
Mar 21st	QP9 sailed from Murmansk with 19 merchantmen, arrived at Reykjavik 3rd April with no losses.
Mar 24th	HMS SHARPSHOOTER rammed and sunk U655.
Mar 28th	SS EMPIRE RANGER sunk by aircraft bombs in position 72°10'N 30°00'E.
Mar 29th	HMS TRINIDAD damaged by own malfunctioning torpedo whilst escorting PQ13. Assisted to Kola Inlet to await repair.
Mar 29th	HMS ECLIPSE sunk German Destroyer Z26 whilst escorting PQ13.
Mar 30th	SS INDUNA sunk by U-boat torpedo in position 70°55'N 37°18'E.
Apr 3rd	SS NEW WESTMINSTER CITY sunk by aircraft bombs off Murmansk.
Apr 3rd	SS EMPIRE STARLIGHT damaged by aircraft bombs in Kola Inlet. (Bombed repeatedly from 15th Apr. until sunk on June 1st).
Apr 8th	PQ14 sailed from Reykjavik with 24 merchantmen, 16 forced to return due to ice and weather damage, remainder arrived at Murmansk on 19th with 1 loss.
Apr 10th	QP10 sailed from Murmansk with 16 merchantment, 1 returned with engine failure. Arrived Reykjavik on 21st with 4 losses.
Apr 11th	SS EMPIRE COWPER sunk by aircraft bombs in position 71°01'N 36°00'E.
Apr 13th	SS HARPALION sunk by aircraft bombs in position 73°33'N 27°19'E.
Apr 14th	SS LANCASTER CASTLE sunk by aircraft bombs in Murmansk.
Apr 16th	SS EMPIRE HOWARD sunk by U-boat torpedo in position 73°48'N 21°32'E.
Apr 26th	PQ15 sailed from Reykjavik with 25 merchantmen including 2 icebreakers, arrived Murmansk 5th May with 3 losses.
Apr 28th	QP11 sailed from Murmansk with 13 merchantmen, arrived Reykjavik 7th May with one loss.
Apr 30th	HMS EDINBURGH damaged by U456 torpedo in position 11 miles ahead of QP11.
May 1st	HMS PUNJABI sunk after collision with HMS KING GEORGE V whilst screening PQ15.
May 1st	German Destroyer HERMANN SCHOEMANN sunk during action against QP11.
May 2nd	SS CAPE CORSO, SS BOTAVON and SS JUTLAND all sunk by aircraft torpedoes in vicinity of position 73°02'N 19°46'E.
May 2nd	HMS EDINBURGH abandoned and eventually sunk by own forces.
May 2nd	HMS/M P551 (on loan to Polish Navy as JASTRZAB) sunk by own forces after sustaining damage whilst escorting PQ15.
May 15th	HMS TRINIDAD damaged by air attacks in Barents Sea subsequently sunk by own forces.
May 21st	QP12 sailed from Murmansk with 15 merchantmen. One returned with mechanical faults.
May 21st	PQ16 sailed with 35 merchantmen. One returned damaged. Convoy arrived in two parts at Murmansk (30th May) and Archangel 1st Jun) with total of 7 losses.
May 27th	SS EMPIRE PURCELL sunk by aircraft bombs in position 74°00'N 26°08'E.
May 27th	SS EMPIRE LAWRENCE sunk by aircraft bombs in position 74°00'N 25°10'E.
May 27th	SS LOWTHER CASTLE sunk by aircraft torpedo 60 miles ESE of Bear Island.

June 24th	HMS GOSSAMER sunk by aircraft bombs in Kola Inlet.
Jun 26th	QP13a sailed from Archangel and White Sea ports with 12 merchantmen.
Jun 27th	QP13b sailed from Murmansk with 23 merchantmen. Joined up with QP13a in Barents Sea. 14 vessels arrived Reykjavik 7th July and 16 vessels arrived Lock Ewe on 8th. Total losses 5 merchantmen.
Jun 27th	PQ17 Sailed from Reykjavik.
July 5th	HMS NIGER, SS HYBERT, SS HEFFRON, SS MASSMAR and Russian RODINA, sunk in minefield off Iceland (part of Convoy QP13).
July 7th	QP13(a) arrived Reykjavik.
July 7th	QP13(b) arrived Loch Ewe.
Sept 2nd	PQ18 sailed from Loch Ewe with 40 merchantmen.
Sept 13th	SS EMPIRE STEVENSON sunk by aircraft torpedo in position 76°10'N 10°05'E.
Sept 13th	SS EMPIRE BEAUMONT sunk by aircraft torpedo in position 76°10'N 10°50'E.
Sept 13th	U589 depth charged and sunk by HMS FAULKNOR.
Sept 14th	U88 depth charged and sunk by HMS ONSLOW.
Sept 14th	QP14 sailed from White Sea ports 15 merchantmen.
Sept 16th	U457 depth charged and sunk by HMS IMPULSIVE.
Sept 17th	PQ18 arrived Archangel with 13 losses.
Sept 20th	HMS LEDA sunk by U435 whilst escorting QP14.
Sept 20th	HMS SOMALI torpedoed by U703. (Sunk under tow 24th September).
Sept 23rd	U253 depth charged and sunk by Catalina escorting QP14.
Sept 26th	QP14 arrived Loch Ewe with 3 losses.
Oct 29th	Independent eastward sailings (Operation "FB") commenced.
Oct 31st	Human torpedoes CHARIOT VI and CHARIOT VIII lost in attack on TIRPITZ.
Nov 2nd	SS EMPIRE GILBERT sunk by U586 (Operation "FB").
Nov 4th	Russian DEKABRIST sunk by aircraft bombs (Operation "FB").
Nov 4th	SS WILLIAM CLARK sunk by U354 (Operation "FB").
Nov 5th	SS CHUMLEIGH stranded on reef off Spitzbergen (Operation "FB").
Nov 6th	SS EMPIRE SKY sunk by U625 (Operation "FB").
Nov 7th	Abandoned hulk of CHUMLEIGH sunk by U625.
Nov 17th	QP15 sailed from Archangel with 28 merchantmen. Convoy scattered by gales.
Nov 22nd	Soviet destroyer SOKRUSHITELNEY capsized and sank in gale.
Nov 30th to 3rd Dec.	QP15 arrived at Loch Ewe with 2 losses.
Dec 2nd	Last independent sailing.
Dec 15th	JW51A sailed from Loch Ewe with 16 merchantmen.
Dec 20th	JW51B sailed from Loch Ewe with 14 merchantmen.
Dec 25th	JW51A part arrived Kola Inlet.
Dec 27th	JW51A remainder arrived Molotovsk.
Dec 30th	RA51 sailed from Kola Inlet with 14 merchantmen.
Dec 31st	HMS ACHATES and HMS BRAMBLE sunk by enemy forces in Battle of Barents Sea. German FRIEDRICH EKHOLDT sunk by British forces in Battle of Barents Sea.

1943

- *A trawlers "river cruise"*
- *An unscheduled dip in the Arctic Ocean*
- *'Jack in Joe's Land'*
- *Trigger-happy Russian guards*
- *On a one horse open sleigh*
- *'Pickfords' special delivery*
- *To sea in a Russian destroyer*
- *Mission to Moscow*
- *A night at the Ballet*
- *Lost at Midnight in Moscow*
- *Life in "Las Vegas"*
- *Breaking the ice - Russian style*
- *A booze-up and a brawl lands Jack in jail*
- *Life in a Russian labour camp*
- *The Battle of Boxing Day*
- *"Scharnhorst" is scuppered*

On 13th January 1943 **David Craig** joined DOVER HILL at Gourock, signing on as Radio Officer and, on boarding the ship, discovered he was bound for North Russian.

We were heavily loaded with fighter aircraft, tanks, guns, lorries and a large tonnage of shells and high explosives. Our deck cargo was made up of lorries in cases, Matilda tanks and drums of lubricating oil covered with a layer of sandbags, presumably to protect them from tracer bullets. Needless to say we were not very happy about this last item.

We left the Clyde on 23rd January and arrived at Loch Ewe on 25th where we lay at anchor until the rest of the merchant ships had assembled. On February 15th 28 merchant ships set out in a gale in the heavily defended Convoy JW53. The escort consisted of three cruisers, one anti-aircraft cruiser, one escort carrier, sixteen destroyers, three corvettes and two trawlers. This was a very good escort and as the daylight hours were getting longer, trouble was obviously expected.

Due to having to maintain absolute wireless silence, the Radio Officers stood their duty watches on the bridge with the Navigating Officers. As we sailed north the gale developed into a hurricane and ships began to get damaged. **HMS SHEFFIELD** had the top of her fore turret torn off and had to return to port along with the escort carrier **HMS DASHER** which was also damaged. Six of the merchant ships were damaged and had to return to Iceland. On DOVER HILL the deck cargo began to break adrift and we were not sorry to see the oil drums going over the side, but when the lorries in wooden cases were smashed up and went overboard things were not so good. But we managed to save the tanks and kept on battering our way northwards. At one stage the convoy was scattered but as the weather moderated the Navy rounded us up and got us into some semblance of order.

The loss of our aircraft carrier meant that we had no air cover and, as expected, a few days later a German spotter plane arrived which flew around the convoy all the daylight hours to keep an eye on us. The next day we had a heavy attack by JU88 bombers, in which our ship was damaged and our gunlayer was wounded by bomb splinters, but we kept plodding on to North Russia. At this part of the voyage we were steaming through pancake ice floes which protected us from the U-boats and the blizzards when they came were very welcome as they hid us from the enemy.

Two days later, on 27th February, we arrived at the entrance to the Kola Inlet. We had not lost any ships to the enemy, a tribute to the Royal Navy and our own D.E.M.S. and Maritime Regiment Gunners on the merchant ships. Of the convoy's 22 merchant ships, 15 were bound for Murmansk and the remaining seven went on to the White Sea ports near Archangel. Little did we know at this time that we would not leave Russia until the end of November. The ocean-going escorts would now refuel and set off homeward with the empty ships from the previous convoy. We were all very tired when we arrived because for the last few days we had either been on duty or at action stations for most of the time. So after picking up the Russian Pilot and setting off independently up the Kola Inlet we were looking forward to having a good sleep when we anchored at Murmansk. We were very quickly disillusioned when, about a mile up the Inlet, we passed a merchant ship on fire with the crew taking to the lifeboats. On asking the Pilot about the ship, which was from the previous convoy, he cheerfully told us that on the way down to meet us he had seen it being attacked by aircraft, obviously a common occurrence. We now understood why we had been fitted with so many Oerlikon and Bofors anti-aircraft guns to enable us to defend ourselves. After two days at anchor we went alongside at Murmansk to discharge our cargo. The port was being bombed most of the time and one of our ships, the OCEAN FREEDOM, was sunk alongside the quay near us. When we had discharged all of our cargo we moved out and anchored about a mile apart on each side of the Inlet. We happened to be on the side nearest the German lines which were only about ten miles away. We were regularly attacked by ME109 fighter bombers which used to come tearing at us about twenty to thirty feet above the water, dropping their bombs as they flew over us just above our topmasts. Our gunners were very skilled and used to open fire only when the planes came well within range. These attacks only lasted about a minute but were very vicious and we had gunners wounded and damage again done to the ship. We shot one plane down into the Inlet and on another occasion we damaged one which got out of range before we could finish it off. The ship anchored astern of us opened fire when the damaged plane came within range and blew it up. We got only half credit for this one so ended up with one and a half swastikas painted on the funnel.

On Sunday, April 4th we were anchored in Misukovo Anchorage, a few miles north of Murmansk, Action Stations sounded and our guns opened fire. Through the pantry we looked out of the door, and saw two JU88 bombers coming up from astern, high up. Our Bofors shells were bursting below them and when they turned away assumed we had beaten them off and stepped out on deck. This was a foolish thing to do, as, unknown to us the planes had released their bombs before turning away. Four bombs exploded close on the port side and one on the starboard and I was blown off my feet. As I got up the gunlayer came down from one of the bridge Oerlikons and pointed out a large round hole in the steel deck a few yards from where he had been standing. It was obvious that the sixth bomb had gone through the main and 'tween decks into the coal bunkers and had not exploded. We informed the S.B.N.O. Murmansk of the situation and were advised that there were no British bomb disposal personnel in North Russia. We then realised that we would have to dig the bomb out ourselves in order to save our ship. The minesweeper **HMS JASON** was ordered to anchor astern of us and to come alongside to render assistance if the bomb should explode, although there was doubt if there would have been much to pick up. Although the DOVER HILL was only a battered old merchantman, she was our home, and no German was going to make us leave her while she was still afloat. The Captain lined the whole crew up on the after deck and asked for volunteers and nineteen of us including our Captain formed our own bomb disposal squad. We had no bomb disposal equipment, in fact we only had a few shovels borrowed from the stokehold - plus nineteen stout hearts when we started digging back the coal, trying to find the bomb. The bunker was full of good British steaming coal which we were saving for the homeward run, so we used a derrick to bring it up on to deck, hoping to replace it when we got the bomb out. When the Russian authorities heard what we were doing, although they had many unexploded bombs to deal with in the town, they kindly offered to send one of their bomb disposal officers to remove the detonator if we could get the bomb on deck. When we had dug about ten feet down into the coal we found the tail fins and, by their size, we decided our bomb was probably a 1,000 lb one. Unfortunately, the Germans also discovered what we were up to and came back and bombed us again, hoping to set off the bomb we were digging for. Between bomb explosions and the concussion of our own guns, the coal would fall back into the area where we were digging and things got difficult at times. We had to dig down approximately twenty-two feet before we got to the bomb, but after two days and two nights hard work we finally got it up on deck.

I was standing beside the bomb with two of my fellow officers as our Russian friend started to unscrew the retaining ring of the detonator, when after a few turns it stuck. He then took a small hammer and a punch and tapped it to get it moving. I can honestly say that every time he hit it I could feel the hairs on the back of my neck standing up against my duffel coat hood. After removing the detonator and primer we dumped the bomb into the Kola Inlet where it probably lies to this day. We then moved back to Murmansk for repairs. Of the fifteen ships which had come to Murmansk in February, one had been sunk and four damaged. On 17th May, in company with three other ships we left the Kola Inlet and set out for the White Sea. We arrived in Economia on the North Dvina River where we stayed until 18th July when we moved to Molotovsk (Severodinsk) and finally on 26th November, with eight other ships, some damaged, we set out for home. Since it was now dark for almost twenty-four hours each day and we could do only seven knots maximum speed we went north to the edge of the ice. Knowing that a Russian bound convoy was coming up to the south of us we expected the Germans to attack it and leave us alone. This in fact happened and we eventually arrived in London on 14th December, 1943, in time to be home for Christmas.

The time spent in the White Sea area was mostly peaceful but our main problem was lack of food and for part of the time we suffered from malnutrition, but we survived.

When we sailed up the Thames towards Surrey Commercial Docks to pay off, with our Red Ensign flying and patches on our deck and side, we were as proud of the old ship as if she had been a spick and span Navy vessel arriving in port. Incidentally, the Red Ensign had a hole in it where an Oerlikon shell had gone through it during the fighting, but it was the only one we had left.

DOVER HILL finished her days as a Naval Special Service Vessel being sunk as a blockship. A kind way of saying that the old ship had taken a bigger hammering than we thought and was no longer fit to go to sea.

Coder Jack Challands drafted to **HMS LORD AUSTIN** thought it was a convoy escort trip to NR and return. Little did he realise on setting out he would be marooned and spend a considerable time before seeing Scapa. Typical of the fact no one ever knows what lies ahead.

HMS LORD AUSTIN was a converted ocean-going trawler, stoutly built to withstand the rigours of the North Sea and Arctic Ocean. She was about 500 tons and a coal burning ship. Her maximum speed made you feel you had Saint Vitus's dance. Our crew consisted of fifty-three officers and men living in very cramped conditions indeed. A number of our crew were ex peace-time trawlermen who were a hard, but likeable bunch of characters.

Our Russian convoy duties were to act as part of the anti-submarine escort. We had A.S.D.I.C. apparatus aboard, depth charge rails at the stern and throwers on each side. Our main armament was one four-inch gun and we also had three, small anti-aircraft guns. We were also acting as rescue ship which meant pulling survivors out of the water, hopefully before the extremely cold water had had its effect.

We joined the Murmansk bound convoy in the North Sea in February, 1943. A severe gale was blowing, the seas were mountainous and this was my baptismal voyage. I wasn't feeling 'very well', but I believe the rule was, if you could walk you were fit for watchkeeping duties.

As a coder my place of duty was in the wireless office behind the wheelhouse. During rough weather it was always a hazardous journey from the mess deck to the wireless office. This involved climbing up an iron ladder to the upper deck, climbing up another ladder which had no protection at all and which was situated in the centre of the upper deck and into the wheelhouse. We had to wait for just the right moment to make this dash up the second ladder. Usually, it was immediately after a huge wave had broken over the bow and the resulting water and spray had completely enveloped the ladder we were waiting to climb. Needless to say, we did not always choose the right moment and in spite of wearing special sea boots, oil skins etc., we often spent our four-hour watch drenched to the skin. This, together with suffering terrible sea sickness, made our lives a miserable lot.

The gale and storm lasted about nine days and it was so severe that several merchant ships and escort vessels were damaged to such an extent it was dangerous for them to continue and they had to return.

At the height of the gale, those of us left in the convoy were ordered to 'heave to' (head into the wind), for this makes life on board a little more bearable and less dangerous. One particularly memorable moment was when the ship rolled so far over we all thought she would finish upside down - indeed some of us did! Our mess deck tables and forms were normally screwed down very firmly to the deck, but they all came adrift due to the continual weight of bodies crashing into them. These all had to be secured and lashed to metal stanchions to prevent them being smashed to matchwood, as the ship pitched and rolled. To make matters worse, we had shipped about three inches of water which behaved something like the sea above us. I didn't hear of any member of the crew who was not feeling sea sick to some extent and this included the peace-time trawlermen. Finally, the storm abated and we began to count the cost. Our life-boat had been damaged beyond immediate repair. Metal guard and hand rails had been twisted and buckled by the sheer force and strength of the water. Our energies had nearly been used up and personally at one stage, my will to survive had gone down the plug hole. However, with the ship now on a much more even keel, we began to pull ourselves together and we realised that the foul and terrible weather had undoubtedly saved many of our lives. I now understand the meaning of 'It's an ill wind that blows nobody any good'. In the conditions the German submarines had to stay submerged, but we knew they were tracking the convoy. Also, the enemy aircraft were unable to operate.

Now that the storm had abated new and fresh perils appeared. I had to answer action stations for the first time in my life. My action station was on the bridge and I was in close contact with all that was happening. On this occasion an enemy spotter aircraft approached at just above sea level. Just out of range, it circled round and round the convoy noting all important details. No excitement this time, but a few hours later, action stations were sounded again and we all knew what was about to happen. I had an ache in the pit of my stomach as I dashed up the three ladders to the bridge. We hadn't long to wait. Specks appeared in the sky, but they slowly grew in size. They were quite high in the sky, but as they came within range of the escorts' guns, the silence was shattered by the hundreds of guns all firing at the same targets. It was quite remarkable that an aircraft could fly clear of all those shell bursts unharmed, but that is what happened. Ships in the convoy were singled out for attack by the German planes as they began their frightening dives. We could actually see the bombs leaving the aircraft and wiggling their way down towards their targets. We had to endure one or two more attacks as the gunners onboard all the ships in the convoy did everything they could. The sky was filled with smoke from the bursting shells and we could hear shrapnel raining down on the ship. With more than a sigh of relief from me, the planes headed back to their base. The score was nil-nil, but how either side failed to score, I shall never understand. I think the German pilots were afraid of so much concentrated gunfire that they came out of their dives too soon and released their bombs from too high an altitude to be sure of accuracy.

Shortly after this attack we received a signal to say that two merchant seamen had been injured by bomb splinters from a bomb which had exploded in the water nearby and we were requested to take the injured men aboard the **LORD AUSTIN** for medical treatment. As a result of this we had to manoeuvre alongside the huge merchant ship while the rest of the convoy carried on course. The two injured men were lowered down to us in strait-jackets and I vividly remember the sides of the merchant ship towering above us with the tiny heads of some of the merchant crew looking down at us. At this point I came to my senses and realised that both ships were at a standstill and were sitting targets for any submarine lurking in the area. Never before or after was I so happy to hear and feel the throb of the engines as the two ships parted company with the injured men safely aboard. Truly, we had a great Commanding Officer in Lieut. Leslie Wathen D.S.C., R.N.R.

Shortly after this incident, action stations were sounded again, but this time it was enemy submarines. The A.S.D.I.C. operator had made a contact and our C.O. manoeuvred the ship to drop and fire depth charges. Full ahead was rung through to the engine room on the engine telegraph and the whole ship vibrated even more as we surged through the water at about eight knots. Our depth charges were duly despatched and there was a short lull. Suddenly all hell was let loose as our depth charges exploded.

It seemed as though the ship was going to break up during the dreadful shaking and noise. It reminded me of a dog coming out of the water and shaking itself dry.

A good deal of our crockery which had survived the terrible weather was broken and many bottles and items of glass lay shattered in the bottom of our large medicine chest. We didn't hang about to see if our charges had found their target, but the contact was lost.

Before arriving at our destination we had to break through large floes of pack ice which made a very eerie sound below deck. We also had to pick our way through a floating mine-strewn area which German aircraft had dropped for our benefit or otherwise. When I did finally set foot on Russian soil, I felt like doing what the Pope always does when visiting other countries - to kneel down and kiss the ground.

During the first few weeks of our stay in North Russia, we transported supplies from Murmansk to the British Naval Base at Polyarnoe. Polyarnoe was a Russian submarine base and sometimes a Russian submarine would return and fire her gun a number of times. We were often startled by this gunfire, especially when it happened in the middle of the night, but we were told later that the number of shots fired denoted the number of enemy ships she had sunk. Sometimes I wondered how the Germans could have any ships left.

Murmansk was quite near to the German-occupied Finnish frontier and it suffered several air attacks every day. We called the Port of Murmansk - the 'Graveyard of Ships'. Sometimes we would tie up alongside a merchant ship lying at anchor to take goods on board and on our return a few days later would find no trace of the ship, the result of it having been bombed and sunk. We used to think what a crying shame this was, having survived all the dangers of war and weather to get there and then to be destroyed.

We were always hoping that another convoy would arrive so that we could return to the U.K. with its escort vessels. The plan was for the naval escorts of the convoy arriving in North Russia to escort all the merchant ships from the previous convoy, which in the meantime had discharged their cargoes and reloaded with timber etc., to take home. This meant an almost immediate about turn for these naval escorts.

LORD AUSTIN, being a coal burning ship could not return to the U.K. with the escorts she had sailed to Russia with. On arrival, we had to coal and water ship. Coaling ship was a time consuming and filthy job especially for the stokers. They would be in the coal hold making sure the coal would not move, thus causing the ship to list whilst at sea. Stripped to the waist with the job done, they would emerge from the coal hold looking like the Black Minstrels.

As a result of the enemy air activity it was decided that all ships should proceed further north to ports in the White Sea and to Archangel on the River Dvina.

During this period we had little or nothing to do, going on a river cruise up the River Dvina which proved very interesting. To help the monotony, a swimming gala was arranged between the crew of another ship and ourselves. I have always been very keen on swimming so obviously I took part in as many events as possible. The starting point was from the side of the **LORD AUSTIN**, but the metal parts were so hot due to the sun that wet cloths had to be put there before we could stand to dive off. The races took place in the water of the River Dvina, but had I been aware then of the pollution in rivers, I would not have dared wash in it, let alone swim in it. In those summer months it was very hot and we had to use mosquito netting over all hatchways. It made me wonder how the mosquitoes could survive such harsh winters when the ice would be feet thick. What extremes of weather they have up there. In the summer, twenty-four hours a day of daylight, and in the winter it never gets really light.

We frequently visited the two clubs in Archangel called the Intourist Club and the International Club. Russian girls would wait outside these clubs for us to escort them inside either to dance or to watch a film. These girls were not allowed inside without an escort and they told us they preferred our company and humour to that of the Russian boys who, they said, were lacking in humour and were very serious.

When going ashore and leaving the dock gates at Archangel it was difficult to escape from the young boys and girls waiting there with hands full of Russian money. A two-penny bar of chocolate or a packet of twenty cigarettes would get you a one hundred rouble note which I think was worth about £4 (cigarettes cost us 4d or 6d per twenty). Apparently the Russians had the money but were so limited in what they could buy, they could not spend it.

Soap and tinned food were also in great demand. Not only could these youngsters barter well but they were very adept at picking your pockets. Mine were emptied and I felt absolutely nothing in the process.

None of us had imagined that we were to be stranded in North Russia all this time and we soon ran out of razor blades. As a result we had to follow naval tradition and put in a request to see the Captain 'to cease shaving', and of course this was granted. After another two or three months had elapsed a destroyer arrived having risked the journey from the U.K. with mail and supplies for us. In no time at all the shop on the destroyer sold out of razor blades.

Amusingly, we again had to put in a request to see the Captain, but this time it was 'to recommence shaving'. I didn't think it was very funny when the Captain leaned forward and with a twinkle in his eye whispered: "It's about time, you look like Henry VIII!" The destroyer also brought us our only lot of mail we were to receive while being in those northern waters. What excitement this caused but what home sickness for the next few days.

I think most Russian people in the places we had visited were desperately short of food. On one occasion, while looking through an upstairs window in one of the clubs in Archangel, I saw a rubbish heap in the back of the club's premises. What amazed me was the number of rats foraging in this rubbish. They were obviously searching for scraps of food. These rats suddenly vanished in all directions as several stray dogs appeared to try and nick their food. Finally, the dogs were driven away by an old man carrying a stick and what looked like an old paint can with a wire handle. He unearthed bits of food with his stick before putting them in his can. Rats, dogs and then a man - priorities upside down.

Most of our ship's company went ashore to enjoy themselves - no matter what the cost. After going out with some of the Russian girls they realised they had to make a visit to the sick bay and ultimately be admitted to hospital for some very unpleasant treatment. During one period, so many of our ship's company were having an enforced 'rest' in hospital that we could not put to sea and, for the first and only time during my naval career, I found myself doing sentry duties with rifle and fixed bayonet on the quayside at Archangel.

It was during this time that I saw rats tightrope walking on and off board ship along the ropes which held the ship to the quayside. Some must have been jumping ship while others were trying to board illegally!

My twenty-first birthday was on the 18th November, 1943 and from my daily rum ration I had saved up a full quart bottle, (illegally I might add). On this day we found ourselves at a port in the White Sea and shore leave had been granted. The four of us who usually went ashore together polished off the bottle of rum and somehow managed to hide our somewhat inebriated state from the Officer of the Watch as we went ashore. We negotiated countless railway lines and other obstacles in the dockyard and eventually found a little cafe-type place. We had to have a light meal before we could order vodka, but having got over the preliminaries we sat back to really enjoy ourselves. Some vodkas later and without warning, one of our party quietly slid forward and finished up under the table. I immediately decoded this signal to read 'we had had enough', and with the help of the other two, managed to get the legless fourth member outside. How we got back to the ship I shall never know, but I remember how I felt the next morning when I smelt the American canned fatty bacon we were to have for breakfast. I shall never forget my twenty-first birthday and especially the after effects. Shortly after this we received the wonderful news that we were to return home.

The continued loss of ships in the vicinity of the Kola Inlet was of great concern to the Admiralty. To bring a convoy safely for 2,000 miles against the worst the enemy and weather could do only to have ships sunk almost in sight of their destination was tragic.

The cooperation of the Soviet authorities was sought, to provide anti submarine sweeps and air cover for the final stages of the passage, when crews were tired and escorts short of fuel, but had little success.

Later, convoys were met by Russian destroyers with communication ratings from Naval Party 100 aboard, but no significant air support ever materialised. In the final reckoning, statistics were to show that 20% of our Arctic losses had occurred in the last short leg of the voyage.

Throughout the passage of the convoys, in spite of the constant fear of attack, with the escorts dashing around and the merchantmen keeping in touch with each other by signal, many a "Jack" retained his sense of humour. The Blohm & Voss shadow plane circling the convoy, at a height out of range of the guns, sending back the convoy position, number of ships etc. to the German air force in Norway was sent the message.

"For Christ sake go round the other way for a change, you are making us dizzy". The German pilot of the "Shad" as it became known replied, to everyone's surprise. "For English gentlemen, anything", altered his course and continued his patrol in the opposite direction.

One of the few British submarines signalled the captain of a destroyer "In the event of attack by enemy surface raiders we propose to remain on the surface". Captain D replied: "So do we!"

The merchantmen had an equal sense of humour. The convoy commodore instructed his yeoman of signals to send to an old tramp steamer: "You are making too much black smoke", who replied: "What do you want me to do, whitewash the bleeding coal?"

A destroyer on its first convoy arrived in Kola Inlet and anchored half-way up towards Murmansk. It was June and someone had obviously overlooked the fact that they were now in the land of the midnight sun. In order to carry out the usual colours ceremony aboard at the end of the day a signal was sent to the W/T Station ashore: "What time is sunset please?" "Sometime late September. Ah, the joys of twenty-four hours daylight!" came the reply.

Another signal sent, no connection with the convoys, to and from whom not known, caused some amusement.

Material for uniform of wrens and matelots being the same and in short supply.

"Wrens uniforms will be held up until sailors needs are satisfied!"

Signalman Maurice Cross explains in comical vein how he

'VOLUNTEERED' FOR THE RUSSIAN RUN

How bored can you get? I asked myself, as I took the ferry from Felixstowe to Harwich for the umpteenth time that month.

Because of numerous breakdowns, my ageing MTB flotilla had paid off a couple of months ago. Most of the crews were absorbed by other flotillas, but signalmen were only carried on senior officers boats (the sparks had to cope on other boats) so in vain I hung about the base, waiting for an S.O's boat. For a time I helped out in the S.D.O. under the beady eye of a man-hating Chief Wren - so I soon got cheesed off with that.

Then I discovered the perfect skive - simply take the inter-docks ferry from Felixstowe to Harwich & Parkstone Quay. Then saunter ashore in each little port, visit the canteens, read the 'Blighty', drink a few hundred cups of tea and perhaps pay a visit to an old friend of mine, aboard a paddlewagon Estuary A.A. guardship, which seemed to be permanently alongside. All this was going on, when lots of you poor sods were commuting between Scapa and the Kola, experiencing various stages of nervous breakdowns - I can only say, "your 'orrible luck, Jack".

The only immediate cloud on my horizon was the niggling fear that there would be a vacancy for a bunting tosser on a certain Lieut. Commander's MGB. He was a very gallant and fearless flotilla leader (DSO and bar, DSC and 2 bars) who casually took on E-boats three at a time - which meant, of course, that he and his crew were not terribly good insurance risks. Fortunately the Lieut. Commander's bunting tosser was lasting the course and looking quite fit every time I anxiously looked out for him, when his boat came in from patrol.

But all this frigging about on ferries, drinking gallons of NAAFI tea and dodging RPOs, gradually took toll and finally, in a fit of patriotic fervour after seeing Noel Coward's 'In Which We Serve', coupled with increasing boredom, I requested to be transferred back to General Service. Once again I took up residence in Jago's Mansions in Guz, until one fateful day I heard the pipe "Signalman Cross report to the Drafting Office". "You've got the **SEAGULL**, the draft bloke said, "she's a sweeper". "Ah", I thought, "that'll be nice - just trundling up and down the English Coast, ashore every other night, with a pint in one hand and a red-headed wanton in the other".

"Where is she based, chief?" "Scapa" he said, "I think she's on the Russian run, but now she's having a refit in Leith". "THE RUSSIAN RUN! NOT THE RUSSIAN RUN CHIEF!!!" I clutched the window flap for support, the chief affirmed: "You'll enjoy the fresh air". I lurched away mentally picturing mountainous seas crashing over ice-covered decks, with tin-fish roaring about like shoals of herring. I decided to raise my morale by enjoying the ministrations of Miss Betty Grable flinging it all about in a Hollywood musical - so off I went to a Plymouth cinema. All was well until the newsreel started. It had condensed all the action highlights of a complete Murmansk convoy into about four hair-raising minutes. Riveted to my seat, I watched aghast as Stukas screamed down in all directions, torpedo bombers barrelled across the waves, tin-fish leaping about like dolphins. High level Focke Wolfes chucked it down, the air was thick with shell bursts, streams of tracers, hurtling bombs and columns of spray raising from near-misses. Billowing smoke rose from shattered ships, as survivors struggled in the icy sea.

"Bloody Hell!" I moaned, groping my way out into Union Street, "Bloody Hell! what have I done? What have I done? Why didn't I stay in Felixstowe, I might have spent the rest of the war quietly chugging over to Harwich and back - too late! Too bloody late!" Into the Long Bar I staggered, only to meet an old signal school oppo, who had a nice easy billet on Berry Head coastguard station and whose main war-effort appeared to be staying awake on watch and keeping his L. & P.A. landlady's daughter happy. He laughed like a chief stoker when he heard of my draft, "Your 'orrible luck mate", he chortled.

So with kitbag and hammock I was away to Bonnie Scotland, and what a welcome - I hadn't been aboard 24 hours before some light-fingered dockyard matey had half-inched my Burberry. But I had a great time in Edinburgh. Far from the bomb-blasted South, it had almost a peacetime atmosphere. I met some lovely Scottish lassies and sank a gratifying quantity of McEwans and Younger's Best. All good things come to an end and much too soon I found myself looking at the slate-coloured, rain-sodden town of Stromness as the **SEAGULL** steamed past the Scapa boom defence.

Scapa - they called it "Home Fleet?" If that's the Admiralty's idea of 'Home', where is their 'Foreign?' - somewhere east of Mars? Scapa - land of the constant drizzle and the permanent bitter wind, with an attendant shower, shitehawks wheeling and shrieking and nagging for gash. No trees on these storm-lashed islands - except when a shore-based matelot brought one back from the mainland, planted it and erected a sign 'The Only Tree In Scapa'. It withered and died and blew down of course, so the matelot hammered a post into the barren soil, nailed his lifeless tree to it, with a new sign 'Still the Only Tree in Scapa'. Scapa - with its tin Fleet Canteen, the floor swilling in beer, where you bought a string of tickets at the entrance, hung them round your neck and exchanged them for pints at the bar. Hoping to gain an alcoholic nirvana, you downed a gallon of dodgy Naafi beer and either joined in, or shouted above, about 20 different sing-songs, drunken monologues and the occasional stoned matelot dancing on the table in his underpants. God rest their desperate souls. I suppose it was just 'Jack' trying to drown the clinging terror of his next Kola Run.

I made one big error when I joined **SEAGULL**. I forgot that my cap-ribbon bore the legend in flaming gold "H.M. M.T.B." It took quite some time to live that down . . . "Stand back men, give him sea-room, here comes the MTB ace, King of the High Seas" etc. It didn't help much when, on the first day out of Iceland, I heaved up my dinner into the North Atlantic. "Well my son", said our old stripey as I hung over the side, "you're on the real 'oggin now, not poncing about the Channel on your MTB - what you need is half a bucket of pusser's peas, washed down with a jugful of pork fat . . . ah! ah! gurg! splosh!

WHAT IS A MATELOT?

In favour of Kids, Oggies, Friday Whiles, Bubbly, Grippo Runs (as long as they are to a Brewery).

He also likes all night in, Beer, Wrens, Punch Ups, Figgy Duff and make and mends, but not necessarily in that order.

A matelot will not go to Church if he can possibly avoid it and yet he will not often be found breaking the Ten Commandments. He will call his oppo all the four letter words that his mind can think of and then share his last tickler with him. He also dislikes Middles, Jimmies, Herrings In, Watch Aboard, Church Parades on the Jetty and Crushers. he has been known to dislike other matelots (if they are foreign or from another ship), Fuelling Ship, Scrubbing Out and Dishing Up, but once again not in that particular order.

A Boy Seaman joins at 15 and is identified by his suit, it has his own name on it.

Ord Sea a man with his cap flat-a-back, wears white hemp instead of a lanyard and has lost his pay book.

Able Seaman is either a sweeper, cook of the mess or is being seen off. One stripe on his left arm means he is a jack. Two tripes he's entitled to a quiet number and three he'll demand one. Crossed guns on his right arm means he didn't listen to his oppo, crossed lightning he won't listen to anyone, crossed flags denotes he can spell.

Leading Seaman wears an anchor on his left arm, the mess wishes it was around his neck. He doesn't "do cook" but has a winger.

Petty Officer One dresses like a sailor and says "Don't cockle your fat" the other dresses like a Railway Porter and does all the cockling. Neither must be disturbed at 1100 hours.

Sailmakers are very scarce they live in a caboosh and have a bottle in the locker.

Gunners Mate is a man with two holes above his shoulders, one is his mouth the other is where his brains should be.

PTI is a man on a chair, or, from here to there - GO.

Master at Arms wears a sword and could be the RPO's Father.

An RPO is identified by a crown and is of unknown parentage.

THE CHIEF

The Chief made his world the sea, his home the Navy, and seamen his people.

He's got an arm like a ship's boom, and he'll go through troubles like a battle-wagon through a regatta.

He's on duty twenty hours out of every twenty-four, because ordinary days are for ordinary people.

He's your Mother, your Sister, your Dad, your Brother, your Teacher, Preacher, Lawyer, Counsellor, Travel Consultant, Yarn Spinner, instant Sea-sick cure, expert on all things female, fashion adviser and friend.

He'll square you off when your ends are frayed, reef you tight when your rigging's slack, watch the cut of your jib, and shift your ballast when you need it.

He reads detective stories on his bunk, can swear for four minutes, twenty-eight seconds without repeating himself (not that you'll ever hear him!) and he will curl your shirt front from a ship's length away when you deserve it.

He'll listen to your troubles, because he's had a few of his own, and he's been known to smile on suitable occasions.

Certain songs can bring a fog to his eyes, and one day he'll probably retire to that chicken farm he sometimes thinks about.

CHAIN OF COMMAND

ADMIRAL: Leaps Tall Buildings with a single bound; Is more powerful than a locomotive; Is faster than a speeding bullet; Walks on water; Gives policy to GOD.

CAPTAIN: Leaps short buildings with a single bound; Is more powerful than a shunting engine; Is just as fast as a speeding bullet; Walks on water if sea is calm; Talks with GOD.

COMMANDER: Leaps short buildings with a running start; Is almost as powerful as a shunting engine; Is slower than a speeding bullet; Walks on water in indoor swimming pools; Talks with GOD if special form is provided.

LIEUT. COMMANDER: Barely clears little huts; Loses tug-of-water with shunting engine; Can fire a speeding bullet; Swims well; Is occasionally addressed by GOD.

LIEUTENANT: Makes high marks when trying to leap tall buildings; Is run over by shunting engines; Can sometimes handle a gun without inflicting self injury; Dog paddles; Talks to animals.

SUB LIEUTENANT: Runs into buildings; Recognises shunting engines; Is not issued with ammunition; Can stay afloat, if instructed in Mae West; Talks to walls.

MIDSHIPMAN: Falls over doorstep when trying to enter buildings; Says, Look at the Choo-Choo; Not allowed elastic for his catapult; Plays in puddles; Mumbles to himself.

MASTER OF ARMS: Lifts buildings and walks under them; Kicks locomotives off the track; Catches speeding bullets in his teeth; Freezes water with a single glance; HE IS GOD!

RUSSIA CONVOY

Have you ever thought what it must be like
To face an Arctic winter's storm,
From the heaving deck
Of an ice-bound ship,
In the early light of dawn?

With steel of the hull so cold to the touch
It would flay the skin from your hand,
And nothing above
But a slate-grey sky,
And far from a friendly land.

With red-rimmed eyes and a face that is gaunt
The result of forced lack of sleep,
And nerves that are stretched
Beyond breaking point
As watch after watch you keep.

Think how it feels to face danger and fear
In clothes that are wet through and cold,
For hours, and days
Or long weeks on end,
No wonder young men grew old.

Do you know what it takes to face a foe
That you may never see nor hear,
Until the klaxon's
Shrill, harsh strident blare
Gives warning that they are near.

Can you guess how it is to see a friend
Die a hard and lingering death,
To be at his side
And not show your tears,
As he draws his final breath.

Think how it feels to be one who has seen
That dead friend now weighted with lead,
Consigned to a dark
And cold friendless sea
When the last Amen is said.

If you can imagine all of these things,
Then I ask you to spare a thought,
For those gallant men
Who were hero's all,
In the special war they fought.

Denis J. Woods

Wednesday 13th January 1943 came my turn soon to become a "Jack In Joe's Land".

In the writers' mess of the RN Barracks Chatham (HMS Pembroke) having answered the pipe of "Up Spirits", as now age of 23 able to draw my tot, and then 'Hands to Dinner", I was ready to return to the office. Came the pipe - 'Writer C.B. TYE report to Drafting Master at Arms'. After three years ashore gaining experience in Admirals Office work, could this be my first ship? Apprehensive, curious wonderment, nervous, I duly reported. A dated stamp on a basic form read "Naval Party 100" with a detail to report to another office. A Naval Landing Party somewhere? What was a writer doing climbing cliffs, landing on a beach somewhere in khaki rig with a rifle on my shoulder? This must be a mistake? With a supply rating, a telegraphist and a signalman, we attended a special briefing.

We were issued with boots, stockings, duffel coats and balaclava helmets and told we were going to North Russia. The communication rating for the signal station and the Jack Dusty (supply rating) and myself for the staff of the Senior British Naval Officer North Russia. Ugh! horrible thought, as it was winter here what must it be like in Russia? Few other details were available. This was it, a very foreign draft - my first.

Friday 15th breakfast at 0600: stood on the parade ground in darkness, loaded with kit bag, hammock and bag of Arctic clothing. Cold, miserable, worried, even scared and tired. If it was cold and miserable in Chatham what the hell would it be like in Russia? 14 hours later arrived in Perth and at 0800 on Saturday 16th January arrived in Thurso, then across the Pentland Firth to Scapa, where a drifter took us to the Polish Destroyer **PIORUN**. The pipes were crackling around the ship all in Polish so didn't know where I was supposed to go - an interpreter showed me to a mess deck. There was no hammock space so I dropped my gear on a locker top. I had a meal of Polish food, did not know what it was, but it was enjoyable after a 24 hour train journey. This was my first time aboard a ship.

We sailed at 2100 on a moonlit night and calm sea bound for Iceland. I watched the land disappear behind me and fell asleep exhausted in my clothes. I awoke needing air but became very seasick for rest of voyage to Iceland, as a passenger. Whilst being made reasonably welcome we were in the way as there was nowhere to sleep - room was so scarce. On arrival the four of us were piped to transfer to the **BULLDOG**. A crowd of moaning matelots in a filthy, dirty, stinking overcrowded mess. My thoughts of 10 days aboard this - Oh God. Taking next of kin forms to the Ships Office, I asked if I could work my passage for something to do. I was allowed to sleep in the office instead of that filthy mess deck, so I slept in an open hammock on the desk. Things were improving I was settled, but we had not sailed. Alas, yet again at 0500, I was told to pack kit bag and hammock for transfer to another ship, **HMS OFFA**. By now I was used to sleeping anywhere fully clothed.

January 21st we sailed for Murmansk. My job allocation was the plot on the bridge - an interesting one, plotting the ship's course and reporting in the log. I felt useful and responsible. I turned in on the deck in a flat hammock as there were still no hooks available and went on watch at 0400 for first stint on the plot. Although the weather was awful and the ship rolled, I concentrated on the job. In desperation I just had to keep awake and not be sick in the bucket alongside the chart table. I tried to ignore it but it seemed to be smiling at me as a useful object. Being constantly bothered about giving the correct information, I suddenly realised if I was the Navigating Officer, where was he then? On one occasion I could swear blind according to my reckoning the ship's position was up Portsmouth High Street moored alongside Woolworths! Fighting the continued seasickness with not much to eat I was determined to do a good job so I spent more than required time on the bridge as this was now a fascinating, enjoyable experience - looking out across the convoy and seeing the destroyers running round the merchant ships like puppies round a mother. Standing on the bridge in a duffel coat, balaclava and gloves, for once I felt a real sailor.

Getting into the danger zone we had a dummy run for action stations. My allocation was Y gun aft magazine, hardly a job for a writer, but I had to do it. I was shown how to put shells in a holder and pull a rope so that the shell slid up to the gun, which had to be in quick and rapid succession.

For the first time I heard action stations with the bells ringing. What a deadly frightening sound. I hoped this was to be the only time, but this was not to be. By 23rd January I became used to a rolling ship and familiar with everything and what to do. Then the crew spotted a plane flying high around the convoy and in surprising jocular vein said we were in for it. They were a jolly crowd so it eased my mind for what was obviously to happen soon.

Out on deck in the forenoon of 24th was found to be the most exciting yet. It was a case of hanging on to the life lines for dear life, moving forward towards the bows, where I should not have been. The sea was breaking over the ship and at one time the deck seemed level with it making me feel a real sailor. Then the excitement turned to fear and the most awful moment of my life. I was well forward of the funnel when a wave knocked me over releasing my grip on the line. I went over the side of the ship, into the sea, realising one minute in the freezing water would be my end and knew I was going to die. My heart was pounding with the shock, fear, cold, my mind in turmoil. Being well forward at the time I saw the ship rise above me, then my shoulder hit something hard. As the ship came back towards me from the port and starboard roll another huge wave had by sheer chance, fluke, extreme luck and good fortune thrown me back aboard well aft, seconds before running out of ship to land on. As she rolled again to starboard hands grabbed me, water rushing all over me - but I was safe. Taken down to the mess, I was stripped and towel rubbed. A mug of rum was poured down my throat and I was wrapped in blankets. Everyone seemed to know what to do as if it was a previous happening. I was still cold for hours, but those hands saved my life. Had they not been there I was a gonner. It was the nearest I had ever been to death.

On an Intercity train many years after the war I poured myself a tot of rum and asked a man to join me. Refusing he enquired whether I was an alcoholic. My reply: each day at 1100 I drink the health and think of the two men who saved my life after being washed overboard from a destroyer during the war. Abrupt and complete silence ensued.

Action stations, no dummy run, this was the real thing. On watch at the Plot, the Yeoman rushed in threw me off my seat put a close angle chart in the Plot and took over as I was not trained for this, and U-boats were about. 'Get to your action station', he bawled, as I ran to Y Gun aft. The convoy was under attack with planes diving all over the place. All I saw before going below to the magazine was every ship opening fire and tracers everywhere. My training in the shell runner was put to the test. I was too busy to be scared. As the carrier came back on the runner, another shell in, pull the ropes, whoosh, up it went with a colossal bang above me, back again for reloading several times followed by the bang. Then came a quiet lull and I thought it was all over. Gazing round at rows of still unused shells I heard the scream of a bomb - or torpedo falling from the sky - screaming with it, waiting for it to land on the ship, knowing that would be the end. A muffled splash followed. The shock reaction to this was to empty my bowels into my pants, shitting myself with fear. The attack over, I walked rather strangely, and somewhat peculiar in stance, back to the mess deck, positively and obviously stinking. I removed the offending uncomfortable underclothes, washed and changed. On recollection my thoughts were: 'Why me?' I'm a passenger, not crew, but aboard a ship in action there is no class, creed, colour, differentiation, rank or rate; its every man Jack.

Nearly the end of the voyage, the sea was calm, by now the cold was excessive, and ice was covering every part of the ship, even below deck. Although I had only a small part to play, a bite of the cherry as it were, I found time for complete admiration for the lads - as we all were then - of **HMS OFFA** and other ships who had done all this several times before. Some had done even ten trips and would be doing so again with more serious and possibly unfortunate consequences than myself.

26th January found us in the middle of a snowstorm, very welcome as there was no trouble. We could steam at only 6 knots, but all was quiet as the mountainous seas had abated and were as calm as a millpond, and after my watch the journey's end was near. My temporary mess mates noticed a difference in me as I was laughing and joking all the time. It was a relief to be my normal self again. Out came the jokes back from this wonderful bunch aboard **OFFA**: "He's a bloody good kid in harbour, but Oh, my Christ, at sea!"

27th January the ship was still making only 6 knots and the sea was calm. I went out on deck as usual and saw something that brought a thrill yet a sigh of relief - land - the snow capped mountains of Russia. My first trip to sea albeit short, had been eventful. The traumatic scare of being washed overboard in freezing cold water in which one lives only minutes, the time battened down in a magazine with an attack on the convoy, the sight of the ships' escorts and the awful cruel sea. I was indeed a lucky man. A trawler took us off the destroyer and I set foot on land, my first visit to a foreign country - I was in Russia. I stood gazing at the surroundings, the strange wooden buildings, wooden jetty, rough roads, snow, ice and for a fleeting moment, although relieved, I felt "The loneliest man in the world".

I reported to headquarters, a disused building converted to become Navy House. I met the Admiral, Base Captain Supply Officer and the PO Writer, who informed me of my duties on the staff of the Senior British Naval Officer North Russia.

Meeting my mess mates, I soon received a full account of the situation ashore here, not all doom and gloom, yet mostly! You get used to it eventually I was told.

Next morning after a rest, I relaxed and during the hour or so of twilight from the continuous darkness of the winter months, I studied my new surroundings. A few dilapidated brick buildings, log cabins without foundations perched on bare rock, barren desolation. One's first impression is a mixture of an American Mining Camp; Cologne, after a 1000 bomber raid, and an urban refuse dump, all situated in the Outer Hebrides. And of course, ice and snow.

Gazing around at the view which was absolutely bleak, barren, desolation. Polyarnoe was no more than a desolate piece of volcanic rock - so why were we here and what was there to do when not working. One had the immediate feeling of being marooned, but hardly on a desert island.

Kola Inlet consists of a long stretch of water with the port railroad of Murmansk at its head. Further to seaward on the eastern shore of the inlet is the bay of Vaenga. On the western shore near the entrance is the Russian naval base of Polyarnoe. Here in comparative, secure shelter, escorts could at last lie alongside the jetties, as it was not until later that our inhospitable allies could be persuaded to allow the ships to do so. Polyarnoe was a very snug harbour. The sides of its narrow entrance overlapping was almost indistinguishable from outside. In the dismal surroundings the crews of the merchantmen, destroyer escorts and minesweepers berthed among them to give anti-aircraft protection, endured sometimes for months on end, a dreary cold monotony, almost perpetual darkness in mid-winter with incessant gales and storms; in the summer endless daylight and daily air attacks.

The Senior British Naval Officer, North Russia, was at Polyarnoe because it was the headquarters of the C-in-C, Soviet Northern Fleet, and became the headquarters of the SBNO who took over the convoys once they had rounded North Cape and were east of Bear island. Some of the convoys were directed to Murmansk and part Archangel. Those for Archangel had to be escorted there and this was arranged with the co-operation of the Soviet Northern Fleet, and the minesweepers based there - **HUSSAR, HARRIER, BRITOMART AND GOSSAMER**.

Similarly the return convoy had to be assembled in Vaenga Bay, escorted from Archangel and brought up from Murmansk, on time.

All this was the main task of the SBNO, who was also in overall command of the SBNO, Murmansk and SBNO, Archangel. For the merchant ships and their crews - the cycle was that the incoming ships remained to be unloaded, ready to return with the next convoy. When these ceased to operate we were left with about forty ships on our hands, and as the months went by with no relief, the morale of the crews was a constant worry. This was another responsibility of the SBNO and his staff, supported by NP. 100.

From time to time there were more RAF than RN operating in the Kola Inlet. 151 Wing and its squadrons of Hurricanes, a gift to the Russians who they taught to fly. A Wing of Hampden bombers was flown out to Vaenga Airfield to hand over to the Russians. With their usual non co-operation they would not be taught anything about the aircraft, and one by one being crashed on training flights. A squadron of Beaufighters were flown out to help the Northern Fleet anti-submarine operations - the same fate happened to them. The RAF Squadron Leader, as Liaison Officer, being so disillusioned and disgusted, flew back to England in a Catalina.

From the same airfield at Vaenga a small squadron of Spitfires operated photographic reconnaissance in connection with the midget submarine attack on the **TIRPITZ**.

Complement of the Naval Base was 72 including the Admiral or Senior British Naval Officer. A Captain RN in charge of the base. Paymaster Lieut. Commander RN the Secretary, Paymaster Lieut. RNR the Base Supply Officer, and our Divisional Officer, a Communication, Cypher and Supply Officer. Lieuts RNVR the interpreters and a doctor.

The ratings were telegraphists, signalmen, and coders, manning the Signal Station at Polyarnoe. The Transmitter Huts they built themselves were high in the hills for more effective transmission because of bad weather. Some were aboard the Russian destroyers patrolling the approach and entrance to Kola Inlet, because of the Russians inability to learn and understand the International Morse Code. There were Sick Berth Attendants, a Chief Petty Officer, Petty Officer and Leading Supply Chief, two supply ratings, a canteen manager, a few seamen for general duties, and in the Admiral's Office a Petty Officer Writer and myself a Leading Writer.

Leading Telegraphist Dennis Whitehouse relates and sums up the function of the Signal Station.

Polyarnoe was like a fishing village, with a wooden floating jetty so only small ships could get alongside. We were billeted in a disused Church. The Top Secret Radio Station was to receive the cargo manifest of every vessel that sailed in the convoy, guns, tanks, lorries, fuel, stores etc.

There were 4 lines of transmitting and receiving. Two to Admiralty in London, one to Murmansk and Archangel and the one known as Area Port Wave which controlled the ships as they came into the area. When the convoy ships were due to arrive in the Inlet they would report their position in code, we would decode it at the Radio Station so we knew exactly where the convoy was, when it was due and ETA. We would then give instructions where to berth, what berths to go alongside or whether to anchor in the Inlet. We also gave cargo uploading positions. A typical cargo manifest of some fifteen ships in one convoy were 2,046 vehicles. 202 tanks, 87 fighters, 33 bombers, 11,500 gallons of fuel, 12,650 gallons aviation spirit and general cargo of 54,320 tons.

There was no social contact with the Russians. Business was conducted through interpreters, who were thus very important people. On our side we had a White Russian whose parents had emigrated after the Revolution, an Australian barrister and a schoolmaster from St. Pauls - all R.N.V.R. Special Branch. The Russians also had a varied selection - a girl in Red Army uniform, a naval commander, and a lieutenant who spoke perfect idiomatic English. We were sure that he had been brought up in England. He denied this. It was the task of the Admiral to negotiate with Admiral Golovko, C-in-C Northern Fleet, regarding essential Russian co-operation in the protection and handling of the convoys. In these negotiations, which were of frequent occurrence, both sides would have their own interpreter, the two monitoring each other, so that there was not much chance of misunderstanding. In Russia, negotiations are successful if they are about something which the Russians want, e.g. convoys - otherwise probably not.

The Russian naval staff were co-operating within the limits of their resources and authority, and the Admiral was always treated with courtesy and respect.

For most of us, service in North Russia was a strange experience - the country, the people, the language, the climate, the N.K.V.D.*, the prison camps, the political system - the whole shooting-match totally unfamiliar. Repellent in some ways, attractive or even fascinating in others.

As there was no direct contact between London and Moscow, all mail and books, secret, confidential matter and so on, came out to us in the convoy escorts. After each convoy's arrival, a small team set out to take the load to Moscow by train from Murmansk; a journey of three and a half days it was also a chance to catch a glimpse of the "bright lights" after a long incarceration in Polyarnoe. Archangel was never bombed and could be regarded as the Las Vegas of the Arctic as there was plenty of entertainment and social activity. Murmansk was virtually bombed out of existence, so Polyarnoe, being first used as a forward operating base for our submarines, became the headquarters of the SBNO when convoys were introduced.

**now KGB*

The whole world knew of the effect on the war in general, and the Russians in particular, with the cessation of the convoys in 1943. We were cut off and virtually abandoned. At first the effect was psychological and only those who have been prisoners of war know what it is like to exist for three or four months without mail from home.

We did what we could and fortunately were a happy and close knit community.

Unfortunately after three months or so the effects were material and we began to run out of everything. The Russians were responsible for the catering but we always supplied this to make the diet more palatable - cabbage soup and black bread was a bit boring. The C-in-C Home Fleet was well aware of the situation and in August 1943 organised a voyage (known as the "Club Run") a high speed dash by two fleet destroyers **MATCHLESS** and **MUSKETEER** from Scapa Flow to Kola Inlet with essential supplies of everything from cypher books to bars of soap, razor blades etc. and mail. Flying a pennant made by a mess deck "wag" bearing the words "PICKFORDS" a wonderful sight for us as they entered the Inlet knowing, guessing and hoping that aboard was fresh food and mail. This continued until the convoys resumed at the end of October and so life gradually became more normal - albeit lonely.

This then was Naval Party 100 - ashore in Russia our need, function and necessity. The lost band of officers and ratings because few knew we were there.

(Many times since then, and to this day, our sea-going colleagues have said: "I never knew there was a Naval Base at Polyarnoe", the reply being: "How the bloody hell did you think you got in and out etc. of the Kola Inlet? Where to moor, oil, unload, preparation and sailing instructions for your return voyage to UK").

Meeting and talking to my new shipmates of NP.100 I was astounded over the length of time they had been ashore here considering the conditions. A letter to medical section at Admiralty from the doctor had stated men should not spend longer than 12 months without relief. The main problem was the Soviet Authorities' reluctance to issue visas for relief of personnel ashore, being of the opinion that the majority of British Servicemen already here were not adequately employed and for many months had been doomed to idleness. Their constant demand for more convoys and materials required more personnel to administer at this end, and surely Admiralty and Senior British Naval Officer were in a better position to know the need. Further requests were made for agreement of immediate grant of visas for additional personnel required; and in future not to withhold visas when considered necessary to ask for them, considering the assistance we were giving in North Russia.

It was further emphasised that of some 170 naval personnel present throughout Russia over 150 should have been relieved months ago, owing to the state of health of the men who are unaccustomed to the climate and other conditions making it necessary to relieve them without further delay. Similar restrictions were made which seemed inappropriate for men sent by an ally to carry out operations of interest to them, in this case especially those who risked their lives bringing the materials to Russia, e.g.

a) No one may land from one of HM Ships or from a British merchant ship except by a Russian boat in the presence of an official and after examination of documents on each occasion.

b) No one from a British warship is allowed to proceed alongside a British merchantman without the authorities being informed beforehand. This even applies to the British Admiral in charge.

c) British officers and men are required to obtain special passes before they can go from ship to shore or between two British shore stations. These passes are often delayed with constant dislocation of the work in hand.

The following directive was sent to all ships visiting Kola Inlet: The whole of the Kola Inlet is a defended area. Officers and ratings ashore are liable to be stopped at any time for identification. Orders given by Russian officers or sentries are to be obeyed promptly.

Sentries are liable to fire at once if not obeyed, without regard to language difficulties.

Libertymen must carry Sailor's Pay and Identity Books. Normally passes are necessary for every officer and man, but exception is made for ships making short visits.

Libertymen landing at Vaenga are to keep to the main road through the village. THEY ARE NOT PERMITTED TO GO BEYOND THE RIGHT HAND TURNING TO MURMANSK, WHERE A SENTRY IS POSTED ABOUT 3 MILES FROM THE PIER.

We were the Harry Tate's Navy. You never saw a scruffier lot of matelots, as replacement clothing was not available. There was plenty of "make" but not a lot of "mend"! Divisions were a farce, especially in the snow; other than blatant untidiness was accepted by the Captain, being aware of stores situation. We would clear out the NAAFI of razor blades and would go without until next delivery; permission to "grow" and/or "shave off" could not apply so was accepted; we broke every rule in King's Regulations and Admiralty Instructions. Our rum issue was more then plentiful, often "sippers" could be "gulpers" because we had a good Tanky so tots were bottled and saved until the week-end for a party on Saturday nights, except the watchkeepers. The few officers would join us for company. The loneliest man was probably the Admiral, he turned up one Saturday night. There was a panic to hide the bottled tots - too late. "Is there not a tot for the Admiral then?" he asked, joined us in an unmeasured tot, a few kind words and returned to his lonely quarters.

Entertainment had been conspicuous by its absence but films sometimes arrived with the mail, shown in a ramshackle cinema, which the Russians were sometimes allowed to see. The only time we were with them, they sat at the back, we at the front. Few words if any exchanged because of language difficulties or the restrictions. The films were censored by Russian officers before being shown. If they showed too much about life in England, even in wartime, only the officers were allowed in. Gracie Fields in "Shipyard Sally" was banned because it showed a lot of the Union Jack and they sang 'Land of Hope and Glory'. We saw the Great Waltz over a dozen times because no others arrived in the next convoy, so we knew every song, words, conversation and dance off by heart, joining in the singing.

Some of the 'Jacks in Joe's Land' became very adept at skiing in the winter. Skis being a commodity fortunately in plentiful supply, ensured good refreshing exercise although more than one party were escorted back to base by rifled sentries for explanation and charges of being out of bounds etc.

The films were the only leisure and entertainment for the base staff and visiting ships, if allowed ashore. The interest, help and initiative of the cypher officer, Lieutenant Bould RNVR, who was in the theatrical profession in London pre-war, a scenic designer for Alfred Black the impresario and a BBC Producer. He wrote to a couple of friends in the theatrical world in London asking for one or two pantomime scripts; on receipt one was Jack and the Beanstalk. James Bould was the producer and decided aptly to call it "Jack in Joe's Land", Joe Stalin being the reigning King of Russia at that time. A stage was built in the basement with curtains and lights. Quite a few had experience semi-professionally in show business so soon - with continuous rehearsal under the guidance of the producer, interested stage hands, and scenery of an Arctic location,the show was on, the first English pantomime in Russia. Two acts, an original misconception in six scenes with Jack the Dame, good fairy, bad fairy, landlord and the cow, and chorus, 6 jolly jack tars. Music accordeon, banjo, uke and drums. The audience and cast: Naval Party 100 off duty, the ever silent Russians sitting at the back, and crews of visiting ships - how daft can you get, but it passed the time away.

So successful was the pantomime and enjoyed by ourselves and welcome visitors, and realising there was talent amongst us, with months, days and hours to produce - when little else to do - the eminent cypher officer James Bould produced a Concert Party known as "We Seven". Accordeonist Ginger Ward, singer Les Sullivan, banjo-uke Nobby Wall, Bill Benton comedian (impersonating Billy Bennett and Max Miller), Jack Dalliber baritone, Alex Downing and Shorty Ancock. Alex was 6'2", Shorty 5'7" did a double act (The Long and the Short and the Tall) so it was chorus, double acts, quick fire gags, sketches etc. Some material was unashamedly borrowed. A lot appertaining to local gossip would be incorporated into the who, our own verses were originated into "That was a cute little rhyme, sing us another one do" becoming a real Sods Opera, Sailors Own Dramatic Society. Again, how daft can you get, but it evoked much needed fun.

The Concert Party being so successful became proficient with a lot of practise and was taken aboard visiting ships to cheer them up a bit, especially those alongside. After the rare occasion of a performance to a Russian audience there was an offer for a Russian girl singer to join the show to add a little sex appeal. This was approved at high level and she sang on several occasions. Great excitement as suddenly a female appeared in an all male company after months. She was called the Commissar's daughter but we doubted that to be accurate.

Giving the concert on the mess deck of **HMS BRITOMART** one evening she asked, and we were given to understand, that she wanted the loo. Alex Downing was the compere and giving her as many instructions as he could, with a mixture of English and Russian hand signals, could not say, or get her to understand, the "Heads" were on the starboard side of the forward mess deck. So references and gesticulations were made to get to the hole in the wall, so it was left, then right etc.

She completely misunderstood the directions, went left instead of right, up instead of down and found herself in a small area with a grating. When a girl has to do what a girl has to do, and not knowing much about British ships' lavatories, presumed this was the place she sought.

Back on the messdeck of **BRITOMART**, Alex was asking for attention for the singer of romantic ballads, Les Sullivan, when an angry matelot, with hair sprinkling from an oil stained singlet and wiping the back of his neck with a sweat rag, bawled out: "Who's been pouring hot tea down my grating!!" This was considered local gossip so at the next concert was included as a cute little rhyme.

"The Britomart's crew are relating, a story they found quite elating, of the Commissar's daughter who, when making water, made use of the Chief Stoker's grating!"

We had the proud distinction of receiving a signal from the Signal Officer of a home going convoy escort congratulating us on our performance and thanking us for the pleasure we had managed to give ships' companies. The most significant point of the signal was that it was addressed to WE SEVEN, repeated SBNO North Russia. Surely the only time in history that an official signal was addressed thus.

IT PAYS TO ADVERTISE ! !

Breingan's Incorp. RABBITS Large Selection	Our aim is to please ! DUSTY's We have the largest departmental store in the district.	If it is civility and smiling service you want - come to the SHIP's OFFICE !

MOVING ?? ....

See "TEDS MEN"

Distance no object

Lorries always available.

We never Sleep ! Messrs. Spry, Page, Pollard, Dennett & Gordon. Night and Day Service. Our Motto - "Come back at 1400"	SUBASE HOTEL Stay with us and like it ! Every modern inconvenience ! Attractive surroundings ! Charming companions ! Food by finest Russian Chefs !	Call and see our "oldest inhabitant" 14 months in North Russia and still sane ? Can be seen daily in the Ships Office No charge !!

Reproduced and photostat copied by C.B. Tye from the original copy kindly donated by Bill Johnston of Whitby, Yorkshire.

SEASON 1942 - 1943

NORTH RUSSIA

Presenting the first English Pantomime in Russia !

Entitled -

JACK

IN

JOE'S's LAND

-o-

- An Original Misconception in 2 Acts.

PROGRAMME

JACK	LES SULLIVAN
DAME	HARRY HALEY
GOOD FAIRY	KEN ANCOCK
BAD FAIRY	BILL BENTON
LANDLORD	RONALD POLLARD
COW	WATT & DAVIDSON

JOLLY JACK TARS

JACK DALLIBAR	ANTHONY EASTON	HORACE WALL
ALBERT WARD	WILLIE JOHNSTON	PHILLIP KING

ACCORDEON	ALBERT WARD
BANJO-UKE	HORACE WALL
DRUMS	W.C. CAISLEY
BOOK BY	JAMES BOULD
ADDITIONAL LYRICS	WALL, BENTON & KALLIN
MUSIC BY	ALL and SUNDRY

PRODUCTION - JAMES BOULD

ACT 1.

SCENE	1	"HOMETOWN"
"	11	"ON THE ROAD"
"	111	"HOMETOWN"
"	1V	"FAIRYLAND"

ACT 11

SCENE	V	"OGRELAND"
"	V1	"ABOARD"
"	V11	"GRAND FINALE - DREAMS COME TRUE"

For the erection of the stage, the lighting and the making of the properties, our thanks are due to - W. Kimpster. A.E. Everton, S.R. Holden and S.N. Thomas

Ronald Frankau and Duggie Byng, who have contributed numbers to the production, send best wishes to you all !!

===================

BECAUSE WE ARE SO FAR FROM HOME
LET'S HAVE "A BLOODY GOOD MOAN"

No BLOODY Tram
No BLOODY Bus
We had to walk
The BLOODY fuss
The sentries stop all BLOODY us

IN BLOODY POLYARNOE

No BLOODY girls
No BLOODY fear
No BLOODY fun
No BLOODY cheer
It's BLOODY dark for half the year

BLOODY POLYARNOE

No BLOODY gin
No BLOODY ale
No BLOODY news
No BLOODY mail
The BLOODY lights they BLOODY fail

BLOODY POLYARNOE

The BLOODY Huns not BLOODY far
No BLOODY roads
No BLOODY car
The BLOODY Russians ne pony mar

BLOODY POLYARNOE

The BLOODY roubles BLOODY down
A BLOODY bath costs half a crown
And even then its BLOODY brown

IN BLOODY POLYARNOE

No BLOODY Scott No BLOODY Whaley
No BLOODY Popeye
No Mirror daily
No BLOODY Jane undressing gaily

BLOODY POLYARNOE

The BLOODY Boats
The BLOODY sink
It's BLOODY cold
The BLOODY drink
The Russian boots they BLOODY stink

BLOODY POLYARNOE

The BLOODY snow
The BLOODY rain
The BLOODY Tigris here again
The BLOODY Tridents the BLOODY same

BLOODY POLYARNOE

The BLOODY cook
No BLOODY need
No BLOODY books
To BLOODY read
A Cabaret is what we need
IN BLOODY POLYARNOE

AND THE COPYRIGHT IS *BLOODY* WELL RESERVED

Washing facilities at Navy House left much to be desired, particularly bathing. Hot water was only available for an hour or so each day, so to prevent arguments we had a roster and each had a limit of no less than eight minutes for a bath in brown water, which did not smell too good. We had a rule that the door should not be locked so if someone stayed submerged or afloat over the time limit he was pulled out to dry off in the corridor. These sessions were noisy banging on the door and shouts of "Your times up, mate". Your next bath could be several days, often a week later, according to the roster.

We also experienced some difficulty to get washing done and dried, especially during winter months.

Jack as usual had the answer - a dhobi woman. At risk of being caught we managed to contact - bribe - call it what you will - an old Russian lady to take on our washing. In return we would keep her supplied with food etc. This worked extremely well until one evening we called round for the dhobying and she informed us it was her husband's birthday that day. That did it, any excuse for a piss up.

Back to our billet, pick up cans of beer and bottled tots, back to dhobi lady's house, small party and very good anglo-Russian relationship. The old Russian got quite drunk, failed to arrive at the submarine base the next day, the result - he got put in jail for seven days for failing to turn up for work. Nearly the end of the dhobi woman, but she carried on at risk to herself - needing the food we supplied.

I remember with sadness and, regretfully, further criticism. Our Cypher Officer and Interpreter, Lieutenant Mark Kallin RNVR, was taken ill on duty with suspected appendicitis and was transported to the Russian hospital at the top of the hill, and diagnosed as having peritonitis. He died either during the operation or soon afterwards. Arrangements were made for a sea burial with a request that his body be delivered to **HMS BLUEBELL**.

As we waited at the jetty, with guard and rifles, prior to start the solemn proceedings, the corpse was brought down the hill from the hospital in a fish box pallet-type coffin in a dirty old van, travelling the bumpy road at thirty miles an hour before screeching to a halt at the jetty. Two Russian drivers dragged the box from the van and dropped it on the ground like a sack of potatoes to the amazement and disgust of those on the ship and jetty. A matelot from **BLUEBELL** rushed down the gangway and hurriedly draped the so-called coffin with the ensign.

Of course from that moment the solemn proceedings were conducted with true dignity and tradition of the Royal Navy as the ship slowly moved out of the Inlet for sea burial in the deep, cold, icy water of the Barents Sea.

Working life was very hectic and extremely busy when the convoys arrived and we often worked into and through the night. Once the return convoy was on its way back to UK there was little to do other than general office work, often creating work for something to do, to while away time.

September would come and the dull rain and drizzle would come to an end. Winter arrived in October and continued until late April or early May of the next year. The wind constantly howling, blizzards, deep snow. Everywhere you looked around all points of the compass was snow and ice with the outside temperature up to 30° even 45° below zero. Being only 520 miles from the North Pole this was not surprising.

Our consolation was being under cover and quite warm as our thoughts and minds went out to those at sea bringing and escorting the convoys in such atrocious weather as well as being attacked en route. We had our raids on Polyarnoe, whilst nothing compared to Murmansk, as the German air force were only 25 miles away in Petsamo, Norway. There is always someone worse off we felt, so could and did not complain. Then came the winter proper, the awful continuous darkness for more than a hundred days, it was dreadful. One became completely disorientated not knowing what time of day it was - constantly looking at clocks and watches, tapping back of the hand as if the watch had stopped. Even so the situation for those at sea was still the worst.

As the blackout of continuous darkness lessened, becoming twilight, but still snowing and laying deeper and deeper, came the whiteout. The communication ratings still had to go on watch to their signal and transmitting huts, and stations scattered around, irrespective of conditions. Imagine thousands of snowflakes falling from the sky where daylight without sun can be seen between the flakes, these were larger flakes of snow falling, blocking out the daylight, complete and utter whiteout in frightening proportions. Signalmen and telegraphists leaving comfortable billets for the log cabins in the hills were ordered to always walk together holding hands, or arm in arm, causing fun comments and mick taking, but done to avoid recurrence of a previous fatality when a telegraphist going on watch alone became confused, disorientated, scared, and lost, took a wrong turning and fell into the Inlet to die in seconds in the freezing water.

After the continuous darkness and the hour of twilight after breakfast it was wonderful to see the daylight with eventually a little occasional sunshine. My office at Polyarnoe overlooked the mountains and the Kola Inlet. There was a balcony the other side of french windows (wasn"t I lucky, especially in summer!) My office curtains were open to let me gaze in wonderment at the sight of light after so long, even a little daylight. I foolishly forgot to draw the curtains to darken ship. Sitting pounding the typewriter, my desk faced the other wall covered in convoy arrival and departure information. Suddenly I heard the sound of a bullet richochet off the wall outside the window. A Russian sentry on the jetty instead of winding the handle on a telephone to advise Navy House a light was shining, and being a trigger-happy chap, like most sentries, used the only warning he knew. Fortunately his aim was bad, an inch or two to the left and it would have been through the window and the back of my head. Reporting the incident to Base Captain I was disbelieved, told I was probably "bananas" and time I went home (a good idea I thought). Next morning in daylight he was convinced when he saw the marks on the wall.

Came the spring, the welcome daylight returned, there were longer hours each day and into the welcome, warm summer. The snow slowly melting and eventually disappearing, one experienced the opposite, though it was still unique. Looking at the hills opposite one would see the sun set with no darkness to follow, to disappear behind the hill on the right, then in half an hour would rise again to the left until you became used to this new phenomenon. When you did, eventually, it was still very strange. Sleep seemed very difficult as the sun would stream through drawn curtains. To pass time until sleep came I would sit on the balcony at 0200 and read a book, feeling alone and lost, yet still marvel at the uncanny situation viewed in the land of the midnight sun.

The never-ending daylight brings an equally strange feeling of depression. The pale sun moving endlessly around the horizon day and night ceased to have any meaning as the sun never really sinks out of sight for 24 hours. As in the months of darkness daylight played havoc, causing the same feeling of disorientation and constant clock watching - seemingly ungrateful, but true.

At the end of the summer and the approach of autumn in mid September, before another winter, there was the wonderful phenomenon of the Aurora Borealis. It seemed strange that this harsh northern area could produce such an awe inspiring spectacle as this - the "Northern Light", the hesitating white fingers groping over the horizon like giant searchlights stretching up into the sky with smaller branches growing from them criss-crossing each other until the heavens are cut into geometrical designs, bands of vapour in all the colours of the rainbow weaving across the starlit sky. Complete fascination and a truly magnificent sight, although a little frightening.

In a more humorous vein, it was more often necessary to play "Silly Bugger" games to brighten the cold winter days when "off duty". L/Tel Dennis Whitehouse was the leader of the "Silly Sod Brigade" and remembers:-

We used to eat at what we knew as "The Corner House". We had a Russian chef who prepared and cooked our meals. There was an arrangement to pick up any "gash" food - spare grub we did not eat - as the Russians were half starving in the village.

A Russian used to come with his horse-drawn sledge, known as a drosky. There was a big wooden tub on the back of it. He would park the drosky at the back of the building so nobody could see it, pick up all left-overs, swill, potato peelings etc, probably taking it home to eat. We would let him in to the galley, give him a tot of rum and sit him by the fire to keep warm.

One day the horse stood outside, the poor creature covered in ice and snow. As it breathed, the whiskers round his nose turned into icicles, so you can imagine icicles four or five inches long hanging off the end of the horses nose - as his breath came out it would freeze. When it was running along the ice used to melt, but standing there this poor, pathetic horse, as thin as a rake, should never have been in the shafts.

We"d had quite a sizeable tot of rum so when we came out for a bit of devilment and fun, to keep cheerful, we would pinch the drosky and park it behind another building, so that when the Russian appeared he wondered where it had gone. We could not take it far as there was nowhere to go and it would be found within half an hour.

Climbing aboard the drosky one got the reins and another a stick and shouted "Gee Up". No one could think of the Russian for "Gee Up" so there was no response. A gentle, considerate whack across the arse, and possible fright, started the horse into a gallop.

Here was a sledge, six inches off the ground with a big wooden barrel full of "gash" and six of us aboard hanging on the back. There was a problem. From the galley to the jetty and water of the Kola Inlet was a hill, with lorries coming backward and forward. "Jesus Christ, what's the bloody Russian for 'Whoa'! to stop the runaway sledge?". No one knew. So we just pulled the rope reins and hoped he would stop. Like hell he didn't. The horse starts to slither and slide on the ice and the sledge goes sideways, we were in a right panic as no one knew what to do as our stupid prank became frightening.

If we decided to stay on, we'd get caught under the runner and be showered with "gash", so we baled out leaving the sledge running down the hill, the barrel goes over the side and slops down the slope, the poor old horse has got it sliding down the side of him trying to stop and us lot, prostrate on the icy deck, laughing our bloody heads off. Hoping no one sees us, or be put on a charge (one wonders what the wording on the charge would be!) we bugger off and hope someone will find it.

There was a column of "Wrens" marching up the road from the jetty. Where we would say, left right, left right, they would say the equivalent in Russian: Trasva Tree, Trasva Tree.

On one occasion we joined in and fell in at the back of their column, causing them considerable embarrassment. There were twelve of them and six of us. The poor girl in charge just did not know what to do, whether to laugh, whether to tell us (in Russian) to "Bugger Off" or what. It delighted the few local population, they thought it quite hilarious, 6 matelots wrapped in woolly furs tagging behind the Russian Wrens. Its a wonder we did not get locked up, or even shot. We did such daft things in Polyarnoe to pass the time when not "On Watch".

The winter of 1942/3 came slowly to its end after many months of Arctic weather. The snow, being so deep, took well into May before it melted completely. As the days of the so-welcome daylight became longer the convoys would once again be sailing in broad daylight and subject to more air attacks - even more particularly with the onset of 24 hours' daylight. Still with memories and concern of the disaster of

PQ17 the previous summer, and intelligence reports that a concentration of powerful German ships were at Altenfjord obviously waiting to pounce on any east bound convoys, and determined to avoid a repetition of the **HIPPER, LUTZOW** fiasco in the Battle of the Barents Sea on New Years Eve 1942, Admiralty raised objections to sailings during perpetual daylight of the summer period and the only response to the threat was a British Battle Fleet to oppose it. But unless a strong carrier force could be provided such a move would be the height of folly. Finally it was agreed and on 30th March, Churchill with great reluctance, had to advise Stalin of the decision and the reasons for it. Stalin was furious and referred to this unexpected action as catastrophic.

We of the Admiral's staff ashore were aware of the situation and the Admiral explained fully to all in Naval Party 100 of the cause, need and reason for the cessation of the convoys and everyone realised that no ships or escorts would enter the Kola Inlet for some time. Likewise, all ships in the vicinity, including Archangel, would not be returning to the UK for some time as no escorts were available for them; so ships and shore personnel became "marooned" with little or no contact with the rest of the world - it caused concern although we knew the reason. At least it was summer, unlike the time before this happened in the winter of previous year.

Many of my colleagues due for relief, having been ashore over twelve months, realised they would have to stay even longer - causing obvious disappointment. There was even less to do with no convoys coming our way: no buzz of activity, the signal stations quiet. We could only wait and see what, if anything, happened.

The Russians were now more friendly and co-operative allowing us to use their football ground which was covered in ashes. Our team played theirs, crews of the base ships joined us. When it became hot we were allowed to walk into the hills to a lake for swimming. On day, to our complete surprise, a party of Russian Wrens came to the lake, undressed to underclothes and into the water. Their hitherto drab uniforms revealed some quite heavenly bodies - eyes popped, spines tingled, such excitement, so sudden after all this time. Jack being what he is tried to swim closer, being repelled with cries of NIET! NIET! We went often to the lake hoping for a repeat performance, but sadly this had been a one off. In April 1943 those living at the submarine base moved to another billet which we soon called Dodge City. The buildings were nearly all log cabins with a wooden pavement and it was just like a scene out of a Western film. Instead of living in separate rooms all ratings were in a large room with bunk beds and soon settled into the new quarters. About 400 yards away was a log cabin where they went for meals which were greatly improved by a cook from one of the ships in Murmansk, drafted in temporarily to instruct the Russian cooks how to cook English dishes.

No ships, so no fresh food or mail. The greatest need of any serviceman in wartime is mail. Contact with home, wives, sweethearts, relatives and friends. Admiralty, realising the concern this was causing all personnel, allowed one cable transmission with a prepaid reply to each man's next of kin, words restricted to 'Is everything alright at home?" My reply was: "Father seriously ill". A few weeks later I was informed via Admiralty he had died. Nothing could be done about it, no normal request for compassionate leave. It was not until months later that I knew the cause of my father's death.

In lighter vein, we had two Harold Wests, one in Polyarnoe, one in Murmansk, both Naval Party 100. A prepaid reply cable was sent advising one Harold his wife had had a baby daughter. The cable came to our Harold in Polyarnoe who had been here awaiting relief for 14 months, quite a shock! A mixture of good and often bad news came with the cables with little detail.

Food soon became a problem, especially fresh food, as what we had in stores were from the last ships in, so it was all canned. There was no flour to make bread, so the Russians let us have some of their hard black bread. Our cook "Wee Jock Watt" did wonders with various recipes of serving the ever constant, fortunately plentiful, corned beef and rice. Stew, mince, fritters and sandwiches, mashed potatoes, condensed milk and custard. For a change we occasionally managed to get some yak meat from the Russians, this had to be cut up in pieces and cooked for 5 hours, then chewed for minutes by which time any flavour had gone - followed often by chronic indigestion, but still a welcome change from corned beef; fruit of course was non existent. Our basic beer ration was halved until we ran out. Fortunately our favourite tipple - rum - did not. We still had our legal issue "Up Spirits" at 1100, some illegal for our bottles for Saturday night, and occasionally a jar, even moreso illegal, seemed to appear. Where would we have been without our "Tanky" supply and canteen assistant? No questions were asked from where it came, to keep our peckers up.

As the weeks became months we began to get somewhat depressed with the idleness and nothing much to do. Although a close knit community, getting on reasonably well, we were becoming frustrated and bored. But most of all the food situation and, even worse, no mail. We were marooned and cut off from the outside world - thank God it was summer. It would have been even worse in winter, so "Jack in Joe's Land" persevered and made the most of the situation.

Admiralty aware of our plight commissioned two fast destroyers **MATCHLESS** and **MUSKETEER** to make a fast passage direct, loaded with stores, food, clothing, films etc. and mail. In anticipation of this we ran a sweepstake with a cash prize of our excess roubles as to how many bags of mail would be aboard the rescue ships. Apart from the minesweepers based in Kola no other ships had been seen. Knowing the ETA we waited patiently, then great excitement as these two destroyers entered Kola Inlet in the sunshine, a wonderful sight. From the topmast of one a pennant flying in the breeze was clearly marked "PICKFORDS". The stores were unloaded - our long awaited mail, 265 bags of it, was not. Because, alas, contrary to strong objections from the Admiral, the Russian authorities insisted that the contents be censored, before being issued to us. So our excitement turned to despair, eventually receiving our mail, by the time it was sorted, a few days later. Silence ensued everywhere for hours as we read what had been happening to our families in UK. Tears of joy and some of sadness, our long vigil was over as we now, once again, had fresh food. I remember to this day our cook carving slices of delicious roast lamb on to our plates, surrounded by piles of fresh vegetables, but by now our "galvanised guts" could not cope with our greed as most were very sick afterwards.

As the summer turned to autumn and the darkness returned, it was October before plans were made for convoys to be resumed and we would return to our normal routine of activity. So came further stores to replenish stock and again thankfully after another long wait and delay - mail. But this time we prepared to obviate the previous situation of censorship, the solution being that two seamen secretly board the ship known to have the mail aboard, unpick the bottom of the bags, extract all the letters, sew them up again leaving only newspapers. The letters were then smuggled ashore and distributed with extreme caution. One wonders what the reaction of the Russians was when the bags were opened, and found to contain only newspapers. We also wondered what would have happened if these two brave seamen under orders had been caught. It does not bear thinking about.

Yet again on arrival of another convoy the cruiser **CUMBERLAND** lowered a boat to bring the mail ashore and attempts were made to confiscate the bags for censorship. The captain of the cruiser sent a signal to Moscow through SBNO stating "Unless this mail is allowed to be put ashore I will turn the convoy round and steam back to the UK". In 24 hours our mail was allowed ashore.

> Russian women were the toughest. Few men could work as hard and as long as they did. They were seen to hump trees about like Canadian lumberjacks; loaded coal aboard ships, sawed up huge logs. They were crane drivers and lorry drivers: were in the Army fighting at the front.

I recall a Petty Officer, no names no pack drill, sneaking away with a Russian woman, going where he shouldn't have gone, doing what he shouldn't have done, crawling back into the mess at Polyarnoe next morning, exhausted. The woman wanted sex with him 5 times in the night. The fourth time he could not make it and refused. The woman opened the drawer of a bedside cabinet, produced a knife and threatened to cut it off, so it was 5 times or else - never again.

SO WHAT IS COLD, REAL COLD - WAR OR OTHERWISE - IN ARCTIC RUSSIA?

> Everyone knew the feeling of cold when you walk around with the natural propulsion of the legs, without feeling anything from the waist down. It can, at times be embarrassing depending how well or not you may be reasonably endowed and wondering if it is still part of the body or not. Best to always be with a mate in case of frostbite when colleague would then rub snow on to the part of the body affected, even if below waist, but is invariably the ears.

Further examples of the extreme cold were recalled by one of **HMS KENT's** crew, Jack "Speaky" Lowe, who was on duty all night on the range finder clad in duffel coat and oilskins. On his return from duty to the messdeck for a well earned and deserved tot, thick ice had to be beaten off his oilskins with broom handles.

Whilst anchored in Vaenga Bay a member of the crew went ashore for a drink at the RAF Mess of 151 Wing. On his return to the ship and entering the cold air he was very sick, his vomit froze solid in his throat and he choked to death. He could not be buried in the ground until April so a coffin was made and he had a sea burial in the Kola Inlet from a whaler. A mate of his who was a bugler insisted he played the Last Post for him. After the solemn ceremony the bugler was brought back aboard with bugle frozen to his lips and was taken to the Sick Bay to thaw the bugle from his lips before it could be released.

> The feeling of being cold. One gets up with it, one walks with it, one goes to bed with it. It seems to wander around somewhere under the skin; it penetrates the bones and sometimes it seems as if it even enters the brain. One can't escape from it. It penetrates under all shirts, sweaters, and jackets, no matter how many one puts on. The second is the feeling of hunger. This feeling has many shadings - from a dull, painful, sharp, unbearable one, which appears as soon as one has eaten one's ration, to being tortured by fantasies.
>
> Soviet records show that of the 26,600 persons who took the basic civilian military training course in the month of November over 6,000 were too ill or weak to finish the course. Of these 800 died of starvation while under training. Another 10,000 were so frail that they could only be given a short course.

Trainees were very reluctant to fail as an allocation to the front-line units meant a different and improved ration scale. As fuel ran out so was electricity power confined to military use from emergency generators. In the short days of November and December, Leningrad must have seemed a city of the dead, shrouded in snow and freezing mists from the Baltic, without light or movement. In the factories, starving and frozen workers toiled for 14 hours a day making armaments, many dropping dead at their lathes.

Medical attention for civilians was virtually nil. In hospitals the absence of electricity, heat, and water made work extremely difficult. The temperature in the wards usually stood between 30° and 35° Fahrenheit. The patients lay fully clothed, with coats and blankets, and sometimes even mattresses, piled on top of them. The walls were covered with frost. During the night water froze in pitchers. The hunger had the effect of causing diarrhoea among the patients, many of whom from weakness were unable to use the bedpans. Sheets on the beds were filthy - no water for laundering. The only medicine available was sodium bromide, which the doctors prescribed under various names.

A Leningrad doctor describes his experiences: "I entered without knocking. My eyes beheld a horrible sight. A dark room, the wall covered with frost, puddles of water on the floor. Lying across some chairs was the corpse of a 14-year old boy. In a baby carriage was a second corpse, that of a tiny infant. On the bed lay the owner of the room - dead. At her side, rubbing her chest with a towel, stood her eldest daughter . . . In one day she lost her mother, a son, and a brother who perished from hunger and cold. At the entrance, barely standing on her feet from weakness, was a neighbour, her horrified gaze fixed on the dead. She too, died the next day.

Telegraphist Nobby Wall's first impressions on arrival. We stepped ashore at Polyarnoe, a Russian naval base in Kola Inlet.

We were to relieve members of Naval Party 100 North Russia. Even in those days our Russian allies kept a strict check on who was allowed in or out. As we came in, those we were relieving had to be prepared to move out.

First impressions were of a wooden quay, backed by a line of log-built storehouses. Beyond stretched an undulating landscape consisting mainly of bare earth, with rocks of various sizes and very little vegetation. In winter, of course, all this would disappear under a white blanket of snow. From the quay, a dirt 'road' ascended slowly towards a mixture of low wooden houses and brick-built terraced buildings; these had been dotted around on any piece of relatively flat ground. The wooden structures formed part of the natural landscape - brick did not. The road continued between the buildings, over a wooden bridge, and climbed towards an imposing structure which dominated the whole area. This, we were to find out later, was the Red Navy Club.

Accommodation was provided in one of the small brick-built flats above the quay. The top floor had been adapted to provide a W/T office, sleeping quarters and a small mess and galley. In summer or mid-winter this presented no problems but, come spring when the thaw set in, the roof leaked like a sieve. However, our predecessors, with a touch of typical naval ingenuity, had overcome this. Much use had been made of bashed-out empty food tins (virtually all our food came out of a tin) to construct an elaborate indoor guttering system in the attic. Archimedes would have been proud of it. From time to time modifications were necessary when the offensive moisture shifted its line of attack.

The unit had been established to provide liaison with the Russian Northern Fleet and a direct communications link with the Admiralty at Whitehall. We received and transmitted signals relating to convoy traffic and weather reports. Recoded versions of German radio signals intercepted by our "Y" group bases in a log cabin in the hills would be forwarded to the code-breakers at Bletchley.

Life was largely routine, even to the regular visits from the German air force. They would nip across from Finland and drop the odd bomb or two. Nothing really serious - more of nuisance raids to keep the Russian defences on their toes. When not on duty watch in the W/T Office, we spent our off-watch time servicing equipment, writing home, chopping logs for the galley fire, walking, or doing some skiing when the daylight permitted. News from home was eagerly awaited, sometimes over long intervals. Letters would be re-read many times.

Signalman John Lowe was a long serving member and a much travelled man across Russia. Having arrived in April 1942 to join NP.100 he did not leave until November 1943, a long, hard, enduring period of 21 months including two long winters when surely one was enough. He relates:-

It was August 1942. Already I had escorted convoy PQ14, PQ16 and PQ17 and now detailed to escort PQ18. We were to go on the Russian destroyer U.S.S.R. alongside at Polyarnoe. Joining the ship I noticed a polar bear, not fully grown, but big enough. The crew of this ship had found it when it was a cub on an ice floe. The crew were all Mongols from South Russia, and had never seen ice or snow before coming north, to make matters worse the ship had never seen any enemy action.

They had this bear chained to "X" gun aft of the bridge, with a very slender chain.

We went out to join convoy PQ18 which we all now know was a humdinger. We got the lot off Jerry - Stuka's - torpedo bombers - high level bombers - U-boats. While all this was going on, the Russians were using 5.5 guns, to which this polar bear was chained. You can imagine the state that it was in, it went beserk, pulling at the chain to get away. At one time I did not know whether to duck from the stuka's or jump over the side of the bridge. After 17 days at sea we returned to Polyarnoe all in one piece, including the polar bear. I was more frightened of that bear than all the Germans.

Shortly after arriving in North Russia, another signalman and I were told to get enough tinned food from the stores to last us three weeks and go to the signal station at Vaenga. This was between Polyarnoe and Murmansk at the top of a very steep hill. We landed with 83 tins of all sorts: sausages, bacon McConachies, biscuits etc. It weighed about three quarters of a cwt. While we were trying to think how to get this lot to the top of the hill - it took us all our time to lift it - a big Russian picked it up, and took it straight to the top.

We were to live on this station, a wooden tower about 15ft. in diameter, for 6 weeks. The only form of heat for cooking was a big wood-burning stove to which we had to wire enamel cups as cooking utensils. This took hours as there was no direct heat and to crown it all we arrived without a tin opener - you can imagine the language, miles from anywhere in the Arctic. We made do with two lumps of iron from the Aircraft dump. The Russians would not give us any food, even though there were 17 of them. They had a big Army type hut with plenty of room but they would not let us live with them, so we were in the tower both day and night. We managed to survive, in fact we had a few spells there, both in 1942 and 1943. It was rough in winter.

One day one of the Russians called me inside, because he said it was 75F below zero. Being very dry cold we did not notice it.

The Russians told us not to worry about the wolves! I went outside one night after hearing a noise there, and about 25 yards away, was a wolf. It didn't seem to bother and just wandered off, presumably looking for food.

The signal station was open to air attack. Quite often an ME 109F would sweep across Vaenga Bay and machine-gun the hillside, sometimes hitting the woodwork, but this didn't do much damage as the station was two poles thick, about 20 inches.

At Vaenga, on the jetty, was a crane with a big nameplate, JOHN SWAW, SALFORD. As this is where I lived I was quite proud of it. I used to point out to the Russians that all their decent equipment was made in England. Just one of our little differences, but generally we got on quite well.

While we were at Vaenga we wore Russian clothes, they were much warmer. As most people knew us, it did not matter. One day a British cruiser came and anchored, some of the crew were given shore leave for the afternoon and as they walked along they met us dressed in our Russian gear. Obviously they thought we were Russians as one of them tried to speak in Russian, and got a shock when I answered back in Salford English, telling him there was no Woolworths or stores here - only thing to do was admire the view!

On Christmas Eve 1942 at Polyarnoe another signalman and myself were once again detailed to join a Russian destroyer, thinking we were going to escort another convoy. On Christmas Day the Captain asked me if it was our "Big Holiday" in England. I said it was so he invited us to have dinner together. We worked 4 on 4 off, which is a bit rough in the Arctic in December. I went down below at 1200; the Captain had sent us brown bear meat, apricots and a half-litre of Vodka *each*. I don't remember much till being called for the 1st Dog Watch at 1600. Waking up, I found I had a big lump like an egg on my forehead. Apparently on going to the "Heads", which were at the stern of the ship (all guard rails are down at sea on Russian ships) and the deck being coated with an inch of ice, it appears I survived this lot, only to fall head-first down the mess deck hatch. I managed to get up to the bridge where my mate was curled up in a corner and shaking him, took his place, at which the Russians were very amused. I later found out we were searching for four Z Class German destroyers, but fortunately did not find them.

After over a year in the Arctic, another signalman and myself were sent to a small village on the opposite side to Murmansk. The signal station was a rickety watchman's hut, open to the weather, and used only at certain times of the day. There were merchant ships at anchor and our job was to make contact with Murmansk.

After a couple of days we fancied some white bread as it was over a year since we'd had any. It struck me that this merchant ship must have some as they usually bake their own. The ship was at anchor about a mile out. I borrowed a rowing boat and went alongside. There was no-one about, so I climbed the gangway, only to be met by a Russian sentry who was not too pleased to see me. He insisted I leave the ship immediately, but I refused, he then drew back the bolt on his rifle and threatened to shoot me. He was told he would be in serious trouble if he shot an English sailor, to which he didn't know what to do.

Fortunately at this time one of the English crew came, which saved a lot of trouble for both myself and the Russian. Explaining who I was and our requirements - a few loaves of fresh white bread - he brought some more of the crew who could not believe we were left in such a dead and alive hole.

They gave me some bread, cigarettes and other things which were scarce in that part of the world. I really enjoyed the bread as we had only dry biscuits and some Russian black bread. It made life a bit more interesting, another episode of life in the company of our Russian Allies. Being over a year since I had left England, we were supposed to go to

Russia for only six months, I eventually left for home after 21 months, much against the Russian's wishes, so had to leave in a hurry.

When **Leading Signalman Ernie Skelton** (known of course as Red) was in his teens he joined the Young Communist League (YCL). At 18 he volunteered and joined the Royal Navy, served on two ships and was then drafted to Naval Party 100. He surely must have been one of the few, if any, to say: "To my immense joy I discovered I was going to North Russia - to the land of my dreams".

Came the day I joined **HMS MARNE** and many cold days and nights later, mingled with a few action stations (blast the Germans, why couldn't they sleep?) we arrived at the Kola Inlet. My signalman colleagues aboard Marne said "Look over there, it is your chosen country".

All I could see were wooden shacks and thought, over the top of the hill there must be more buildings. There were more shacks, the homes of many Russian families. That was the beginning of my disenchantment of the land of my dreams, the USSR.

During the following 18 months my experiences of the communist ideology were shattered when one saw the abject poverty in which the average Soviet citizen lived, whereas the officers of the Red Army and Northern Fleet lived in comparative comfort. Many uncomfortable situations were experienced during my stay.

I had to join the Russian destroyer **BAKU** as liaison signalman to escort part of convoys from Kola Inlet to the White Sea Port of Archangel.

Conditions on the ship were primitive, you could not get a bunk to sleep in until a Russian got up, either to change watch or go to the toilet. When I returned to Polyarnoe I was infested with lice and crabs. The food we ate was black bread and fish head soup. Subsequently we took our own food aboard, corned beef and biscuits.

Going to a dance I found that due to shortage of females it was not uncommon to see two Russian matelots dancing together. This was not too bad, but when they tapped you on the shoulder and asked for a waltz then you knew it was time to "return to base". When in an attempt to do what was natural, and as the Russians were not allowed to fraternise, one would give a matelot 50 fags for the loan of his coat and hat. So in the event of "clicking", your silhouette would appear to be Russian and not an English sailor.

Back at Polyarnoe Ernie Shelton was detailed for duty to a signal station, a remote outpost in a small village, Michukov, situated half-way up the Kola Inlet towards Murmansk. The purpose being to communicate with and assist merchant ships and escorts in their passage to Murmansk to unload and return to U.K. or into the White Sea to get round to Archangel.

The signal station was manned by two signal ratings and a few men of the Soviet Northern Fleet. It was here he learnt the Russian language, if only of interest to communicate with the men of the Russian Fleet, but mainly to avoid being shot over any misunderstanding.

We slept in a dark, dirty and most uncomfortable building, did our own cooking on a small wood burning-stove. This arrangement was reasonably acceptable barring the important function of toilets, which left much to be desired:

The communal toilet was a small hut placed on the end of a jetty. Each morning one joined a queue to do what came naturally. If the tide was high it dropped in the water, if low on the banks of the Kola Inlet - either way the whole exercise was far from pleasant. For some, if not most of the Russian villagers we were not good bomb aimers! It was decided something had to be done to try to find improved independent conditions - but how? We cut the top off a large tin that previously contained dehydrated potatoes. A pole was fixed over the top to act as a seat. A small amount of water was put in the tin and after each use more water was put in as a primitive flush. Time of course came to change tins, fortunately readily available, and saved for future use. Removing the filled tin exposed a block of ice consisting of many layers of excretion: my oppo's, mine, my oppo's, mine, adnauseum! We then decided to place the heavy tin on the jetty near the communal centre.

Early next morning before the queue formed the villagers formed a group around the ice block, lots of discussion. Finally a Red Army man kicked it into the Inlet, it sank, eventually thawed out and the British waste joined the Russian and made its way round the Kola Peninsular.

Then one day things began to improve, in fact quite exciting, when a woman doctor aboard an ice breaker offered sex for a tin of "Tickler" (naval pipe tobacco). The frustrated, unhappy Ernie decided to take advantage of such a tempting offer.

Pinching a rowing boat and armed with the issue contraceptive and essential prize, the randy rower went across the Inlet.

I went aboard, presenting myself at the door of the doctor's cabin, only to find this rather aged female (bearing in mind I was 20) who said: No Tickler, No Sex. Gleaming inside I gave her the Tickler only to find she meant a tin of TICKNER jam from Grimsby. The romance ended before it began.

I rowed the distance back, even more frustrated, and spent many weeks in the hope of the remote possibility of finding a tin of TICKNER jam.

When VE day arrived (we learnt two days before the Russians) we spliced the mainbrace. Two days later when they were informed by Pravda that the victorious Red Army had single handed beaten the Nazi hordes, we had to stand for three hours at the quayside listening to the Marshall of the Red Army, then an Admiral, then down to the party workers, how they had done it alone. I often wondered what some of our colleagues who had been lost en route to Polyarnoe and back had died for and am convinced the average Russian was not aware of their sacrifice.

When we eventually paid off NP100, the collection of junk and things was piled into a heap for anyone to take if they so wished. An old lady decided to look over the rubbish to see if she could find anything, whereby a Red Army man armed with a submachine gun told her to move on. She said: "Go away young man, I have grandchildren your age". The Red Army man then struck her with the butt of the gun and knocked her out cold. That really made up my mind that the Young Communist League and the USSR were not for me.

Wee Willie Johnston known as Malinki Matroos (the little sailor) the youngest member of Naval Party 100, a coder with events he never thought he would experience on his first draft at the age of 19 has vivid recollections.

I served both in Polyarnoe and Murmansk according to the roster. Life at the Naval Base was fairly good with the others in the company. We got on very well considering we did not have many amenities for relaxation, so we made the best of what we had. Considering the conditions there were of course sad times, such as when we had convoy survivors living with us or at Vaenga Hospital across the bay. We shared our NAAFI rations with them, cigarettes and clothing as they had little or nothing but what they stood up in. Our own supplies of clothing were far from adequate, waiting two or three months for replacements. One would go on divisions with a uniform that had darns in it and the Captain knowing the situation could only say "At first opportunity get a replacement."

In winter because of the intense cold we were allowed to wear what notice board described as "Pirate Drag". This was duffel coats, balaclavas, heavy boots, stockings, longjohns, jerseys, scarves and mittens, anything to keep the biting cold Arctic weather out. We drew our NAAFI issue twice a week, being allowed four cans of beer on Wednesday and four on Saturday, plus soap, toothpaste and razor blades etc. and whatever else in stock providing the ship carrying supplies had got through without being sunk. We kept our beer ration until Saturday for a party. We bottled some of our tot each day to go with the beer so the scene was rather hilarious and noisy. Being a close knit community the officers used to join us for company.

We had had quite a number of air raids and after she was sunk had the **EDINBURGH** survivors in Polyarnoe. They were put up in a Russian school, which way lying empty available for them. There was a particular young lad who was a cabin boy on one of the merchant ships, a fellow Scot about 15 or 16. In one particular heavy raid, carrying him from the sub-base building to a make-shift air raid shelter, built into the cliff at the back, I had to carry him because he had an arm and a leg amputated, and was unable to walk. I was only 19 coming up to 20 and my thoughts were: "There but for the Grace of God go I". It could so easily have been me that lost the arm and leg, and some of the people who thought that Communism was such a great thing, should remember the sacrifice that many of our men made, and got little or no thanks from the Russians for their efforts.

The bombing at Polyarnoe was nothing compared to Murmansk where we had 103 air raids in a period of eight days. They came the same time each day, every hour on the hour, you could check the watch by them. Buildings you saw one day were missing the next. Behind Naval Headquarters was an ack ack battery. I was the duty coder receiving an important signal. Army personnel were with us as port central unit. With everyone evacuating the building I stayed to complete the signal and was then handed a tin hat by the REME Sergeant. "Come on Jack, it's time you got out of here lad, the guns are going and bombs are starting to drop." We made our way at a gallop down six flights of stairs. On the last we could hear the German aircraft screaming down. A deafening sound the whole building shook the doors flew open and flames shot up the stairs past the alcove we had sheltered in. Safely and luckily outside we met the Commander RN of the Headquarters saying: "That was a large bomb sir, to shake the building like that". "That was more than a bomb, you're lucky to be alive" he replied. The anti aircraft battery had shot the plane down before it could release its bombs so both had hit the building. The whole place stank of burnt flesh there being no survivors.

Just one of many examples, too numerous to mention, of the bomb attacks on Murmansk and the ships in the harbour whilst the war materials were being unloaded. To be attacked whilst in convoy en route and yet again at the destination was all too frequent. Murmansk, then, was a heavily bombed city, the aftermath as if black ghosts were moving in twilight over the snow in a kind of deathly silence. Everywhere there were remains of property, desolate brick chimneys, crumbling walls sticking up through the snow. Murmansk itself, especially in winter, was like some ghastly vision of a northern hell. Everybody remarked upon the funereal muffled deadness of the town's streets, and the miserable inhabitants shuffling about in the snow. Later when the snow melted away the sight of charred rubble was even more depressing, especially the awful smell in the air over the scene of desolation.

Back in Polyarnoe with his continued roster of watchkeeping, and now being summer, Willie Johnston walked alongside the jetty to relieve the middle watch man.

It was broad daylight, a lovely sunny morning - time 0345. I noticed a lifeboat being rowed in the bay. Thinking the Russians were energetic, rowing about at that time of the morning, I wondered why? I stood at the edge of the jetty watching this small boat approaching. As it came alongside I realised the assumed Russians were in fact survivors. One of them looked up at me in my duffel coat and jolly jack's cap and said: "Are you British mate"? Yes I'm just going on watch. "Where is this place?", he asked. This is Polyarnoe, the Russian Naval Submarine base, there is a British Naval base here also.

Noticing that many on the boat were only party clad, I asked: "Who are you?" "We are survivors from the BOLTON CASTLE" a ship I knew had been sunk a few days ago. I helped them out of the boat and escorted them to the control post. Here, the Russian sentry was not at all happy about allowing them to proceed as they had no passes or visas. Through sign language and words of Russian which I had learnt during my time here, I got him to phone his superior who contacted our interpreter, who allowed the survivors through and into the base - straight to the galley for gallons of tea and the now proverbial corned beef sandwiches. We provided shakedowns in the corridors and utilised the empty beds of the men who were on watch until they recovered from their ordeal and awaited passage in the next convoy to the UK.

PQ17 must be one of the most outstanding events. Working at I did in the coding office, we got the reports hour by hour, day by day, the positions where ships were being sunk and the position of the convoy, it was heartbreaking. There was so little we could do but score the ships out as they were reported sunk till a mere handful were left at the end of the day. It all seemed so tragic. Did the man in London make the wrong decision because he didn't have sufficient knowledge, or incorrect knowledge? Should it have been left to the senior officer on the spot? It certainly didn't leave a very good taste in anybody's mouth that all these men and ships had been lost, simply because someone in London had told the convoy to scatter because of a threatened attack from capital German ships which, in fact, never sailed. The convoy of course was such a tragic loss, which we could ill afford in those days. Further convoys were halted during the summer weather, which after all was 24 hours of day-light and of great assistance to the German U-boats and air force. So there was a lull before the convoys resumed again: when the weather, or rather the 24-hour daylight, drew to a close.

TO SEA IN A RUSSIAN DESTROYER *with L/Tel Les Sullivan*

Notice to prepare to board a Russian destroyer, was always short, but the few preparations necessary were quickly completely.

The number one priority from our point of view, was a sack, an ordinary common or garden sack, into which would be put the necessary sustenance for two people, covering a trip of approximately four days. This would depend on what was available in the stores and usually consisted of things like baked beans, sardines, span (of course), fruit, not forgetting the tin opener! As our time would be spent entirely in the wireless office for the whole trip, we would not have access to cooking facilities - so, 'straight from the tin' had to suffice.

The (Gremyashi type) destroyers were Italian built, very fast and tending to be a bit top heavy. This was more noticeable when manoevring in a sea. There were three wireless offices on board, one of which was situated on the upper deck just abaft the funnel, forming part of the main upperworks - the best target to aim for in action! This was the one allocated to the British telegraphists. The Russians did not read International Morse Code and did not have access to the necessary code books. It was our job to read the signals, decode them and pass them to the Liaison officer. The fact that a Bofors type gun was mounted on each side of the platform on which the wireless office was situated, made it very difficult to read signals when these guns were in action. It was a constant irritation to COs of ships of the escort that the Russians persisted in opening fire with close range weapons at aircraft that were no more than specks in the sky! I recall an incident at night when the main armament was brought into action firing at an iceberg that was identified as an enemy battleship. But that was better than having the opposite occur.

Conservation of ammunition did not appear to be a Russian practice and after one particularly sustained action with aircraft, it was not possible to open the office door, it being jammed with a considerable depth of shell cases, and still don't know if they hit anything!

An ordeal to be suffered aboard the destroyer was a visit to the heads, the only place where the crew were allowed to smoke and you really had to be in need to sit in a cubicle, without a door in an area inevitably packed with seamen, creating an atmosphere that was never experienced on a British ship! All the Russian ratings appeared to carry a newspaper which they tore into strips to serve as cigarette papers. Into the news paper was put a peculiar tobacco, this looked like bird seed. The ends were twisted tight and when a match was lit the atmosphere of the heads - which was already devoid of anything like disinfectant - was filled with an extremely pungent smoke, alien to a lot of rubbish bonfines including old motor tyres. The last thing you wanted was a bit of constipation to prolong your stay!

On one occasion my colleague and I agreed to join the Russians on the messdeck - which was only possible on return to harbour. We had to crawl through small hatchways to reach the messdeck where their meal was being prepared. Large tins of fish, like tuna, had been opened and placed on the mess table alongside large piles of black bread. With a piece of bread in one hand and a fork in the other to take the fish from the tins we proceeded with the meal - all accompanied by sips of vodka. This was followed by the almost inevitable tin plate of compot - a very pleasant mixture of small fruits and berries stewed in a sweet juice. This was well known to us ashore as 'Jungle Juice'.

Although the whole atmosphere on board Russian destroyers was completely different to that on our own ships, the crew really did their best to welcome us and be as friendly as their way of life allowed. We were very grateful for their efforts in getting us things like white bread, butter and sugar for our tea and coffee - which they did not get themselves.

Our stay on board was only a short one each time but it is unique to be able to say that one spent time at sea in Russian destroyers.

L/Telegraphist Les Sullivan travelled from Archangel to Murmansk the long way round.

After being with Naval Party 100 at Polyarnoe for a very rugged nine months the Admiral arranged for a party of us to go to Archangel for a break. We took passage - free of all duties - in **HMS BRYONY** - a Flower class corvette. The ones that could roll in damp grass! Upon arrival we were refused permission to land. Russian officialdom was at work and it took a lot of negotiation by our authorities to get permission for some of our party to be accommodated in the Intourist Hotel. The rest elsewhere. On arrival at the dock gates after a 'run ashore' we were informed by the signalman on duty that the **LORD AUSTIN**, a trawler, was to take our party back to Polyarnoe. After another 24 hours it was then arranged for a party of about 8 or 9 of us to take the train back to Murmansk. The train left late one afternoon and 24 hours later was still in a siding just outside the town. There were no lights in the train so we removed one from the rear of the last carriage and had sufficient light to play cards for the rest of the five-day journey. At intervals, the engine stopped to enable the crew to take on logs for the fire from huge stacks at the side of the track. Kadalashka station used to change hands frequently between the Russians and the Germans so a couple of miles outside the station the crew were informed which lot had the station today and the answer decided whether the train stopped at the station or got up all the steam possible to go through like the clappers of Hell! Luckily the Russians had the station when we arrived.

Signalman Eric Rathbone on draft to join Naval party 100 was to find it a little unusual and different from the start. Boarding a Dakota at Hendon Aerodrome he flew to Belfast, a flight of three hours. Within 2 hours he was aboard the **ULSTER QUEEN** a brand new banana boat commandeered by the Admiralty after been converted into an anti-aircraft cruiser. The same evening he sailed to Iceland to join PQ18, a convoy of forty ships. This was to supplement the losses in the previous convoy PQ17 ordered to scatter.

Two days later PQ18 was attacked by one hundred aircraft; five merchantmen were sunk and three others by U-boats. The next day a further attack by a hundred torpedo and high-level bombers with loss of two more ships, one being blown to pieces. Yet again three days later a further attack by fifty aircraft as the convoy neared Archangel. In a period of five days the Merchant ships were attacked by no less than two hundred and fifty aircraft with the loss of eleven ships.

On arrival at Archangel three of the remaining ships became stuck on the Dvina Bar. Jerry taking advantage of this made several further attacks on the defenceless merchantmen which **ULSTER QUEEN** protected until they were refloated. Still not satisfied, German aircraft again returned to bomb those now at anchor.

Next day, more than relieved after such an experience as a passenger, on draft, Eric joined a small party of other signalmen and took passage in one of the escorts for a fast run through the White Sea round to Polyarnoe, which is where he was supposed to be.

I was very thankful to be ashore but with the same impression as others; very dismal, very cold, with blizzards and heavy snow, and this was still only September: so what must mid-winter be like. Settled in at the naval base I was allocated duties at the signal station. One night another signalman and I returning to our quarters after being on watch had to pass through a gate guarded by a Russian sailor, where pay books had to be shown and stamped.

At 2000, after passing the sentry, he shouted something at us and then we heard the click of his rifle bolt. Two very frightened matelots fell down in the snow as a bullet whizzed over our heads, then, pandemonium as Russian officers appeared. We explained we had acted normally and that no harm had been done; the officer apologised then hit the sentry in the face.

Another night, again returning from the signal station after being on "watch" it was snowing heavily causing us difficulty in walking. We reached some wooden steps and half way up we saw a reindeer, which was most unusual; the animal saw us and slid down the snow-covered steps. My "oppo" and I vaulted over the rails and finished up waist deep in the snow. Nobody believed us with cracks about "where was Father Christmas!" Several days later many reindeers were seen nearby to make our story more convincing.

This then was our function, purpose and need as Naval Party 100. Ashore in Russia, but what was there to do to occupy our minds when not on duty; to fight the boredom of isolation and inactivity; the dull, dismal days of darkness, perpetual snow and ice and the freezing cold: knowing and realising our stay would be, at least, twelve months. We were not allowed to speak to the Russians, especially the girls, the Red Army Wrens. If we did they were the ones who were in trouble, so no female company.

The whole area was restricted and guarded by sentries, so we were completely impounded in a Camp on the shores of the Kola Inlet.

Telegraphist Les Lawrence of HMS Westcott gives his views as a visitor to Polyarnoe.

I looked forward to setting foot on Russian soil with keen anticipation. I suppose I thought that even the humblest dwelling would exhibit the grandeur of the Kremlin, expected that the people of Russia would recognise that the journey up was at best tedious and that their gratitude would be expressed in many gratifying ways.

Whatever I expected, I was not prepared for the desolation and raw boredom of Polyarnoe seen from the sea. From the quayside the snow, masking any pavement there might have been, gave the place an unfinished look, the buildings were ugly and the absence of people completed the "ghost town" impression.

Matelots on board summed up the general feeling of disappointment with remarks like: "It's like Scapa without the beer" or: "Wonder where they go for their summer holidays".

Since we were used to our female members of the armed forces taking up only non combatant roles, the sight of a young armed female soldier patrolling the quayside was an eye opener. Jolly Jack's efforts to lure her onboard or even to get her to accept a bar or two of nutty were met with a stony stare. Her reluctance to behave in a more friendly fashion was influenced, so we were told, by men who could be seen hovering about who were rumoured to be OGPU members.

Since it soon became apparent to those with amorous tendencies that Polyarnoe was not Paris or even Pompey, ships' companies looked around for other things to relieve the monotony. However, realisation that the front line was not millions of miles away, coupled with the privations of the Russian people, made me come to terms with their jumpiness or suspicion.

"THE GIRL BACK HOME"

On leaving school a pleasantly serious, auburn haired Reigate girl was faced with the problem of what to do. "I want a job where I can be shut away from everything", she told her father, who had other ideas. "Nonsense!" he replied. "You'll learn to type like all the other girls". Obediently Jean Metcalfe did just that, she found a job as a typist with the B.B.C. She had been on the staff for 3 years when one spring day a girl came over to her desk and whispered: "Jean, guess what! They want you to do a microphone test". Jean wondered who's idea it was. They were looking for women announcers, and someone must have heard Jean on the 'phone and put her name forward. As a result of that test, and her father's insistence that she should learn to type, the eager confident Jean Metcalfe went on the air and became known to the millions of serving wartime personnel as "the girl back home".

Jean had deserted her typewriter for the microphone as compere for her Forces Favourites programme. The idea being to make us feel less than a 1,000 miles or more from home. Soon, in slit trenches, desert outposts, aboard ships at sea and at far distant airfields, servicemen by the hundreds of thousands were listening in on sets ranging from service receivers to battered wonders strung together by "morse bashers".

The troops became so attached to the programme that tank men in the desert were forbidden to tune in when in action: one tank driver got so preoccupied with Jean's voice his vehicle crashed. The rest went on and ran into an ambush resulting in casualties.

For us her sweet dulcet tones kept us in touch with home and we, like millions of others were in love with her. Unfortunately, not everyone agreed, but they were a small minority. One man wrote from Bristol saying he didn't like the programme or the sickly pathos in her condescending tones, and a women listener declared she could not stand the sound of her voice. They were obviously not over 1,000 miles away from home, least of all ashore in cold, bleak North Russia in the month of November 1943. When we first heard the voice of the girl back home, as we were then at long last getting mail out, as the convoys had resumed, I wrote to Jean Metcalfe asking for a request and not to forget the chaps in North Russia. She replied, she was surprised to hear that we were there, presuming like so many others the Navy were only at sea escorting convoys. I could of course not tell her where, and to my surprise and extreme joy Jean said she would put on a special programme if I sent her several requests. Without delay I roped everyone in on it. Then awaiting patiently, and listening to every one of her programmes we heard in those ever sweet dulcet tones "Now we go from the heat of the desert to the other side of the world to the Arctic wastes of North Russia, where we find leading writer Chris Tye and his colleagues of a special Naval party there, with requests from all the lads at the Naval Base". What excitement! So it was definitely "Good On Yer" Jean Metcalfe. But what mattered even more to her was that compering Forces Favourites enabled her to fulfil an old ambition as she worked "shut away from everything", compering the programme from a compact glass panelled cubicle, hidden monastically in the warren below Broadcasting House. "Shut away from everything" Jean may have been, and wanted, but she certainly did not shut us away from home.

On return to U.K. I wrote to Jean at the B.B.C. thanking her for all she had done for the lads overseas and especially us. A kind invitation was received to have lunch with her. A special pass was sent to enter the nerve centre of the B.B.C. in the hub of the universe. What a pleasure and how enjoyable this was, but I was to be confronted with a shock; not the meeting with Jean Metcalfe, "The girl back home with the golden voice", but an interview with Audrey Russell, of "Radio Newsreel", who asked me to make a broadcast, on my experiences in North Russia. She seemed to think it was something special for a naval rating to have been ashore there, and also been to Moscow. As requested, I wrote several sheets on the subject, which was censored by the B.B.C. and the Ministry of Information. Several weeks later, I entered the studios, surrounded with flashing lights, and sat at a table opposite Audrey Russell, in front of a huge microphone which to me seemed about 18 inches by 9 inches. Fortunately it was a recording. I fluffed my lines, my nervous hands rustled the papers I was holding and could be heard by everyone: the thoughts that my words were going out all over the world frightened me. After three dummy runs it was accepted and duly broadcast the following week in Audrey Russell's Radio Newsreel. A full report on my visit to the B.B.C. was sent to Polyarnoe, and appeared in our own magazine "Northern Light", by the editor who took over from me when I left. This indeed was a very happy end to my 12 months in Russia and Jean Metcalfe mentioned my visit in her continued programme "Forces Favourites" with the many requests that followed for the lads ashore in the Arctic.

When "Forces Favourites" closed down in 1945, "Family Favourites" continued with male announcers in London and Hamburg. The B.B.C. then decided to have a woman at the civilian end and Jean was the obvious automatic choice. The voice in Hamburg was Cliff Michelmore: on his last Sunday there Jean called "Well Cliff, I do hope you enjoy your holiday". Nobody except a few close friends knew he was coming home to get engaged to his opposite number, Jean Metcalfe. The two had made up their minds months before after Cliff decided when on leave to look in on the London end. They were married in March 1950.

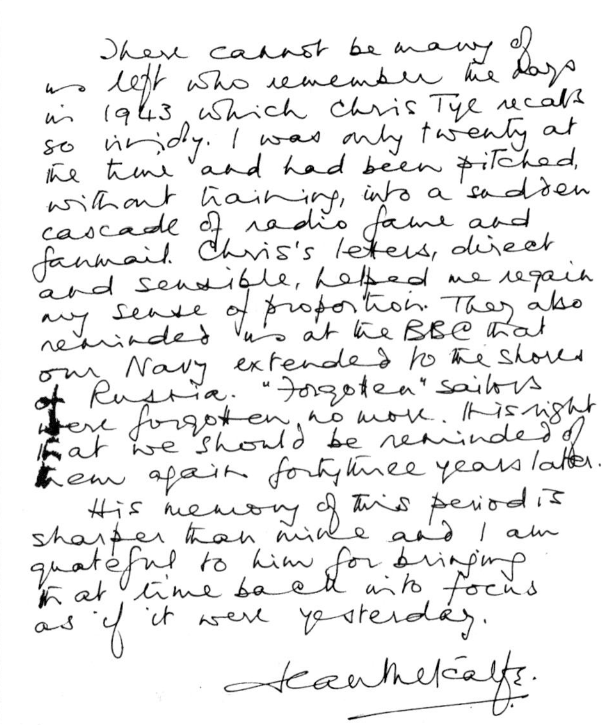
There cannot be many of us left who remember the days in 1943 which Chris Tye recalls so vividly. I was only twenty at the time and had been pitched, without training, into a sudden cascade of radio fame and fanmail. Chris's letters, direct and sensible, helped me regain my sense of proportion. They also reminded us at the BBC that our Navy extended to the shores of Russia. "Forgotten" sailors were forgotten no more. It is right that we should be reminded of them again forty three years later.

His memory of this period is sharper than mine and I am grateful to him for bringing that time back into focus as if it were yesterday.

Jean Metcalfe.

As another winter approached and having had no leave for nearly a year, a Friday while on compassionate leave, my thoughts were: "Oh God, I can't stand much more of this, I'll go bananas". I would look at ships returning to UK with envy, obsessed with becoming a stowaway on one of them going home, and taking a chance of ending up in Davy Jones' Locker.

In the depths of depression I received some wonderful news. The Admiral's secretary announced he was going to Moscow and I was to join him, also Leading Telegraphist Alex Downing and Leading Supply Assistant Andy Anderson. Unlike other watchkeepers who had leave in Archangel we had not had any since arrival.

Our purpose was the delivery of confidential books etc and to arrange accommodation in Moscow for the Admiral who was soon to leave us. The excitement kicked the depression and although it was now winter it just did not matter. To get away from Polyarnoe, although not to UK but to Moscow, I just could not wait or believe it. Within 2 days, loaded with confidential documents and enough food for a 3 or 4 day train journey, the Secretary, a Paymaster Lieutenant Commander, Alex, Andy and myself went by RAF launch in a raging blizzard to Murmansk to board the train for Moscow; ahead of us a journey of over 1,000 miles taking three and a half days. We spent the night at Intourist Hotel - three of us in a room with single beds, already sampling a piece of welcome luxury. The receptionist was a nice girl and spoke good English, all rather exciting as I had not spoken to any females for a long time, least of all in English. She thought I was the same age as her son, 17, and queried my paybook re the date, a good start to any journey.

Next morning it was still snowing with a blizzard, so I wondered what we were in for. We embarked on the train to Moscow, 12 coaches all of different categories. Right forward is about 6th class - hundreds of soldiers packed together (the smell was horrible - cigarettes, awful scent). In the middle, us, considered 2nd class and further along 1st class - curtains on the windows and quite posh but still the acrid smell of cigarette smoke. Each compartment had two 2-tier bunks, the CB's (confidential books) and stores took two and "Sec" and I were to sleep on the bottom two. Andy and Alex were in the next compartment. 0930 under way so the 4 of us had a Moscow Conference - our instructions for the journey. My first impression of the train was deadly, rough, dreary, untidy, rickety and noisy. We spent the time together in one compartment. An unusual situation this, 3 matelots travelling with a Lieut Commander. He must have felt the same, although the boss was good company. Our first "dummy run" meal was excellent considering conditions, tinned meat and potatoes cooked on 3 methylated spirit Tommy Cookers followed by pears and cream. When conversation dwindled we went to sleep with difficulty. At the end of the first day the Secretary produced a surprise bottle of Scotch and throwing rank and rate aside had a sing along to pass the time.

Marusha - the carriage attendant, a sweet young girl - 19, took a liking to us as we joined the train. She did not speak English, so we taught each other different words. The next day was same routine. Dinner and supper, a few tots, singing, a few canned beers in the evening to wash down the corned beef, baked beans and pickles. A game of cards, and as much sleep as was possible. The sec was very happy, as we were, and enjoyed this unusual role for an officer, even joining in a bit of fun.

As the train rattled noisily and lurched along the track through the snow-capped countryside of the Russian Steppes he would take "rounds" every morning. Standing out in the corridor in true naval style, feet well apart, hands behind the back while Alex, Andy and I got on with the tidy up, cleaning, scrubbing out and getting the whole compartment absolutely shipshape and Bristol fashion. One would go out in the corridor and report: "Ready for Rounds". He would come in with a bit of exaggeration as a joke wiping a white scarf here and there as they do in the real Navy, let alone trains, checking we had made a thorough good job. When he was satisfied he would say "all correct" and give us one of his wonderful salutes and we would give him one back. Then he would pipe "Up Spirits" and get the Scotch out.

On the journey we ate caviare. How could we possibly afford this? It was very cheap, only a few roubles. It was bought at a station halt and was wrapped in newspaper. One of the few luxuries on the train journey.

Alex was noted for his super custard and more so his toast, particularly in view of the meagre facilities on the train, especially so in our particular carriage. Threading a piece of string through the bread and lowering it into the depths of the big, old wood-burning stove outside in the corridor, he produced smoky yet very acceptable toast.

On one occasion in both directions the trains passed very close to the Finnish border. The soldier guards on the train manned the windows with rifles, big guns as well, loaded, pointing towards the direction the trouble would come from and we were given instructions to lie on the floor until we had passed the danger zone. When on occasions the train would appear to travel faster we could only assume that since stopping at the last station we had picked up some unusually drier wood. Everything runs on wood, engine, hot water boilers, so at every station there were piles of wood floating all over the corridors. Should we have ever ran out of fuel there were plenty of trees around, although they would be wet. We started to imagine having to stop en route, get out to cut down trees in order to continue our journey but fortunately the need never materialised.

By the third day we were very organised. Sleeping became more comfortable as we were nearing Moscow and weather improved, so no need for a blanket and a thick coat. Chatting to Russians in a coach down the train was a new experience, there being no restrictions as in Polyarnoe. We asked them along to join us, a Russian Officer who spoke a little English, his wife and another "busty wench" all sitting in our compartment; this was indeed an unusual pleasure, and, Alex, having brought along his Balalaika, played and sung Russian songs. They liked the Sec's whisky so stayed a while. We also met other interesting people, far more friendly than people north; a Polish airman, a Russian colonel,

ATS girl and a female railway engineer. Our Russian had improved a lot since the train left Murmansk, given more chance to practise.

At the end of 3 days having travelled through the Siberian countryside of pine trees and snow it became more interesting, lighter with the sun shining on the snow on the hills, a welcome sight. We had arrived at Moscow after our journey of three and a half days. I said goodbye to Marusha, very sentimentally, and was touched by her disappointment at my leaving and more so her request for a photograph. I promised to call and see her in Moscow, such a tearful farewell made everything already different. A large car from the mission, in which were loaded the sacks of CB's, took us to the English Mission known as ENGLISKY MISSI. What a fantastic place, just like the best hotel in London. A house, 5 colossal rooms, beautifully lit by a great chandelier in the middle of each; immediately three waiters rushed around and gave us dinner. Here were 10 army and 2 navy personnel giving us a great welcome and anxious to meet us. They certainly lived in the height of luxury, together with being waited on. It was all so friendly, especially the Russians, it made us feel wide awake and alive by comparison. Even further luxury, a hot bath before dinner, a fantastic welcome party until the early hours, a soft bed with clean sheets, waking next morning in broad daylight.

The first day our guide took us round Moscow. It was wonderful to see people, busy streets, trains and buses again. Being in No 1's although only one badge killicks, the so-friendly Muscovites thought we were officers and saluted as we passed. We visited Kremlin Red Square, St. Basils Church and Lenin's Tomb and many other marvellous buildings, thence to a cocktail bar in Gorky Street, a balcony all around, and oh so pretty waitresses, not in drab uniform, who actually spoke to us. 3 champagne cocktails and a liqueur later we were elated with enjoyment. In the evening a display of fireworks, Moscow's salute for taking another town at the front. From then on we were on our own each day.

Soon after leaving the mission, Andy ran away with a nice Russian girl. We walked the streets meeting many girls who could speak English. This was good fun, quite exciting as unusual. In search of a restaurant, we entered finding it to be an Actors Club. Bold as brass we walked up and down the main hall until a very gushing, English-speaking lady made us very welcome - introducing two professors and three Russian airmen. One, an air ace with the Order of Lenin, had an interesting conversation about Spitfires and Hurricanes, sent out from England. Then came my first visit to and use of the Metro.

It was strange to see the word Metro instead of the usual "Underground". Descending the hole in the ground you stand in amazement that you are, in fact, in the Metro, and underground. It was intended as a show-piece but quickly became a prize exhibit for foreign statesman and delegations. A symbol of the new Soviet Society, as a lone sailor underground it was the same.

The metro was to be more than just an efficient method of urban transport and much money was wasted in certain aspects of the construction which could have been put to better use, having regard to the poor living conditions in the capital at the time. Therefore a great amount was spent on the luxurious decoration of the stations with which their pilasters, statues and vast areas of marble were little less than underground palaces.

The stations of the Metro are finished with polished marble, granite and glazed tiles, adorned with sculptures bas-reliefs and mosaics. The Muscovites are proud, and rightly so, of their underground palaces with their spacious, airy, well-lit halls. The first 14 stations of the Metro alone are finished with more marble than was used in all the palaces built by Russian Tsars in the last 300 years. Soviet architects, sculptors and artists took part in building the stations. Not only is it comfort and convenience it is indeed a work of art.

In 1940 there were 13 stations, now there are 115. 117,000 commuters are carried daily through the 115 stations. Seven and a half million passengers journey in one day over a length of 122 miles. 7,300 trains a day carry the millions up and down hundreds of escalators. 20 express trains are made up of 130 carriages, meaning there's a train every 80 seconds travelling at a speed of 50 mph - all controlled by automatic devices. The stations are open from 0600 to 0100 each day.

Passengers can press a button on an electric map. When lit up it shows the best route to any of the 115 stations and tells how long it takes to get there.

The fare, once you are down the hole, is the same as it always was - 5 kopecks for any length of journey which is 3p. You don't pay any more until you come out and go back again. For 7 kopecks you can have a monthly season ticket using it as often as you like and still make a profit. (London Transport take note).

On one of the occasions during my stay in Moscow whilst amongst the crowds and gazing at the splendour of it all with great admiration, I found myself travelling in a compartment entirely on my own. Thinking how lucky I was, on alighting at my destination I was sworn and shouted at in Russian, and from all the gabble and gesticulation and my rough knowledge of the Russian language, realised that this compartment was reserved for pregnant women. Not knowing it at the time, for I was a lone sailor in a foreign country admiring the view of the fantastic Moscow Metro.

At the British Mission our hostess felt that our leave in Moscow would not be complete without a visit to the Bolshoi Theatre, particularly as the performance was "Swan Lake". We were allocated two tickets each; Alex Downing, being the tall, good looking one, kept his promise to visit Marusha (our train attendant) at her home a distance away in the suburbs of Moscow, inviting her to join him at the Bolshoi Theatre. He travelled by tram and eventually arriving at Dulvorski, an area of wooden shacks and slums. After difficult enquiries the shack-type home of Marusha was found to be spotlessly clean and homely. They returned to the Bolshoi Theatre where I was supposed to meet them. Going into a building and a gallery box my first thought was surely it should be larger than this. On stage were colourful costumes a lot of talking in Russian but no sign of an orchestra or music, something strange here. Realising with concern, I was not in the Bolshoi Theatre and because of my meagre knowledge of the language I was directed a few streets away and there, however could it have been missed the first time? was the massive, and so obviously the famous Bolshoi Theatre. Bolshoi is Russian for big - huge would be more like it. As I walked, somewhat bemused, even a little scared, into the auditorium I just stood awe-inspired at the magnificence of it all, knowing I was to see the most famous of all ballets "Swan Lake".

Around me in the auditorium were many young girls seeking admittance. So with a pretty girl on my arm I had only just met, the closest I had been to a female for nearly a year. She spoke only a little English, myself a little Russian but it seemed not to matter. We were together, she needed a ticket, I needed company - perfect. Lost in the vastness of the building and the splendour, our tickets took us to a box in the gallery. You have to arrive and be seated 30 minutes before the start of any performance, this gave me the opportunity to gaze at the young girl and the wonderful surroundings. The velvet curtains, crystal chandeliers with a background of gilt balconies and the red and golden interior, created a majestic, ceremonial atmosphere known all over the world. The pride of the Russian people and Soviet musical culture, 203 years old with a seating capacity of 6,000. The 5-tiered hall is 63 feet high, 75 feet long and 80 feet wide, the length of the stage is 100 feet, 21 feet longer than the audience. The whole theatre is lit by ornate 19th-century lamps creating a vast palace of gilded stucco, scarlet velvet with the glittering effect of crystal.

All kinds of miracles took place on stage, providing effects of lightning, fire, fog, snowstorm, even earthquake, the unique lighting controlled from a console. The scenery and costumes are made in 22 shops by 400 craftsmen. Unbelievably 3,000 people work these stage miracles: singers, dancers, two full symphony orchestras, one stage orchestra, engineers, stagehands, dressers, make up artistes, nine hundred in all in the opera, ballet, orchestra, chorus and mime group. Two thousand people of various traders are in its many shops. It has its own print shop, a museum and a belfry (as bells are required in some opera scenes). For over two hundred years the Bolshoi Theatre has had a choreographic school, entering its third century full of enthusiasm. I was told that it always seeks the new in art and intends to continue to acquaint people through its art with the immortal as well as the best modern works of the classical heritage.

A real fire in Khovanschina, a real fog in Midsummer Nights Dream. In Lyudmila the talking horse is most impressive and in Sleeping Beauty endless vistas of fairy kingdoms achieved by the use of a revolving panorama 260 feet long. The audiences watching more than fifty performances on stage per month not only applaud the artistes, but marvel at the magnificent stage scenery.

Swan Lake was no exception: the music of the large orchestra, so many dancers, the ballerina herself all giving a fantastic performance made it a wonderful evening of sheer enjoyment. However it was marred and spoilt by the British troops billeted in Moscow who, because there was nothing else to do, had been to the ballet so often and seen "Swan Lake" so many times. Olgei Lepreshenskia, the ballerina, would have to do 32 foueltes one after the other spinning around on her toes 32 times, and when doing so they would, in unison with the twirl, shout Oneee, Twooo, Threee, Fourrr in time with her. The Russians did not like this very much in spite of the tremendous applause they gave her each and every performance.

Now completely alone for the first time in this large city, my mind full of everything that had happened and unable to contact Alex in the mass exodus from the theatre, I had need to return to the British Mission by means of tram packed solid with people, hanging on the back, climbing on the roof as was normal. After 10 minutes I alighted with difficulty at what I thought was my stop and with horror realised I was on the wrong tram and going in the opposite direction. I could not make myself understood to any Russian because of meagre knowledge of the language so was walking around aimlessly, completely lost and nearing the curfew time of 2200, just gazing around. I was soon picked up, not by helpful pedestrians but two burly Russian Police, taken to the station and put in a cell for the unforgivable crime of enjoying my evening, and being in the streets after 2200 - fighting hard to make them understand. None of them could speak English so my Russian was put to the test. Following my constant NE PONNY MIATE (I do not understand) their constant PUTCHY MOO (why?) through fright and nerves I said slowly YA ENGLISKY MATROOS (I am an English Sailor) BOLSHOI DOM (big house) ENGLISKI MISSI (British Mission) MOSKVAW (Moscow) BOLSHOI BALLET OLGA LEPRESHENSKIA. The reply after all my effort was NE PONNY MIATE. NIET ENGLISKY MATROOS - at least six times I repeated, what a good job I was not drunk were my thoughts, it was difficult enough to send it out sober, although I might have been more calm if I'd had a drink. Arms were waving, fingers in imaginary gesticulating holes of a telephone, then in desperation ENGLISKY MISSI PAJOLSTA (English Mission please). Some thirty minutes later the most welcome sight of all - a British Army officer, an interpreter and two soldiers stood there offering the most wonderful words in English: "Come on, let's get you back to the Mission, shipmate", what a relief, my final plan had worked. It was a good laugh, but only afterwards, and I forgave them for their oneee, twoeee, threee, fourrr at the ballet!

Not all the fatalities of the convoys were committed to the sea. Like those who went down with their shipmates and perhaps moreso, those so alone from a lifeboat by survivors, too cold and weak, could hardly lift them over the side, or to utter words before they sank into the cold grey forbidding sea.

A number were buried ashore at Murmansk, in a cemetry at the top of a small hill overlooking the port, attended by the Russian women and children, and covered in leaves of the mountain ash.

By the gate is a memorial in Russian and English which reads:- *This memorial erected in memory of the warriors of the British Commonwealth of Nations and the United States of America who brought help to the Soviet Union during the Patriotic War 1941-1945.*

Not only naval personnel served ashore in North Russia. Naval Party 100 and 200 were not only part of the role of the R.N. The RAF were with us nearby at Vaenga.

The Army too served in Russia, Royal Engineers and REME operated the port control at Archangel and were at the British Mission in Moscow with various duties.

At Murmansk, high on the hill overlooking the Kola Inlet, at the end of the convoy route, stands a massive granite memorial, over 150 feet high, of a Russian soldier in memory of those who fought at the front and those who brought the supplies to the very inlet the statue overlooks.

Inscribed on the base plaque are the words:

"TO THE DEFENDERS OF THE ARCTIC REGION"

Naval Base Polyarnoe from Destroyer.

Meacon Hut, Vaenga - Mid-winter

Submarine surrender to HMCS Nene.

Naval Base Polyarnoe

'We Seven' Concert Party.

"Winter Olympics" Naval Party 100.

Sailors on skis.

Icebreaker Lenin.

Icebreakers off Archangel.

Captain of Icebreaker Lenin

HM Trawler 'Chiltern'.

Hauling timber to build 'M' cottage.

'M' cottage from South.

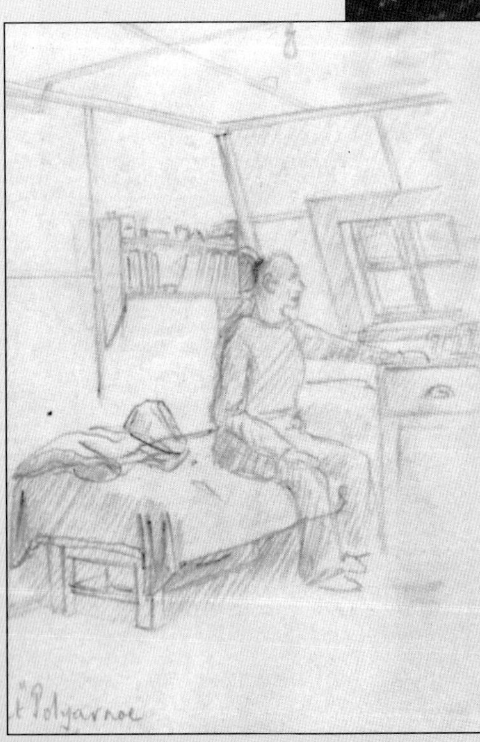

"Meacon Hut" Polyarnoe, June 1994

Meanwhile in Archangel, referred to in jest as the Las Vegas of the Arctic, were Naval Party 200, having the extra facilities of clubs, hotels, entertainment, cooks and waitresses and the risky, secret meetings and relationships, with the girls. But, nevertheless, the worst of the weather, fewer air raids.

The river Dvina being frozen over with ice up to 6 feet thick meant living in temperatures up to 50° below.

A few served aboard the Russian destroyers, especially the icebreakers crashing through thick ice to make a channel for the incoming and outgoing merchant ships also to avoid them becoming ice bound and "marooned" until the thaw many months later.

These men were the liaison communication ratings assisting the Russian captains and crew as they were not familiar with the International Morse Code.

On return from these hazardous trips they deserved the extra facilities, especially after the living conditions experienced aboard the ships to which they were seconded.

In Spring of 1943 **Edward Robson, Leading Signalman**, was informed he was on draft with the somewhat unenlightening title of Naval Party 200. These numbered parties could be for anywhere in the world - some of them small, highly secret operations, others for huge bases like Durban or Trincomalee. Naval Party 200 turned out to be Archangel, which sounded a bit uncomfortable but full of interest and excitement. About 50 mustered together with this party including some destined for Murmansk and Polyarnoe, Russian ports near the Norwegian border and well north of the Arctic Circle.

A few days later, with kitbags and hammocks, the party entrained at Chatham bound for Scapa Flow. The journey took about 12 hours. Arriving in the dark we were then hustled on to a picket boat and taken to what seemed to be a pre-war islands steamer now serving as a transit base.

My first view of Scapa Flow next morning was that it was a very bleak environment surrounded by grassy, rock-strewn landscape with not a tree in sight. A motley collection of vessels were scattered about. Later than afternoon we embarked on the destroyer **MAHRATTA** and sailed, doing a steady 20-25 knots in a choppy sea. We were informed that we were proceeding to Murmansk with mail and essential stores. Owing to huge convoy losses in the 24 hours daylight of the Arctic summer, sailings were restricted to fast naval vessels which could outrun U-boats, surface raiders and dodge aircraft. Convoys now ran only in the winter months under cover of darkness from November to April.

At 0200, dozing on the mess deck, I was aware of a change in speed and the vessel crashing through waves whipped up by wind from a different direction. We were tearing back to Scapa at over 30 knots. The Russians had apparently refused to issue visas and we would not be allowed to land, so the long journey back to Chatham began.

I was very disappointed, as the anticipation of the interesting experience of seeing an exotic, distant part of the world seemed to be off. It did however give us some idea of the suspicious nature of our remote 'allies', who apparently had no compunction in committing quite large parties to unnecessary journeys and expense.

We spent nearly six months messing about between Chatham and Cookham Camp with conflicting rumours that the draft was either on or off. Then in early October we all mustered again and the same long journey to Scapa was repeated. This time we were dumped on an old First World War Dreadnought **IRON DUKE**, anchored in the Flow.

We were on the "Duke" for about two days, then embarked yet again on **MAHRATTA** - this time on her own as our party had been reduced to about 30. It was now freezing cold and we headed north into grey, choppy seas and cutting winds. I recall thinking that about 5 minutes or less in that freezing sea would see anyone off.

You didn't get your passage for nothing in the RN and were expected to work watches with the regular ship's company. I was therefore on the bridge or flagdeck for 4 hours at a time. We continued north with ice building up on yards, stays and decks. The ventilation trunks on the mess decks were encased in ice and icicles like stalactites drooped from the vent ports. The bitter, freezing cold penetrated everywhere. We eventually arrived at Murmansk and were instantly conveyed (in the dark) by lorries to what was apparently an old hospital block, some miles from the main town. It was a depressing, hopeless environment. A loudspeaker on a telegraph pole, blared out a constant, distorted noise of speeches interspersed with selections of classical music. One soon recognised the Soviet National Anthem and a favourite overture was Rossini's Thieving Magpie.

One of the first impressions was the sweet, sweaty odour which seemed to pervade all Russian buildings and work-people. Part of this was contributed by the horrible herbal tobacco they smoked, hand rolled in a torn-off scrap of newspaper. The combination of the smouldering paper and coarse tobacco, known as 'mahorka' has to be smelt to be believed.

Packed, frozen snow lay on roadway and paths, it was in fact difficult to discern where tracks or rough ground ended or began. A few hundred yards from the buildings one emerged on to a wild, moorlike landscape, whose main plant life appeared to be a sort of bilberry.

I spent the time reading and trying to swot up Russian, translating all the signs and printed notices with the help of a dictionary. I could now at least read the letters and words albeit rather slowly. We had few duties, seldom saw any officers, most of my companions seemed bored to death. One or two of them caught "crabs" and this was the first time I had seen this unpleasant parasite which bores under the skin causing violent itching and a nasty rash.

After about a week we were taken to the quayside and embarked on a fleet minesweeper bound for Archangel. It was a most cramped but uneventful voyage. Most of the party and ship's company spent the time playing cards, so I took up a hand.

We eventually sailed up the Dvina - the White Sea had not yet frozen over completely - and from Vozkressensky Quay we and our gear were lorried to Karl Marx House, a large, single storey, wooden building on the banks of the Dvina about three quarters of a mile from the centre of Archangel.

Coming into a small hall through the two sets of doors was a rack of about twenty Sten guns, the first I had seen. The whole time I was there we were never instructed how to use them. I often wondered what the Russians thought as they seemed more likely to be turned on them than the German enemy.

Part of the site of Karl Marx House was a group of small huts which housed three radio transmitters and generators for emergency power. The keys and operators were at Norway House half a mile away and the lines ran with telephone wires on poles through the streets.

There would be about 30-40 personnel at Karl Marx but as a number were watchkeeping and others at sea or other duties a full complement was seldom there at one time. There would be about 10 telegraphists, 3 signalmen, the remaining population were coders, writers, supply assistants, petty officers and a motor mechanic who looked after the generators and also acted as chauffeur for a three-ton truck, jeep and a motor cycle.

We were in the larger rooms holding eight or ten beds and a few wooden chairs. Very bare but the space was most welcome after cramped mess decks and the seething mass of humanity in barracks. Accommodation was however relatively confined as the personnel we were relieving were still on hand and would remain so for a few weeks until the next convoy. Many of these had been in Russia when the base opened in 1941 and some were suffering from an over-indulgence of both alcohol and sex. I was keen to learn the ropes from my predecessor as soon as possible but found him rather aloof and most uncommunicative to the extent I felt he despised us 'new boys' and considered himself on a different plane. Whether he was any good as a signalman I was unable to assess. I should think he had forgotten most of it. He always looked as if he could do with a good bath but I did envy him his mastery of the language which surpassed that of any other Englishman.

The food was fantastic for wartime. RN Stores were supplemented by exotic Russian items such as smoked salmon and caviare. Large plates of smoked salmon lay on the table, this was often neglected by many of my less knowledgeable mates who much preferred the good old John West, pink or red, canned fish, which was also in abundance from our Naval stores. I ate more smoked salmon in three months than most people consume in a lifetime. The caviare was a little more difficult. It was in half pound slabs and my first few tastes did not arouse much excitement. It just seemed to be a glutinous fishy-flavoured mass. Knowing its high cost in the west and its exalted reputation, I persevered and found it an acquired taste and soon looked forward to the delicious salt, sea tang much prized by gourmets. A cheaper, red variety, which resembled a dollop of juicy, fish-flavoured frog spawn, was not so appetizing. We were waited upon hand and foot by the kitchen staff, most of whom were quite attractive young girls, they were hand picked by the authorities as 'trustworthy' Soviet citizens and were expected to report any titbits of interesting information to party members. They did not appear to know any English or at least gave the outward impression of not doing so. Over the months my colleagues became very friendly with some of them so the Soviet authorities often removed them. Later, I was suspicious of a girl who fraternised ardently and continued at the base over a long period. For the staff it was obviously a prized job, with access to so much food when the rest of the population was starving.

As the months passed, a few of my more ignorant compatriots treated the staff like dirt with complete disregard for their feelings. Coming back from an icebreaker trip one day, after witnessing the terrible deprivation in surrounding towns, I was appalled to see one youth feed a full, untouched plate of corned beef to one of our two Alsatians - which were about the only dogs left in Archangel, the rest had been killed and eaten long ago. I noticed the poor girl serving us blanch with disgust, knowing that her own family and friends could have relieved starvation with that food. A heated argument ensued which almost came to blows. He developed a very strong anti-Russian complex - after coming out to Archangel with quite strong Communist tendencies. Not a good advertisement for the English way of life, and an ignorant bore who gained little pleasure from anything in life.

On one occasion we completely failed to get on the air with an important signal to London and the Captain lent me his Humber Snipe and chauffeur - the only car on the site - to drive out to the radio station. The guards on the gate refused to let me in, but eventually a senior member of the staff in a non committal manner half agreed to comply. In view of his aloof and disdainful manner I was not too confident but by the time we got back they were merrily transmitting to Admiralty, it must have been the large, shiny car which did it, as Russian officials were seldom impressed by mere ratings.

To avoid frequent trips to the radio station it was decided to erect a mast for better reception and transmission of signals to Admiralty. Ed Robson witnessed with admiration, the erection of this new wireless mast at Karl Marx, using only very basic implements. Owing to the low power of the transmitters it was considered improved clarity could be gained by increasing the height of the aerial. So with the help of our Russian joiner, three or four long straight fir trunks were joined end to end with steel collars, which also carried the guy rope shackles. It was built up on the ground and using an antique hand winch, hoisted vertical. The base of the mast was set in a short, heavy log which acted as a pivot or roller-bearing on a base of small trunks secured between 4 heavy posts driven deep into the ground. It was nearly 70ft high and weighed well over a ton with all its guys and shackles. No officers seemed to be involved, although presumably they had authorised the project, the mast was still there in perfect condition when leaving Russia months later. A brilliant piece of seamanship and innovation.

In Archangel, and other bases, timber was the main construction material, almost all pavements consisted of long, thick planks. In winter these were covered with a layer of ice and snow but at least they were more or less anchored in place. During spring and autumn before the complete thaw or freeze-up, you had to watch where you were stepping, as a loose plank could pivot and freezing, muddy water could spray over you as it splashed back. House occupants were ordered to clear away heavy falls of snow off the pavement surrounding their building and were often fined for not doing so. As there was so little traffic and the streets very wide, miniature mountains of snow in the gutter - or where the gutter should have been - did not cause much inconvenience. It was always eventually cleared from main thoroughfares.

Late in 1944 there was great activity at Norway House. At the time we were unaware what was afoot as it was all top secret. It turned out to be a heavy bombing raid on the **TIRPITZ** (German battleship) in a Norwegian fjord. Bomber Command decided: owing to the range and exceptional size of the bomb load the planes had insufficient fuel for the return journey to their English bases, so it was planned to drop the bombs and fly on to a much nearer airfield in North West Russia, refuel and return home. The raid was most successful and the **TIRPITZ** was sunk or so completely disabled she was out of the war. She was a great menace, particularly to the Russian convoys, and we had few vessels powerful enough to take her on. This seemed to be one of the few occasions when we had full co-operation from the Russians but it was also very much in their interest as well.

The heat and sun although very welcome after the dreary winter brought with it plagues of midges and even the flies seemed more vicious than their English brethren. Another objectionable experience was meeting the horse-drawn, open dung cart, plodding steadily through the streets. We were fortunate in Karl Marx having a rather vintage WC but most Russian houses at that time did not go in for such advanced sanitary appliances. A hole in the floor of a small closet at the rear of the building had to suffice. This was emptied periodically by the staunch individual with the dung cart, who gained access to his 'stock' by means of a trapdoor at ground level. In winter the smell would be fairly well contained but in hot weather the stink defied description. I sometimes wondered where these tons of manure went - probably just dumped in the river. It certainly stank pretty badly too. One of our chaps accidently dropped his Ronson lighter down one of these primitive earth closets. He could see it glint in the smelly depths below but did not have the courage to attempt to retrieve it.

As was experienced at other bases only infrequent deliveries of mail in the summer months though the odd destroyer or submarine brought essential stores and mail to Murmansk at intervals and a courier arrived by train occasionally. There was always a great rush to write letters to catch returning convoys or individual vessels.

At the stuffy, smelly, Post Office I became known to the assistants, some of whom became very friendly. One in particular, finding I was a stamp collector, kept selections of the better used copies for me and in return she welcomed the odd bar of chocolate or cigarettes. I took her out to the International Club one night but wished I hadn't as she disappeared overnight into a labour camp. When I asked her colleague where she was the only reply was "sovsyem nye boodyet" which translated literally means 'completely finished'. The cold dread of those words still chills me to the bone. I had agreed with her before that she would let me know if she was moved but the poor girl never had the chance and was arrested because the authorities did not trust her to fraternise with foreigners. I thought with horror what a ghastly system it must be where people just disappear overnight without trial. Like most of the ordinary folk I met in Russia she was just a hard working, lively person, incapable of doing anyone any harm but she had posed a threat to that system by learning too much about the free world.

The Archangel street scene was understandably depressed and drab owing to the war and lack of consumer goods, but even in times before the conflict things would not have been much brighter. Absolutely no attempt was made to smarten up premises even in the town centre. Shop windows carried no advertising and it was often difficult to know from the outside what many of them would have for sale even if they had had any stock. Posters in the streets carried only giant portraits of the ubiquitous Lenin and Stalin and exhortations to the workers to strive even harder to support the Red Army. Another frequent gaudy poster proclaimed "Death to the German occupation". The distorted blare from the loudspeakers echoed down the streets and I felt sorry for those inhabitants who were unfortunate to reside next to one.

Whilst talking to one of the senior administrators, an elderly artist noticed I was regularly referring to a Russian dictionary and asked me if I was interested in learning the language. She offered to give me some private tuition which was readily accepted and we agreed a time and date for one afternoon at the club. She spoke fluent English so her assistance would be most helpful, particularly with colloquial and grammar complexities. It was, however, disappointing to discover that she was obviously trying to obtain a detailed timetable of the movements of myself and others on the base, and a schedule of our activities. The strain of both trying to translate her questions and carefully phrasing my replies to give no information of value away, was so exhausting I gave up after two sessions. She had obviously been planted there by the NKVD (Peoples Commissariat for Internal Affairs - the much feared Secret Police) - to glean all possible intelligence from the English and other visitors to the Club. Vodka and beer was on sale in the bar, so they picked up some quite useful information from some of our more indulgent colleagues. Apart from a cursory warning when we landed, to act with discretion and not upset our Russian hosts, I do not recall ever having been forewarned of the tactics likely to be encountered in such places as the club. Perhaps our own senior officers were not aware of the dangers or thought none of us knew anything of much military or political use.

Female labour was used everywhere in Archangel. Even the heaviest labouring jobs used gangs predominantly of women. They used to pick away at snow and holes in the road, wrapped up in heavy drab padded jackets and thick headscarves. It seemed very ungentlemanly to us naive English.

It was rumoured that if a member of a family died during the winter, the body was placed in an attic or outhouse if one existed, where under freezing conditions it was preserved. The remaining family members continued to draw the food ration until Spring when the thaw forced them to dispose of the body. There seemed to be a spate of funerals at the outset of warmer weather.

> Although Ed Robson's draft was to Naval Party 200, ashore he soon found himself seconded for duty in the Russian ice-breakers with some awful experiences. The Yeoman at the base told him to meet the next convoy into Archangel and was to take an Aldis lamp and batteries and join Ice-breaking Tug No. 6 at Vosskressenski Quay:

At the appointed time we were taken by jeep to the quay and on board met the Russian interpreter. The tug was about 250-300 tons - quite a substantial little vessel but didn't look much like an ice-breaker. I subsequently discovered she was not too effective in thick, solid ice, but her engine power could easily cope with mush and broken pack ice which was more than enough to strand a merchant ship.

I was given a bunk in a space aft, which also accommodated several petty officers or the Russian merchant navy equivalent. They were very friendly and seemed to have terrific respect for the RN and its personnel. We put to sea almost at once and were told that it would be next day before we met up with the convoy. My Russian was very limited at this time, so conversation with my seafaring allies was somewhat stilted. A picture of a serious-looking gentleman was attached to the bulkhead and to make some sort of chat, asked them who it was. They told me with pride that it was Andrei Zshdanov, who had made his name as a great leader in Leningrad and was now a member of the Supreme Soviet. They were most impressed with my wristwatch, which my parents had given me for a 21st birthday present. In Russia, then, only high officials sported wristwatches, the rest of the populace had to make do with large, heavy pocket watches. Some of them attached these large dials with a strap to their wrists and they really did look ludicrous. They were even more shattered when they saw the Rolls razor next morning, they had never seen anything like it before. It was quite like being in the jungle and showing the natives a gramophone for the first time. What I think really puzzled them was how a mere rating could own such things when their own propaganda had informed them that in the West, officers and landowners were the ruling class: ratings were like serfs and all but a few were living in Dickensian, poverty-stricken conditions far worse than in the USSR. Some months later when next on board this tug, I was incensed to learn that the political representative had told them that these possessions together with the quality of the uniform were special issue by the UK Government to give the impression to outsiders that all was well in England. It had to be realised that the average Russian had little idea what went on outside the USSR and were brainwashed by their own one-sided propaganda.

We had the first meal on board in a small saloon amidships. The food was quite revolting. Greasy cabbage soup of sauerkraut flavour, followed by 'Kasha' (literally translated as porridge) consisting of greasy, boiled buckwheat with odd bits of chopped meat scattered amongst it. There was black bread and expecting this to be something like a rather coarse English wholemeal, took a small piece from the basket on the table. It can only be described as tasting of a mixture of sand and vinegar and bore no resemblance to any bread ever sampled. This bread was the staple diet of the Russian people, at the worst they were down to a ration of only 100gms per day, but could only manage three mouthfuls, despite being hungry. To our spoilt English palates it was scarcely edible. The thought that I might have to survive on this awful food for a week or more was dreadful.

The Russian interpreter appeared to be a weedy, pasty-faced little man with small, round, steel rimmed spectacles. I thought he looked rather out of place amongst happy-go-lucky seafaring men and, in fact, I think it was about his first trip to sea. He was a graduate of Leningrad University and was fluent in English, with a fairly extensive vocabulary which he was always trying to extend. He had never been outside Russia and his English accent was not too good. I had a feeling there was something insincere about him and was sure he was a Communist Party member and we became bored stiff by his long discourses on the superiority of the Russian way of life. Later I was to dislike him intensely and perhaps rather unwisely got into arguments with him. He sometimes introduced me to ship's personnel as: "This is Signalman Robson - a very patriotic Englishman". It was said with a slight sneer and which hinted I was also an anti-Soviet.

Our vessel ran into heavy mist and we took some days to rendezvous with the convoy which was also late. Ice was only scattered and thin. After guiding the ships to the estuary we made various signals organising pilots to take the vessels in across the bar and then had to wait for the pilots to arrive. Whilst waiting we tied up alongside an American liberty ship and invited ourselves on board for a decent meal. After three or four days of Russian food I sat down in the American crew's quarters and tucked into ham and eggs, great slabs of cream gateau and ice cream. It was heaven and I have seldom appreciated a meal so much. I had several meals on board one or other of their ships and the food was always superb. They also restocked me with a Dutch brand of pipe tobacco and gave me one of their throw-away corn cob pipes which I found smoked beautifully cool. I used it for months. In turn they were bursting for information about life on shore and I warned them that there was nothing much to look forward to.

As winter closed in, the ice became thicker and the river Dvina froze over hard. Only an ice-breaker the size of LENIN could keep a narrow channel open and later even this was closed. Our next trip was to be on board the ice-breaker LENIN which was lying at Molotovsk and involved a train journey from Archangel. The railway station was on the south bank of the river so we had to cross the river which at that point must be about 450-500 yards wide. Our transport took us and our gear - kit bags, Aldis lamp and batteries - to the crossing point about half a mile upstream and we trudged across the ice to the centre of the river. There was a stream of Russians tramping across in both directions, some with heavy sledges and others humping heavy loads. Where the ice-breaker had cracked a channel probably 30ft wide, were floating wooden duckboards about 3ft in width. These were encrusted with slippery ice and bobbed about in the water. We had been issued with high leather jack boots which we wore with thick sea boot and normal stockings to keep out the cold. They were not however the ideal footwear for retaining a grip on the ice. Russians universally wore Valinkees, a sort of wellington made of compressed felt. They were useless in wet weather as the felt became sodden but just the job for hard frozen snow and ice - very warm and gave good adhesion.

It was really scary, slipping and staggering across the narrow boards encumbered with baggage, the icy water of the Dvina flowing beneath. Apart from freezing to death if you fell in, you could easily be swept under the ice, to be washed up on some distant White Sea shore, weeks later. The worst part was when you had to pass someone coming in the opposite direction, perhaps with a bulky load. It was easy to lose your balance if they brushed heavily against you and they took it all in their stride and made no allowance for our unsuitable footwear. I understood a number of people did fall in during the course of the year. Some lucky ones suffered no more than an uncomfortable wetting and frostbite, others were never seen again.

Having negotiated this frightening obstacle we crawled up the bank on the opposite side and some distance along a well-worn snow track came to the sidings of the railway station. There are seldom any platforms on Russian provincial railway stations. You just clamber across the tracks and climb up into the train from ground level. There were only 2nd and 3rd class coaches, the 2nd class was pretty full but the 3rd was packed to suffocation. People were crammed into rough hewn, timber joist types of cages and also down the central gangway. Our coach was fitted with wide 'shelves' in compartments face to face on either side of the central gangway. The middle shelf was hinged so that it could be fastened back, enabling the passengers to sit upright during the day or for short journeys, but to sleep stretched out six to a compartment at night. We chugged along at about 20 mph and our fellow travellers settled down with their 'Isvestias' and 'Pravdas', occasionally tearing off a piece to roll themselves a fag. The ubiquitous Russian odour, hot, sweaty and sweet, assailed our sensitive English noses. They were however quite matey and chatty and apart from the 'foreign' smell I put up with it like any other travellers enduring war-time journeys. Some of the more affluent looking smoked 'papirosas', posh Russian cigarettes mounted on a cardboard tube.

It seemed to be hours before we reached Molotovsk, where a Russian-driven jeep took us to a small house which served as a mini English outpost. I was never quite clear as to what the purpose of this little base was. It was manned only by a Lieut. RNVR, a telegraphist and Russian cook/general maid. It did however provide us with a reasonably comfortable billet en route to the quayside.

Early the following morning we were up and away, slithering and stumbling over a rough, icy track to the docks several miles away. My kit bag and the heavy, lead acid Aldis batteries became more weighty at every step. The kit bag was weighted down with tins of food and chocolate to eke out the awful Russian food.

We were met at the gates by our interpreter, a well-built, cheerful, friendly man of about 35. He spoke good English, but with an American accent. We found we could not gain access to the quay without a special docks pass. I had been issued with an official pass by the Russians in Archangel (for specified English personnel). This had to be produced for rail travel and when demanded by police, etc. It was apparently no use for the port of Molotovsk and despite the interpreter's obviously persuasive arguments, the quayside gate guard refused to let us through. After much discussion we were allowed to proceed with an armed sentry to the docks police office, where we were scrutinised and a check made, presumably with the ice-breaking controllers. They marched us back to the gate and deposited us in a hot, smelly hut outside. We then went on to the quayside and walked about half a mile to the LENIN moored at the far end behind a row of ships we had brought in a week or so earlier. Whilst on the quay, I was astonished to see thousands of tons of war material of every conceivable type, some of which seemed to have been there for months and the piles were constantly being added to, as more and more ships got through. It was apparent that the rail network was incapable of moving it fast enough. Food consignments - which could easily be pilfered by the starving population - and very urgent goods were moved first. One would have thought however during the summer lull, when only odd loads were arriving, they would have cleared the backlog from the previous season. It also seemed that their administration was bureaucratic and inefficient and this must have contributed to the chaos.

On this trip I was with an RNVR Lieut. He was a bearded young man of about 24. He took everything in his stride and nothing seemed to worry him. Partly because of this and his amenable approach to everything, all my trips with him went extremely smoothly, at least as far as our part of the operations were concerned. His dry sense of humour and lack of pretension was most appreciated.

The LENIN looked like an old 1890's heavy cruiser with wide beam and twin tall, erect funnels. A couple of 3-inch or 4-inch guns had been mounted fore and aft with a few heavy machine guns to ward off aircraft. She was about 6000 tons, coal fired; the design was exceptional in that one of the triple screws was mounted below the bows deep under the waterline. This made her very manoeverable and the captain was adept in exploiting this facility, working the ship in and out of congested ports and anchorages with ease.

Three of us had a cabin on the port side just aft of the large saloon, below the wheelhouse and bridge. The saloon was rather dark as it was panelled in heavy mahogany but the general impression was one of Victorian luxury and solidity. Heavy brass fittings - lamps, ports and brackets, etc. were of high quality and obviously dated from a more affluent age. This was confirmed when strolling on the afterdeck, I saw a brass plate above the engine room companionway which revealed that she was built as the "Alexander Nevski" in 1913, by Wallsend Slipway, Newcastle. It was quite exciting joining up with this ship, built only 20 miles from my own home and I felt that this could be a good omen, also a wonderful advert for British craftsmanship and their ability to build something of lasting quality.

Eventually LENIN got under way and we ploughed out to sea and the beginning of the ice. Almost immediately we were crunching through thick ice, making a channel for three or four merchant ships, who were returning in ballast or laden with timber, which was about the only export Russia could spare.

Except in very extreme weather the Barents Sea, in the vicinity of Murmansk, is fairly free of ice all the year round. The White Sea tends to freeze over completely between November and March. The entrance to the White Sea from the north passes through a fairly narrow channel or throat - known as 'the Gorla'.

It is here that the heaviest ice was encountered, conditions being made more difficult by high easterly winds piling up huge icefields on the western shore. Our job was to lead the freighters out to clear water in the Barents Sea and bring back five loaded vessels from a recently arrived convoy. The ships followed us in single line ahead, keeping to the broken channel. LENIN seemed to have no difficulty whatsoever in pushing through ice over two feet thick.

Although the technique of ice-breaking was never explained, it was apparent that the ship did not actually cut through thick ice, like a snow plough, shifting snow. The hull was cut away at the bows just on the waterline which enabled the whole weight of the forepart of the ship to ride over and bear down on the edge of the ice, fracturing it into huge slabs which splashed back into the water. Above six feet thick, progress was slower as the ship lost momentum owing to the resistance and pressure of the ice on the side of the hull, then we would go astern and take a run in the cleared channel until the next barrier of virgin ice was encountered. The clang of the engine room telegraph resounding throughout the ship, the thump of the 8000 hp engines and the crash of the breaking ice against the hull, diminishing in sound volume to a gentle crunch as speed reduced and momentum was lost against the restraint of the solid ice ahead.

On the bridge it was fascinating watching great chunks rearing up contrasting the whiteness of the snow-covered floes with the grey water beneath. Often seen were families of seals, clumsily trying to put some distance between the ship and themselves, sometimes too slow and occasionally getting squashed between the ship and the unbroken ice edge.

A fair amount of signalling occurred both outward and on the return ship with the heavily laden vessels and sometimes hours at a time were spent on the bridge and at night often hove to if the ice was heavy, as it was not advisable to show other than very dim navigation lights, owing to random reconnaissance flights by Junkers 88's. The further north we were the more spectacular were the Aurora or Northern Lights. These great moving curtains of light were quite brilliant some nights and lit up the snowscape with eerie, if faint reflections.

In the Barents Sea the handover was successfully accomplished and the trek south proceeded with reasonable speed. Occasionally a ship became stuck and LENIN had to run back to re-open the channel. It was noticed that despite her age, she had a fair turn of speed for this type of vessel and could crack up a good 18 knots in free water.

A few days later we arrived off Molotovsk. Whilst waiting for them to proceed with pilots, we went down to dinner and the captain appeared with a bottle of vodka, suggesting we drink to the completion of a successful operation. Being teetotal, I did not drink either beer or spirits. The captain started apologising for not having any rum or brandy, thinking it was the vodka I didn't like, so, as he was a decent sort and language difficulties could not make my attitude clear, decided to try the vodka and downed a huge tumblerful. It was surprisingly good and my palate was so dulled I even relished the fish soup and greasy millet kasha with meat shreds, which constituted our evening meal. I fear from then on I was an enthusiastic drinker and sampled any alcoholic tipples that were on offer.

We left the LENIN late that night and made our way to the little English base where the Russian lass knocked up a very tasty omelette from the tinned dried egg imported from England. It was surprisingly good. We then endured a smelly train journey back to Archangel and that awful crossing of the Dvina, but at least the baggage was lighter as we had eaten all 'iron rations' on the voyage.

The next trip was again from Molotovsk on the much newer Russian-built ice-breaker, JOSEF STALIN. She was the biggest and most powerful of their breaker fleet at about 10,500 tons. Built on the same principle as the LENIN with twin screws aft and one forward - no doubt the Russians simply studied the sample they had and constructed a larger version.

I found myself sharing a cabin with two Russian petty officers. They were very chatty and hospitable and took me down to the main mess for lunch, before which I was plied with liberal quantities of vodka, or so I thought. But it turned out to be almost neat spirit, distilled from either potatoes or wood, being ignorant of the fact that you were supposed to dilute it with equal parts of water. So my first mouthful of the almost neat spirit therefore nearly blew my head off, much to the amusement of my hosts, who then diluted this 'fire-water' for me. As a result, I was fairly drunk and back on my bunk recovering, when the inevitable call came "signalman wanted on the bridge". On my way, I brought up the last meal and some of the spirits outside the wheelhouse. I left it for them to clean up and no doubt the resident political officer was able to make some capital out of the 'disgusting habits of the British'. Fortunately the signal, to a minesweeper, was fairly short and simple, just as well for I was still not in very good mental shape to tackle anything complex.

Ice and weather conditions were very difficult on this voyage. We crunched out to the Barents Sea and collected six or seven ships from the escort, comprising both RN and Russian destroyers and then re-entered heavy ice fields in the White Sea. For days we seemed to be straining to make progress south with painful slowness. In one 24 hour period, it was noticed, after a furtive glance at the chart, that we were actually a mile or two further back than on the day before. The whole convoy was drifting in a giant ice field. It was bitterly cold and the ice was thickening all the time. One day it was so bad that we had all ships stuck and even the STALIN was finding it difficult to manoeuvre. The Luftwaffe then chose that moment to fly over the ships with a couple of Junkers 88's. The Russians got very excited and let fly with everything, but no bombs were dropped. It was just a routine spotting flight.

Off watch with my petty officer friends below I was getting along famously. We had long rather exhausting discussions on every subject under the sun from religion to food and drink. They were most interested in my past sea time experiences on Atlantic convoys and the North African landings. They had an enormous respect for British seafarers and nothing was too much trouble for them. They lent me a pair of 'valinkees' from the ship's store to replace the heavy leather boots, which even with thick sea-boot stockings, left your feet icy cold after standing about for hours on an open bridge in 30-40 degrees of frost.

One day whilst exploring the STALIN (without making it too obvious) I found a door open to a fairly large cabin and looked inside. The walls were draped with red and black crepe or some similar material and the first impression was that a story of Edgar Alan Poe had come to life. It was apparently a 'Krassny Oogolok' - Red Corner. A sort of shrine to communism and the Russian way of life. I learnt that all ships of any size have these 'corners' which are used for political indoctrination and a quiet retreat for individuals to contemplate, no doubt, the joys of the Soviet system. All rather bizarre.

Thinking his ice-breaker service days were over and back to a comfortable billet, Ed Robson found himself yet again back to sea in a Russian ship, this one a trawler and recalls even worse conditions.

The trawler was old, slow and shabby - built in the 1920's. I was given a tiny cabin right in the stern, just over the screw. When she was steaming the vibration was quite alarming. It felt as though the rivets were being shaken out of the plates. The cabin had a small steam heater which was impossible to adjust and one had to shed the voluminous Arctic clothing immediately on entering or dissolve in a pool of sweat. I sometimes opened the port during daytime but the freezing blast of icy air then reduced me to a shivering wreck in a matter of seconds. The cabin led off from the main saloon or mess where I dined with the interpreter, skipper and mates. The tropical heat in the cabin was much enjoyed by the resident population of cockroaches, ever seen in such a small space, or such giant specimens. They scurried across the deck as I entered and switched on the light. It was an ideal spot to study the lifestyle of the cockroach, if only they had not been so prolific. I spent some time trying to reduce the overcrowding by squashing them, but gave up, as if anything, the population seemed to multiply. The cabin also had an unpleasant background odour, reminiscent of decomposing rodents, but it may have been dying 'roaches.

The trawler's sanitary arrangements left much to be desired. I used to dread the 'call of nature'. The mates and some of the crew used a tiny W.C. in a cubicle on the port side. The pan was a small, round, cast iron contraption, lacking a seat and about three feet above the rim was a stout pole from bulkhead to bulkhead. If you sat down you had to lean forward with the pole across your back and shoulders. Its purpose was apparently to deter people from standing on the rim. It was undesirable to sit on the actual pan and you needed to be a contortionist to crouch over the rim. Another disgusting feature was that the soiled paper was placed in a box at the side. The small orifice of the pan would be choked if you dropped the bits of used Pravda down it, so the stink was appalling. I mentioned this curious pole arrangement which brought hysterical laughter - as it was thought I had tried to sit on it like a parrot on a perch.

I noticed on my inspection tour of the upper deck that they had two or three fat pigs in a sty which also did not smell too sweet.

My private food supply was almost exhausted after a few days and I had the depressing thought of spending Christmas day aboard, so kept a large tin of Maconochie's meat and vegetables and a couple of bars of chocolate for my Christmas dinner. Food was very short on the ship. Even the Russians looked hungry and it is surprising what you can eat as starvation begins to creep up. I even relished the fish soup and sucked the revolting head floating in it. I had never been so hungry, having reached the stage when all you can think of is the delicious meals you have had in the past. I was so relieved when we entered harbour that I hurried back as fast as possible to Karl Marx and wolfed down a massive meal. The date was 24th December!

Having completed my voyaging away from the base - I had often been back only for odd days between trips - I was rather out of touch with what had been happening. One very unpleasant aspect was the large number of our people going sick with VD. Russian girls were in the main quite attractive and many of my mates lost no time in fraternising with them. Many girls lived on their own - families were split up, all men of military age were away and any offer of food, chocolate or cigarettes in the starvation-afflicted city was a welcome fee for their 'services'. What our people did not realise at the time was that a particularly virulent strain of gonorrhea raged through the female inhabitants. This was partly due to the fact that many Russians had dosed themselves fairly liberally with the recently available drugs and a resistant strain of the disease had become widespread. During the summer of 1944, I estimated that almost 50% of the numbers left on the base were infected by the disease in varying stages of intensity. M & B tablets, our then usual remedy, seemed to have little impact, but I think subsequent variants or the introduction of the new penicillin drugs probably cleared it up later. I was very glad I had not had the chance to indulge owing to being away at sea and had no intention of doing so now. The poor physical state and appearance of some otherwise healthy young men was then to me a strong deterrent.

Ed Robson had many other trips to sea in ice-breakers with similar appalling conditions. Spending more time at sea than ashore as his draft to Naval Party intended, he gained experiences he never thought would happen or be seen. From all these his most vivid and upsetting memory of time ashore was en route from Archangel to join a ship:

We were walking down to the quay, with all our gear, and passed on the way a great shambling mass of about 60 or 70 men, escorted by armed guards with dogs. They came trudging past us from the direction of the port. It was a contingent from the nearby labour or concentration camp. They were clothed in heavy padded jackets, worn and dirty, and rough cloth caps were pulled down over their heads. A look of numbed, hopelessness was expressed on their faces. I could imagine the cold, the starvation diet and foul living conditions they would have to endure for years. Probably their only crime was that they had criticised some aspect of Soviet life and were therefore considered to be enemies of the state. They now provided cheap labour for that system. This chance meeting with concentration camp victims in the icy dawn of Molotovsk, a terrifying condemnation of a ruthless, brutal system. I was told that the port of Molotovsk was built entirely by convict labour. It was a depressing, expressionless place, probably haunted by the ghosts of those who died, slaving to construct it.

Writer Joseph French arrived in Archangel from Murmansk to join Naval Party 200 in the depth of an Arctic winter. Getting over the ice-bound river from the station to the town opposite, and after the grey barren scene around the Kola Inlet, the sight of the cluster of wooden dwellings untouched by the bombing, as in Murmansk, was surely something of an improvement. The scene did change as he subsequently found in the summer, when there was green vegetation with almost tropical heat and mosquitoes abounding.

But during the winter it all appeared grim with so many people around you, seemingly without hope, going about daily tasks with bleak prospects ahead of them. There was deep snow, with roads kept clear by an army of strong-limbed Russian women dressed in the usual drab padded coats, malinki boots, fur caps pulled well down, just showing pale under-nourished faces beneath. Wooden-planked pavements where deep snow, trodden down hard, had lifted the level near to adjacent buildings and deep ditches forming open sewers beneath. The smell from the sewers in summer was always predominant and the largest rats ever seen were running around pavements and in the houses for scraps of food.

My billet was at Karl Marx House by the banks of the River Dvina, and these were reasonably comfortable as the whole building was well heated with wood-burning fires. In Russia there was always a plentiful supply of wood and huge logs were stored in the yard, sawn up ready for use. The fires for the heating of the premises were fed by elderly Russians, glad no doubt to have a good job where plenty of square meals were provided. At Karl Marx House this job was carried out by a very polite Russian of the old school who was affectionately given the name of Wilson "the gentleman's gentleman", bowing to us in the corridor when we met, in the manner of a gentleman's servant. I remember once we got him drunk, as he was very partial to alcohol, after having sunk a whole bottle of our NAAFI supply of gin, and afterwards regretted getting him into trouble for having to sleep it off when on duty later.

There were many more opportunities for entertainment in Archangel than at Murmansk - two cinemas the ARC and EDISON, a Bolshoi theatre, a circus and a sports stadium. There was also the International Club, with entertainments where regular invitations were issued to the British and American personnel with reciprocal events organised by the British Mission in return. I took part in most of the entertainments that were going - there were also dances arranged at the International Club, with a supply of attractive dancing partners provided. It became obvious that many attractions laid on had other motives behind them in that questions often guardedly directed seemed to imply more interest in what was going on in the secret activities of the British Naval Base than interest in the social attractions.

Compared to Polyarnoe and Murmansk this was surely the Las Vagas of the Arctic!

In the town itself there was continual noise from loud speakers positioned at every corner - all radio sets were taken away from the public and the only news available was from the public speakers with Russian music in between. Joe remembers when the Russian national anthem changed from the "Red Flag" to what we termed "Uncle Joe's" anthem. This was played at long length every half hour, so that if you were anywhere near the speaker system, life became unbearable.

Our relations with the Russians deteriorated over a period of time when pressure was being applied to start a second front, and failure in this respect was conveyed to the public in the news bulletins. British and Americans were being subjected to disgraceful behaviour by certain local elements by being pushed and jostled in the street and having pockets picked by young members of the populace.

I remember attending a local celebration concert organised by the Russians and after partaking of the generous refreshments provided, sat down to watch a very dull Russian film. I was joined by a very pleasant American who, like me, did not like the film, so we conversed about the current situation with the Russians. I found him to be most interested in the opinions of the lower ranks of the difficulties in conducting everyday affairs with our Russian counterparts. I did not discover till afterwards that I was conveying my very frank opinions to the American Ambassador Avril Harriman, at that time the President's right hand, who had come up for a visit to see for himself the difficulties experienced by the British and American personnel.

Some of us were interested enough to try to learn something of the language. I did go for lessons at first, but it was so laced with propaganda and with certain questions that were fired at you when alone with the instructor - a very intelligent lady who was no doubt high up in N.K.V.D. circles - I gained the impression that the purpose was to gain access to some of the more secret work that went on in the naval base.

Certain members of the female Russian staff - serving at table at Karl Marx and Norway House - were so obviously listening to conversations that afterwards one would be certain they would be reporting daily to N.KV.D. Headquarters. At table or in mess rooms one never referred openly to the N.K.V.D. but substituted Y.M.C.A., and if disgusted at one of their acts, did not express feelings by calling them "bastards"; everyone knew what this meant. One of the female reporters did ask a less suspecting naval rating why Y.M.C.A. was a "basket" which she thought was a "container"!

There were very grave risks if involved in "skulkering" or exchanging chocolates, cigarettes, and other supplies which were short, for jewellery or other favours. This was going on all around us. It was so sad to see advantage taken of conditions where top prices were available to supply the Soviet citizens able to afford it through agents, when there was so much suffering around us. It was not possible to give food away without risks, as the recipients might face serious consequences if found with it. The Soviet authorities took a very dim view of any admission that Russians suffered disadvantages compared with British and American counterparts.

Russian passes were issued to British personnel to obtain admittance into protected premises but, although provided with photographs inserted with instructions to give free passage, one point not taken into account was that the sentries on duty could not read and the policy was to shoot first and ask questions afterwards.

Except for a very few, one could say at that time that after the age of twenty-five no education was provided, so these people could not read or write. Younger people did have some evidence of education and for the very young there was much keenness to learn and this particularly applied to testing out their knowledge on the English language which was taught in all schools, along with French.

There were difficulties experienced in setting up the naval hospital at Vaenga over admission of the first contingent of doctors and sick bay staff. When another contingent for sick bay cover was required for Archangel, similar difficulties arose. The doctor and ratings for the party were hurriedly despatched on a departing convoy without visas and were refused admission. The party returned on the same convoy to enable passports and visas to be obtained and then dispatched for a second time to go through the risks of sea passage once again.

The very heavy casualties for which the Archangel sick bay hospital party might be needed did not afterwards arise but, safe to say, there were heavy demands on the medical staff for treatment of V.D. cases, both from base staff and ship crews detained in the port for long periods. There was also treatment needed for frequent bouts of dysentery and of course other casualties.

There were further problems for the medical staff when a merchantman arrived and berthed at Archangel. The ship was surrounded by floating logs and a seaman trying to get aboard fell between the logs and was drowned. Another serious incident on the ship resulted in an enquiry. This involved the cook aboard who ran amuck and attacked members of the crew with a carving knife and attempted to set fire to the ship. This was a serious case of mental breakdown caused by stress and resulted in the man being sent home for medical treatment.

Remembered are the spontaneous reactions of the British when faced with the cruelty to animals accepted as normal by the Russians. The man with the horse laden with far too many logs on the sleigh, with the poor horse falling to the ground unable to pull that size of load uphill in the snow. The man was standing over the fallen animal striking it hard with a heavy stick. The British in a body flew to the aid of the poor horse - the stick was wrenched from the hands of the Russian and smashed to pieces, the traces undone and horse lifted to its feet. Some of the logs forming the far too heavy burden taken off and pitched into the ditch; remaining logs strapped on. Horse coupled up to sleigh, man lifted back on his seat without stick, and the horse given a pat to move forward, which it could do with its lighter load. I wonder now if it helped, as the man departed shaking his fist at the British interference. But I am afraid this was the soft reaction of everyone present, who could not stand by and witness this act of cruelty to an animal.

There were other serious incidents in Archangel and I remember much discussion over the affair of two merchant seamen smoking in a timber yard who were accosted by a Russian civilian appearing rudely to threaten them, pointing out that smoking was not allowed. Under the impression they were under attack, one hit out knocking the Russian down. He may have been slightly drunk but although one stood aside both were arrested. It came to light that the Russian official was a very important member of the "Party". Both men were put on trial for "hooliganism" with the result one was given five years and the other two years imprisonment. Very harsh punishment indeed. Appeals lodged reduced the sentences but only the intervention of Mr Eden with Stalin was said to have enabled a free pardon to be issued to both men after about four months imprisonment.

Often, action taken against Soviet citizens was even more harsh than that awarded to foreigners. Joe recalls an incident at the docks when a party in the forced gang of labourers broke open a case from a British ship and drank from the blue cans, thought to be Barclays lager. As this was anti-freeze and poisonous, several men lay dead at the dockside. Others, were very ill. Efforts by the British naval doctor with a stomach pump saved a few and they were able to get up and walk around. As soon as they were on their feet the militia arrived with guards and the men were taken by the side of the ship and shot out of hand. No trial was necessary for these men, as stealing from stores at the docks was punishable by instant death.

It was amazing how the Russians seemed to keep tabs on everyone - it was perhaps because every action was regarded as suspicious and so many people were employed watching each other and reporting. There was the case of "Tamara" who fell in love with a British seaman who wished to marry her. This was not possible as Stalin had forbidden and refused permission to all Soviet nationals to leave the country for whatever reason, and this included marriage to foreigners. They could marry if the foreigner took out Soviet citizenship but this was wartime and this situation could not be accepted.

In this tragic situation an attempt was made to smuggle the girl out of the country by giving her passage as a stowaway on the ship without, of course, the knowledge of the Master, but helped with the full knowledge of the seamen in the crew. The girl was missed by the Soviet authorities and the ship was stopped and searched by a Russian naval vessel at the Kola Inlet and the terrified girl arrested. The ship was then allowed to proceed.

Speaking to friendly Russian contacts in their own homes was just to get away from the feeling of being watched outside. The thing that was so different when out of doors was to see everyone hurrying along - no little collection of housewives chatting over events at street corners. In winter one could understand but in summer this was missing. The answer given was that people were afraid to call attention to themselves as at street corners they were being watched by the militia who might wonder what was going on and perhaps a search of their homes might prove fruitful. These searches when carried out were brutal, causing much damage to effects, with floor boards being ripped up to see if hidden food stocks were there from the black market.

It was a great day when news came through of the commencement of the Second Front, so often requested by the Russians. Crowds in the street cheered us. We were kissed by attractive ladies in the town - and after a rapid search for a British tune to play on the loudspeakers, the radio station came up with a Scottish air - By yon bonny banks and by yon bonny braes - which was played every half hour. There was a special edition of "Pravda" printed in English with a picture of General Eisenhower on the front page with headline "Allied troops land in Northern France, take invasion beachheads". It was the first time Allied actions took over the front page of a Russian newspaper.

The other major event was the arrangements for the reception of British R.A.F. bombers at Archangel for the attack on the **TIRPITZ**. Attempts had been made previously to put the **TIRPITZ** out of action as she represented serious danger to the convoys, but these had little effect. A 12,000 pound monster bomb called the "Tallboy" was prepared for the job which was thought to be capable of piercing the Tirpitz's tough hide.

TIRPITZ 42,900 tons, 8 15" guns, 12 5.9" guns, 16 4.1" AA guns. Launched 1 April 1939.

Sailed to Trondheim from Kiel January 1942, was attacked by Stirlings and Halifaxes end January. Sortied out to attack PQ12 but attacked by Albacores from **HMS VICTORIOUS** and mission aborted. Threat of **TIRPITZ** instrumental in the fatal scattering of PQ17. Attempt on **TIRPITZ** made by "Chariots" - 2 man Human torpedoes in Oct. '42 a failure. **TIRPITZ** joined Scharnhorst in February 1943 at Altenfjord. September 1943 **TIRPITZ** attacked weather station on Spitzbergen - the only time its main armament fired in anger. Late September she was attacked by X craft midget subs. Badly damaged. Two VC's won by

R.N. Spring 1944 attacked by Barracudas from **H.M.S. VICTORIOUS, FURIOUS, EMPEROR, SEARCHER, PURSUER** and **FENCER** - disabled for three months.

Then in September 1944 Lancasters from 9 and 617 RAF Sqns (The Dambusters) flew to Yagodnik airbase near Archangel to attack from North Russia. Damaged, no longer seaworthy. Limped 200 miles south to Tromso which brought her in range of Lancasters operating from Scotland. November 12 1944 again attacked by 9 and 617 Sqns (Wing Cmdr J.B. Tait). Hit in Magazines by "Tallboy" bombs and turned turtle - over 1,000 sailors lost with her.

In September 1944 two squadrons of R.A.F. bombers cruising at treetop level over enemy territory to avoid German radar flew on to Russia to stage a surprise attack on the battleship in Norway's Alten Fjord. Using the mountains to shield their approach, 27 Lancasters attacked from the south-east. It was reported that the planes scored only one hit but one "Tallboy" was sufficient to make the ship unseaworthy. Subsequently the Germans moved the ship to Tromso and in November 30 Lancasters from Scotland sank her.

The arrangements to receive this large influx of bombing planes at Archangel did leave a lot to be desired as there were many defects in the preparations. Bombers were seen everywhere having had to land on flat territory wherever they could, but most of them were serviceable and put into the air again.

In lighter vein the story of the poor chap who lost his teeth. With "gummy" face and looking sick, he reported this fact to the assembled company in the S.B.N.O's office. After answering a series of questions, given hesitantly, one gathered that the most likely spot where they might be located was the Russian toilet at the International Club where he was sick after a drinking bout. Questioned had he looked there, he said it only caused him to be sick again, so he gave up. Questioned again 'have you any roubles?' - answer 'about 500'. Call for Russian driver Alexis - Skulka - 'how much to search for this man's teeth?' - settled for 200 roubles, duly handed over. Instructed to come back at 1600. After lunch there were complaints in the office about the smell. 'What's the dirty old newspaper doing on your desk?' Opened up - false teeth just as they came from the toilet. Gingerly holding the edges, conveyed package some distance away so smell faded in the distance. At 1600 in comes chap with no teeth. 'Yes - package over there, teeth found'. Smile of great joy over his face, picks up teeth from paper just as they came from toilet and pops them into his mouth!

There were many happenings in connection with our work in Archangel which may now be forgotten, many perhaps would be better to bury deep in the ground and forget. There was however a job to do there. Not always appreciated as it should have been by the Russians - we did our best in spite of all the obstacles placed in our way, often by Russian officials with limited knowledge and capabilities, operating always under the watchful eyes of the dreaded N.K.V.D.

Bob Risley, Ord. Sig. after a long, arduous train journey from Murmansk, also arrived at Archangel to find the river frozen solid and lorries going across to halfway, down which was a passage of broken ice caused by the ice breakers. Crossing this stretch on frozen planks carrying kit bags and hammock was far more frightening than the bloody U-Boat attacks! His journey continued on horsedrawn sledge to Karl Marx Dom, Archangel.

Bob records his main duties being on a Russian ice-breaker to take a convoy out of Archangel, up the River Dvina and through the White Sea which was frozen solid, up to the open sea by Murmansk, and to bring another convoy back to Archangel. These trips could last up to 2 to 3 weeks, and living as one of the Russian crew, and being the only Englishman on board, was not a pleasant experience.

Black bread, cabbage soup, fish head soup, and beans if we were lucky was our main diet. One night the ice was particularly thick and as we were not making much progress, it was decided to stop for the night. We were about 50 yards from the nearest ship and I got permission to go over the side and walk back over the ice to visit her to see what I could scrounge. The look-out on deck couldn't believe his ears when I shouted up to him in English, because I was in fur hat, Russian coat and velinkis. A ladder was lowered and I went on board. I told them who I was and asked if they had any spare food. I returned to the Ice Breaker (LENIN) with a duffel bag full of tinned food, a loaf and fags, and nearly got mobbed by the crew. They had never seen such food, I was their friend for life!

I was only 18 and being on board for 2 or 3 weeks at a time, and only hearing Russian spoken, and broken English of the interpreter, really got to me. I used to be frightened of forgetting how to speak English, and used to lie in my bunk at night talking to myself. After taking one convoy to the edge of the ice field I was transferred from the ice-breaker to the Acting Commodore's ship, a Norwegian tanker, as liaison signalman, to take her into Murmansk. As we were just forming into line ahead to cross the bar we were hit in the stern by a torpedo. A few of the crew were killed including two DEMS gunners. Luckily I was on the bridge at the time and was taken off by a Russian tug. Again I was landed at Vaenga Hospital. Next day I was taken to the same Russian tug that had picked me up. I was told I was being taken to **HMS LARK** which had been torpedoed. She was badly damaged and listing but the Russians decided they could salvage her. When we got to her I had to scramble on board to act as liaison signalman to the towing tug. I shall never forget the sight and the smell below decks where she had been hit. What a bloody mess! Fifteen survivors were still on board, one of whom was Jimmy Edwards.

One of the more pleasant memories was coming ashore at Archangel from the ice-breaker after leaving the **LARK** and bringing another convoy back. I had been away for about a month without a proper bath, haircut, or a change of clothes and was beginning to look and smell like a Russian. Making my way through Archangel to NP 200 pulling my little hand sledge with my batteries and Aldis lamp on it, I bumped into three others. "Come on, we are going for a drink in the Intourist". "Not in this state, I want a bath and a haircut". "Come and have a drink, and you can get a haircut in the Intourist". So being easily led I went with them. Vodka and black bread was the order of the day. An hour later, well and truly stoned, they took me for a haircut and shave. It was a woman barber. I remember slumping in the chair and the woman pulling me up by the ears and the sound of the hand clippers going over my head. I kept drowsing and she kept lifting me up. The next thing was my head feeling very wet and cold. When I cam round and focussed in the mirror she had shaved my head as bald as a coot. God, was it cold!, that sobered me up.

Before we left Archangel a concert and party was organised for the Russians. Seeing ten matelots dressed as ballet dancers in little frilly skirts, tights, and wellies, what a sight. For the finale we sang the Red Flag in English. The Russian audience gave us a standing ovation, but if they could have understood the words we would have been shot!

Joseph French having served with Naval Party 200 in Archangel during the severe Arctic winter with the River Dvina frozen solid, recalls the joy of the arrival of spring, equally shared with the Russians. The rapid change from winter to summer was quite a phenomenal experience.

The great May Day celebrations were over and it was noticed that a feeling of expectancy prevailed. The townsfolk were anxiously awaiting for the signs of the expected thaw. With more pleasant prospects ahead, the inhabitants of the large city looked hopefully towards the future and appeared to be in the act of throwing some great burden from their shoulders.

At last the temperature began to rise and slowly the snow began to disappear and the resultant slush to drain away through the ditches and sewers to the river. For the first time in many long months, brilliant sunshine appeared to help this good work and, almost within the space of a few days, it was with some amazement that we saw green shoots clearly visible on all the trees and shrubs. The frozen river, into which all the surplus water was pouring, succumbed to the inevitable and, as if groaning in great agony, gave final vent to its feelings. Great cracks appeared on its icy surface, forming weird and mystic patterns in all directions, from the banks to the centre passage, still being kept clear for traffic by the hard-worked ice breakers. By the eighth day of this amazing month the weird patterns had already broadened into great chasms and, soon afterwards, massive blocks of ice were being caught by the racing current of the already swollen river and were crashing their way out to sea. All traffic was suspended and crowds of happy people lined the banks to watch the events move towards the climax. Suddenly distant thuds coming from the upper reaches of the river told the inhabitants that the Red Air Force was in operation against Russia's oldest enemy. Bombers assisting in the final destruction were dropping high explosive charges at the "bottle necks" where the river twists and turns, so that no temporary stoppages would delay the great clearance.

By the late evening the sun was still throwing its rays on the spectacle and, as most of the ice had gone, ferry boats and other craft could be seen venturing forth, dodging to and from to avoid smaller particles still floating in the strong current.

As the current swelled in intensity the strong sunlight played on the water and made artistic patterns on the moving objects which charged relentlessly on towards the open sea. It seemed strange that the daylight and sunshine would last so long but, at this time of the year, the daylight continues until well on towards midnight and then, after a few hours of semi-darkness, the dawn breaks again.

Looking around us the transformation was astounding as, for the first time, we saw the town in its true guise. The ravages of winter were in the past and all the grim reminders of habitual dreariness with which we had become accustomed, and which were accepted as the real thing, seemed to have been swept away by some great supernatural power. One of the most surprising changes was in the people themselves as during the winter they were, in appearance, completely colourless. Now all that drabness had gone, and they blossomed out in the most amazing collection of summer garments. Now that climatic conditions no longer compelled them to wear the accepted dismal garb, they threw off the grey padded coats, the ear-flapped fur caps and the tall jackboots and emerged in a sea of colour. In their best summer frocks the girls looked particularly attractive and with their gay dresses and attractive headgear compared favourably with the crowds on the promenade of an English seaside resort in mid-summer. Mingling with this sea of colour were the smart uniformed figures of the men and women of the Red Army, Navy and Air Force who had for the occasion discarded their thick heavy greatcoats, and were smartly turned out in new summer uniforms bedecked with coloured ribbons and flashes.

All around us every thoroughfare was decorated with flags and bunting, and it was hard to believe that this was the same town that we had been living in for the past six months. That all this could have happened so quickly was unbelievable and something of a revelation.

Before these astounding events everyone appeared at their worst, moving about their daily tasks as if it required extreme effort. There were no smiles, as the grim winter privations and the accustomed suffering of indescribable hardships required all one's willpower to just push one foot before the other. Now all this was over and the people looked forward to the better times ahead, which would mean more food, more warmth and more comfort, and for the first time we looked around at a sea of smiling faces. We realised what it meant to them and we joined them in their rejoicing. It was as if a magic wand had been waved over us and a completely new picture appeared.

As we watched, we saw that the sun was slowly beginning to sink towards the distant horizon, and it was evident that the curtain would soon fall on one of the most amazing series of events ever witnessed. In the background were the shrieks and hoots of the ferry boats still engaged in dodging the ever-diminishing blocks of floating ice, mingled with the continual hum of cheerful conversation of the passers-by, and the joyful shrieks of the youthful elements of the population still lining the banks in anticipation of more good things to come.

To end this day of days came one of the most glorious sunsets ever witnessed. A magnificent rose-tinted sky as a setting for the glistening, deep-red orb, which slowly and, it seemed, reluctantly, disappeared beyond the distant sky-line, leaving its last rays to enhance the brilliant patterns made by the moving ice and water around us.

Leading signalman Bill Loades at Archangel got himself in a right load of trouble following 'a few' at the club, and being arrested for stealing the hat off the head of a 17-year-old Russian youth. He and his mate were being pestered in the street for chocolates and cigarettes and he jokingly took the Russian lad's hat. He forgot he had the cap and later burnt it. The Russians said there had been a brawl and Bill was sentenced at a military court to a year's prison for assault and being a hooligan.

This sentence caused a secret storm between the Russian and British governments. Churchill and Stalin kept in touch with events after exchanges between the two Foreign Secretaries Anthony Eden and Molotov. After a short stay in prison Bill was marched through the streets at gunpoint and taken on an 18-hour train journey to a labour camp in a remote forest region, 450 kilometres from Archangel.

He joined about 1,000 prisoners in the camp who were forced to work up to 12 hours a day, sometimes longer, living on meagre rations and enduring freezing temperatures. The work was loading and unloading supply trains for the Russian war effort with a rest day every 10 days.

Prostitution was rife, payment being by food and cigarettes, theft commonplace. Prisoners became ill and he saw some die. Like most British personnel serving ashore, he had a working knowledge of Russian and recalls a phrase coined in the camp "we work like elephants and eat like little children"; prisoners were told "more effort for more bread". He was terrified and wondered whether he would survive. His agony eventually ended after four and a half months following negotiations between the British Embassy in Moscow. Eden wrote and said the sentences were a serious threat to friendly cooperation between the allies and was causing bitterness among the British servicemen.

Bill was then removed to another part of the prison because he was not allowed to see his mates in the street; semaphore messages and communication was made by another signalman using two cigarettes as the flags thus enabling them to converse visually with each other's knowledge of the code. Food parcels were delivered to the prison but never reached his cell.

S.B.N.O. Archangel signalled to 30 mission Moscow informing them that on 29th November three British service personnel Ord. Tel. Prior, Leading Sgmn. Loades and Army Signalman Pemberton were involved in a street scuffle with Russians who were demanding cigarettes and chocolate. Blows were exchanged between Prior and a Russian. Prior was seized and taken in a lorry to militia headquarters where he was detained. After strong representations his release was obtained the following day.

2. The Russian authorities then demanded that these three men be handed over to them for investigation at once, but S.B.N.O. Archangel refused to do this, stating the view that the charge against them should be handed over to Archangel where the case would be investigated and tried.

3. They were however insistent and were told we were unable to accede to their demand without referring the matter to Moscow and had accordingly deferred the matter until 6th December at which time they state the men must be handed over.

4. In answer to the question as to whether the men would be returned to S.B.N.O. Archangel immediately after investigation, the Russians stated that no guarantee could be given but that if they were considered not guilty they would be, otherwise they would be kept under arrest, and it would be for the prosecutor to decide whether they should be tried by Russian authorities or not.

5. Immediate instructions were requested as Archangel did not propose to hand over men who were confined to their quarters, without orders from Moscow.

The People's Commissariat for Foreign Affairs were made aware that on the 23rd December, William Prior and William Loades were tried by the Military Tribunal of the N.K.V.D. Troops of the Archangel District for offences committed.

2. The charge against Prior was that he assaulted passers-by in a hooligan manner, resisted arrest and assaulted two workers of the People's Commissariat for State Security, and then attempted to escape while under arrest. The charge against Loades was that he behaved in a hooligan manner and stole a hat from a Russian citizen, hit him when asked that his hat should be returned and subsequently destroyed it. The court sentenced Prior to four years' correctional labour and Loades to one year's imprisonment.

3. The Embassy understood that the lawyer who defended Loades and Prior at the trial in Archangel had prepared appeals for submission to the President of the Supreme Court of the U.S.S.R. and that these appeals be heard, expressing the confident hope that every consideration be given to the arguments advanced. In addition to these arguments, the Embassy should submit the following considerations ad misericordiam.

4. In the first place it appears, from reports received by the Embassy, that Prior and Loades were pestered by a crowd of boys and youths asking for chocolate and cigarettes as they left the International Club, some of these youths were still following the men when they turned into the main street of Archangel where the incidents which form the Subject of the charges took place. It appeared that the men had some cause for irritation and considered to have acted under provocation. Applying more particularly to Loades, who stated that the youth whose hat he stole was one of those who was pestering him for chocolate and cigarettes.

5. As regards Prior, it appears that his alleged attempt to escape was no more than an effort to inform the British naval headquarters of the fact that he had been arrested and that he was not aware of what was going to happen to him.

6. At the trial, the method of translation adopted by the interpreter, who reserved his translation until after the end of a long statement or series of questions and answers and then only summarised from memory, had the effect that Prior and Loades were at no time fully aware of the progress of the case against them or in a position at the time to deal with any particular allegation.

7.The Embassy understood moreover that the defending counsel did not see the defendants until immediately before the trial and did not see the documents until the previous day. They were also informed that Loades, who was given an opportunity of studying the documents some time before the trial was not shown the indictment against him until the day before the trial opened.

8. The Embassy considered that these factors may possibly have led the court to impose heavier sentences than it would otherwise have done. The prosecutor asked that the sentences should be such that the British authorities could point them out as a concrete example to all British service and other personnel. This request conveys the impression that the sentences imposed were more severe than they need have been, as the court was asked to take into consideration another motive than the guilt of the accused.

9. The embassy hoped that the foregoing considerations, as well as those contained in the appeals which have been prepared for submission to the President of the Supreme Court of the U.S.S.R. would be taken into account if and when the sentences were reviewed. The Embassy would of course have preferred that the men should be handed over to the British naval authorities and sent to the United Kingdom for disciplinary action. In this connection the People's Commissariat realised that Thomas Devine, who was sentenced by a military court, was released on probation, and that he was sent to England to be dealt with there. If this were not possible the Embassy hoped that the sentences would be amended as requested in the appeals and in the light of considerations advanced hitherto.

On the 29th November, 1943 three British service personnel, Telegraphist William Henry Prior, Acting Leading Signalman William Hedley Ernest Loades and Signalman Eric Jack Pemberton, Royal Corps of Signals, left the International Club at Archangel at about 17.15p.m., with the intention of returning to their quarters. They had each drunk about three or four tots of red wine, which was said to contain about 20% vodka and all three admitted to being slightly intoxicated, it is probable that they were happily drunk but had no intention of looking for trouble. In Bennerskya Street they were pestered (as all British personnel were persistently and aggravatingly pestered) by the inevitable crowd of small boys and youths asking for chocolate and cigarettes. These youths are a familiar feature of the streets of Archangel and a constant source of annoyance to foreign visitors, for not only do they pester but shout obscene remarks in English when refused. Many are expert pickpockets. Some of the youths were still following the three men when they turned into Pavlina Vinogradova, the main street of Archangel, on their way home. It was in this street that the incidents, the subject of their charges, took place.

There is a great deal of conflicting evidence as to what actually occurred and the order in which the incidents took place.

The Russian's alleged that the three men were all together the whole time until shortly before Prior's arrest. They were singing and behaving like hooligans. That Prior stopped a woman in military uniform but that she got away. That he then stopped a second woman and put his arms around her, but she struck him in the face with her bag and also got away. It was then alleged that the three men overtook a man who was consistently referred to as an invalid of the 'patriotic war' and that Prior caught him by his wounded arm which was in a sling. According to the official translation of the indictment, '. . . . this man made a remark that he felt pain and again stated he was an invalid of the patriotic war, Prior hit him in the face, and he fell to the fence. Loades is alleged to have stolen a cap from the head of a youth aged about 17, and described as a 'Russian worker', an innocent passer-by on his way to get his food tickets, and when asked to return the cap, Loades was alleged to have hit him in the face.

It was further alleged that two members of the N.K.V.D.,* one in the uniform of a Captain and the other in civilian clothes, passed the three men, when Prior, without provocation, hit the officer in the face, knocking him down.

The militia and members of the N.K.V.D. then approached and the three men scattered. Prior was arrested and after a struggle, taken to Militia Headquarters in a lorry.

To the British authorities stated that Loades admitted he was singing and made remarks to women passing by, but these were of a friendly nature. All three men denied that any woman was stopped or molested. The women were not traced, made statements, or had given evidence.

Loades further admitted that he took a youth's cap at or near the junction of Bennerskya and Pavlina Vinogradova and some 300 yards from where the youth stated it was taken. His explanation was that at this junction he was pestered by a youth for chocolate and cigarettes and to teach him a lesson snatched his cap, intending to compel the youth to follow him for it for some distance and put it inside his greatcoat. In the excitement following Prior's arrest he forgot about the cap, and when he came across it among his belongings two days later, burnt it.

All the three men categorically denied the incident of the alleged assault on the invalid or indeed that they noticed anybody answering to his description. Prior stated that the whole way they were pestered by boys and youths but took no notice of them until he was suddenly hit in the mouth, when he hit back and knocked a man down. He was not certain whether he hit the man who hit him or somebody else. Prior then alleged that he was set upon by a number of men who knocked him down, and after handling him very roughly put him in a lorry and took him to Militia Headquarters. He admits fighting back, but states he did not realise it was the militia who were arresting him.

Pemberton stated that while he was walking next to Prior, Prior swung half round and bumped into him, and that Prior hit out and knocked a man down but that it was too dark to notice whether the man was in uniform or not. He and Loades then each took one of Prior's arms and hurried him away, but when a party of men was seen approaching they scattered and mingled with the crowd. Later Prior was seen being put into a lorry. Loades and Pemberton returned to their quarters, Pemberton reporting the incident on Prior's arrest.

It was not possible adequately to reconcile these conflicting accounts, but the balance of probability appears to be that the three men were walking down the pavement, not giving way to passers-by and probably jostling people in their way. This might well be how the alleged assault took place. The three men overtook him, bumped him into the fence and injured his wounded arm. There seemed a more reasonable theory that he was seized by his wounded arm, (which was in a sling) by the men overtaking him hit and knocked down. The three men appeared to be telling the truth when they were interrogated separately and all denied that they had ever seen a wounded man. This point was dealt with in some detail as the wanton assault on an invalid of the patriotic war and was a feature of the interrogation and trial. It was said that no British person had seen the invalid who was stated to be in Murmansk, and although he did not attend the trial, his evidence, in the form of a statement was read and accepted in it's entirety by the court.

The statement was made before the prosecutor in the absence of the two accused men or their lawyer, and they were at no time afforded the elementary right of an accused man to cross-examine or test the truth of the allegations made against them. They were, therefore, placed at the grave disadvantage at their trial of being faced with a damaging piece of evidence which they were only able to refute as a whole and upon which their lawyer did not comment.

There is little doubt that Prior did knock the officer down, but according to Prior only after he himself had first been hit by somebody.

After his arrest Prior was put into a lorry and taken to the Militia Head Office of the Archangel district, struggling all the way, succeeded in jumping off the lorry once, but was re-captured. In Militia Headquarters he was roughly handled and resisted the whole time until his hands were tied, and then, according to the statement made by Divisional Officer and repeated to the court, he was knocked down and kicked when on the ground. One of the charges of his indictment was for an assault on a Militia Officer which took place at the time. Later Prior's hands were untied and he was taken to another place where he slept the night. Next day he was questioned by Russian officials through an interpreter, and a written statement was taken. Meanwhile, strong representations were being made by S.B.N.O. Archangel for Prior's release and eventually at about 1800 hours on 30th November, Prior was released after again being questioned by Russian officials through an interpreter.

On 4th December, the Russian authorities required the three men concerned to attend before the Public Prosecutor for interrogation and on 7th December, in accordance with 30 Mission's Moscow's instructions, the three men were accompanied by a Lieutenant R.N.V.R. and a Captain of the office. The Lieutenant as an interpreter.

The interrogation was conducted by the Prosecutor through a Russian interpreter and the three men were heard separately. The first interpreter was a receptionist from the Intourist Hotel. A girl of apparently 18 years of age whose command of English was pathetically inadequate for the purpose and there were many mistranslations, some apparent on the face of them as when, she quoted Loades as saying that he was born in 1924 but that his father had died in the last war. Subsequently a second interpreter was called for Pemberton's interrogation but he proved equally incompetent. The Prosecutor soon realised the position and at his request, a great part of the interrogation was conducted through the Lieutenant R.N.V.R. As a preliminary to his interrogation, each witness was asked a number of questions, one of which was directed to ascertaining his political views. The form of the interrogation of Loades and Prior assumed their guilt and they were asked questions such as: "Witnesses have stated you knocked an invalid down. Why did you do it?" The statements were not taken down by the Prosecutor as they wee made, but a summary from memory was made at the end of the interrogation and signed by the witness. Certain discrepancies were noticed by the Lieutenant and where possible, corrected before the statements were signed.

Loades was a bad witness and at first repeatedly denied that he knew anything about a cap being stolen. When however, he was definitely assured by the Prosecutor that there would be no charge against him on this score and also warned of the penalties for perjury, he admitted taking the cap, creating a bad impression.

Pemberton was a good witness, giving his evidence clearly and well.

Prior was interrogated last, and it was apparent that the atmosphere of the enquiry was definitely antagonistic towards him. Several additional people came into the room to hear his statement, and a third and more experienced Russian interpreter was called. Prior had already made a statement when in custody and he was questioned upon what he had already said and signed a further statement.

At the end of the interrogations, which lasted seven hours, Prior was detained in custody on charges of hooliganism and resisting arrest, but Loades and Pemberton were allowed to leave.

On the following day Loades was re-called for further interrogation and confronted with the youth, who, however, was unable to identify him as the person who took his cap. Notwithstanding this initial setback the Prosecutor made bricks with the state of Loades previous statement and Loades was formally charged with hooliganism and stealing the cap, but was released on S.B.N.O. Archangel's undertaking that he would be produced at the trial.

On the same day Prior, while being conducted from Militia Headquarters to the Archangel prison, attempted to escape when passing British Naval Headquarters, but after shots had been fired, was recaptured.

Subsequently Loades again attended at the Prosecutor's office with the Lieutenant R.N.V.R. when the documents in the case were read over to him. The Prosecutor told him that a statement had already been taken from Prior regarding his attempt to escape, but that Prior at first refused to sign it as he was not satisfied with the interpretation and had asked to see the interpreter. The Prosecutor said that he had told Prior that he would get no sympathy and only then did he sign the statement. Further, that Prior had been marched through the streets carrying his two kit bags and accompanied by an escort of three soldiers with fixed bayonets. it may be that the indignity of being treated as a dangerous criminal even before his trial may to have some degree contributed to Prior's determination to escape.

The trial of Prior and Loades took place on 23rd December, before the military tribunal of the N.K.V.D. troops of the Archangel District. Another Lieutenant R.N.V.R. (an interpreter) and a Captain attended. The court consisted of a Captain (President), a senior Lieutenant and a junior Lieutenant. The two accused men were represented by a Russian lawyer, who saw then for the first time in court and who had only seen the documents in the case the previous day. Apparently Soviet law does not permit a prisoner to be seen before his trial. After the formal preliminaries for covering the court had been complied with, the prisoners were called upon to plead to the indictment. They were then called upon to make their statements in defence, upon which they were questioned by the Prosecutor and their own lawyer. Only when the two men had completed their evidence were the witnesses for the Prosecution called. The evidence was not translated step by step, but only when witnesses had completed their evidence were the witnesses for the Prosecution called.

In his closing speech (which was fair on the evidence before the court) the Prosecutor asked that the sentences should be such that the British Authorities could point it out as a concrete example to all British Services (and other) personnel. He asked for 5 years for Prior and one year for Loades.

The closing speeches of the defending lawyer were of a much higher quality than his previous efforts. He took the point, which if a good one, should have been taken earlier, that as a civil claimant for the value of his cap was not a competent witness in criminal proceedings. This point was replied to by the Prosecutor and again pressed by the defence, but was not settled or even considered by the court. The final speech for the defence concluded with a suggestion that the sentences might be such as would enable the two men to continue to take part in the struggle against Hitler, or Facism. A summary of the two closing speeches on both sides was translated at the end from notes made by the interpreter.

The prisoners were then asked if they had any final word to say, and both, dispirited and frightened, spoke shortly and with great feeling of their deep regret for all that had happened, of their friendship for the Russians, and their desire to return home. These speeches, which might have carried weight with a British jury, lost their point in interpretation and met with the single observation 'Tak' from the President.

After an absence of 50 minutes the court accepted all the evidence against the two men and sentenced Prior to 4 years in a correctional labour camp, and Loades to one year in prison. Before then it had been impossible, notwithstanding repeated requests, to ascertain the whereabouts of the two men. It was stated that permission to communicate with them being entirely at the discretion of the governer of the prisons they were in.

The proceedings which lasted 7 hours resulted in Loades and Pemberton being released but Prior was detained in custody at Militia Headquarters and it is stated he will be removed to a Russian gaol today where he will remain until his trial by a Russian Civil Court.

Charges against Prior are (1) Hooliganism in a public place (2) Resisting arrest with violence.

The case now looks more serious than originally anticipated as Russians state medical reports are in their possession showing that 6 persons including 1 N.K.V.D. Captain and 1 Militia Lieutenant are suffering from facial injuries alleged to have been caused by Prior.

Request was made for Prior to be detained in British quarters and S.B.N.O. Archangel gave personal undertaking as to his custody and also to produce him at the trial but this was refused.

The atmosphere of the enquiry was definitely antagonistic to Prior.

Such incidents as these put British personnel in Northern Russian ports in a most invidious position. If they do nothing they are liable to be robbed; if they resist and a scuffle develops, they are liable to be charged with hooliganism and sentenced to long terms of imprisonment. The Embassy therefore strongly supported the representations which the Senior British Naval officer at Archangel had addressed to the local representatives of the Peoples Commissariat for Foreign Affairs urging the necessity of effective measure to stop the continual pestering and pick-pocketing to which British personnel were subjected.

It would not escape the notice of the People's Commissariat for Foreign Affairs that incidents such as those described reports illustrated a state of affairs which is conducive to such occurrences as led to the arrests of two British Servicemen serving in North Russia.

Whilst in prison Bill Loades made a further personal appeal through his Lawyer.

TO THE PRESIDENT OF THE HIGH COURT OF USSR.

Loades William - British subject confined in Archangel prison.

APPEAL ON PROCEDURE

The Military Tribunal of N.K.V.D. Forces of the Archangel area have sentenced me, William Loades, to one year imprisonment and a fine of 300 roubles as civil claim payable to the youth involved. This sentence I cannot recognise as correct for the following considerations:

1. The witness appeared in this case as the offended party and civil claimant, but was nevertheless admitted to give evidence as an impartial witness. Furthermore he received a compensation of 300 roubles. The court has thus allowed a direct infringement of the criminal code.

2. The charge against me was having hit the worker in the street on the 29th November, snatching and failing to return his cap.

These charges against me are borne out only by the suffering party. No other person has confirmed that I had ever hit him. The fact that I have taken off a cap from a youth who followed me asking for chocolate and cigarettes, I do not deny, but at no time did I hit him.

The reason for removing the cap is explainable by the fact that this youth together with a whole group of others followed me and my friends through several streets and persisted in demanding chocolate and cigarettes. As we refused them so they abused us.

Jocularly I tore off the cap from one of these boys continuing the walk on and presuming that this youth will also continue to follow me whereupon I would return his cap to him.

Soon the incident occurred with my comrade Prior and in the general commotion I failed to return the cap to its owner. Returning home I forgot altogether about the cap and on the following day when convincing myself how useless the cap was I burnt it.

This was all the crime that I have committed for which the tribunal sentenced me to one year's imprisonment.

I consider that the alleged offence has neither been proved nor confirmed and is based exclusively on the evidence of the claimant whose evidence is not admissible as evidence of fact.

Considering the verdict against me to be unfound, I request you, citizen President of the High Court to call for the documents on this case and to order the withdrawal of the action against me because of insufficient evidence. I further request that the recommendation given to me by SBNO Archangel be taken into consideration, to the effect that I was working as a signalman since the 4th February 1943 and served in the British Fleet since 1939 and my character was good hitherto.

Signed

Lawyer

Neither the British Embassy nor the Senior British Naval Officer Archangel had any idea where these men were imprisoned and in order that a visit could be made urgent appeal was sent to Senior British Naval Officer North Russia and subsequently three days later from the British Embassy.

TO........ S.B.N.O. NORTH RUSSIA

FROM..... S.B.N.O. ARCHANGEL

Prior and Loades.

On 24th December I wrote to Narkomindel representative that I might be advised the whereabouts of the two men and at the same time requesting that arrangements might be made for them to be visited by an officer once a week. A further letter was sent on 17th January and at least twelve requests have been made to the same effect.

2. Nothing but evasive replies have been received and was informed that the question could not be settled locally but would have to be referred to Moscow.

3. For your personal information it was learned that men were in a prison in the town and that they were able to signal from the prison to ratings in the street. Provisions and cigarettes were left at the prison for them but the men have since disappeared from that cell.

4. Request Russians may be pressed to supply information as to their whereabouts and to grant permission for an officer to visit them regularly.

His Majesty's Embassy presents its compliments to the People's Commissariat for Foreign Affairs and, with reference to its memorandum of the 7th January, 1944, in which it requested the People's Commissariat to arrange permission for a British Official to visit the places of detention of William Prior and William Loades, has the honour to state that on the 7th February the Senior British Naval Officer at Archangel was still without information regarding their whereabouts in spite of his having repeatedly approached the local representative of the People's Commissariat for Foreign Affairs.

2. The Embassy have accordingly the honour to enquire where these two men are detained and to renew its request that permission should be given to a British officer or other official representative to visit them at regular intervals.

Sir Archibald Clarke the British Ambassador in Moscow then sent an urgent appeal to Monsieur Molotov explaining the concern of Mr. Winston Churchill and Mr. Anthony Eden and a further request from Mr. Eden to Monsieur Molotov for his personal interest and sympathetic help - regretfully to no avail.

PERSONAL MESSAGE FROM Mr. Anthony Eden

TO MVM Molotov

I am anxious to enlist your personal interest and sympathetic help in connection with the sentences of four year's correctional labour and one year's imprisonment passed last December on Prior and Loades, two naval ratings from our shore establishment at Archangel. These sentences and those previously passed on British personnel who had got involved in brawls ashore when drunk have caused much bitterness amongst our people and it was because of these incidents that we suggested to the Commissariat for Foreign Affairs that in the case of all offences except serious ones against Soviet citizens or property British personnel in North Russia should be tried by British authorities and that similar Soviet personnel in this country should be tried by the Soviet authorities. This proposal is similar to the arrangements which we have found it convenient to make with our other allies. But so far we have had no response from your authorities. As it is of course impossible to guarantee that other incidents might not occur at any moment I beg of you to do all you can to ensure that our proposal meets with a favourable response in the very near future.

About Prior and Loades. I do not of course want in any way to condone the offences committed by these men and it is very proper that they should have punishment for them. But sentences of the severity of those imposed are not given for similar offences in this country and they simply are not understood by our men. The bitterness caused by them increases the possibility of further incidents and may prejudice the full co-operation between British personnel and their Soviet allies in North Russia. What answer can I give if I am asked in Parliament why our Russian allies are so treating men whose only purpose in going to Russia is to facilitate delivery of supplies? I therefore hope that as Prior and Loades have already spent about two months in jail since they were sentenced they should be considered to have learnt their lesson and should be sent back to this country at the first opportunity. Please do your best to assist me in removing this serious threat to that full and friendly co-operation which we want to see prevalent in Archangel between Russian officials and population and British personnel.

PERSONAL 17th March 1944

Dear Monsieur Molotov

I enclose herein a personal message which Mr Eden has instructed me to deliver to you from him about two British naval ratings, Prior and Loades, who were sentenced at the end of December to four year's correctional labour and to one year's imprisonment respectively on charges of hooliganism.

2. This is a matter about which both Mr Churchill and Mr Eden feel very real concern, and I should have asked for an interview to hand you Mr Eden's message personally, had I not been reluctant to take up more of your time than is absolutely necessary. As it is, I ask you to regard this letter as containing the comments and explanations which I should have made to you orally, had I been discussing the matter with you face to face, which I shall hope to do the next time we meet.

3. In the first place I should have mentioned that our naval personnel at Archangel have several times been assaulted by gangs of hooligans who try to pick their pockets, and that when they leave the International Club they are constantly pestered by a swarm of boys asking for cigarettes and chocolates. If our men leave the Club drunk - as Prior and Loades did - trouble is almost bound to arise, and I should have urged that full consideration should be given to this provocation when sentences are passed in such cases.

4. In the second place I should have asked you to remember that our men are stationed in the Northern ports, under what I am sure you will agree to be for them trying conditions, so as to help the flow of supplies to the Soviet Union. If they misbehave themselves, they must be punished. As you know, we should much prefer to punish them ourselves, but until agreement on that point can be reached, they must be punished by the Soviet authorities. But punishments which go beyond what would be imposed for similar offences in the United Kingdom cause resentment among their comrades, and might give rise to ill-feeling at home. I would therefore venture for my part strongly to endorse Mr Eden's plea that Prior and Loades be released forthwith, so that we can send them away. As Mr Eden says, they will have learned their lesson, and I am sure that such an act of grace on the part of the Soviet authorities would not be interpreted by their comrades as meaning that any further misdeeds of the same kind would not be treated with due severity.

(Yours sincerely)

(signed)

Archibald Clark Kerr

British Ambassador, Moscow

Bill Loades relates his personal experiences in the Russian prison and subsequently a labour camp for the theft of a youth's cap, hooliganism and a slight alleged brawl:

On 23rd December I was taken to the prison in an open lorry guarded by soldiers with machine gun and rifles. The first night I spent in a dungeon, a cellar cell 10 x 6 with no light or heating although the temperature outside was at least twenty below zero. A wooden box was the only furniture in the room, there was no bed and it was extremely cold and damp.

On the following morning, December 24th, I was taken to a prison office where all my particulars including fingerprints were taken down. Only the usual questions were asked regarding my occupation etc., but they included the question "to which party I belonged", which was also asked me at the time of my trial. I gave the same answer as before, namely that I had no party affiliation. There was no interpreter present so had to manage as best I could, with the few words of Russian I had picked up.

After the formalities were concluded Prior and I were placed in a cell on the second floor in the women's quarters. Although we had to continue to wear our uniform, extra underwear was issued. We were given water and some soap. The soap was, however, of very inferior quality and crumbled as soon as it was placed in water. Our guards, women - since we were in the women's section - were very considerate to us. In exchange for a few cigarettes they would smuggle through an extra piece of bread for us. But we felt very hungry. Our ration consisted of five hundred grammes of bread issued in the morning, together with a warm brew. At midday we had a bowl of similar brew and kasha (cereal) or cabbage and a bowl of soup in the evening. No contact with other prisoners was allowed. Fifteen minutes daily exercise in one of the prison squares was arranged for us quite separately from all other prisoners, (so that we should not meet them). Bribed by a few cigarettes the guards would allow us occasionally to extend the period of daily exercise from fifteen minutes by another two fifteen minutes. We saw no brutality or maltreatment of prisoners but when we passed the other cells prisoners would shout requests for something to smoke.

Whilst we were in the cell in the women's quarters one of the girl prisoners in the adjoining cell recognised me. She was at one time friendly with a British rating so hence knew me. The American prisoner who was with us in the cell showed me how, with the help of our aluminium mug, wetted at the bottom, I could talk to the next cell using the mug as an amplifier. This we did. It appeared that the girl had her house searched after her friend the rating had left Archangel. A few items of British produce, probably chocolate, were found at her house and she claimed that because of this she was sentenced to eight year's imprisonment. She had been in prison for some six months when I arrived, waiting to be sent out to one of the labour camps. As I understood it, workers for the labour camps were being drafted from the prison and the prison was used as a clearing house or sorting depot for labour. I could see no distinction in treatment, or the nature of the work allocated to Prior and myself, although he was supposed to undergo four years' punishment in a correctional labour camp and I one year in prison, we were both treated exactly alike right through the three and a half months I spent with him. Another girl prisoner who was kept in the dungeon for the past three months also called out to me whilst taking exercise in the prison square. A girl of about twenty who was a waitress in the Intourist Hotel. She had formed a liaison with an American merchant seaman by whom she became pregnant. Her husband, a Russian seaman, to whom she confessed, immediately went to the N.K.V.D. and lodged a complaint, whereupon she was arrested and imprisoned. The baby was born to her in the prison. Whether she was kept in solitary confinement in the dungeon because she became hysterical I would not know, as only a few words could be passed at the time due to the watchfulness of the guards. The baby was born to her in the prison hospital and after the birth of the child she was put back into the dungeon, the baby being taken away from her. Apparently she knew something about the baby, since she was able to tell us that the baby had been very ill due to lack of care and attention. I could not see what she looked like, as she was speaking through a small window and we could only hear her voice.

We felt extremely hungry not only because the quantity of food we received was inadequate but also because, at the time, we were not used to that kind of food. The window of our cell faced onto the street and we managed to attract the attention of a passing woman and asked her to communicate with our friends and to tell them that we were in need of food. Apparently she did so because soon afterwards we began getting parcels of food. It was the same girl who later drew our attention to the fact that some of our friends were outside trying to talk to us and that a parcel had been delivered. We were thereupon warned by the guards that if we continued to shout to people outside we would have our windows blocked. Instead we were moved to the men's quarters.

On the 19th January we were removed from the women's quarter and placed in a cell in the men's quarters. This cell was much inferior to the previous one. It was full of cracks through which the wind blew, the roof was leaking and we had to sleep fully dressed with as much extra clothing as we could lay our hands on and even then felt cold. All our complaints regarding the conditions which we made at the morning rounds to the officer of the guard produced no results. Occasionally one of the male guards, after we had been transferred to the men's quarters, would come into our cell, probably with a view of getting one of our cigarettes and we would have a chat with the help of a few words of Russian. The guards were able to tell us about our ships passing the Dvina, in which we were interested, inasmuch as we hoped to be sent back home in one of the outgoing convoys. The female guards would not talk to us, but once a week one of the male prisoners would be sent into our cell to scrub the floor.

Fortunately we continued to receive parcels of food from outside until on 23rd February we were told to get ready to leave the prison and Archangel for an unknown destination. We had no opportunity of communicating with our friends to tell them we were leaving. At about 10.30 we were marched through the streets of Archangel in full uniform together with about fifty to sixty Russian prisoners guarded by eight machine guns and four police dogs. We marched across the ice-bound Dvina to the station and were immediately placed in a prison truck. Whilst in Archangel jail we wrote three letters to the British Mission, we were assured that these letters had been delivered but have learnt since that none of these letters reached their destination.

Yertzowa, the station at which the labour camp to which we were taken, was situated eighteen hours, train journey from Archangel on the direct line to Moscow. It is approximately 450 kms from Archangel and some 200 kms from Volodga. There are some fifteen or sixteen labour camps around Yertzowa, all situated within two or three kilometres of each other, and there are about a thousand prisoners in each camp. Every camp seems to have its own special task allocated to it and Yertzowa is the clearing house for labour and work. In some of the camps they make sledges and carts, in others they cut wood or repair clothing worn out at the front. In our particular camp we were engaged loading and unloading railway trucks. This camp seemed to be a marshalling yard surrounded by barbed wire with the railway lines running through it.

Before joining the camp we spent three weeks in quarantine. During this period we were not supposed to work, were given a bath every ten days and shared a large room with several prisoners.

As soon as we arrived our uniforms were taken away from us and we were given some old clothing to wear. The rooms were infested with vermin and rats were running freely about the floors. Because of the vermin we could not sleep on the wooden benches, without mattresses, which constituted our bunks, but preferred to sleep on the floor before being driven away by the rats; we finally slept on the table. Whilst in quarantine, we had received two rations of bread, issued to us at lunch and dinner time, weighing 550 grammes all told. Were also given baked cereals and soup three times a day. We, as well as the Russians, could not manage to exist on these meagre rations, so were constantly hungry. On the fourth day after our arrival in quarantine, one of the camp inspectors visited us and ordered that we be issued with more food, better clothing and should be moved to other quarters. We were thereupon issued with an additional two hundred grammes of baked cereal in the morning and a vegetable dish in the evening, were given new clothing and moved to the caretaker's quarters where good mattresses were supplied to us.

But even that food was not enough for us to live on and although, whilst in quarantine, we were not supposed to work, we volunteered to do so for the sake of extra bread that we would get. For three days we were loading wood on to a lorry in a sawmill nearby. Then the next ten days we were bailing hay in the prison stables within the camp. The foreman was, however, dissatisfied with the number of bales we produced daily and the extra 100 grammes of bread received whilst loading was not issued to us bailing hay. With the help of a very antiquated hand bailing machine we were producing forty bales a day, as the other members of the team, two girls and a male invalid, did little or nothing to help us. We had to produce eleven bales per worker per day in order to earn the extra hundred grammes of bread, whereas we actually produced forty bales instead of fifty-five. After ten days' fruitless work we refused to continue. Two days later our quarantine period was over and we had to work without extra rations.

After we left quarantine we went over to the main barracks where there were eighty men per barrack. We were lodged in what appeared to be the best barrack; it was fairly clean, there were no vermine but plenty of rats. We were assigned to work in the food depot, which was very fortunate for us inasmuch as we could, when not being watched, throw a few potatoes into the fire, or quickly mix some flour with water putting it equally into the fire. By the time the outside of the potatoes or cake was charred, the inside became edible. According to the amount of work we managed to do per day we received extra food which amounted some days to one hundred grammes, but on other days to two hundred. Of course, as soon as we left quarantine our extra food of baked cereal in the morning and the vegetable dish in the evening were discontinued but we managed to get a cake of baked cereal on most evenings.

We normally worked from about 07.00 hrs until 18.00 hrs. One day of rest was granted every ten days. The days of rest were fixed as the tenth, twentieth and thirtieth of each month. In February the day of rest was the 29th. The working hours, with a break of one hour per day for lunch, were kept punctually, but on a few occasions we were made to work late, 22.00 hrs or 23.00 hrs. Whilst working at night we had a guard over us, to prevent our escaping, but there was no guard during the day, other than at the gates of the camp. On one occasion whilst working at night, Prior asked the guard for permission to leave for a few minutes, but the guard kicked him with his boot, ordering him back to work. Otherwise there was no brutality applied to us and we did not see any physical violence being used against any of the other prisoners.

The extra food was not enough to sustain us; I sold a pair of knitted gloves to another prisoner for eighty roubles. For this amount I was able to purchase one glass of local tobacco and about five hundred grammes of bread. Prior sold his blue scarf for a hundred roubles and a blanket which he brought with him to prison for four hundred roubles. We occasionally succeeded in disposing of our underwear, which we were due to surrender on washing day in exchange for clean underwear, and all the money realised went towards the purchase of extra bread, some tobacco and, occasionally, some potatoes. Some of the prisoners who had work given to them on parole in the village were mainly concerned in trading, but sometimes we also succeeded in buying seed cakes, which are the residue of the seeds after the oil has been pressed from them and on which the horses were normally fed in the camp. Some of the horses' food went to us and I was eating quite a bit of it. "It makes your mouth come out in blisters but it fills your stomach".

The camp in which we were situated consisted of about a thousand prisoners, six hundred men and four hundred women. The prisoners were of all ages from sixteen upwards. One man of seventy-nine was still working in the camp - he had spent the last nineteen years in labour camps all over the country as apparently no prisoner was allowed to remain in the same camp too long. All the prisoners I spoke to, here we could mix freely with all prisoners, claimed to have been imprisoned because of political offences.

Although the men lived in separate quarters from the women, there being an inspection and counting of prisoners during rounds every night, there was no attempt to interfere in the relations between the male and female section in the camp. Prostitution was very widespread among the women prisoners. The men could visit the women's barracks quite freely during the day and vice versa. The women usually received in payment two hundred grammes of bread or the equivalent in money. The prison authorities knew that this was going on but could do little to stop it; only when caught in the act would a woman be sentenced to five days' solitary confinement, but the man was not punished.

I cannot say whether there was any disease due to this state of affairs in the camp, but the general state of hygiene in the camp was in any case very low indeed. Some of the women were known as the mistresses of one man who, in exchange, would look after them and supply them with extra food. The men who received parcels from home or had a job which enabled them to steal more were able to keep their own mistresses.

The women were usually given the lighter duties in the camp to perform and they too would receive extra bread for extra work. Apparently they preferred to earn their extra bread by prostitution. There was only one case of marriage in the camp. The woman became pregnant and married the man. There was also one couple, a Polish woman and a Russian man who were sent to the camp together; the opinion in the camp was that they were sent to prison because of their marriage.

The camp was run to a large extent on lines of self-government by the prisoners. The entire prison staff, including administration and guards, consisted of about fifty or sixty people. The management of all labour within the camp and the running of the camp itself was carried out by the prisoners, practically without any supervision. The foreman, chosen from amongst the prisoners, would get the day's work allocated to them, or they would be given a particular task. It was up to them and the prisoners to organise the work and to distribute according to ability and physical strength.

The camp hospital was staffed by doctors - prisoners. The dentist was equally a prisoner. They had quite well-equipped surgeries for outside patients. Most of the administrative and office workers were also prisoners.

Any breach of discipline would, however, be most severely dealt with by the camp authorities. For fighting in the camp a sentence of two years would be imposed, for attempting to run away the sentence was ten years. I don't know what the sentence was for stealing, although general in the camp. Somehow no serious attempt seems to have been made to stop stealing. Not only were prisoners stealing food stuff from one another but anything they could lay their hands on. Almost anything could be sold or exchanged for bread or other food. It was not known whether there was a large element of criminals at the camp or whether it was hunger that drove them to steal. Twice a week there was a cinema performance at the camp, the entertainment side being similarly taken care of by the prisoners. Concerts were organised, some of which were extremely good and included well-known artists - also prisoners in the camp. The concert party was allowed to travel from camp to camp but most artists had to work during the day. Only a few, presumably, very talented artists, were exempted from hard labour. Amongst the latter was a well-known composer who was allowed to spend his days composing music. Prisoners criticised the regime quite openly but no derogatory remarks were ever heard against Stalin, who was agreed by all to be a very great leader. Criticism of the Government was almost unrestrained, although several agents were suspected in the camp reporting subversive remarks to the authorities. Whether the critics of the Government simply didn't care or whether the agents or suspected agents were known to them and they were wary of them is not known. The paper "Britanski Soyuznik", published by the Embassy's Press department in Moscow was frequently seen in the camp. It was probably sent by friends outside. There was a large number of educated people at the camp, some of whom had occupied responsible and important posts in their time.

The woman in charge of the linen was a well-known ballerina in Moscow in 1937. She then received a sentence of eight years, allegedly because of her association with a British engineer, and she still had one year to serve. Whether she would be freed at the end of her sentence remained to be seen. Most of the prisoners, irrespective of their sentence, seemed to remain in prison long after they have served their sentence. A Pole who spoke English and seemed generally an educated man, had to serve a sentence of three years for some political offence. Although he was already in his fourth year he still remained in prison. A Hungarian, who acted as English interpreter at the camp, similarly arrested for some political offence, long passed the five-year sentence passed on him. He had no idea when he would be released. The general impression was that the only time prisoners would be released was when they could be sent to fight at the front. A Captain, also a prisoner in the same camp, was, until eighteen months ago, a representative of the foreign trade department in Archangel, connected with the unloading of incoming convoys. He claimed that the sentence of ten years imposed upon him was due to the fact that he was friendly with members of the British Naval Staff in Archangel, many of who he could name and he asked for regards to be given to them.

Another person, a woman, similarly claimed that she was in the camp because of her friendly attitude to members of the American Mission. She named several senior American Officers, asking that regards to given to them and to say that she was sentenced under Paragraph 58, which all prisoners know to be the paragraph under which political prisoners are sentenced.

One other prisoner was not quite sure under which heading his offence came, political or criminal. He had told his foreman in the factory what he thought of him and for this was sentenced to five years' hard labour and three years' loss of civil rights. Many of the girls on the camp were extremely well dressed, much better than the girls in Archangel. They were receiving parcels from home and as all prisoners were allowed to wear their own clothes without any prison markings on them these girls could dress as they pleased.

Those who volunteered for the front and were accepted, were put in uniform and sent for training, or direct to the front if they were trained soldiers, without any leave or a chance to see their family. One man had spent ten years in camp, he was sent away direct to the front and all his requests to be given leave to see his family first met with no response.

We seem to have been treated with some consideration, not only by the fellow prisoners but also by the camp authorities. It was at the suggestion of the second camp director, a Russian, that the prisoners addressed a petition to President Kalinin admitting their offences as due to ignorance of Russian customs and under the influence of drink and concluding their petition by asking for pardon so that "they may redeem themselves by shedding their blood for the great Allied cause".

The camp director tried to impress upon the prison authorities the need to treat the British prisoners with some consideration as they were used to a "different standard of living".

Before leaving the camp to return to Archangel he arranged for special food supplies to be given to us, in fact he sent them to the kitchen to select whatever was required. "This was the first occasion in three and a half months that I had a really square meal".

Letters sent by the prisoners to the Naval Staff in Archangel never reached their destination in spite of the camp director's assurance that they would be delivered. He also took away Prior's passport which, he said, he had sent to the British Mission in Moscow. A paper had to be signed whilst in camp, but the contents of the document, written in Russian, were never explained. My diary, which I kept in camp, and all other letters and papers written in English were taken away before we left the camp.

On the 27th March, Prior and Loades were suddenly informed that they were to get ready to return to Archangel. The same day they were, in the company of a guard, placed in a prison truck and brought back to town, where a closed passenger car awaited them to take them to the town prison.

They were taken back to the same cell in the men's quarters but the cell had, in the meantime, undergone considerable changes. The cracks and leaks had been closed up, furniture, including a table with a white table-cloth was in the cell and new mattresses had been placed in the bunks.

Loades was told to change into his uniform and he was thereupon released. He was ordered to proceed "straight to the Mission". By that time he was, however, frightened to such an extent that he misunderstood the instruction to mean that he was to walk "in the middle of the road".

Thus, walking in the middle of the road, from prison, Loades arrived at the Mission in the afternoon of March 28th. Prior remained in his cell and the supply of food and comforts was resumed. Whether, or when, he was released remains unknown.

In spite of the previous constant pestering by the Russians, especially the children, for cigarettes and chocolate from seamen of the visiting ships in Archangel the following memorandum was sent to Ships Masters and Captains in the Port.

SUBJECT: Trading and Bartering.

. . . .

FROM: The Senior British Naval Officer, Archangel.

TO: Masters of British Merchant Ships in DVINA Ports.

DATE: 26th February, 1944 REF: 3997/113

. . . .

The Soviet authorities have informed me that they take a very serious view of the selling and bartering of cigarettes, chocolate, provisions etc., landed from merchant ships which is a breach of Soviet law and that they are determined to put a stop to it.

2. Special Soviet police in uniform and plain clothes are now on duty in Archangel, Bakharitza, Ekonomia and Molotovsk with instructions to apprehend anyone seen in the streets or elsewhere selling or exchanging cigarettes, chocolate or provisions.

3. I wish to warn all Merchant Service officers and men of the grave consequences attendant upon their breach of Soviet regulations. Once they are arrested, there is little hope for them. They are taken into custody and appear before an Examiner and after a further interval in custody are tried by a Civil Court. The sentences of these Courts are very severe and range from one to five years in a Soviet gaol or concentration camp.

4. It is therefore of the greatest importance that no Merchant personnel should lay themselves open to these penalties.

5. Masters of all ships should immediately on arrival warn their crews, in this sense, that no one is to take ashore with him more cigarettes, chocolate etc. than is necessary for his PERSONAL consumption. Any member of the crew found with an excess amount should have his shore pass withdrawn at once.

Signature

Captain R.N.
S.B.N.O.
Archangel.

As a further illustration of life ashore in North Russia the following is an excerpt from a report sent to Admiralty in September 1943 from the Senior British Naval Officer, North Russia, regarding the difficulty in obtaining reliefs from UK as passports are required, even in wartime, and these take considerable time to obtain. Hence a twelve month station often runs into eighteen months:

Included in the party which recently left here for UK by destroyer are three Officers (two from HMS . . .) and three ratings from Polyarnoe.

The two Officers from HMS . . . have gone haywire and the other Officer from Murmansk is heavily depressed and gaga.

A Petty Officer has gone mad and might do anything given the opportunity.

A Petty Officer from Armament Party is in a complete daze.

A Canteen Assistant who passes the time by cutting girls names on his forearm with a razor blade.

Also going home are eighteen Merchant Navy seamen suffering from Chronic Stomach troubles or Mad, this includes one who imagines he is a bear.

Yes . . . we are carrying on successfully, but I hope you can do everything possible to remedy this situation. Our life is no bed of roses but their's in the merchant ships must be ten times worse.

. . . .

MORE NAUTICAL HUMOUR FROM MAURICE CROSS

Clear Lower Deck! Clear Lower Deck!

"All right chaps, listen carefully. You will shortly be going ashore, so remember this is Archangel, Soviet Russia, and not a trip to 'Aggie Weston's in the U.K. There will be armed Russian sentries around the docks and also on certain street corners. They are very trigger-happy because of spies reporting shipping movements, so if you hear any shouted commands, come to an immediate half - don't say 'Bugger off' and saunter past, because if you do so, you may end up shot full of little holes. I repeat, if challenged you will come to a halt, shout 'Engliski Matross' and flash your paybook. I have been informed that last week a drunken seaman was shot dead after he told a sentry to 'piss off'.

Now the only place for you chaps to go, is the International Club. There will be young ladies there, who are hostesses and not ladies of easy virtue - so don't try any funny business, or you'll rapidly find yourselves sawing wood in a freezing labour camp. Do I make myself clear? Righto chaps, off you go and enjoy yourselves!

....

"Sons of Sea Cooks"

I can well appreciate that the life of a small-ship's cook was fraught with aggravation. Being nagged by the cooks-of-the-mess, wrestling with pots and pans in a heaving galley, plus the super-heat of an oil-fired stove, all combined to keep the chef's temper at boiling point.

Any enquiries from cringing shipmates usually met by a menacingly wielded butcher's knife and the query "What do you bastards want?" Even the Chief POs adopted a fawning attitude when talking to the chef - even if he was only a killick! I suppose he was in sole charge of the most important item onboard - FOOD! As such, he appeared to be immune from the usual disciplines. I recall an Asdic exercise off Scapa, when we were chasing after one of our submarines. Our 'pinging' results were not exactly marvellous, so the captain was getting a wee bit niggly and started flinging the ship around like a ten-foot motorboat, with hard-a-starboards every other minute.

Suddenly, the chef, red with fury, leapt up through the galley skylight, brandishing a huge ladle and screaming loud obscenities at the bridge. The general trend being "How the frigging hell could he be expected to cook when the mad bastards on the bridge were chucking the ship around like a frigging Austin 7". With a last angry flourish of his ladle the chef disappeared down the skylight. The captain turned to the O.O.W. and drawled, "My word, the chef seems a little put out".

....

Hardships!

During one Russian run, in a Force Nine gale, I paid a visit to the Heads for a pee. I was grimly hanging on to the steady-bar whilst performing, when suddenly the wild gyrations of the ship caused a matelot, his trousers round his knees, to shoot out of the cubicle, crashing head first into the bulkhead, then he was flung backwards back into the cubicle and on the next shot back out and again back inside. Where upon I heard a voice cry out in despair, "Christ, too late, too bloody late!"

I could only guess at the misery and the unspeakable shambles inside the cubicle - with about three inches of water swilling about the heaving deck, adding to his private hell.

AND THE "NAUTICAL ALPHABET"

(Or an O.D.'s guide to the Royal Navy)
by Bill Johnston

"A" is for anchor, all ships have them fitted,
"B" stands for buntings, a few quite quick witted,
Its also for beer, which most matelots drink,
"C" is for chokker, a naval expression,
When linked up with crusher it causes depression,
"D" must be draft chit, a bad one brings drips,
Its also defaulters to muster midships,
And duff's from the galley, some heavy as lead,
Oh, and poor dockyard mateys, who work till they're dead,
"E" is for engines, or eats if they're big,
"F" of course foreign, and tropical rig,
"G" stands for gannets, they'll eat the mess bare,
And gash of course, too, that's for rubbish or spare,
"H" is your hammock, its use understood,
or hard lying money, both useful and good,
"I" is inspection at divisions on Sunday,
Don't get picked up Jack, or you've had it on Monday,
"J" stands for jankers and jaunty as well,
Both rather grim, and together just hell,
"K" gives you killicks, the less said the better,
It's also for kye, and that's hotter and better,
"L" brings you loafing, or leave with its charms,
"M" well that's matelots and master at arms,
It can give you the middle, or bring make and mends,
Or maybe for Malta the Med. to defend,
"N" leads to N.A.A.F.I. and nutty, what matter,
It's Navy and Nelson and ends up in natter,
"O" must be officers, so varied, so many,
Scrub round them says Jack, we could do without any,
"P" is patrolman, so grim and unfunny,
It brings in the paybob to dole out your money,
"Q" is the quack, he'll take charge of your ills,
And in moments of stress dish you number nine pills,
"R" yes it's rum mate, with all it's delights,
And it's also for refit, I hope one's in sight,
"S" for a smoke since it's stand easy teatime,
It's scranbag as well and alas some more seatime,
And slops too and sippers, not gulpers you glower,
That brings us to stokers and they are quite a shower,
"T" gives us ticklers and maybe your tot,
Telegraphist's too, crashing out dash and dot,
It's tanky as well, and tinfish by the score,
"U" was for U-boats thank heavens no more,
"V" will be Victualling, of that not a doubt,
"W" for writers and warrants you shout,
It's also the wardroom but let's keep this polite,
Watchkeeping took are you duty tonight?
And don't forget weekends and watertight doors,
And let's add the Wrens chum, a shrill voice implores.
"X" is the X-ray in depot you had,
"Y" Brings in the yeoman of signals my lad,
It also means you, I remembered in time,
So roll on your twelve mate, it helps this to rhyme,
"Z" could be zig-zags, it's the end, I've reached zero,
If you can do better ops then you're a hero,
I could add plenty more to this long winded caper,
But to tell you the truth, I've run right out of paper.

Between the innocence of infancy and the recklessness of adultery comes that unique specimen of Humanity known as a Seaman. Seamen can be found in Bars, in Arguments, in Bed, in Debt and intoxicated. They are Tall, Short, Fat, Thin, Dark, Fair but never normal.

They dislike Ships Food, Chief Engineers, Writing Letters, Sailing on Saturdays and Dry Ships. They like receiving Mail, Paying off Day, Nude pin Ups, Sympathy, Complaining and Beer.

A Seamans secret ambition is to change places with the Owner for just one trip, to own a Brewery and to be loved by everyone in the world.

A Seaman is a Sir Galahad in a Japanese Brothel, a Psychoanalist with "Readers Digest" on the table, Don Quixote with a Discharge Book, the Saviour of Mankind with his back teeth awash, Valentino with a fiver in his pocket and Democracy personified in a Red Chinese prison cell.

A Seaman is a Provider in War and a Parasite in Peace. No one is subjected to so much abuse, wrongly accused, so often misunderstood by so many as a Seaman. He has the patience of Job, the honesty of a Fool and the Heaven-sent ability to laugh at himself.

When he returns home from a long voyage no one else but a Seaman can create such an atmosphere of suspense and longing as he walks through the door with the magic words on his lips:

Have you got the Ale in then ??????

On 15th November 1943 convoys to Russia were resumed. JW54A sailed for Murmansk. A week later JW54B was on its way, both arrived without incident. JW55A sailed on 12th December comprising nineteen ships with escorts, supported by the Battleship **DUKE OF YORK** with Admiral Bruce Fraser Commander in Chief Home Fleet aboard and duly arrived Murmansk unmolested. British Intelligence learnt that the Germans were aware of the resumed convoy movement, so Fraser assumed tht some action could be imminent and felt certain that the German Battlecruiser **SCHARNHORST**, confirmed as being in Altenfjord in Norway, would venture out to attack the convoy. His assumption was correct as German Admiral Donetz, aware of the resumed convoys, informed Hitler of his intention for **SCHARNHORST** to put to sea, along with destroyers of his battle group, to strike, attack and destroy the next convoy.

On 20th December JW55B comprising nineteen ships escorted by ten destroyers sailed for Murmansk. At the same time returning convoy RA55A sailed from Murmansk; twenty-two empty cargo ships escorted by eight destroyers and the Cruisers **NORFOLK, SHEFFIELD** and **BELFAST** with Rear Admiral Burnett aboard. Hopefully to trap and attack the **SCHARNHORST**, Fraser in **DUKE OF YORK** with Cruiser **JAMAICA** and the destroyers **SAVAGE, SCORPION, SAUMAREZ** and **STORD** headed north, en route making the four "S Force" boats practise mock torpedo attacks in preparation for the action which was surely soon to come.

By 1200 on 24th December a German reconnaissance plane, the ever present Bloem Voss "Shad", had reported JW55B outgoing convoys, composition, escort, position and speed, to HQ in Norway. The convoy was 400 miles north east of Admiral Fraser's cover force and Admiral Burnett covering the return convoy was well to the east. So as to be closer together for the impending attack, escorts were ordered to slow down the advance of convoy for three hours whilst **DUKE OF YORK** and escorts increased speed to 19 knots, Fraser then ordered Burnett to transfer four of his destroyers to JW55B and divert the return convoy further north, so that now fourteen destroyers were in the escort. Christmas Day, 25th December 1943, the crews of the merchant ships, escorts and covering force were rolling and crashing about in rough seas, blizzards, gales, the snow and the ever present ice, with little chance of a Christmas dinner proceeding forward, waiting nervously but intently for something to happen, guessing and knowing it surely would.

Meanwhile at the naval base at Polyarnoe we were more fortunate as the real bad weather had not yet reached us, but it was snowing, and compared to those at sea we were cosy and warm in our billets. The recent renewed convoy had brought us fresh food and poultry, even razor blades and replacement clothing so we were now a smarter group; food and drink was plentiful, including our illegal bottled tots. There was no point in Bing Crosby dreaming of a White Christmas, this was guaranteed as the snow lay all around, very deep and crisp and even, as it had been since September. Paymaster Lieut Kenneth Clarke RNR Base Supply Officer, our Divisional Officer, strapped on his skis and precariously went into the hills and the old, lonely signal huts to wish them a Merry Christmas and to see they had a turkey and sufficient food and drink. On his visit to the Admiral he found that rats had eaten his turkey so a replacement had to be found. After a drink at each visit and in spite of the worsening weather our Divvy O seemed to have enjoyed his rounds and the run home being down hill was a lot easier. The Admiral's turkey was replaced somewhere along route. Our thoughts were with families at home and our shipmates at sea - not so lucky as us.

In Altenfjord, Norway, not far from us, amidst a Christmas card setting, silently at anchor was the mighty, majestic German Battlecruiser **SCHARNHORST**. The Admiral had done his rounds, Xmas dinner had been eaten, cigars were being smoked, mess decks gaily decorated: the 2000 seamen aboard were very happy. Rear Admiral Erich Bey had left the Tirpitz, now out of action in the Fjord, came aboard **SCHARNHORST** to take command of the ship and her escort of five destroyers **Z29, Z30, Z33, Z34** and **Z38**.

At 1700 Admiral Bey gave the order to "prepare for sea". His intention and orders to attack and destroy JW55B. Whether friend or foe, the time of "good will to all men" was shattered and soon "all hell was to be let loose". The Battle of North Cape was about to begin, the second heavy ship attack on the convoys to Russia. By now, at sea, **SCHARNHORST** and the destroyers were heading into a typical winter Arctic gale. Bey was worried about his destroyers in such weather and signalled Navy Group North that their action would be drastically impeded by atrocious weather. The reply: if this was impossible proceed alone - his first awful mistake. British Intelligence picked up the message and passed to **DUKE OF YORK**. "Admiralty appreciates **SCHARNHORST** at sea" - just what Admiral Fraser wanted to hear.

The situation on Boxing Day. Admiral Fraser, **DUKE OF YORK**, was heading east (200 miles SW of convoy). Admiral Burnett, **BELFAST**, was heading west (150 miles east of JW55B). Admiral Bey, **SCHARNHORST** was heading north (100 miles from convoy) into the trap laid and baited by the Commander-in-Chief. At 0920 the cruiser **SHEFFIELD** sighted the German battlecruiser. **BELFAST** fired star shells to illuminate the target. The Battle of North Cape had begun. Two 8-inch shells from **NORFOLK** struck, one destroyed her radar the other starting a fire. Taken completely by surprise **SCHARNHORST** turned to the south-east to head for the convoy she was at sea to attack. Burnett anticipating this moved placed his cruisers between the convoy and **SCHARNHORST**.

DUKE OF YORK was by now closing the gap. At 1200 **BELFAST** picked up the battlecruiser on radar and by 1220 the cruisers were near enough to open fire at five miles. Admiral Bey was now aware of the remarkably efficient radar system of the British having already been found twice in the dark and atrocious weather. During the afternoon **SHEFFIELD, NORFOLK** and **BELFAST** and the fourtenn destroyers continued the trail of **SCHARNHORST** who was now into the trap Fraser had planned and rehearsed with **JAMAICA**. At 1617 **DUKE OF YORK's** radar picked up the German battlecruiser still unaware of the presence of the British battleship. At a range of 14 miles **BELFAST** again illuminated the target with star shells. Immediately the ten 14-inch guns of **DUKE OF YORK** and the twelve 6-inch guns of **JAMAICA** inflicted severe damage on the enemy ship. Admiral Bey, having by now ordered his destroyers to return to base because of the bad weather realised his mistake. **SCHARNHORST** was now alone and a single target and in an attempt to escape then came under fire from **NORFOLK** and **BELFAST**. By 1800 **DUKE OF YORK's** shells were falling direct on the target destroying her forward turrets and boiler room, reducing her speed considerably. Admiral Fraser then ordered **DUKE OF YORK** and the cruisers to hold their fire and sent the destroyers **SAVAGE, SAUMAREZ, SCORPION** and the Norwegian **STORD** into the attack, as previously rehearsed, with torpedoes on the port and starboard sides of the stricken **SCHARNHORST**. Bey now realised he had lost the battle though his diminished fire power killed and wounded men in the attacking **SAUMAREZ** putting four of the torpedo tubes out of action. The German Admiral now had just two alternatives, surrender and scuttle his ship hoping to save lives or maintain the honour of the German Navy and fight to the finish - his last signal to Donitz and Hitler "WE SHALL FIGHT TO THE LAST SHELL. LONG LIVE GERMANY AND THE FUHRER. SCHARNHORST ONWARDS", immediately followed by the Captain to his crew "I SHAKE YOU ALL BY THE HAND FOR THE LAST TIME".

The torpedoes from the attacking destroyers and the shells from **DUKE OF YORK** and the cruisers caused fires and heavy explosions, **SCHARNHORST** was torn apart and reduced to a barely-afloat, blazing wreck, her original proud sleek silhouette no longer recognisable, the skies around creating a reddish purple glow. **MUSKETEER, MATCHLESS** and other destroyers now closed for their own attack with three more hits. At 1937 Fraser ordered **JAMAICA** to go in and finish her off with torpedoes. Bey ordered **SCHARNHORST's** crew to "abandon ship". The great majestic battlecruiser blazing from end to end, down by the bows, rolled over helplessly after an enormous explosion, slipped forward by the bows and disappeared into the raging sea. She had been hit by 11 torpedoes from over 50 fired at her, 13 shells from **DUKE OF YORK's** 14-inch guns and at least 12 from the 8-inch, 6-inch and smaller guns of the cruisers and destroyers.

From **SCHARNHORST's** crew of nearly 2,000 there were only 36 survivors picked up from the freezing seas by the destroyers **MATCHLESS** and **SCORPION**. The Battle of North Cape went on through Boxing Day 1943 commencing at 0844 with the first sighting by radar of an unidentified large vessel until 2100 when **SCHARNHORST** was reported sunk.

A major factor affecting the **SCHARNHORST's** demise was the poor quality of their radar, which was a gunnery-radar system, and could not give a picture of the whole horizon and it's accuracy was never closer than 2 degrees.

If the German system had been equal to the Royal Navy's, she probably could have picked off the Force One cruisers at long range, and forewarned of **DUKE OF YORK's** approach, could have had it away at 33 knots.

Admiral Bey in **SCHARNHORST** contributed to his ship's fate by sending his destroyers back to base because of the heavy seas. Also, his concern for his 'little ships' made him break W/T silence by contacting Kreigsmarine H.Q. which alerted a British monitoring unit that **SCHARNHORST** was at sea.

So, superior British radar, superb British gunnery, the courage of the destroyer crews, combined with Admiral Bey's clangers, sealed the fate of the Battlecruiser **SCHARNHORST** in those stormracked waters off the North Cape.

With **TIRPITZ** out of action and **SCHARNHORST** sunk, the threat of surface attacks on future convoys had been eliminated.

Leading Signalman Arthur Goldsmith, whose action station was on the bridge of **HMS BELFAST** remembers.

The weather was bloody foul, heavy seas and the inevitable cold. On Christmas Day 1943 the crew did not enjoy their dinner of hard dry biscuits and soup, washed down by endless cups of Kye (ship's cocoa), but this was soon forgotten when, early on Boxing Day, **BELFAST** got the first echo sighting of **SCHARNHORST**. Signalling **NORFOLK** and **SHEFFIELD** they were going to illuminate the target and orders from Admiral Burnett aboard **BELFAST** and for **NORFOLK** to engage. After salvoes on both sides contact was unfortunately lost until later in the day when Scharnhorst made another move to attack, this time within a distance of only 5 miles and we were receiving a lot of near misses, too close for comfort. We then received a signal from C in C Admiral Bruce Fraser aboard **DUKE OF YORK** that the target was within range and to again illuminate **SCHARNHORST** with star shell; as these burst over the enemy there were flashes on the horizon as the **DUKE OF YORK** opened fire. It was an awe-inspiring sight seeing this huge, magnificent battlecruiser speed into a trap from which everyone knew she could not escape. **SCHARNHORST** took a hit forward and another aft until following hits slowed her down. By now she was being pounded by gunfire from all sides with all ships, including the destroyers, having a go with guns and torpedoes and was now on fire and well alight. I had a very clear view from the bridge - an amazing sight although sad to see, but this was war. The awful smell of cordite and burning, so heavy in the evening Arctic darkness, thinking of those on board **SCHARNHORST** who stood little chance of survival once in the water, having a choice of death in the sea or the flames, whilst the majority had no choice at all, being trapped in the bowels of a raging inferno. Having survived the action of gun-fire and torpedoes now came certain death. Then followed a large explosion muffled as though under water followed by silence. As **BELFAST** steamed slowly through the area we put on a 20-inch signal projector to act as searchlight and saw wreckage, bodies, men clinging to wreckage.

Before leaving Kola Inlet to search for **SCHARNHORST** the Russians presented the ship with a reindeer known as Olga who was put in the hangar but was doomed to become an action casualty. During the battle, with the gunfire, shrapnel, cordite and burning, she became so distraught the ship's butcher put an end to her plight with a meat cleaver. Earlier, during the rare occasional lull in the battle, the Rear Admiral was asleep on the deck by the bridge, for a pillow a folded duffel coat on a metal fire hose holder. Trying to wake him with an urgent signal, not being allowed to touch an officer, least of all an admiral, I shook the duffel coat hard which became detached from the holder; as a result the admiral crashed his head on the metal, cutting his ear. He was not very pleased as I realised the first blood of the action was down to me. Rear Admiral Burnett did, after all, have a large head, hence his nick-name "nutty", but not through love of chocolate!

Leading Seaman Eric Parry was aboard **SCORPION** when ordered to attack the **SCHARNHORST** with torpedoes.

I could hear the orders from the captain to various officers so it became obvious we were close to the enemy. I thought at one time we were going right alongside as we seemed to be looking down the muzzles of **SCHARNHORST's** armament.

Our captain was calm with his orders - the S class destroyers being encouraged to attack on their own with torpedoes. **SAVAGE** and **SAUMAREZ** were on the battlecruiser's port quarter, **SCORPION** and **STORD** on the starboard. We closed at a range of 2,000 yards: **SCHARNHORST** could have blown us out of the water. I could hear the torpedo officer calling off the fish as they fired, swinging away we fired all eight and heard them running towards **SCHARNHORST**, two hits were reported. Gunner (T) reported to bridge "all torpedoes fired" the captain replied: Good, let's get the hell out of here". As we turned away we could hear muffled explosions. The S force attack over, **VIRAGO, JAMAICA** and **BELFAST** followed by **MUSKETEER** and **MATCHLESS** went in. By now **SCHARNHORST** was a dead duck. About 1930 I saw this once magnificent battlecruiser go down by the bows with her screws still turning as she rolled over and sank.

In company with **MATCHLESS** we were ordered to move in as close as possible and pick up survivors. Being stopped, the asdic crew were sweeping the area in case U-boats were about. We were now attempting to rescue the poor bloody crew of the **SCHARNHORST**, what few were left, as few survived. The survivors were drenched in oil and half dead with cold, and swallowing fuel, some were injured. One of them, a very "arrogant Nazi", seemed to want to die rather than become a prisoner of war. Whilst hanging on to the scrambling net over the ship's side he refused all help from me and my mates, but we finally pulled him aboard where he still struggled and was very arrogant and defiant. He was dragged on deck but refused to sit. He fell down and started to cry. I went over to him, pulled him to his feet, at the same time receiving a blow to the chest. Stripping most of the oily clothing from the young seaman, he was only 19, known as "Hans", we discovered a shoulder wound which was bandaged with a hankerchief.

The next day the survivors were transferred to the **DUKE OF YORK**. As the "arrogant Nazi" left he walked over to me, put his hand on my shoulder, stood for a moment and smiled, shook my hand vigorously and then got into the boat. Opening my hand I found an oily, soggy photograph. I never saw him again but was proud to have known him. A German sailor, some poor mother's son who, in a small way, was saved from the cold Arctic waters of the North Cape.

Stoker Petty Officer Wilf Birke in the engine room of **SCORPION**:

"The old SCORPS" went in faster than designed to do, the pointers on the oil fuel gauges had gone past the MAX 160 lbs square inch and were tapping the stop peg trying to make another circuit. On deck the **SCHARNHORST** looking like a silver model against a dark background would have made a beautiful picture. I could see the 14-inch shells of the Duke's broadside - like a single decker bus with the windows lit up going along a bumpy road.

We took 30 of the survivors aboard. **MATCHLESS** took the other 6. One of them speaking good English said to me: "Little ship make smoke then bang". Not a single officer was saved. The nearest we got was a commander with his left eye hanging down his cheek; we got him up the stern as we were moving away but on reaching guard rail level he spat at us, let go and dropped down to be mangled by the propellers.

If I'd had a grabbling hook I could have landed the **SCHARNHORST** battle ensign as it floated past on its broken staff.

Able Seaman Bob Tanner aboard **SAVAGE** - with his special duties as navigator yeoman and at sea bridge messenger - was very much aware and involved in the 'S' Force attack. With some six or eight mock attacks on the **JAMAICA** during the previous days he knew exactly what was to be expected. Fraser of **DUKE OF YORK** having believed that "practice makes perfect".

On morning of 26th December I was on watch on the bridge as starboard look-out heard the cruisers were engaging the **SCHARNHORST**. We closed up at action stations late in the afternoon and ordered to take up position with the other 'S' boats for a torpedo attack. On the way in we were criss-crossing the wake of the **SCHARNHORST** turning maximum degrees to port then maximum degrees to starboard: as we approached the battlecruiser shells began falling close to us.

Because of the speed of our attack not all torpedoes went in as time was needed between firing and hitting for the "fish" to become primed for action. The reason for fewer hits than those released, similarly applied to **SAUMAREZ**, **SCORPION** and **STORD**, but nevertheless, between us, it was still a successful high-speed exercise causing further excessive damage to **SCHARNHORST** - practically stopping her in her tracks for the following cruisers to attack and finish her off. After the final action we could see **SCHARNHORST** in her death throes blazing on the horizon.

Thinking it was all over, again action stations sounded and we closed up following a radar contact with an unidentified ship. Our immediate thoughts were the **LUTZOW** was out again to assist **SCHARNHORST** but it was the damaged **SAUMAREZ** limping back to Kola after the damage received in her part of the action. Next morning we were joined by **SCORPION** to escort the crippled **SAUMAREZ** with her dead and wounded into Kola Inlet.

S Force, **SAVAGE, SAUMAREZ, SCORPION** and the Norwegian **STORD** had achieved success with good planning and ardent rehearsal in a combined operation.

Petty Officer Tony McAllister aboard **SAVAGE**, the leader of 'S' Force.

Having practised the mock attacks over and over we were very alert when the time came to attack. Admiral Fraser ordered us in astern of him at full speed to close to 10,000 yards. We went flat out at 30 knots, seemed as if we would ram **SCHARNHORST**, turned hard 35° to port, gunwhales awash; aft depth charge deck was really under. I was lucky not to be washed over the side. All torpedoes fired: we got to hell out of it at same speed.

Petty Officer Leading Torpedo Operator Dick Squires was aboard **MATCHLESS**.

My action station was on the torpedo tubes, positioned at the control and firing position - in a little 'tin hut' perched on top of the tubes and just large enough to contain one man - together with the firing sight, firing levers and communications to the bridge and the tubes crew. The weather was attrocious with heavy seas being shipped inboard at regular intervals. The 'tin hut' turret offered no real protection as each wave managed to deposit my share of the Arctic Ocean through the sighting port right into my lap. After nine hours (and two cups of 'Pusser's Cocoa'), I was a sorry sight but, like everyone else, was engrossed by the task on hand, being kept informed of progress via the control officer on the bridge. Then came the order we all awaited: "Ready Port". I made the preliminary settings on the sights, removed the safety pins and firmly concentrated on the aftermost firing lever - the one that is pulled first. The tubes were being trained to port, the came the fiercest sea of them all, the tubes lurched, I butted the bulkhead, the telephones went dead! The tubes were jammed and the communications had capitulated to the elements. The turret door opened and the Gunner (T) appeared at the opening and said: "Tubes jammed, Squires, we are going to try a starboard attack if we can find our way around the other boats". But before we could do this, the eerie glow that was **SCHARNHORST** disappeared below the waves. Then came the order "Rescue Stations all available hands man the guardrails", but I could not join them as my legs had become numb with cold, so could not move them and was half lifted off the tubes to the warmth of the messdeck, and to the tot-bottle. The toast was, "After that bloody lot, every Boxing Day will be a bonus" - and it still is!!

Radar Operator John Horton aboard **MATCHLESS** was available to man the guard rails to rescue survivors.

The searchlights were switched on wreckage, bodies, and cries for help were everywhere. Four survivors were rescued, covered in dirty, slimy oil, taken to the messdeck, given rum to fetch up the oil they had swallowed, washed, given dry clothing and put into hammocks hardly used by a tired ship's crew. One of the survivors was very belligerent so he was kept away from the others, on his own, on the tiller flat. He was thought to be an SS man as the other survivors were afraid of him.

Edward (Curly) Morris Boy 1st class age 17, was aboard **JAMAICA** on the run to attack the **SCHARNHORST**.

During the action I was the port lookout. The battlecruiser was quite visible, being engulfed in flames, and I saw men running along the deck jumping into the sea. Silhouetted by flames from the superstructure, we torpedoed with our port tubes at 1,000 yards, did a 180° turn and fired our starboard tubes - four hit, one missed and one misfired - soon she was gone.

Helmut "Harry" Boekhoff was one of only 36 German survivors from the crew of the battlecruiser **SCHARNHORST** sunk on Boxing Day, 26th December 1943 in the Battle of North Cape. His rate, equivalent to RN, was Leading Seaman in the communications tower of the battlecruiser, relaying information from lookouts to gun crews.

Harry Boekhoff recalls his experience in the action, as the enemy:

We first contacted the **BELFAST** in the morning then again in the afternoon, we were being bombarded on all sides and fighting the whole fleet in the end. It was difficult to think of time - we slipped away but the destroyers came after us.

People were being killed and the wounded taken down to the hospital. I just got on with my job, you don't think about dying as you never think it is going to happen to you.

All my mates were killed on my deck, I kept wondering what had happened to our destroyers, why had they gone back to port? Earlier they were supposed to be with us when we made contact. Admiral Bey gave no thought to his men; he followed instructions to the end to get the convoy - we could have got away along the coast instead of turning round and steaming right into it.

Then came the final stage, we did not see anything, were just hit, there was an awful explosion, I heard Admiral Bey say "The English are firing by radar". We realised the end had come when the first three torpedoes came in, the water had come up to the commandant's bridge, the ship was going over. I saw blokes jumping from the searchlights thinking they would hit the water but crashing 36 feet into the bridge. Hearing the call "abandon ship" I was one of the last to get off.

The sea was terrible, very rough, you cannot help anybody, everywhere people were grabbing each other, I had not managed to put on a life jacket; I got on to a raft and was picked up in a net, otherwise I would not have had a chance in that sea. I vaguely remember being on board a ship wrapped in a blanket and someone putting a bottle to my mouth, as if I were a baby - there was rum in it. The British sailors were very nice to us - there was no bitterness because seamen generally have a bond.

In all the action, drama and sadness of the Battle of North Cape there is humour on the messdeck of **SEAGULL** as **Signalman Maurice Cross** in lighter vein gives "a Seagull's Eye View".

'Twas Christmas night on the oggin, or rather Boxing Day, and I had the middle watch. It was the usual dark, filthy Arctic night with a gale force 9 to 10, causing tinned Christmas pudding to jingle inside me like a leaden weight. The gyro compass had packed in, so the captain was dead niggled - especially when the quartermaster reported that the magnetic compass card kept veering off course under the malign influence of the Magnetic Pole.

"Tell the radar op. to report any variation on our distance with that tanker" the captain shouted above the wind's howl. Then the radar packed in. "What!" roared the captain, "Get the radar mech. off the gyro and up here on the radar".

The best part of the watch was 'Jimmy the One' emerging backwards from the chart caboose with his duffel coat hood tossed back, when we hit a millstone and three tons of oggin crashed down on the bridge - most of it down Jimmy's neck. Squealing with rage and shock he leapt to the wind-dodger, shook his fist at the raging elements and shouted "the slings and arrows of outrageous bloody fortune!!"

The W/T office buzzer clamoured Emergency! Emergency! I nipped across to the W/T voicepipe, swiftly pulled up the string (highly technical stuff in those days) and removed the pink signal form from the container. It was from Whitehall W/T. "Admiralty appreciates that **SCHARNHORST** is at sea" T.O.O. 0319. "Appreciates! Appreciates!" snarled the captain, "I don't appreciate it. Get that bloody radar working Number One, or we'll be up that tanker's backside or half way across Bear Island". We were homeward bound on Convoy RA55A. After the **SCHARNHORST** message panic stations started, both convoys (one coming, one going) were told by Sir Bruce to push off north out of the way. But not before he pinched four of our fleet destroyers (**MUSKETEER, MATCHLESS, OPPORTUNE** and **VIRAGO**) to join the Murmansk-bound JW escort and later join Force One Cruiser Group.

So our convoy was left to the ministrations of V & W destroyers, corvettes, sweepers, etc. Up north we steamed, away from **SCHARNHORST's** 11" broadsides. The wind reached force 11. Ruddy great waves the size of the Mendip Hills thundered by. Our radar and gyro were back in action, so the captain had regained his usual sang-froid. Then one by one the V & W's flashed, "Heaving-to, to ride out the weather". Because of our shorter, round-bottomed shape, we were riding the giant waves like a rollercoaster, while the long, lean V & W's, were plunging head-on and shaking their guts out. So to our amazement, especially the captain's, we in **SEAGULL** found ourselves Senior Officer of the escort. Fortunately our radar and gyro were still working or we may have led them all across the North Pole. The captain rose to the occasion magnificently and struck Nelsonian poses on the compass platform - no doubt already anticipating the scrambled egg on his cap.

As we carried only four V/S staff, we bunting-tossers were on permanent watch as Morse was flashed about in all directions. "Well chaps, what do you think of being Senior Officer of an ocean-going escort?" beamed the captain. "Bloody terrible", I thought, but said: "Splendid sir, splendid" (Creeping again). What has this got to do with the **SCHARNHORST** caper did you say? Well not much really. I just thought that you 'flash harry's' on the big ships and the fleet destroyers might like to know what the other half were doing, as the big bricks and tinfish were flying about down south. Not that I was breaking my neck to be with you brave lads of course. If it came to a choice of 11" projies whistling through the bulkhead, or shipping it green up with RA55A, I knew where I'd rather be; you guessed it - in the bar of the Seven Stars, with a pint in one hand and a blonde in the other!

On return and arrival at Kola Inlet the 36 survivors were taken aboard **DUKE OF YORK** and allocated accommodation for their return to the UK. Admiral Bruce Fraser addressed his officers. "Gentlemen, the battle against **SCHARNHORST** has ended in victory for us. I hope that if any of you are ever called upon to lead a ship into action against an opponent many times superior you will command your ship as **SCHARNHORST** was commanded today"; and on the ship's notice board gave the following report of their function and action this day.

26th December 1943

Closed Up for Action Stations at 0830

Action completed at 2000

Stood Down from Action Stations at 2200

First engaged enemy with 14" armament at 20,000 yards at 1630

Total number of 14" projectiles fired - 446

Total number of 5.25" projectiles fired - 800

DUKE OF YORK sailed back to UK with the **SCHARNHORST** survivors aboard, they had been fitted out with trousers, blue jerseys, slippers, shaving kit, combs and brushes. As **DUKE OF YORK** came close to the position where their ship sunk they were told to assemble and be ready for a visit from the British Commander in Chief Admiral Bruce Fraser and the captain and officers of his ship. Through an interpreter Fraser asked each man his age, profession, where he lived, why he joined the Navy, then said to the company "We honour a brave opponent even if he has been beaten. The British people harbour no hatred against you. Have no misgivings about being taken to England just do as you are told and you will be all right". At the position the **SCHARNHORST** had been sunk a wreath was laid on the water, an interpreter announcing in German on the tannoy the ceremony was to honour the brave crew of the **SCHARNHORST**.

THE LAST DRAMATIC ACTION - FOLLOWING TORPEDO ATTACK BY SAVAGE, SCORPION, SAUMAREZ AND STORD

1901 hrs	**DUKE OF YORK** and **JAMAICA** opened fire at a range of 10,400 yards. **NORFOLK** opened fire but checked after two salvoes as she was having difficulty in keeping **SCHARNHORST** in sight. Between 1901 and 1928 hours it was observed that the enemy's speed had fallen from 20 to 5 knots.
1915 hrs	**BELFAST** opened fire. Range 17,000 yards.
1925 hrs	**JAMAICA** fired three torpedoes to **SCHARNHORST's** port side, one of which misfired. Range 17,000 yards.
1927 hrs	**BELFAST** fired three torpedoes to the starboard side at a similar range to **JAMAICA**, but could only claim one 'probable' hit. Both cruisers hauled round to fire their remaining torpedo tubes, meanwhile **JAMAICA** engaged **SCHARNHORST** with gunfire.

1928 hrs **DUKE OF YORK** checked fire because of the number of our destroyers in the vicinity.

1931 hrs 72nd Sub-division of the 36th Destroyer Division (**OPPORTUNE** and **VIRAGO** attacked at a range of 2,100 yards. One hit reported.

1933 hrs 71st Sub-division of the 36th Destroyer Division (**MUSKETEER** and **MATCHLESS**), attacked from the north-east on **SCHARNHORST's** port quarter; **MUSKETEER** fired four torpedoes at a range of only 1,000 yards. Two or three hits observed between funnel and mainmast. **MATCHLESS** followed, but could not deliver her attack as a heavy sea hit her torpedo-mounting while the tubes were being trained. The traversing gear was so badly strained that the attack could not be delivered from that side. When **MATCHLESS** had hauled round and came in again to attack again on the **SCHARNHORST's** port bow the battlecruiser had sunk.

1933 hrs **OPPORTUNE** on the 72nd Sub-division of the 36th Destroyer Division fired another salvo of four from 2,500 yards and secured a hit.

1934 hrs **VIRAGO** of the 72nd Sub-division fired seven torpedoes from a similar range and secured at least two hits, she also opened up with gun-fire whilst retiring.

1937 hrs **JAMAICA** fired another three torpedoes from 3,750 yards. Two underwater explosions were recorded after the appropriate 'running' time, but hits were not directly observed as **SCHARNHORST** was obscured in clouds of smoke.

1948 hrs **BELFAST** fired starshell to illuminate the target for further attack, but only drifting wreckage could be seen. **MATCHLESS** reported that **SCHARNHORST** was no longer afloat.

VESSELS THAT TOOK PART IN THE BATTLE OF NORTH CAPE

(including convoy escort and support ships)

H.M.S. Duke of York
H.M.S. Belfast
H.M.S. Jamaica
H.M.S. Norfolk
H.M.S. Sheffield
H.M.S. Ashanti
H.M.C.S. Athabaskan
H.M.S. Beagle
H.M.C.S. Haida
H.M.C.S. Huron
H.M.S. Impulsive
H.M.C.S. Iroquois
H.M.S. Matchless
H.M.S. Meteor
H.M.S. Milne
H.M.S. Musketeer
H.M.S. Onslaught
H.M.S. Opportune
H.M.S. Orwell
H.M.S. Scorpion
H.M.S. Scourge

H.M. Nor. S. Stord
H.M.S. Virago
H.M.S. Westcott
H.M.S. Whitehall
H.M.S. Wrestler
H.M. Nor. S. Acanthus
H.M.S. Dianella
H.M.S. Honeysuckle
H.M.S. Oxlip
H.M.S. Poppy
H.M.S. Gleaner
H.M.S. Seagull

Scharnhorst

Z.29	R.56	U.277
Z.30	R.58	U.314
Z.33	R.121	U.354
Z.34		U.387
Z.38		U.601
		U.716
		U.957

The grand old "Duke of York"
had two thousand men,
Bruce Fraser sailed to the top of the world
Sank "Scharnhorst"
and sailed back again.

SNOOPER AIRCRAFT SIGNALS CONVOY

CONVOY SIGHTED RUSSIA BOUND

HITLER'S NAVY ORDERS STEAM UP

ATTACK CONVOY AS SOON AS FOUND

ROYAL NAVY'S NET IS CLOSING

NAZI RAIDER TURNS AROUND

HELTER SKELTER BACK TO HARBOUR

ONWARD CONVOY SAFE AND SOUND

RETRIBUTION IN THE MAKING

SCHARNHORST BEATEN BROKEN DOWN

TO THE "S" BOATS AND THE CRUISERS

LET OUR THANKS BE MOST PROFOUND

Don Tuffin

Who Sailed The Unknown Region

It was grim on the Arctic convoys,
Though no pen could fully tell.
Of the damnable conditions
In this dismal, frozen Hell.
Well, someone had to be there.
It was just a job, I guess.
And sometimes a wandering seabird
Shared our silent loneliness.

In a climate few could long endure,
Whose hazards have no rival.
The enemy oft took second place.
In the struggle for survival.
The constant foes throughout the years,
Were the elements, no less.
Wind, wave and snow, iceberg and floe,
Shared our silent loneliness.

For God's fresh air and exercise,
We had tramped the upper deck,
At Scapa Flow, and Iceland, too,
We spent hours on the trek.
But not around Bear Island.
If you came up from the mess,
The chill hand of death reached to grip you.
None could walk in such loneliness.

Distant escort in a Battler,
Gave us little satisfaction.
As we tried to lure the Germans out
And bring their ships to action.
For Jerry knew our tactics,
And in this wilderness.
A solitary German aircraft
Shared our silent loneliness.

We were generally shadowed,
And with each successive plane,
The element of surprise was lost,
Our efforts rendered vain.
But one day fate would favour us,
For in this game of chess
The Duke of York and Scharnhorst,
Would meet in this loneliness.

I was home on leave on Boxing Day,
Had just paid off the Howe,
The frozen wastes and Arctic gloom
Were but a memory now.
Then suddenly some stirring news
Burst forth from the wireless
My thoughs reached out to friend-and foe,
Who fought in such loneliness.

I rejoiced; they had sunk the Scharnhorst,
But I grieved for her hapless crew
And remembered my many comrades,
At rest in these waters, too.
For someone had to die there.
It was just their turn, I guess.
Now two thousand German seamen
Shared their silent loneliness.

It was grim on the Arctic convoys
Though not easy to explain.
Of eight hundred ships which sailed there,
Full one hundred still remain.
And if you're ever sent there.
You'll have company of the best.
The ghosts of five thousand sailors,
Roaming in silent loneliness.

After the sinking of the **SCHARNHORST** in the Battle of North Cape, and before the return of the survivors, as prisoners, to the UK Admiral Bruce Fraser came ashore to Polyarnoe from the **DUKE OF YORK** for a visit to the Senior British Naval Officer, and the Signal Station to thank us for our small part in the recent battle.

Accompanied by his Flag Lieutenant he stepped ashore from his launch, slipped and fell headlong into the snow. The Flag Lieutenant brushed the snow from his resplendent uniform before proceeding to the Base. The Admiral was immediately approached, pounced on and pestered by the ever present Russian children begging for chocolate and cigarettes. "Chocolata, Cigaretta Pajolsta" they screamed.

"Flags, what do these children want?"

"Chocolate and Cigarettes Sir but you must say "Niet" ". The Admiral showing off his meagre knowledge of Russian replied: "Sorry Son Neit Chocolata and Cigaretta". The screaming reply was **F...ing Bastard, F...ing Bastard!**

Shocked, surprised and aghast Admiral Bruce Fraser turned his head in shame:

"Flags, judging by this boy's knowledge of the English language, there must be many British sailors ashore here!"

1944

- *A Gnat with a deadly sting*
- *Half a ship is better than none*
- *Chilly times on the "Chiltern"*
- *Take-offs and landings from an unsteady flight deck*

The great news I had received previously about my leave to visit Moscow after eleven months at the naval base, and having returned, came an even more exciting notification. Christmas was over - our hectic Boxing Day at the signal station with the "Battle of North Cape" going on virtually on our doorstep - and now my relief was taking passage in one of the escorts of the next convoy. I was to return to UK on 3rd February 1944 taking passage in **HMS SPEEDWELL**. I breathed a sigh of relief as excitement came over me.

As **SPEEDWELL** steamed slowly out of the inlet heading for the Barents Sea I glanced back at what had often been referred to as "The Arsehole of the World, with Polyarnoe right up it" and thought, thank goodness, at last I'm leaving this godforsaken place.

One has often heard it said when something interesting or exciting has happened: "I feel on top of the world". We had been there, literally, not all that exciting but unique.

After an uneventful passage, except for being virtually unconscious for three days with seasickness aboard such a small ship in heavy seas, we arrived back in UK.

At Thurso, Northern Scotland, I went straight to the Post Office to phone home to say I was safely in Scotland. Standing at the counter was an extremely attractive girl. She sensed I was gazing at her as I just could not keep my eyes from her. Walking across to apologise for looking at her in that way, I asked if I could just talk to her. Her natural reply, but with a delightful smile, was: "Why?"

"I have just come back from North Russia where I have been for twelve months and you are the first girl I have spoken to in a very long time; please forgive me". Realising my intentions were honourable and friendly, further conversation ensued. Now Russia seemed far away and meeting and talking to this attractive girl made me feel I really was home at last.

On 25th February 1944 whilst escorting a north bound convoy JW57 **HMS MAHRATTA** was sunk in the Barents Sea by a "Gnat" Torpedo from **U990**. Of the 220 men aboard only 17 survived: another victim of the dreaded torpedo containing one and a half tons of high explosive. The listening device fitted in the head of the weapon enabled it to home in to the noise of the ship's propellers.

A target travelling at more than 24 knots or less than 8 knots was generally immune. **HMS MAHRATTA** was between the two.

The Acoustic Torpedo nicknamed the "GNAT" (Giro Navigational Acoustic Torpedo).

The enemy were apparently using a torpedo which followed a ship's course striking her in the stern. Intelligence provided indisputable evidence that they were equipping U-Boats with several of these acoustic weapons.

This deadly torpedo was intended primarily to destroy escorts so that a convoy would be left unprotected and at the mercy of ordinary torpedoes. The new weapon could be fired at extreme range in the general direction of an escort. It would then hear her propellers and automatically alter course towards the target, faithfully following her zig-zags until it hit and blew off the stern of the ship.

Admiralty experts, however, established some measure of defence from the "Gnat". If escorts steamed at no more than eight knots, or not less than twenty-four, they were immune. Analyses of widespread attacks showed that the torpedoes were hard to shake off between these speeds but could not hear propellers outside them. There was a snag; at seven knots the escorts were too slow for the convoy, and at twenty-four knots the convoy was too slow for the escorts.

Another defence was the introduction of a device known as "FOXERS" which would, it was hopefully supposed, attract the "Gnat" and explode it well astern of the target. It consisted of a series of wires trailed over the stern on the end of which were long strips of metal. The theory was that the metal strips would be tossed around in the wake, fifty yards astern and clustered together, making a din the "Gnat" could not fail to hear above the noise of the propellers. But again, this created yet another snag. It made so much noise the ASDIC equipment became practically useless to warn of approaching U-Boats.

As if the run up was not enough, **Jimmy Edwards** found himself torpedoed at the end of the journey, in the approach to Kola Inlet. The name of the ship was not too appropriate, the **LARK**, a victim of "Gnat". While waiting for the return convoy to assemble, Jim was detailed for jobs about the ship during the forenoon. He recalls:

I went down into the tiller flat astern for the afternoon watch. Hearing the pipe 'afternoon watch men to dinner' no one needs telling twice when grub was up. On the mess deck our 'tot' was waiting for us, there was also another 'tot' for one of the lads from the same mess and taking it to him on the quarter deck I said: 'See this off mate - down in one'. They had just reached the mess deck on their return, when the "Gnat" torpedo hit them. His mate was standing with three more of the lads when he was cut in half; one was never found at all, and one was picked up by a Russian MTB and died of exposure, the other only had a sprained back.

Jim thought he had a charmed life that morning, the tiller flat was no more, for when the lads went on deck the 'tinfish' must have been running, moreover had he not had the afternoon watch, he would have been in the mess when the torpedo struck at 11.40 a.m. The U-Boat fired another one but as they had been turning to starboard it passed by.

LARK was towed into the Inlet, other bodies found in the wreck were removed for sea burial.

The **LARK** was so badly damaged with her stern blown off she could not return to UK. Considered now as scrap she was handed over to the Russians for whatever use they could make of it.

A similar incident happened on 11th December 1944 to **HMS CASSANDRA** who had her bows blown off by torpedoes from a U-Boat (now known to be a "Gnat") but causing similarly devastating damage.

CASSANDRA's introduction to convoy work was in November 1944 when, with six other destroyers, escorted two troopships, EMPRESS OF AUSTRALIA and SCYTHIA, transporting 11,000 repatriated Russian ex-prisoners of war and slave workers of the Germans, arriving in Murmansk on 6th November.

Her next was JW62 arriving safely with 30 merchant ships on 7th December. Returning with RA62 heading for the UK she left on December 10th. Other escorts were ahead of the convoy to drive off the U-Boats near the entrance to Kola Inlet. They then formed a patrol some 150 miles out.

At 0600 on 11th December a U-Boat blew the bows off **CASSANDRA**. It was amazing she did not sink, the damage control party had done their job and although surrounded by casualties the ship was towed stern first back to Kola, to go into the dry dock whilst still afloat: more bodies were found in the mangled wreckage and transferred to **HMS CHILTERN** for sea burial. 62 of her ratings were killed.

Able Seaman Morris Birkett, aboard at the time **CASSANDRA** was struck, relates:-

On the night prior to the explosion, December 11th 1944, I had the middle watch (midnight until 0400) along with my operating 'oppo'.

The watch was uneventful and at 0400 I said goodnight to my oppo, not realising that we would never meet again. He went to his hammock in the forward mess deck, and I to mine, just outside the canteen hatch. Going to sleep straight away I was next aware of flying through the air and landing flat on my back on the deck. (Apparently the time was 0602).

After laying awhile trying to figure out the situation I heard water running and the deck seemed to be wet. Suddenly, I thought I'm going to have to go in the 'drink' - where is my lifebelt? Before starting to look for it, I had already forgotten about it.

I was next aware of two figures standing at the open mess door. They were both waving their arms, indicating to me to come that way. (I realised later how important that action was as some shipmates in a concussed state had run the wrong way into the open sea).

I was directed to the wardroom, which had become a sick bay. Here I was inspected by the ship's surgeon - wrapped in a blanket and given a shot of something which put me to sleep again.

When next I woke I appeared to be in a straitjacket, on the iron deck, for transfer to another ship which I could see coming alongside. I said: "I want to be sick". The reply came: "Be sick then, don't worry about the deck".

After a couple of days I was able to move about and talked with others about what happened. Nobody really seemed to know anything clearly - was it a mine or was it a torpedo?

Petty Officer Stoker Sid Lay, also aboard **CASSANDRA**, had a similar plight.

The torpedo hit forward and the bow, right back to 3 gun, broke off. Those who survived were amazed to think we were towed to Rosta Dry Dock without sinking, a credit to the damage control party shoring up the bulkhead.

Eventually, in dry dock with the water pumped out, the extent of the damage was realised, everything had gone forward of the canteen flat. One body was found, naked, not a stitch on. Hammocks slung belonging to those on watch, had shells in them blown up from the forward magazine.

The cold room had been flooded so there was no need for offal, this was removed by the Russians whom we described as "zombies" being expressionless. As the meat and offal was taken off the ship it was being eaten, although the cold room had been under water for weeks.

In the dry dock it became very cold and heaters had to be put in the remaining mess decks. Life aboard was very uncomfortable, we slept on camp beds under the mess table being no room to sling hammocks; there were layers of ice on the bulkheads; our food was tinned stuff and black bread.

The idea of fitting a new bow, so that **CASSANDRA** could return to UK, presented many problems as materials sent out were in ships that had been sunk. So the Russians were persuaded to do it using their own wood and steel, and the work, carried out by mere youngsters, men and women, took several weeks.

With a renewed bow **CASSANDRA** - a peculiar sight - sailed for the UK, the crew apprehensive as to whether it would make it in rough weather, or at all. But as credit to the Russians, no more than a bucket of water was found in the bulges at the end of this unique voyage.

Sid Lay eventually arrived in Chatham on July 1945 after an enforced stay in Russia of 7 months.

With **Signalman Bill Proctor** aboard **VIRAGO**:

On arrival at Kola Inlet, destroyers **HARDY, VIRAGO, VENUS**, and Norwegian **STORD** were immediately refuelled and rushed out to escort an incoming convoy who were having a particularly bad time because of the icefield that had encompassed Bear Island.

They sailed at 28 knots and after a day or so could just see the convoy in the murky light. Sailing in line ahead came across eight to ten U-Boats in a virtual line, port to starboard all sitting on the surface, not one spotted the destroyers coming up astern, their look-outs must only have had eyes on the approaching convoy. It was not until Hardy started ramming through the line they were seen, and tried to go down as fast as they could, not all of them made it one of them off starboard bow, in perfect position for ramming.

This was **VIRAGO's** opportunity and she was given the job as her Captain had previously sunk five U-Boats, two by ramming and three by gunfire. Bill reported U-Boat bearing green 45 Sir, on surface. Skipper said to Jimmy shall we have a go at it? It will only take a few minutes then we can return to the line. By the time they reached the U-Boat it had started to submerge, but the stokers reported to bridge, it had been hit. Another U-Boat was still on surface bearing green nine-0. The question was should they go to starboard to attack but it was thought it would take too long as **HARDY** and others were now some two miles away.

Turning to port to rejoin, as the destroyers and convoy appeared as one bunch, a loud explosion was heard. The captain stood to attention, saluted, saying there goes another brave merchantman. On getting closer it was realised the **HARDY** had been hit by a gnat torpedo whilst doing only 18 knots. The only way to beat the gnat torpedo was to steam at 24 knots which was too fast to catch up or 8 knots wherein the revs were not fast enough for the screws to attract.

VIRAGO immediately went alongside to pick up survivors. **VENUS** and **STORD** circling around dropping depth charges to disorientate the U-Boat instruments.

Bill called **HARDY** "which side alongside" but received no reply. Then two more explosions and smoke was completely engulfing the stricken ship. Everyone thought it was the end but when the smoke cleared **HARDY** was in the same position. Everyone was relieved, Bill flashed again "which side alongside" but still no reply, then kept calling her pennant number. He thought everyone on the bridge who could signal must be killed, although some movement was seen.

The **HARDY** never went down, the **STORD** had to finish her off with two twenty-one inch fish. The armour-plated hulls were only three-sixteenth thick and were known as the eggshell destroyers - were expendable - and expected to go down from one torpedo. It took two to sink **HARDY**. Eighty men were picked up jumping from fo'c'sle to fo'c'sle, **VENUS** rescued the rest. Fourteen men died mostly those in the stern.

Yet another victim of the notorious destructive Gnat torpedo (Giro Navigational Acoustic Torpedo).

In August 1944 on return to the Royal Naval Patrol Service Headquarters HMS Europa Lowestoft - known to all as the Sparrows Nest because, as in peacetime, it was the town's Municipal Park - **Steward Bill Taylor** heard the top priority was to get a draft out of Lowestoft as soon as possible.

To be called to the Drafting Master-at-Arms office to discover one's luck was exciting, as it could be anywhere like Australia, South Africa or the West Indies. Having just returned from Grimsby, the largest minesweeping port in the U.K., one was looking for sunshine away from the war, but alas Bill was told: "Mark your bag 'Chiltern' ". The next day a whisper came to us that someone had seen the **CHILTERN** in NORTH RUSSIA. Nobody wanted to believe it was true. After 14 days the order was to mark our bags Scapa Flow. It was true, it was North Russia.

23 souls had been selected by the Lords of the Admiralty to go to Russia as replacement of the present crew of the **CHILTERN**.

What was the **CHILTERN**? We knew it was a trawler but what was her function and purpose? To visit ships around the Inlet, deliver and collect stores, sea burials, or in the event of a jerry coming down from Petsamo only 20 miles away to evacuate the S.B.N.O. and his staff. **CHILTERN's** duties extended as far as Archangel.

It was night when we arrived at Kola Inlet and anchored in Vaenga Bay. After breakfast I could not wait to see Russia. There it was, silent, cold, most uninviting. I kept saying to myself, I am on top of the world, 500 miles from the north pole and here for at least twelve months.

Whilst surveying everything around me a trawler approached. It looked so small and although I had served on trawlers since 1938 I never realised how small a trawler was until now. Could this be the **CHILTERN** I wondered, the intercom confirmed it was the "one and only" **CHILTERN** and now alongside. Her crew were radiant, all smiles with the thought of returning to the U.K.

When a skipper takes over a ship he signs for the ship lock, stock and barrel and debt. It did not take our skipper E. Creaser RNR long to realise that the outgoing crew were over £200 in debt and that would be our problem. The outcome being he refused to sign the ship over. This caused raised eyebrows. The 1st Lieutenant in Polyarnoe told him he had got to sign for the ship but our skipper refused. All the time this argument was going on the sailing time for the return convoy was getting near. The lads waiting to go home realised they would miss the boat and **CHILTERN** would have two crews.

By this time the Senior British Naval Officer, came into the argument. It was only then, on his assurance that there would be a clean sheet and a new inventory, the ship was signed over, and with relief the old crew were allowed passage to the U.K.

We said "goodbye" to the lads and set about making the **CHILTERN** our home. I immediately went to my cabin to sort out my bunk and settle in. On my first night aboard I found to my horror the ship was infested with rats. They were in the bed, under pillows in duffel coats and oilskins. There were thousands of them, just everywhere, big fat rats, I could not sleep because of the noise they made. It became a sport trying to kill them. The champion rat killer, a stoker, had his own technique. Using an oil can with a flexible spout he would blind the rat with oil then hit it with his fist. This method accounted for a large number of rats but we could not win as they were still coming aboard off the wooden jetties simply by running up the mooring ropes on to the decks and the rest of the ship was theirs.

We had many talks by officers from the base at Polyarnoe on our behaviour and conduct with the Russian authorities and the people as we soon found out there was a large gulf in between. The first month was taken trying to store the ship with food. This became first priority as there was little in the NAAFI stores. This brought the skipper to his feet again, this time in conflict with the base supply officer who by the end of the month had to repay every man aboard the **CHILTERN** £5 for unused victualling allowance. This was repeated the second month: so how did the old crew get £200 in debt if there were no stores to buy? It never did get sorted out. We were very short of food for the 12 months and begging and stealing soon becoming the order of the day. My priority was to get aboard all visiting ships, contact the butcher and baker to buy or beg for meat and bread.

The routine of going to the sick bay for "Durex" was soon shattered by the sick berth attendant . . . that none were available. As there was no fraternising with Russian women, they would not need any. Three of the crew had reason to visit the medical officer . . . VD was diagnosed. The next day the surgeon lieutenant commander came aboard to see the skipper as to why the men had not gone to the sick bay for "Durex". They did, but you did not have any as it was considered unnecessary. Next day a sick berth attendant came aboard presenting the skipper with a box of 144 brand new "Durex" - I was later introduced to the woman who was the cause of all the trouble - over sixty years old, with a mouth full of metal teeth gold, silver and steel, it was like a scrap yard!

CHILTERN's job was to deliver stores all over the Inlet, stealing and pilfering was not considered a crime as at times it was necessary to survive. One occasion we had a cargo of whisky. The address of the valuable cargo was destined for Moscow. The British, Australian and Canadian Embassies. We had the cargo overnight in a barge, so big was the consignment it was to be the undoing of three of the crew. They made so much noise breaking into the whisky they awakened the skipper from his sleep. His words: "I'm not taking the can for this lot". Captain's Report of course. Found guilty and sentenced to three months' imprisonment to be served in the U.K.

Another job for the **CHILTERN** was sea burial of RN personnel who had been killed in action on the convoys or had died in Russia. One ship was lying at the Rosta dry dock waiting for dry docking for weeks. When at last it was in the dock four bodies were taken from the wreckage. The admiral was reluctant to have any person buried in Russia as relatives would want to visit the graves of loved ones, yet this was an impossibility. On one occasion we did carry in a cargo of War Graves Commission gravestones, so there were some graves ashore.

Contrary to belief that Kola and Murmansk are ice free all the year round, on at least two occasions in the winter of 1944-45 **CHILTERN** was ice-bound. The first time we were returning to Polyarnoe from Vaenga when we had pack-ice coming in from the sea, getting thicker until it became continuous, unbroken from bank to bank. I was with the skipper on the bridge who reassured me the ship would break it's way through the ice, this was 0100, five minutes later we were high and dry on top of the ice showing four feet of the bow exposing the keel. Problem now was how to free the old girl without damaging the propeller. Eventually, after an hour of drama, she freed herself. **CHILTERN** had already experienced a broken propeller. The Russians were able to replace it, but put it on the wrong way round and made it go astern instead of ahead, an embarrassing situation for any ship's skipper.

Another occasion of Kola being frozen, the trawler needed a boiler clean and went past Murmansk to a village known as Drovanoy, a collection of wood huts plus an ocean liner with it's bows blown off and a workshop for ship repairs. It should have been a seven day job but to everyone's amazement the trawler's triple expansion engine was taken out and laid in the snow. We had no water, electricity, heat, and the temperature was nearly 50° below freezing. Water was carried from a stand pipe, shore electricity by supply line failed at least once an hour. Drovanoy was on the opposite shore to Murmansk, a small ferry took an hour to cross. On one occasion the skipper and I went across for a hopeful meal. We returned to the ferry to get back to find the Inlet frozen over once more. There was not one ship moving. We had to stay at a hotel for one week looking across the river where the **CHILTERN** lay stranded.

We knew food was getting low so how to get supplies became top priority. On the 5th day the **CHILTERN's** crew came to the hotel. They had walked across the Inlet to Kola village, across the river at the narrowest point and back up the opposite side of Murmansk. They had come to tell us of the desperate food situation and how the crew were living on tea and corned beef, being all that was left on board. Eventually the ice thawed and we returned to the ship.

The refit came to an end, the Russians managed to put the engine together again. Before the boiler clean the trawler would do 9 knots, after she did 7.

The day **CHILTERN** raised steam and sailed away from this terrible, awful place was the best day of our Russian experience, but not without one more small problem. We proceeded to Rosta to coal ship. In theory the best coal was Welsh steam coal sent out from the U.K. and discharged on the quay coal wharf for the ships to use. Somehow the best Welsh steam coal had been replaced with Spitzbergen coal, which was almost dust. As soon as the ship made fast at the wharf an army of Russian women descended on the ship and worked all night nonstop. The job completed, came the task of cleaning the ship, the dust from inferior Russian coal got into every corner and it took two weeks to get the ship clean.

On 8th August 1945 **HMT CHILTERN** sailed from Polyarnoe for the last time arriving home after 8 days of heavy going in a 324 ton Trawler, built to fish out of Fleetwood and Lowestoft, doing only 7 knots.

A gallant, hard-working fishing trawler had served her time in the war, especially North Russia, for every purpose needed, with more variety than any other small ship in the Navy.

When the ship was handed back to the owners in 1945 the fishing nets from 1939 were still in the mess deck hold, but after the rats had been at them for 5 years were found to be of no further use.

In August 1944, a further gift was made to the Russians, for use by the Northern Fleet, of the battleship **ROYAL SOVEREIGN**, following a complete refit in America.

A skeleton crew came to England to sail with the ship to Russia in Convoy JW59. On arrival the battleship was renamed **ARCHANGELSK**, considered to be a very bad omen to change the name of a vessel at any time. To Royal Navy personnel it was nick-named the "Tiddly Quid" and "Regal Rouble".

The **ARCHANGELSK** never fired a shot in anger but during firing practice of its massive guns shot down a Catalina aircraft which happened to be passing overhead at the time. Fortunately no one was killed, the pilot and crew of Americans, on an official visit, were rescued by a ship in the area.

There was considerable distress and concern when it was noticed, on many occasions, lines of dhobying strung across the upper deck, dressed overall with a difference!

The battleship was never used and was returned to UK in a very filthy state, known in our Navy as "Shit Order", with rumours that it had been used as a "floating brothel".

The battleship **ARCHANGELSK** (neé **ROYAL SOVEREIGN**) sailed to Inverkeithing in Scotland for breaking.

Master-at-Arms Sid Conley having done quite a few Russian Convoy runs in **NIGERIA**, Convoy JW64 then in **NAIRANA**, an escort carrier, considers it is not easy to make comparisons or segregate the good, the bad or the bloody awful, but most of them would fall under the last category. However JW64 and the return RA64 in **NAIRANA** were by far the worst. There is no doubt that they suffered the most continuous and lethal attacks by enemy aircraft coupled with the most appalling weather conditions ever experienced.

The combined air and U-Boat attacks were being constantly pressed home with some determination. The size of the air attacks were more than previously experienced often numbering 40 aircraft split into five groups of eight attacking from various directions. JU88's were dropping torpedoes like confetti, how so many failed to find the target was nothing short of a miracle.

As with so many Russian convoys my sympathy and admiration on the round trip went to the small ship sailors in the escorts. The sea conditions on occasions were the worst that could be encountered anywhere in the world. It must have been sheer bloody hell aboard those boats with hurricane force winds and the freezing seas. Only those who served can know what it was really like. The strain of being continually closed up at action stations and under constant threat of attack from aircraft and U-Boats and to have imposed upon them the onerous task of shepherding the stragglers, meaning little or no rest twenty four hours a day, plus the constant buffeting from the seas. Some of the lads would, I'm sure, would have been happy to have changed places with the U-Boat crews just for a few hours to slip below the surface of the sea to enjoy the warm, dry comfort of being on an even keel.

As a big ship sailor I watched them with pride and felt deeply the tragic loss of the **BLUEBELL** which was very close to us at the time. I was in the fore well deck when she was hit. The shock of seeing the ship disappear with the whole of her ship's company was horrific.

For those who served in the escort carriers it was a different world, the prime object of the carrier was to keep her aircraft airborne as and when needed. **NAIRANA** with her 835 Squadron and our sister ship **CAMPANIA** with 813 Squadron achieved this to a remarkable degree having regard to the atrocious weather and frequency of air attacks and the 24-hour anti-submarine patrols by the Swordfish, with their open cockpits. You have to appreciate life on a carrier with the skill and courage of the aircrews, particularly those with small flight decks as so much of the flying was at night, and particularly hazardous in bad weather when each take off and landing was a feat of skill and cool nerve. Getting the fighters safely aboard in a sixty-knot wind with the carriers stern rising and falling fifty feet was due to the skill of the batsman. Many times I watched Swordfish taking off in blinding snowstorms from a pitching flight deck, disappear from vision as they struggled to "lift off" and thinking "Come back safe, lads", sadly, sometimes they did not. One aircraft struggling to take off from **NAIRANA** was struck by a cross sea, the Swordfish slid to starboard, smashed into the oerlikon and catapulted over the side. Miraculously the **ONSLAUGHT** had the crew out of the sea in minutes and they survived.

Unfortunately for the fighters, the perils of take off, landing on and engaging the enemy aircraft was not the only thing they had to contend with. Despite warnings given to captains of the merchantmen over the R/T aircraft were damaged by anti-aircraft fire and some were shot down by the guns of the convoy ships.

On one occasion **NAIRANA's** most experienced fighter pilot had to dive through a very heavy anti-aircraft barrage from the escorts to shoot down a JU88.

The flight deck aircraft handling parties did a magnificent job. Working on a snow-covered flight deck being whipped by gale force winds can be a frightening experience, the wind can lift an aircraft and the handling crew and deposit them over the side as there are no stanchions or bulkheads on the deck against which one can secure and make fast.

Many aircrews' lives were saved by the efficient way the handlers carried out their duties. Frequently there were unavoidable crash landings, aircrews being quickly released and the aircraft secured or in some cases put over the side.

Very good work was also carried out, in the same difficult circumstances, by the Fleet Air Arm maintenance crews with repair and servicing aircraft ready in time for the next anti-submarine patrol flight. Bearing in mind that the total aircraft defending the convoy was 835 Squadron's fourteen Swordfish and six Wildcats from **NAIRANA** and 813 Squadron's twelve Swordfish and six Wildcats from **CAMPANIA**, they achieved a remarkable success over the numbers and superior aircraft which the enemy threw against them, plus keeping the U-Boats under control.

On another occasion the convoy was under heavy torpedo bomber attack. The **NAIRANA** helmsman swung the ship so violently to port to miss a torpedo it temporarily jammed the rudder making two circles out of control, narrowly missing collision several times.

Having rolled in ships "East of Suez and west of Panama" was nothing compared to the return journey with head winds of seventy knots. Forty degrees of roll was considered the safety limit for escort carriers. Standing in the port catwalk **NAIRANA** went into a roll to starboard and just kept going over and over. With my chest pressing hard against the ship's side, my eyes level with, and looking across the flight deck all that could be seen was this massive bloody steel island carrying her over, certain that she would never recover and silently screaming "come back you ugly, ungainly cow". Hanging, poised for what seemed an eternity, then ever so slowly beginning to climb back. In those few seconds I felt proud of the ship and remorse for the mental abuse.

To every manjack that sailed in the convoys to Russia I believe they can justifiably recite with pride that old naval ode "Hardships, you bastards don't know what hardships are!" Having seen a few officers and men from all branches crack under the strain I always thought: "There, but for the grace of God, go I".

Others sailed to Russia with the Fleet Air Arm aboard what were known as "The Woolworths Carriers".

The origin of these carriers, **SEARCHER, STRIKER** and **TRACKER** amongst a few - or Banana Boats as they were more affectionately known by those who served on them - were based on a type of merchant ship originally designed to carry fruit mainly for the banana trade. The bananas were carried in box section holds, so that the fruit was more or less ripe when the ship reached its destination.

During the war the Americans, who built these ships, found that by the elimination of the interior hold bulkheads when under constructions they virtually had a ready-made aircraft hangar, and by building a flight deck above the superstructure, with a lift forward and one aft, they had a cheap, constructed carrier. Operating within the main squadrons of American Wildcats, Hellcats, Corsairs and eventually Seafires, they served with some distinction.

Because of the swiftness and low cost that these carriers could be constructed in the American dockyards - as opposed to the cost of a conventional aircraft carrier - they got dubbed with the nickname "Woolworths".

Earlier in January 1942 on approaching Kola Inlet one ship was lost and another damaged by a mine. This started a battle; with German minelaying around, and closing ports, this created a problem. Minesweepers were sent out together with experts to show the Russians how to cope with the various types, contact, magnetic and acoustic. In spite of this training more than one ship having battled through with the other enemy, the weather, and under attack all the way, became the victim of a mine.

Having agreed to the immense task of getting convoys through, surely some effort could have been made to make their waters safe from U-Boats with the minesweepers made available. Also at the end of a hazardous voyage, they could have provided fighter cover with the Hurricanes supplied, and the training given how to fly them being only an hour's flight away. Not one of the Hurricanes the previous convoy had delivered, ever went out of sight of land to help and perhaps save ships being attacked in the approach to their shores. Requests and pressure for the need to cover the convoy from Bear Island to Kola Inlet were met with the often repeated "NIET".

1945

- *Sailing on a floating bomb*
- *Sadly, Bluebell's do not survive in the Arctic*
- *The end is in sight - but not yet*
- *"They followed us into port like little lambs"*
- *"We are still alive"*

Convoy JW65 entered Kola Inlet on 21st March 1945 **OPPORTUNE** and **ORWELL** were allowed no time to relax and were ordered to Rosyth where with minelayer **APOLLO**, loaded up with mines. On 16th April orders were received to sail to Murmansk. The group, **APOLLO, OPPORTUNE, OBEDIENT** and **ORWELL** sailed at 18 knots in Operation Trammel to lay a deep anti-U-Boat minefield in the approach to Kola Inlet being an area where U-Boats, protected by unusually bad and persistent asdic conditions, lay in wait for convoys.

For many months the Russians had refused British demands to mine the area until losses sustained by recent incoming and outgoing convoys to UK and their own losses in Archangel forced the ally to give way.

The fast passage to Kola Inlet had its hazards for destroyers carrying two long lines of mines 30 port, 30 starboard sitting on large, square steel and mooring cable containers. The mines coupled on launching rails lowered over, restricted the free movement forward and aft along quarterdecks. Spray formed into ice which day and night had to be chipped and scraped off mines and horns making it a daunting task, but it had to be done otherwise stability of the speeding destroyers was at risk.

The minelaying squadron arrived on 21st April and the operation very nearly became sabotaged by the obstinacy of the Russians. Instead of allowing the squadron to lay mines right away they insisted on the ships going to Polyarnoe to be inspected and to embark liaison officers. Thus patrolling U-Boats, sighted and were warned off, the squadron's intended mines could not fail to be seen crowding the upper decks of the destroyers and **APOLLO's** role was unmistakable. The ships that had been exposed on entry to the inlet had now to emerge and carry out the lay. It was an unnerving evolution, the ships in rigid formation had to steam at a slow 10 knots on a steady course to lay their mines with Russian officers plotting the position of each mine as it dropped off the stern of the parent ship. Russian obsessional distrust of their British ally became counter-productive for in the ships of the mine-laying squadron gyro compasses repeating positions allocated to their officers were all offset by a few degrees so that it was impossible for them to accurately plot the position of the minefield within their territorial waters.

In spite of damage from U-Boats all went well and then to the alarm of the Russian liaison officers the squadron led by **APOLLO** steamed back at high speed to Polyarnoe over the minefield to prove they had laid a deep field. Next day on 23rd, having the previous evening entertained highly critical Russian liaison officers, the squadron left at high speed arriving at Scapa Flow three days later.

On the 25th a U-Boat blundered into the new minefield while the squadron was still on its return passage and they received from SBNO North Russia a signal which congratulated them in "quick dividends".

Ron Thake was aboard the minelayer **APOLLO** heading for Russia to take part in Operation Trammel in company with **OPPORTUNE, OBEDIENT AND ORWELL**. The destroyers had 6 mines aboard clamped each side of the quarterdeck. **APOLLO** had no less than 160 on board.

Imagine his thoughts and feelings and the other crew members as they constantly gazed upon the most lethal of all cargoes. If one single mine can sink a merchant ship what could happen to a minelaying cruiser carrying 160, does not bearing thinking about.

Fortunately the passage was fast, not being a convoy escort, and weather calm. One can only imagine the extreme relief on completion of the laying, more so after the delay experienced on arrival at Kola Inlet.

Russia still required convoys to continue to meet inflexible demands from a relentless ally, too many convoys, one out and one return had to be run. It mattered not that cargoes from previous JW convoys of motor vehicles, artillery, tanks, locomotives and thousands of tons of other war material lay in the snow deteriorating. A scene that destroyed the morale of every seaman in the convoys. A reduced escort was required to deal with U-Boats who might not have received orders to cease fire and proceed to nominated ports to surrender. JW67 departed from Clyde on 12th May 1945 and arrived Kola Inlet without problems on 20th May. Three days later on 23rd May the last allied convoy departed from Kola Inlet. It is unlikely that any of the seamen manning convoy ships had any other feelings than an intense sense of relief at leaving this awful place.

Except for the discomforts of early Arctic spring sea conditions the last passage, uneventful RA67, arrived at the Clyde on the last day of May.

If the cargo from JW66 was still deteriorating in the snow it is assumed that the cargo from JW67 suffered the same fate, the result of the still consistent demands of the Russians, making one wonder how much of the many previous convoys, cargoes were actually used, considering the perils, suffering and loss of life and ships getting it there.

Later in the war, on 17th February 1945, **Stan Kirby** was aboard **HMS ZEST**, Convoy RA64 had assembled ready for return to UK. The Flower class corvette **HMS BLUEBELL** was sweeping at the entrance to Kola Inlet. **HMS LARK**, sweeping ahead of the convoy was torpedoed, but safely towed into harbour, then a merchant ship was hit by the same U-Boat, sinking while being towed in. Then sheer horror to crews of other ships in the vicinity to witness, at 1530 hours, **HMS BLUEBELL** being torpedoed by **U711** and blowing up, with loss of all hands but one.

Stan was less than a mile away at the moment the torpedo struck - she disintegrated in a huge orange flash and a great pall of smoke. In less than 30 seconds she was gone.

ZEST made toward her at best speed to pick up survivors. We were at the scene in a matter of minutes. There was wreckage and a great deal of oil fuel, we could find only three survivors, two engineer room ratings and one seaman P.O. (now known to have been the buffer Albert Edward Holmes). He was well clothed against the cold, including a one-piece kapok-filled suit and a 'Mae West'. The other two were actually on watch below when the torpedo struck, and had no idea how they came to be in the water. Wearing just a shift and a pussers overall they had little protection against the intense cold of northern waters, no buoyancy aid and were covered in the ship's fuel oil which had laid on the surface with the consistency of blancmange, and they both had difficulty keeping their head above in order to breathe. With hands slipping on the oil which clung to them, we had difficulty lifting them on to the iron deck of **ZEST**. They walked into the fo'c'sle where we cleaned them up and were unmarked. Although they had walked along the iron deck into the fo'c'sle they shortly afterwards collapsed and died, whether from shock and exposure, or the oil inside them, or a combination of both, one can only guess.

Once under way again, I had to get back to my action station, but had a chance later to talk to the buffer. He had just come off the bridge and stood at the guard rail by the sea-boat (skiff), he put his gloved hand under his arm and withdrew his hand to get something out of his pocket. At this moment the torpedo exploded, instinctively he put his bare hand to his face as protection against the flash (the imprint of his hand could be seen on his face where the flash had burnt the uncovered skin. The skiff and the 'griping spar' pinned him against the funnel casing, the ship was already sinking, the water covered him quickly and he was going down with the ship. "I thought this was the end", he said, but then suddenly broke free, due he thought to the buoyancy of the gear he was wearing. As he broke surface he felt his head push through the oil which was congealing on the surface in the intense cold, at this point he saw **ZEST** approaching. It seemed to take ages to reach him, but it was only minutes. It was difficult to believe she had gone so quickly, and not surprising that only three survived the explosion.

Sid Conley was the Master-at-Arms in the escort carrier **HMS NAIRANA** and had a similar experience of the horror.

BLUEBELL was steaming close on our port side. I had come on to the upper deck probably hoping to see the shore side and was looking at **BLUEBELL** when she was hit by torpedo.

Of the many sinkings I witnessed on the Russian run none was so amazing as the loss of **BLUEBELL**. She simply disappeared off the surface of the sea. I recall seeing a terrific explosion of bluish purple flame, and temporarily had difficulty in focusing my eyes. Then searching the sea for sight of survivors or wreckage, but there was nothing. It was as though she had never actually been there.

Leading Telegraphist Oliver Nelson was aboard **HMS WHITEHALL**; he also witnessed the tragic loss of the Bluebell at the start of escorting the return convoy.

Early on the morning of the 17th the fleet destroyers, who were well able to take care of themselves, began going out and they got clear away without any loss. Then we had the problem of getting these 30 merchant ships out of the Kola Inlet. The only way to do this was in a jumble. If we'd tried to go out in an orderly line ahead we'd have been torpedoed one at a time as they put their noses out, so all hands to the pump and off we went, and it worked. Unfortunately, **LARK** was torpedoed, which was one of our group; we had already lost the **DENBIGH CASTLE**. Then the **LARK**, began stooging around trying to get the merchant ships out and into some sort of order. By mid afternoon we'd got all the ships out without any losses of merchant ships, only the loss of one escort ship. About tea-time they were all out and the signal went up "take night steaming positions". Everybody started diving around getting onto course for home. Our position was well up front and on the plan, **BLUEBELL** was going to tuck underneath our stern and stay with us all night, unless anything happened needing her of course, or needing us.

We were steaming around; there were 30-40 ships getting into double formations lying ahead in eight groups, 8 lines close escort. Torpedoes were flashing all over the place. It seemed there must have been three or four hundred torpedoes fired at this group of ships and it was amazing it was not a really bad day for loss of shipping. But again the discipline, good lookouts and prompt actions saved lots of lives.

BLUEBELL was coming up to tuck under our stern and we were going ahead to take up our position, ahead of the convoy on the close screen, then our asdic boys suddenly shouted out "a torpedo to port". **BLUEBELL** caught it, she was just behind us with no chance at all to do much in the way of avoiding action at her slow speed. The torpedo, at least one, or probably two, hit her. There is no doubt that her magazine went up because it was not only an underwater explosion, there was a really huge upper deck explosion. With flames going up into the sky, the ship actually disintegrated. We went over the spot a couple of minutes later, but there was very, very little, not even a lot of oil, the whole lot had gone. We were not able to stop and search for survivors, but were on the lookout; there was no chance that there were any survivors. Other ships in the vicinity did likewise but we saw no survivors.

The last sinking of a naval escort was on 29th April 1945 only 10 days before the war ended. Every man jack aboard the ships were thinking: "Thank God this bloody lot will soon be over, it's gone on long enough".

It was the men on these last convoys who had been sickened at the sight of tanks and munitions standing idle on the shore at Murmansk, now derelict and unwanted, as their thoughts were with their shipmates who lost their lives getting them there, and perhaps even themselves could have suffered.

Stalin's constant demands for more, more, and now they were left on the shore with no attempt to remove and use for the purpose shipped. Sick and sad hearts but nevertheless happier, they were on their way home to UK - never to experience another awful convoy; except on 29th April 1945, homeward bound, the frigate **HMS GOODALL** was torpedoed soon after the return convoy RA66 sailed from Kola Inlet.

Her fo'c'sle was destroyed when the magazine exploded, taking the bridge back to the funnel. The Flower Class corvette **HMS HONEYSUCKLE** was sent in to attempt to rescue survivors, but oil fuel gushing from the stricken ship caught fire by a lifeboat calcium flare and very soon the sea itself was ablaze. One of the ship's company of **HONEYSUCKLE** went aboard to try to rescue the wounded but was driven back. As **HONEYSUCKLE** moved away astern her own paintwork was burning. 44 were saved from the **GOODALL**, 98 were lost - virtually on the eve of the end of the war.

Telegraphist Bill Bates was aboard **GOODALL** and as a survivor relates:

I was trapped in the emergency wireless cabinet, about 3 feet square, amidships. The water came in from a fractured main and mixed with the battery acid, I could hardly breathe and had a burning sensation in my eyes. The lights went out and the gear stowed in the cabinet was falling all over the place, I soon became disorientated. The door suddenly opened and the fire was only a few feet away. Men and parts of men, were lying on the deck outside.

I stayed with a wounded man but was unable to get forward or aft because of fire and exploding ammunition, so was ordered over the side with the wounded men.

We were the last to leave by floatnet and the sea fire was very close. We joined up with three men and managed to stay ahead of the flames. As I could hardly see or breathe I became unconscious. When I came to, fortunately, the others had gone. I felt a rope fall across my head and managing to turn my head I saw **HONEYSUCKLE** twenty feet away. Being unable to fasten the rope, I rolled it round my arms and let go of the net. I made it to the side of **HONEYSUCKLE**, the rope came adrift, then somebody came over the side, down the scrambling net, into the water and hauled me aboard. It must have been a near impossible task being six foot tall and twelve stone.

As I lay on the deck a rating raised my head and said: "I think this one has gone". It took all my remaining strength to open my eyes to let him know I wasn't. We were treated like kings, were taken below, given dry clothes, cigarettes and blankets. I fell asleep almost immediately and on being awakened was told to muster for transfer to **HMS VINDEX**.

Leading Seaman LTO Arthur Bartle was aboard **HMS HONEYSUCKLE** and witnessed the sinking. They had been carrying out a sweep at the entrance to Kola Inlet to ensure safe passage for the ships of a returning convoy. During this procedure **GOODALL** was struck by torpedo forward and **HONEYSUCKLE** was ordered to the scene. He stood in horror and amazement at the damage, destruction and subsequent fire of both ship and the surrounding sea.

The bows as far as the bridge were completely blown away, the fo'c'sle was bent up and over the bridge like the lid of a sardine tin, down at the bows and up at the stern there were many small fires.

HONEYSUCKLE closed in, bows on to the stricken ship's stern, in so doing, one of **GOODALL's** twin rudders penetrated our bow above the water line. A few of us went over the stern to assist the wounded but were ordered back owing to the danger. We managed to get off all that were still alive and others who had gone over the side were picked up.

There was a dreadful stench of fuel, the tanks were full in preparation for return convoy. The fire on the ship ignited the fuel, it roared like an express train as it swept across the water engulfing our ship's port side, burning away the paint, cracking porthole glass and small items along the ship's waist. We returned to harbour to land survivors; whilst doing so, a senior engine room rating, injured badly, asked: "Hookey, could you let me have some tickler? I shall have to go to hospital, don't suppose we shall get any there". I was able to give him a tin, cigarette papers and matches. You would have thought I had given him a block of gold.

On returning to UK the weather as usual blew up, the forepeak started to flood. Our buffer managed to jam a bale of cotton waste into the hole and shore up.

On arrival back at Greenock on VE Day our ship looked a sorry sight, yet nothing compared to the damage and destruction of the ship we had left behind.

HMS GOODALL, the last to go of the gallant little ships who escorted the Russian convoys in the past years, perhaps with added sadness, being homeward bound and within a few days of the end of the war. . . . .

"THE ADMIRALITY REGRETS"

Green downs of rich and verdant pastures
Stretch before his vision as he lies
Entombed in steel beneath the silent ocean.
It is a dream . . . because he slowly dies.

Surrounded there by glittering wheels and gauges,
He sees them not, nor hears his fellows groan;
His mind returns to distant places,
The green hills of his Sussex home.

Ten minutes more of clear but tortured thinking,
What then? . . . just madness as his life is closed,
He is too cold to think of life that's wasted,
Too great the price that depth charge has imposed.

Back on those hills in a little cottage doorway,
A figure stands, the sunlight on her hair,
And in that scene of Springtime English beauty
Why should her heart be filled with cold despair?

The legend on that little slip of paper
Clutched in her hand has caused her sudden dread,
The words she reads, and knows the awful answer:
"The Admiralty regrets" . . . is what they said.

By J E Forbes

On May 7th 1945 fifteen German submarines, escorted by five Canadian frigates which captured them off the coast of Norway, shortly after Germany surrendered, arrived at the picturesque port of Loch Eriboll, 15 days later after a 500-mile voyage. Also taken into custody was the commander of the U-Boat flotilla who wore the Iron Cross with oak leaves and said he was the senior submarine officer, a captain, in the Arctic Ocean and Barents Sea.

The U-Boats were separated in the company of a German submarine depot ship and four merchant vessels. The enemy craft were ordered to proceed to a Norwegian port while the Canadian ships took up escort positions around the U-Boats. These operating with the Home Fleet were escorting a convoy to Murmansk when ordered to intercept a group of U-Boats reported to be travelling south along the Norweglan coast.

Although information was vague the escort frigates went full speed and covered 250 miles before intercepting. Officers and crews were very excited and could barely contain themselves when the U-Boats were sighted. They were at action stations and ready to blast them out of the water.

Signals were sent to the depot ship ordering all vessels to shut down their engines. An executive officer from one of the frigates boarded the German depot ship to accept the surrender from the commander of the U-Boat flotilla who advised, under orders of the German High Command, he was withdrawing his command from Narvik and proceeding to Trondheim. He would comply with surrender and said that all ammunition had been landed. The German vessels carried no mines, and torpedoes had been rendered harmless. They were then warned that if they attempted to scuttle or submerge they would be destroyed and no mercy shown.

The U-Boat flotilla commander then sent a signal: "Farewell U-Boats, we have worked well together. Don't be down-hearted. Goodbye".

Lieut-Commander Eric R. Shaw R.C.N. Commanding Officer of **HMCS NENE** relates his part in the surrender of the U-Boats:

Escort group 9, five Canadian frigates one being my ship, left Londonderry to join the escort force for Convoy JW67 out and RA67 homeward. Rumours of peace being imminent abounded as we sailed, allied forces being at the gates of Berlin and were expecting this long and real Cold War to end at any moment. At 0800 on VE Day altering course to take position in our group my first lieutenant came with haste and speed to the bridge to report:

"Captain, 8am news on BBC states Admiral Doenitz has ordered all U-Boats to remain surfaced and surrender". Signals were sent for instructions on what should happen in view of the BBC announcement. "Proceed as original instructions: further will be sent". Then a signal from unidentified escort.

"Am attacking bogey U-Boat contact, intend to continue until ordered otherwise", then the final signal for "all systems go". "Proceed north to position off Trondheim, Norway, to take over surrender of all U-Boats, tenders and accompanying vessels".

So it was goodbye to JW and RA67 - we were on our own with a special mission, with great excitement, yet on guard for possible problems.

At 0230 on May 17th the U-Boats were sighted. We all went to action stations and at maximum speed to close the group. On reaching them took up strategic boarding as a checkout procedure. A noticeable minority showed semblance of hostility, but most were philosophical, many being glad it was all over. There were twenty craft in all, four supply vessels and a beautiful yacht belonging to the King of Norway with the German flag officer on board. The surface craft were instructed to proceed to a Norwegian port, they desperately wanted to come with us as unless they were to surrender to the Norwegians they would be taken by the Russians and in view of the horrors their armies had inflicted on the Soviet people, very little mercy would be shown.

We then put a communications officer and two ratings on board the German senior officer's boat and set course for home; but not quite so simple, as things began to happen. On board **NENE** we had three crew members who were bilingual in English and German so were invaluable during the voyage.

They came peacefully enough although one, more defiant than the rest, flaunted a skull and crossbones painted on the black flag of surrender.

The sleek and powerful yacht and the four depot ships having been despatched to Norway, the U-Boats under our command were in two columns, line abreast with engines stopped. With our crews at action stations and still all weapons manned, in case they were not as innocent as they seemed, we threaded our way through the columns to interrogate and ascertain they had complied with surrender. German officers crowded the conning towers dressed in seagoing best, prepared to be dumb; evasive smiles and shrugs of the shoulders greeted our questions as we neared the U-Boats: you could feel the hostility in the air.

These former terrors of the deep, the U-Boat crews - although friendly, seemed very scared. Others were smiling, treating it all as a joke amongst themselves.

The convoy got under way in two columns, the U-Boats bunched together as close as safe navigation allowed with the frigates patrolling up and down the wings. As night came we ran into a storm and as the weather deteriorated this caused problems. The conning tower staff and the boats took a bashing, and were forced to submerge. 9 surfaced submarines can stand just so much and no more, appearing to be under water, as often on the surface with tons of water pouring down the conning tower hatches. Constant watch was needed, fearful that if we looked away one of our charges would go missing.

The suspicion was aroused when one asked permission to submerge to make a minor repair owing to bad weather, but surfaced within the allotted time.

A rumour "a buzz round the ships" stated that prior to sailing from Norway the skipper of **U992** was ordered to wear full uniform until further orders. This meant he was to be tried for treason, the charge "for severe derogatory remarks about Hitler", in the presence of an under-cover Gestapo agent amongst the U-Boat crew. For this reason he was the happiest man in the group to get to sea. When the surrender order was issued it blew the Gestapo member's cover. The rumour continued, and when the U-Boat asked for permission to submerge to correct a problem the crew member was ordered forward to check if the gun was properly secured. Whilst he was there the U-Boat submerged, leaving the Gestapo agent to a fate he had consigned to others.

We could almost feel sorry for these beaten enemies, so close to or in the soaking cold water, as even we were "shipping them green over the bridge". Nevertheless we were constantly on the lookout for treachery and the possibility that one or two with more venturesome spirits might make a bolt for it, or even the fanatical Nazis might attempt to scuttle their craft in spite of the cold water.

On arrival at Loch Eriboll on 18th May EG9 group, each escort was instructed to have a U-Boat on each side, their crews were co-operative, well behaved and efficient. The captain, 25 years old, spoke perfect English. I had tea with him in the conning tower: in return he had breakfast with me aboard **NENE** to discuss his trip to Lochalsh for internment with his other officers and U-Boat crews. He was beaming when told they would be home in six weeks.

Unlike the commander of the U-Boat on our starboard side who thoroughly spoilt the relationships by putting a two-foot gash in our hull - either by design or sloppy handling or still bitter to the end. We had difficulty with him, a dyed-in-the-wool Nazi.

The situation was still tense, even more so when he came aboard and gave a Nazi salute. I told him to get back on his boat and come aboard my ship properly or I would take disciplinary action. To improve his manners one of our petty officers offered, if I gave the order, to throw him in the salt chuck, but a threat of a cold bath in Scottish waters changed his attitude. He was so brainwashed he found surrender hard to accept.

Prior to this final incident and approaching the end of the arduous voyage, before entering harbour came relief and reassurance of all previous problems, as signals were now being sent in "plain language". **HMCS NENE** intercepted a most heartening message from the senior officer of the U-Boats:

"Comrades so near England we have to carry out a mission and obey the law of their people. We must obey the orders of our Fuehrer and take a bite of the sour apple. The weapons of our U-Boats are out of commission. All that remains for us is to carry out this last mission and turn over our gallant U-Boats" Franze.

HMCS NENE's Commanding Officer Lieut Commander Eric Shaw, "Skipper" as he was affectionately known by the crew of this happy-efficient ship, said on entering harbour. "They followed us into port like little lambs" still, perhaps, with the temptation to scuttle lurking in the minds of one or two of these beaten mariners, the wolf pack who years, or even a month ago, could have wreaked terror and havoc on the shipping of the world.

"WE ARE STILL ALIVE"

Slowly the jumbled mass of strange sensations stumbled into Jack's mind. Cruel reality built the picture, piece by piece, the fearsome darkness, the nauseating stench of oil fuel, and the crawling pains that slowly burned over his body.

The picture brought a wave of fear that grew to a sickening terror. His cry of "Help" was a naked appeal of dire distress, born of frantic hope.

Clinging to the oar Jack tried to lift his head above the waves of oil fuel, but the effort nearly tore the oar out of his hands. He must hang on. This dominant order came persistently from inside and must be obeyed. Every few seconds Jack could hear his cry of "Help" like a gramophone playing the same groove continually.

Another sensation tore through his body like sharp electric shocks, in quick succession they followed until his stomach felt like jelly. He knew the reason even before he heard the explosions, depth charges, and he was feeling the terrific vibrations set up by the explosions. The pain in Jack's stomach was much worse, now almost too much to bear, but the inner force wouldn't let him go, so he hung on and kept up his perpetual cry of "Help".

The explosion brought back a flood of memories, he remembered the "Action Alarm", how he had put on his lifebelt and stumbled in the dark to his station on top of the engine room. The engineer had stood beside him and together they had looked around trying to find out what was happening in the darkness. The alarm had meant submarines. Where? How many? They did not know.

The crew's panic was followed by two terrific explosions, one almost the continuation of the other, a huge enveloping flame and the deck buckling as though a giant had kicked a tin can. The deck opened, Jack couldn't remember whether he fell into the engine room, or whether the engine room came up to him, but he was squatting on a big steam pipe. The scream of escaping steam told him that he was being scalded, but he couldn't feel the pain, he crawled amid the maze of twisted pipes, as he sucked in the hot steam, still he kept crawling on. The next Jack remembered was the sea, not the ordinary sea that rose and fell, this was a mad whirlpool of motion, bubbling and gurgling and huge bursts of air breaking the surface. Something struck his head and a black cloud wiped away the nightmare.

Jack met the floating oar and together they drifted away from the wreckage. The depth charge explosions reminded him of other ships making their attack on the submarine, perhaps they would be back soon to pick him up.

The remote stars moved slowly across the sky but Jack did not see them, all he knew was the oil, the pain and the terrible darkness, perhaps he had always been there. He did not know which was real and which was a dream. Perhaps he would wake up and see the woman he knew, he remembered her now, her smile and her body, warm and sympathetic. She made him feel important, Yes, a necessity of life, but how about now, he felt only the horrible fear of being alone. He could see two children who played together, scrambling with noisy exuberance to hug him, their interests free and easy. They did not know any fear. Now their familiar faces were near his own and after noisily pressing their lips to his cheek they said "Good night, Daddy" and scampered away with the woman. A few minutes later the woman returned to sit near him; first he eased off his shoes, then lit a cigarette and gently fondled her hair in contented abstraction. They did not talk very much, just sat close and enjoyed the peace and quiet of each other's company. Here was the one woman he did not have to pretend with, she knew him so very well, in fact she knew more about him than any other person, but he wasn't worried, rather he felt happy.

The dream was slipping, in spite of his clumsy efforts to hold and enlarge the pictures. The true, cruel reality broke through his thoughts, shattering the broken pieces of his dream to oblivion.

The choking oil was there, clogging his hair, burning his eyes and as he opened his mouth to cry, some of the oil slipped inside, he tried to spit it out again but the effort had meant more oil. As the water chilled his body the pains became less and less, even the demand to hold on wasn't quite so loud.

A sound other than his cry attracted his attention: "Who are you?" Jack lifted his head and opened his eyes to see a dim black shape a few feet away. Suddenly he became alive with fear that welled up inside him, perhaps the figure had come to take the oar away from him. It was his oar, right from the beginning he had clung and obeyed the inner force to hold on, hold on. Desperately Jack clutched the oar, but the voice came across the darkness. "Won't be long now, keep going, they will be back soon". He did not answer, strange though that voice was saying similar things to the one inside. Why did they want to know who he was? It did not seem to matter that he was Jack.

The cold water was slowly taking the warmth out of his body. He did not mind because the pain was somehow going also. The dream seemed too far away to try to recall and his cry of "Help" wasn't coming very often.

Jack wondered about the gentle vibrations he could feel, gradually they grew stronger, until he willed his head to life, alas he couldn't make the muscles and flesh obey. Two oil-fuel covered mad men. He did not feel able to fight for the oar, but he wasn't going to let go, the oar had been his since time began. Except for the voice inside, he would not care what happened, but he must obey, must hold on.

The two figures struggled frantically alongside Jack, why can't they be quiet he thought in despair. Now other voices broke in, suddenly Jack felt his cheek touch something hard and his cheek was roughly pushed across the oar. Looking up he could see a steep wall with faces peering over the top. The two black faces were passing a rope under his arms, now they were tying the rope in front.

Now, many voices could be heard, one very authoritative voice was saying: “Hurry, I will give you two minutes, there are submarines around here”.

Voices were shouting: “Let go, we can’t pull the bloody oar in as well”. Why must he let go, for ages the inner voice had commanded him to hold on, hold on, they did not understand, they did not know, and Jack hung on. Frantically the rope jerked under his arms, and the two dark figures were yelling urgently: “For Christ’s sake, let go”, then he felt his fingers torn from the oar. The two black faces were left behind as Jack swung in mid-air, cold air that chilled him to the bone. Clutching hands pulled him over the rails and gently laid him on something soft. “Where is the oar?”, the one question tore through his mind, he struggled wildly to find the oar. Suddenly he gripped something too small to be an oar, but this was warm so he hung on and lay back.

Jack new he was still making his cry of “Help”, he couldn’t stop, somehow the periodic movement of his throat and lips were automatic.

These strange happenings, the explosions, the steam, the oil, the cold water, the darkness, why couldn’t he be left alone; perhaps then he could sleep. Two dark faces peered at him and said: “We made it, Jack”. Another voice cut in: “He won’t let go of my arm”. “All right”, said another, “you will have to walk alongside the stretcher”. Movement and banging followed, then Jack felt something tearing into his eyes - “Light”.

Quickly his clothes were removed and a patch of his arm cleaned, then the needle plunged in to give him morphia, he slowly relaxed, he did not remember having his fingers prised away from the arm he had so grimly held on to.

Cleaned and placed on a small bed with high rails around, Jack was examined by the doctor, first the extensive burns, the bruised head and the jagged wound in the stomach.

As the doctor gazed down on his patient, he felt a challenge. This man must live, he deserves to live and with the help of God he shall live. Only give me the chance dear God to keep life in this torn, burnt body.

Then began the fight, injections, cleansing, oxygen, jelly for the burns and medicine to counteract the oil fuel in the stomach. Slowly, carefully, the doctor worked, bringing to bear his knowledge and training and the jumbled panorama of medical science.

After seventy-four hours the doctor gazed down at his patient, trying to make a decision from the facts and symptoms he had collected. The man was slowly dying of starvation, the liquid food was not giving the results. There must be a break where the stomach was injured. After methodically weighing the facts in his mind, he reached his decision, to leave the man meant death within twenty-four hours, to operate gave a slim chance of life. The doctor turned to his two assistants and gave the order: “Prepare for an abdominal inspection operation”.

First the operating table was screwed into position, the instruments boiled, swabs, gauze, needles, catgut, oxygen and chloroform. Every detail was checked and the number counted. While the doctor scrubbed his hands, his mind was following every move he expected to make, he wanted to feel sure, he wanted to keep this man alive. He MUST win.

The chief assistant gave the anaesthetic, the doctor checked the instruments; next he held his hands up to probe his fingers into the gloves. Everything depended on those hands, could they obey, to a fraction of an inch, the orders from the brain and be guided by his eyes? Slowly the doctor found the poised position, the necessary point of balance to counteract the roll of the ship. He cut in a straight line, about six inches, cutting layer by layer, probing aside the muscles till finally the intestines lay there slightly bulging out of the opening. Instantly, he saw he was right, puss and foreign matter were gathering there, perhaps even now the deadly germs had done their work. With probing fingers the doctor pulled out a section of intestine, quickly searching along the length. The doctor found the break, a jagged hole, quickly the instruments flew, guided by his delicate hands.

But, stop! the assistant was saying something: “Breathing has stopped”. Quickly the assistant changed from chloroform to pure oxygen, while the other man massaged the heart. “Breathing again, sir, pulse weak”.

On the doctor worked, he found another break, he was sweating and constantly the assistant had to pass gauze over his brow. Even this was done without apparent notice by the doctor. The life was in the balance and by now the assistants had caught the spirit of the challenge - “Fight for his life”. The younger assistant had never seen an operation before, but he pressed his white lips together and kept on the job.

Twice more the patient stopped breathing and each time oxygen was used. With grim determination the doctor worked on, first swabbing out the puss with antiseptic gauze and hoping against hope that there were no other breaks in the thirty-odd feet of intestines. Quickly he pressed the intestines back, they would find their proper position when food passed through. The one regret the doctor had was that sulphanilamide had not so far been distributed to ships. The wonderful new drug that was able to kill all the germs, just by sprinkling about a tablespoonful inside the cavity before closing.

Layer by layer the doctor stitched the cut together until the stomach was closed, then he stitched down and up to give the cut strength. The catgut would dissolve in about ten days and obviate the necessity of pulling out the stitches, which might open the wound again. The muscles had been pressed into position and the stitching completed, then the cut was covered with gauze and cotton wool to protect and finally bandaged into position. Then the doctor stood back to wait and hope.

After the instruments had been checked, the swabs counted, all three sat back and smoked, they did not talk very much. The doctor had no regrets about his decision, he had played his last card, he must wait and hope for the result.

The next twenty-four hours found the doctor keeping almost continuous watch, except for a quick meal in the wardroom, and slowly saw his patient improve. But alas, true to all life, circumstances cannot be guided all the time by forethought, there is always some situation you are not prepared for and the result will often change situations beyond recognition. Some people call this freak circumstance, luck or bad luck, perhaps for the want of a better explanation.

Quietly the patient lay, when suddenly the stillness of the ship was rent by the clash of alarm bells. Action Stations. To Jack that meant one thing, submarines, on lifebelt and away to his station.

Before the doctor could stop him Jack had sat up and fallen over the side of the cot, crawling along the deck on hands and knees, leaving a trail of bandage and bed clothes. Quickly the doctor and assistant jumped to lift him back, but Jack was fighting frantically, with his bandaged hands and arms. He knew what those bells meant - submarines. At last they managed to put him back, the doctor plunged the hyperdermic needle into Jack's arm and slowly Jack relaxed and closed his eyes.

Too late, the movement had undone the work, the excitement and fear had done even more damage.

Exploding depth charges shook the ship, she twisted and turned to execute intricate manoeuvres, while the doctor, ignoring the noise, did all he possibly could to repair the damage. Very quietly the doctor cursed his fate; but for the damn bells he would have succeeded.

Much later, when the sound of guns and depth charges had ceased their noisy salutes, the doctor gave his final check-up. Jack was slowly getting worse, slowly slipping back to the state where nothing is really heard or seen.

Twelve hours later Jack opened his eyes, he thought he had felt the arms of the two children hug him and kiss "Good night, Daddy", but his eyelids were so hard to open that by the time he had succeeded they had gone away. Perhaps they would come back later, anyway the woman would come in a few minutes and Jack closed his eyes to rest and wait for her. But she never came and Jack never opened his eyes again. Slowly the doctor pulled the sheet over his face, then sat at the desk making out the report and certificate. Quite a long report, everything he had done was down in black and white. The naval authorities had a habit of cutting down on the report, usually "Died on Active Service", that's all.

The assistants did not move until the doctor had left, then they prepared for the last irretrievable resting place.

A fellow officer walked into the wardroom and seeing the huddled figure of the doctor, a glass in his hand, was going to ask the question "How's the patient, Doc?" But he suddenly stopped and turned away to leave quietly, the question was not necessary because he had seen the answer written on the haggard lines of the doctor's face. The regret was there, in the slowly rolling tears of silent and motionless anguish.

Slowly he drank, looking straight ahead without seeing the glowing fire, no one had the heart to stop him and finally he slumped forward. Quietly, he was carried to his bunk and placed under the sheets, quite drunk.

The next day Jack's body was carried on deck and placed on a plank facing outboard.

A number of men listened to the short service given by an officer who distinctly avoided the eyes of two of his listeners. They stood together with dry eyes. They had known Jack well and liked him, they were the two black faces who together had struggled to push him alongside the ship. They had worked, fought and drunk beer together.

For our tomorrow Jack gave his today. We are still alive.

"JACK'S STORY IS AN EPITAPH TO ALL WHO DID NOT SURVIVE"

THERE - BUT FOR THE GRACE OF GOD

There are no roses on sailors' graves,
Nor wreaths upon the storm-tossed waves,
No 'last post' from the 'Royals' band,
So far away from their native land.
No heartbroken words, carved on stone,
Just shipmates' bodies floating there alone,
The only tributes are the seagulls' sweeps,
And the teardrops - when a loved one weeps.

TO THOSE WHO SURVIVED

Almighty God we especially remember before thee all those who
gave their lives, afloat or ashore in Arctic waters during
1941 and 1945. Those who have suffered, been maimed,
disabled or blinded, and those whom the war has left weakened
in body or mind, grant that they may never be forgotten
and grant them O Lord thy peace, and enable us, each one,
to do our part for their comfort and help
Through Jesus Christ Our Lord
Amen.

AND TO THOSE WHO DID NOT RETURN

They shall grow not old
As we that are left grow old.
Age shall not weary them
Nor the years condemn.
At the going down of the sun
and in the morning
"We will remember them"

FROM

THE REAL COLD WAR

Between the sailing of the first convoy PQ1 on 9th September 1941 and the last JW67 on 12th May 1945 nearly 1,000 ships sailed outwards to Russia carrying between five and six million tons of cargo, not all of which arrived. The cash value of the material carried in this joint Anglo American project amounted to £430,000,000 and included 5,000 tanks, 7,000 aircraft 12 complete freight trains with engines, hundreds of thousands of tons of high explosive and high octane spirit and the medical supplies the Russians said "niet" to landing.

From the outward bound convoys 62 merchant ships were lost, half of that number from PQ17 and PQ18 and of the return convoys 28 ships never made port. The Germans lost 32 submarines and over a hundred aircraft during their attacks on the convoys.

Our naval losses were severe: 2 cruisers, 6 destroyers, 3 sloops, 2 frigates, 3 corvettes and 3 minesweepers with a loss of 1,840 gallant young men.

The Royal Navy called on more than 200 warships to form escorts drawn from 8 light cruisers, 4 anti-aircraft cruisers, 4 anti-aircraft ships, converted merchant ships, 14 escort carriers, 102 destroyers, 17 fleet sweepers, 18 sloops and frigates, 24 corvettes, and 17 asdic trawlers.

During 1941-1945 the Russians had sneered at the war material which we delivered as being but a drop in the ocean, compared with their needs, but from the way the Germans directed their utmost energies in trying to stop the Arctic convoys, it is clear *they* did not think so, for they came to realise that the materials the convoys carried could well be the deciding factor on the Eastern Front.

Mr Maisky, the wartime Soviet Ambassador in London, was eventually able to say to a British audience:

"The Russian convoys are a northern saga of heroism, bravery and endurance. This saga will live for ever, not only in the hearts of your people, but also in the hearts of the Soviet people, for without it our common victory would have been impossible".

and a German Vice Admiral, writing after the war, said that

"Between August 1944 and April 1945 the 250-plus ships on the Arctic run carried over a million tons of war material", and that this *"Allowed the Russians to equip a further 60 motorised divisions which gave them material superiority at focal points of the battles".*

It became difficult to escape the conclusion that the Russians did not really care much for the supplies being delivered to them by the convoys, at such cost in lives, ships and war supplies which could ill be spared. Perhaps Stalin made these demands to sap the allies' strength so that they would be less able to stand up to Russia after the war and, maybe even as a punishment, for not opening the 'Second Front'. One has a sneaking feeling that nearly all our efforts to help them were misplaced.

It leaves the impression that the Russians actually wanted our ships to be sunk and demanded equipment, which they could not use themselves, simply to stretch our supplies and thus weaken us. It is a sad thing to have to say that about an ally, but it seemed that Uncle Joe Stalin's mind worked that way.

Whilst impossible to prove, thoughts are that little of the equipment sent - tanks, vehicles, aircraft, aviation spirit etc. scraped together, to give to the Russians - was any use to them, unfit for the climate, handling, and not tough enough to stand misuse by the wooden, peasant soldier. Their own equipment seemed far more suitable.

"HE THAT OUTLIVES THIS DAY AND COMES SAFE HOME

WILL STAND A TIP-TOE WHEN THIS DAY IS NAMED"

APPENDICES

CONVOYS TO NORTH RUSSIA (PQ AND JW)

CONVOY	SAILING DATES	VESSELS SAILED	VESSELS ARRIVED	REMARKS
Dervish	21.8.42	7	7	Trial Convoy.
PQ.1	29.9.41	10	10	
PQ.2	17.10.41	6	6	
PQ.3	9.11.41	8	7	1 ship returned, ice damage.
PQ.4	17.11.41	7	7	
PQ.5	27.11.41	7	7	
PQ.6	8.12.41	7	7	
PQ.7	26.12.41	2	1	1 sunk by U-Boat.
PQ.7b	31.12.41	9	9	1 torpedoed but towed to Murmansk
PQ.8	8.1.42			HMS MATABELE sunk by U-Boat.
PQ.9	1.2.42	7	7	Joined up and sailed together from Reykjavik.
PQ.10	1.2.42	3	3	
PQ.11	6.2.42	13	13	
PQ.12	1.3.42	16	16	Capital ship support; HMS SHERA capsized.
PQ.13	20.3.42	19	14	2 bombed and sunk; 2 sunk by U-Boat, 1 sunk by surface craft. HMS TRINIDAD torpedoed, German destroyer Z26 sunk.
PQ.14	8.4.42	24	7	16 returned, ice damage, 1 sunk by U-Boat.
PQ.15	25.4.42	25	22	3 torpedoed by aircraft; HMS PUNJABI sunk in collision.
PQ.16	21.5.42	35	27	1 returned damaged; 5 bombed; 1 torpedoed by aircraft; 1 by U-Boat.
PQ.17	27.6.42	36	11	1 grounded; 1 returned damaged; 23 sunk (10 bombed; 3 torpedoed by aircraft; 10 by U-Boats): figures do not include 3 rescue ships, 1 bombed and sunk.
PQ.18	2.9.42	40	27	3 sunk by U-Boats; 10 by torpedo bombers; 5 sunk by aircraft or mines after arrival at Kola Inlet.
JW.51A	15.12.42	16	16	
JW.51B	22.12.42	14	14	HM Ships ACHATES and BRAMBLE sunk by surface ships: German destroyer FRIEDRICH ECKHOLDT sunk.
JW.52	17.1.43	14	13	1 returned to Iceland due to lack of speed.
JW.53	15.2.43	28	22	6 returned to Iceland, weather damage.
JW.54A	15.11.43	18	18	
JW.54B	22.11.43	14	14	
JW.55A	18.12.43	19	19	
JW.55B	20.12.43	19	19	SCHARNHORST sunk by covering forces.
JW.56A	12.1.44	20	13	Convoy put into Akureyri due to weather; 5 returned; 3 sunk by U-Boats.
JW.56B	22.1.44	16	16	HMS HARDY sunk by U-Boat.
JW.57	20.2.44	42	42	HMS MAHRATTA sunk by U-Boat.
JW.58	27.3.44	49	48	1 returned, ice damage.
JW.59	15.8.44	33	33	HMS KITE sunk by U-Boat.
JW.60	15.9.44	30	30	HMS DENBIGH CASTLE sunk.
JW.61	20.10.44	29	29	
JW.62	29.11.44	30	30	
JW.63	30.12.44	35	35	
JW.64	3.2.45	26	26	HMS BICKERTON sunk.
JW.65	11.3.45	24	22	2 Merchant ships and HMS LAPWING sunk by U-Boats off Kola Inlet.
JW.66	16.4.45	22	22	
JW.67	12.5.45	23	23	

CONVOYS FROM NORTH RUSSIA (QP and RA)

CONVOY	SAILING DATES	VESSELS SAILED	VESSELS ARRIVED	REMARKS
QP.1	28.9.41	14	14	
QP.2	2.11.41	12	12	
QP.3	27.11.41	10	8	2 returned owing to weather.
QP.4	20.12.41	13	11	2 put in to Murmansk.
QP.5	13.1.42	4	4	
QP.6	24.1.42	6	6	
QP.7	12.2.42	8	8	
QP.8	1.3.42	15	14	1 straggler sunk by surface craft.
QP.9	21.3.42	19	19	
QP.10	10.4.42	16	11	1 returned to Murmansk; 2 bombed and sunk; 2 sunk by U-Boats.
QP.11	18.4.42	13	12	1 straggler sunk by surface craft. HMS EDINBURGH torpedoed by U-Boat, subsequently sunk.
QP.12	21.5.42	15	14	1 returned to Murmansk.
QP.13	6.6.42	35	30	4 and HMS NIGER sunk in British minefield; 1 damaged and beached.
QP.14	13.9.42	15	12	3 sunk by U-Boats; HM Ships LEDA and SOMALI and RFA GREY RANGER sunk by U-Boats.
QP.15	17.11.42	28	26	Convoy scattered by gales, 2 sunk by U-Boats.
RA.51	30.12.42	14	14	
RA.52	29.1.43	11	10	1 sunk by U-Boat.
RA.53	1.3.43	30	26	3 (2 stragglers) sunk by U-Boats; 1 floundered in gale.
RA.54A	1.11.43	13	13	
RA.54B	26.11.43	9	9	
RA.55A	23.12.43	22	21	1 returned to Kola Inlet.
RA.55B	31.12.43	8	8	
RA.56	3.2.44	37	37	
RA.57	2.3.44	31	30	1 sunk by U-Boat.
RA.58	7.4.44	36	36	
RA.59	28.4.44	45	44	1 sunk by U-Boat.
RA.59A	28.8.44	9	9	
RA.60	28.9.44	30	28	2 sunk by U-Boats.
RA.61	30.10.44	33	33	
RA.62	10.12.44	28	28	
RA.63	11.1.45	30	30	
RA.64	17.2.45	36	31	2 sunk off Kola before joining convoy escorts; 1 returned to Kola; 1 sunk by U-Boat; 1 straggler by torpedo aircraft; HMS BLUEBELL sunk by U-Boat.
RA.65	23.3.45	25	25	
RA.66	29.4.45	24	24	HMS GOODALL sunk by U-Boat or mine.
RA.67	23.5.45	23	23	

TOTAL NUMBER OF CONVOYS TO AND FROM NORTH RUSSIA 76
CONVOYS COMPLETED WITHOUT LOSS OF MERCHANT SHIPS BY ENEMY ACTION 53
CONVOYS COMPLETED WITHOUT LOSS OF MERCHANT SHIPS OR ESCORTS FROM ANY CAUSE 36

TOTAL VESSELS ESCORTED TO RUSSIA 811
TOTAL VESSELS ARRIVED IN RUSSIA 720
TOTAL VESSELS ESCORTED FROM RUSSIA 715
TOTAL VESSELS ARRIVED IN U.K. PORTS 680
VESSELS LOST BY ENEMY ACTION 87
VESSELS LOST BY OTHER CAUSES.................. 7
VESSELS RETURNED TO DEPARTURE PORTS 32

ANALYSIS OF RUSSIAN CONVOYS

	1941	1942	1943	1944	1945	TOTAL
Number of convoys to North Russia	8	13	6	9	4	40
Number of ships in convoy	64	256	112	284	95	811
Number of convoys from North Russia	4	13	6	9	5	37
Number of ships in convoy from N. Russia	49	188	93	249	136	715
Ships obliged to turn back due to ice or weather damage	45	21	8	6	1	40
Ships sunk by U-Boats	1	24	4	7	5	41
Ships sunk by aircraft	-	36	-	-	1	37
Ships sunk by surface vessels	-	3	-	-	-	3
Ships sunk by aircraft or mines after arrival in Kola Inlet						5
Ships foundered in gale						1
Ships sunk in British minefield						5
Ships sunk sailing independently plus a fleet tanker and rescue ship						8
Total number of ships sunk						100

Gross Registered Tonnage: 605,837

U-BOATS SUNK DURING RUSSIAN CONVOY OPERATIONS

U-Boat	Date	How sunk
U665	24 March 42	Rammed by HMS Sharpshooter during QP.9.
U585	29 March 42	Depth charged by HMS Fury during PQ.13.
U589	12 Sept. 42	Depth charged by HMS Faulknor during PQ.18.
U88	14 Sept. 42	Depth charged by HMS Onslow during PQ.18.
U457	16 Sept. 42	Depth charged by HMS Impulsive during PQ.18.
U253	23 Sept. 42	Depth charged by Catalina aircraft on patrol.
U644	7 April 43	Torpedoed by HMS/M. Tuna on patrol.
U314	30 Jan. 44	Depth charged by HM Ships Whitehall and Meteor during JW56B.
U713	24 Feb. 44	Depth charged by HMS Keppel during JW57.
U601	25 Feb. 44	Depth charged by Catalina aircraft during JW57.
U472	4 March 44	By rocket and gunfire by Swordfish aircraft from HMS Chaser and HMS Onslaught during RA57.
U366	5 March 44	By rocket and gunfire by Swordfish aircraft from HMS Chaser.
U973	6 March 44	Ditto.
U961	29 March 44	Depth charged by HMS Starling supporting JW58.
U355	1 April 44	Depth charged by HMS Beagle and aircraft from HMS Activity during JW58.
U288	1 April 44	Depth charged by aircraft from HM Ships Activity and Tracker during JW58.
U360	2 April 44	By Hedgehog missiles from HMS Keppel during JW58.
U277	1 May 44	Depth charged by Swordfish aircraft from HMS Fencer during RA59.
U674	2 May 44	Ditto.
U959	2 May 44	Ditto.
U361	17 July 44	Depth charged by Liberator bomber on patrol.
U347	17 July 44	Depth charged by Catalina aircraft on patrol.
U742	18 July 44	Ditto.
U354	22 Aug. 44	Depth charged by Swordfish aircraft from HMS Vindex during JW59.
U344	24 Aug. 44	Depth charged by Escort Group 20, HM Ships Keppel, Mermaid, Peacock and Lock Dunvegan during JW59.
U394	2 Sept. 44	Combined rocket and depth charge attack by Swordfish aircraft from HMS Vindex and Escort Group 20, HM Ships Keppel, Whitehall, Mermaid and Peacock during RA59A.
U921	30 Sept. 44	Depth charged by Swordfish aircraft from HMS Campania during patrol.
U387	9 Dec. 44	Depth charged by HMS Bamborough Castle during RA62.
U365	13 Dec. 44	Depth charged by Swordfish aircraft from HMS Campania during RA62.
U425	17 Feb. 45	Squid attack by Escort Group 9, HM Ships Lark and Alnwick Castle off Kola Inlet.
U307	29 April 45	By gunfire from HMS Lock Insh detached from Escort Group 19 during RA66.
U286	29 April 45	Combined depth charge and gunfire from Escort Group HM Ships Loch Shin, Anguilla and Cotton.

During World War II a total of 30,248 merchant seamen died. This was 13% of all who sailed. 4,654 were reported 'Missing presumed dead', 4,707 were wounded and 5,707 were taken prisoner.

Over 80% of all operational U-boat crews died at sea. The sinkings of German U-Boats were:-

1939	9
1940	24
1941	35
1942	87
1943	237
1944	242
to May 1945	151
	785

246 of these were sunk by ships

245 were sunk by shore based aircraft

45 were sunk by shipborne aircraft

48 were sunk by combined ship/aircraft action

21 were sunk by submarines

62 were destroyed in bombing raids

16 were sunk by mines laid by aircraft

9 were sunk by mines laid by ship/submarine

7 were sunk by Soviet forces

40 were sunk by accident or marine causes

17 were scuttled before surrender of Germany

29 were lost through unknown causes

WAR EQUIPMENT SHIPPED TO NORTH RUSSIA

From Britain:

Between October 1st, 1941, and March 31st, 1946:

5,218 tanks
7,411 aircraft
4,932 anti-tank guns
4,005 rifles and machine guns
1,803 sets of radar equipment
4,338 sets of radio equipment
2,000 telephone sets
473,000,000 projectiles
9 Motor Torpedo Boats
4 submarines
14 minesweepers

Total value £308,000,000 plus:

Raw materials, foodstuffs, machinery, industrial plant, medical supplies and hospital equipment to the value of £120,000,000.

Statement by the Prime Minister in House of Commons, April 16th 1946 and 3rd report on Mutual Aid, 1946.

From United States:

Between March 11th, 1941, and October 1st, 1945:

14,795 aircraft
7,537 tanks
51,503 jeeps
35,170 motorcycles
8,701 tractors
375,883 trucks
8,218 anti-aircraft guns
131,633 sub-machine guns
345,735 tons of explosives
1,981 locomotives
11,155 flat cars and wagons
540,000 tons of rails
Over 1,050,000 miles of field telephone cable
2,670,000 tons of petrol
842,000 tons of chemicals
3,786,000 tyres
49,000 tons of leather
15,000,000 pairs of boots

Total value $11,260,343,603 plus:

Food shipments to the value of $1,312,000,000

POSTSCRIPT

In 1984 the author was seeking the whereabouts of a shipmate. He was contacted, along with 35 others, who said they never thought they would ever hear anymore about Russia, least of all Chris. B. Tye. At a subsequent reunion aboard **HMS BELFAST**, he was a founder member of the North Russia Club as Secretary for Convoy War Veterans of World War Two Arctic Campaign, including those ashore. By 1989 the membership reached 750 throughout the country and overseas. Many shipmates were reunited after 45 years, especially from the cruisers **BELLONA** and **CUMBERLAND** and destroyers **KEPPEL** and **MATCHLESS**. In 1985 Leonid Zamyatin the Soviet Ambassador in London was acquainted with the existence of the North Russia Club.

In 1986 520 Soviet Medals to commemorate the 40th Anniversary of the end of the war were presented at the Embassy to members of the North Russia Club in appreciation of their efforts through 1941-45. This started a "medal mania" throughout the country.

In 1987 the President, Secretary and Assistant Secretary were invited to Russia as guests of the Soviet Union as a delegation, attending many important meetings in Moscow, Leningrad and Murmansk. In 1988 a party of 120 members, with their wives, visited Russia as guests of the Soviet War Veterans, visiting Moscow, Leningrad and Murmansk - taking part in the ceremony of Victory Day on 9th May, the author having the pride and pleasure to lay a wreath at the base of the huge monument overlooking the Kola Inlet.

A visit was also made to the war graves of seamen, who died in Russia, at a cemetery, in Murmansk, both RN and MN. One from the first destroyer sunk in the conflict. A cruise liner took the party down the Inlet to the Barents Sea where wreaths were laid on the waters where our ships were sunk, followed by a special, poignant ceremony in memory of our lost shipmates.

This became an annual pilgrimage, especially on the 50th anniversary, thus giving and maintaining a true bond of renewed friendship between the two countries.

Two survivors from the lifeboats of SS INDUNA, Bill Short and Austin Byrne, had an emotive reunion at a club annual dinner after 43 years, as have many ratings since, from various ships, through the auspices of the North Russia Club.

In the words of Alexey Nikiforov, Counsellor to His Excellency the Soviet Ambassador at a reunion dinner.

I knew it was really necessary to be here. I wanted to tell you that the Soviet Government has indeed decided to make awards to all of you, these medals which will be presented, on two occasions this year in London, and later to members who join the club. I must tell you, and I would like to stress this, that it is only due to you, due to your efforts, to your contribution to our common struggle in that most difficult, most bloodiest of the wars that we emerged victorious. I must say that all my meetings from the British Navy, first of all yourself and I have been in several occasions speaking at the Greenwich Naval College. I was always struck by their friendliness, by their attitude of people, who probably have white seas before them and have white hearts to welcome others, but I would like in particular to mention one person who I have been priviledged to meet in India. It was Lord Mountbatten. He struck me as an extremely noble person, and a very pleasant person to speak to. I was reminded of him when I came here and tried Rum, because I was told he being a very sober person, among his other qualities, he introduced the new law so to say denying the Navy the 11 o'clock tipple, but I must tell you he was sober in other respects as well. Only today you could read in the Times one of the quotations from his address where he says, in a very serious mood of course, that presently we have nuclear weapons and nuclear war is an absolutely impossible thing to wage, and nuclear weapons are not the weapons to wage the war with. We share this thought and we are deeply indebted to him for these noble quotations.

With that I would like to thank you once again to thank you all and wish you every happiness in your lives, because I do think that we must continue to be allies, but God save us not in any war but in struggle for better life and for peace.

In the words of the Soviet Military Attache at the presentation of Commemorative Medals at the Embassy in London.

Dear friends, and I hope I may say dear comrades in arms.

I am very pleased to welcome you all to the Soviet Embassy, and for some of you, maybe, it is an occasion when after 40-odd years you find yourself once again, as it were, on Soviet Territory. I trust that this time, you feel much more safe and sound than during your last stay in Murmansk.

Today is a very special occasion for us all and the Ambassador asked me to convey to every one of you his personal congratulations with the high award of the medal which was issued on the occasion of the 40th Anniversary of the Victory, our common Victory, in a very hard struggle, in a live or die struggle, and that was the victory over Fascism, over evil forces who tried to conquer the world, to enslave other nations, to quash everything our Revolution and our people stand for, and at that moment of extreme danger to our civilisation, freedom and socialism the Soviet Union and Great Britain came to be allies in a common struggle. Both countries paid a very high and heavy price for their freedom to fight off the invasion, to crush the enemy, and to liberate Europe. My country lost over 20 million people. We always appreciated the help of those who came to our aid, who fought shoulder to shoulder with us.

We remember all those glorious British people who paid the ultimate sacrifice, who did not return to their homes.

So today my dear friends, I have the honour to present you with the Commemorative Medal as a token of our gratitude to you. Let it be a memento for you of our alliance, in the most trying period in the history of mankind. I am convinced that our two countries have to be allies now, allies in the struggle for world peace. My country does its level best to avert a nuclear catastrophe and I hope that you are familiar with the far-reaching disarmament proposals put forward by General Secretary Gorbachov; of his plans to eliminate nuclear weapons and the chemical weapons package of the proposal and agreement reached at Reykjavik. All these proposals as well as our practical steps are aimed at improving international situations averting the danger of war.

Please accept on this solemn occasion, our heartfelt congratulations and very best wishes for you all. I would like now, on behalf of the Presidium of the Supreme Soviet of the U.S.S.R. to present you with the memorial medals with which you have been awarded.

In the words of Leonid Zamyatin Soviet Ambassador to Great Britain. On the occasion of a Reception at the Soviet Embassy to commemorate the 50th Anniversary of Commencement of the Northern Convoys.

"I am pleased to have this chance to pay my deepest respects to those who in times of imminent hardship helped my country to overpower the forces of Fascism. Ask anyone in the Soviet Union what was the most significant allied contribution to our war effort and you will hear two things - the opening of the Second Front in Europe and the Northern Convoys. (Hear, hear).

Important from the military point of view the D-Day came three years into the war, but it was in the autumn of 1941 when the first ships with weapons, ammunition and food arrived in Murmansk. Then, the soldier in the trench realised he was not alone in his fight. A source of tremendous emotional support. The Commonwealth played a significant part in sustaining our military capability at a time when most of our industry was either destroyed or relocated to unoccupied regions. In all more than 1,400 ships took part and many were sunk, taking away the lives of more than 3,000 seamen. I propose to stand in silence to commemorate their heroic deaths .... Those brave men, who in the icy northern waters who did everything possible and impossible to help their fighting comrades, I would like to express the deep gratitude of the Soviet people for their heroic efforts. Having paid a great price for our victory we will never forget those who stood by us in the flames of the war. Who were the first to give us a helping hand, sometimes paying with their lives. Fighting the common enemy and having produced an unprecedented example of effective co-operation in the interests of democracy, peace and freedom for the people of the world. Successful against the little states, the aggressor failed to reap the fruits of his barbaric acts.

Many of you I am sure often wonder, just as I do, whether we can achieve the same level of co-operation in peace as we did in combat. My answer to this should be a definite Yes.

SOVIET THANKS

Survivors of the Arctic convoys who braved appalling conditions to take arms and supplies to Murmansk and Archangel during the Second World War were paid a moving tribute by the Soviet Ambassador Leonid Zamyatin.

Mr Zamyatin told more than 100 former seamen, who attended a reception at the Soviet Embassy in London to mark the 50th anniversary of the first convoy, that the people of his country felt deep gratitude for the sacrifices made by the Royal Navy and Merchant Navy.

He also announced that further commemorative medals would be presented to convoy participants who had not previously received one.

THE WHITE HOUSE

WASHINGTON

July 1, 1992

I am pleased to send greetings to all of the Allied veterans who are gathered in Glasgow to commemorate the 50th anniversary of the sealift to Murmansk and Archangel. I commend the North Russia Club of England for sponsoring this reunion.

Although it is difficult to believe that a half-century has passed since World War II, time cannot dim the significance of the material and food that you and your bold companions conveyed to the Soviet Union during that epic conflict. I know that many of you, military and civilian, lost good friends and comrades in that perilous operation and that you remember them today. Thanks, in no small part, to their sacrifices and to your willingness to brave ferocious attacks from sky and sea, the Soviet army, in concert with that of Allied forces, was able to beat back the forces of Nazi Germany and turn the tide to victory.

As we in this country celebrate the 216th anniversary of America's independence, we also celebrate new ties with Russia and the other states that replaced the USSR. During President Boris Yeltsin's recent visit to Washington, we signed treaties to reduce dramatically our nuclear arsenals, and we agreed to many other cooperative efforts. This new cooperation to build a safer and more peaceful world is reminiscent of the Allied effort during World War II that your sealift helped to strengthen. Today, we can truly celebrate the triumph of democratic ideals, and each of you can take pride in your contribution to the groundswell of freedom that continues to sweep the world.

Barbara joins me in sending best wishes for a memorable reunion.

G. Bush

10 DOWNING STREET

LONDON SW1A 2AA

THE PRIME MINISTER

Organisers of "Dervish".

Fifty years ago, Britain, and the Soviet Union, stood side by side, against daunting odds. These were dark times; but they showed how much, our two countries can do, when we work together, towards the same goals. We owe a great deal, to those brave men, who took part, in the Arctic Convoys. Many of them, selflessly gave their lives, in the hope, that we, would be free. We will remember them. Some of their more fortunate comrades, will be present, at the events in Murmansk, and Archangel. We wish them well, as we stand on the threshold, of a new era, of co-operation, between Britain, and the Soviet Union.

Copies:

Northern Fleet.
Murmansk Exec. Committee
Archangel Exec. Committee.
Ministry of Merchant Marine.
Eternal Memory to Soldiers.
Soviet War Veterans Committee.
British & American Veterans.

August 1991

CLARENCE HOUSE
S.W. 1

4th August 1993

Dear Mr Skinner

I write to tell you how much Queen Elizabeth The Queen Mother appreciated your message of birthday greetings.

The Queen Mother was touched by your very kind thought and I am to convey to you and to all Veterans of the Russian Convoys and Arctic Campaign of World War II Her Majesty's sincere thanks for the loyal sentiments expressed in your letter of 15th July.

Yours sincerely
Alastair Aird

Private Secretary to
Queen Elizabeth The Queen Mother

Peter A. Skinner, Esq.,
Secretary,
North Russia Club.

BUCKINGHAM PALACE

1st October, 1992.

Dear Mr Skinner

Thank you for your letter of 23rd September with which you enclosed a message to The Queen from the North Russia Club.

I have laid this before Her Majesty who has commanded me to send you the enclosed reply.

Yours sincerely

Robin Janvrin

(ROBIN JANVRIN)

Peter A. Skinner, Esq.

BUCKINGHAM PALACE

C.B. Tye, Esq.,
The President,
North Russia Club.

I am commanded by The Queen to convey her warm thanks to you, the Officers and Members of the North Russia Club for your kind message of loyal greetings, sent on the occasion of your eighth Annual Reunion at Northampton.

Her Majesty was delighted to receive this message and sends her best wishes to all concerned for an enjoyable and successful occasion.

PRIVATE SECRETARY

24th October, 1992.

GLOSSARY

AB	Able Seaman
BARRACK STANCHIONS	Shore based navel personnel
BATTLEWAGON	Battleship
BOATS	Submarines are known as
"O" Boats "M" Boats "S" Boats	Ships of a Class, names beginning with relevant letter, and usually group each together as a Flotilla
BUNTING TOSSER	Signalman
BUZZ	Rumour
CPO	Chief Petty Officer
CRUSHER	Regulating Petty Officer
DHOBYING	Washing
DIVVY O	Divisional Officer
ERA	Engine Room Artificer
ETA	Expected Time of Arrival
FRIDAY WHILE	Shore leave Friday to (while) Monday
GALLEY	Ship's Kitchen
GASH	Rubbish
GASH SHUTE	Rubbish over the side
GUZ	Devonport
HEADS	Ship's Lavatory
HOT BUNKING	Due to shortage of space, someone coming off watch would get into the bunk of someone coming on watch
JACK DUSTY	Supply Assistant
JANKERS	Ship's Cell or Gaol for offenders or defaulters
JAUNTY	Master-At-Arms
JIMMY THE ONE	First Lieutenant
KILLICK	Leading Hand
KR & AI	Kings Regulations and Admiralty Insutrctions
KYE	Ships Cocoa (in blocks)
L & PA	Lodging and Provision Allowance
LSA	Leading Supply Assistant
LSBA	Leading Sick Berth Attendant
L/SEA	Leading Seaman
LTO	Leading Torpedo Operator
No. 9	Tablet/pill for constipation
OA	Ordnance Artificer
OGGIN	The Sea
OPPO	Mate, Opposite Number
O/SEA	Ordinary Seaman
PIER HEAD JUMP	Last minute posting
PO	Petty Officer
POMPEY	Portsmouth
PTI	Physical Training Instructor
RATTLE	A reprimand/rollicking
2 $^{1}/_{2}$ RINGER	Lieut-Commander
SCRIBE	Writer
SDO	Signal Distribution Office

GLOSSARY CONTINUED

SHIPPING 'EM GREEN	Waves over Forecastle and Bridge
SHITEHAWKS	Seagulls
SKATE	Sailor consistently on a charge or in trouble
SNOTTY	Midshipman
SPARKS	Telegraphist
STOKES	Stoker
TANKY	Seaman in Stores
TICKLER	Cigarette/Tobacco
TOO	Time of Origin
WAVY NAVY	RNVR
WINGER	Best Mate

INDEX

The author returning to Russia in 1988 for the annual pilgrimage, points to Polyarnoe whilst on passage down the Kola Inlet for the poignant ceremony of laying wreaths by the Russians and British on the waters at the entrance where our ships were sunk at the end of their hazardous voyage.